MW01628469

PUBLIC UNIVERSITY SYSTEMS

PUBLIC UNIVERSITY SYSTEMS

Nancy Zimpher, Jason E. Lane, and James R. Johnsen, Series Editors

Public University Systems

+ + +

LEVERAGING SCALE IN HIGHER EDUCATION

EDITED BY JAMES R. JOHNSEN

JOHNS HOPKINS UNIVERSITY PRESS | *Baltimore*

Printed in the United States of America on acid-free paper
9 8 7 6 5 4 3 2 1

Johns Hopkins University Press
2715 North Charles Street
Baltimore, Maryland 21218
www.press.jhu.edu

Library of Congress Cataloging-in-Publication Data
Names: Johnsen, James R., 1957– editor.
Title: Public university systems : leveraging scale in higher education / [edited by] James R. Johnsen.
Description: Baltimore, MD : Johns Hopkins University Press, 2024. | Series: Public university systems | Includes bibliographical references and index.
Identifiers: LCCN 2023057609 | ISBN 9781421449715 (hardcover) | ISBN 9781421449722 (ebook)
Subjects: LCSH: Public Universities and colleges—United States—Administration. | Education, Higher—Aims and objectives—United States.
Classification: LCC LB2341 .P83 2024 | DDC 378.1/010973—dc23/eng/20231227
LC record available at https://lccn.loc.gov/2023057609

A catalog record for this book is available from the British Library.

Special discounts are available for bulk purchases of this book. For more information, please contact Special Sales at specialsales@jh.edu.

CONTENTS

Foreword, by Ronald Heifetz vii
Acknowledgments xv

Introduction 1

Part I: Structure and Functions

1. Structure and Functions 17
Aims C. McGuinness Jr. and Dennis P. Jones

2. Accreditation and Quality: System Perspectives 50
Peter T. Ewell

3. Is Responsive and Adaptive Collective Bargaining Possible, or Is This Déjà Vu All Over Again? 59
Daniel J. Julius

4. Public Systems and the Financing of Postsecondary Education 81
Paul E. Lingenfelter

5. Reallocating Resources 106
Robert C. Dickeson

Part II: New Models

6. Student-Centric Systems 127
Tristan Denley

7. The Lean University System: Focusing on Value 145
Steven J. Patin

8. Online Systems 171
Wallace E. Boston

9. Partnering with Purpose: Collaborations for the Future 195
Demarée K. Michelau

10. Lessons from Multi-Stakeholder Consortia for Public Higher Education Systems 217
Stakeholder Alignment Collaborative

11. The International Engagements of Higher Education Systems in the United States: What's the Current State, and What Does the Future Hold? 242
Jason E. Lane and Jessica Schueller

12. Leveraging Systems to Increase Diversity, Equity, and Inclusion at Institutions of Higher Education 264
Khaleel Seecharan and Darren Greeno

13. The Emergence of Intelligence Machines and Cyberspace: Framing the Challenge to University Systems and Suggesting a Three-Level Strategy of Resilience 281
Mark Hagerott

Part III: Leading the Future

14. Shared Governance in University Systems 301
George Blumenthal

15. Governing Large: How Public University System Boards Can Help Shape the Future of American Higher Education 319
Kevin P. Reilly

16. Making Change Happen 339
Allison M. Vaillancourt

17. Systems Heads 360
Nancy Zimpher and Rebecca Martin

Conclusion 383
James R. Johnsen

Contributors 393
Index 399

FOREWORD

I have had the opportunity during a 40-year career at Harvard's Kennedy School and as an advisor here and abroad to hear thousands of stories from people trying to lead their organizations, communities, and societies toward worthy goals. Nearly everyone succeeds on some issues and fails with others—this is true of people around the world running countries, international organizations, global businesses, and nonprofits; people in the middle of organizations; people practicing leadership from the streets; people in national, state, and local politics; and people in education, religious institutions, government agencies, militaries, and movements for social justice. In one way or another, nearly all are eager to improve the world around them, yet along with their high aspirations come frustrations with achieving progress as broadly as they seek.

My job in listening to these stories has been to develop a theory of practice and methods of teaching that might help people "increase their batting averages." Trained as a physician, I learned early in my professional life that most diagnostic data come from listening to the story of the person with the complaint. Medical examination and tests are critical sources of data, but "taking a history" is primary.

I've learned from these stories that the most common sources of failure in leadership are diagnostic. People often move too fast to debate solutions and spend too little time on the diagnostic part of the work. They assume too quickly that the situation is amenable to expertise, and then move toward partial or unsustainable solutions, or move with the wrong approach altogether, such as linearly rather than iteratively.

So, the first challenge I've faced as a leadership educator is to develop and teach professional students the diagnostic difference between technical and adaptive challenges, and how the former are addressed through hard-won knowledge developed over generations that enables us to solve myriad critical problems by applying our managerial and authoritative expertise along with our repertoire of organizational designs and solutions. In contrast, adaptive challenges arise when the gaps between our aspirations and the situation demand responses beyond our authoritative expertise, responses that will generate new capacity in people and organizations, and therefore demand that those of us with authoritative knowledge become accustomed to operating beyond anyone's authoritative expertise and to develop adaptive strategies of engagement and discovery.

Ironically, the tendency to make the classic diagnostic mistake associated with leadership—treating adaptive challenges as if they were technical problems—is strongly reinforced by institutions of higher education, of which Harvard is a primary example, because we strengthen people's self-identification as expert problem-solvers. We feed the presumption that all problems are amenable to expert solutions, "if only the key parties would listen." In medicine, we listen for data amenable to our expert analysis and solution set, and the patient is then supposed to follow to our prescriptions. Yet after cardiac surgery, only about 20 percent of patients change their habits of smoking, eating, and exercise. We physicians call these "compliance failures," yet these are failures of our own diagnostic processes and modes of engagement. For example, we rarely, if ever, ask patients and their families: Does the smell of home cooking play a part in making your home feel like home? What losses would you and your family need to accommodate to eat different food?

Indeed, generally in higher education, in one way or another, we tell our students, we will educate you to know best. You will become the next generation of "go-to" people, the experts, the ones with the answers to the challenges of our world, meriting authority. Inadvertently, however, we have done our part to contribute to the current distrust and polarization in America by generating the attitude, Why listen to people across America who have less or different education, if we know best?

Many challenges that land on the desk of executives arrive as a bundle of technical and adaptive problems with different ratios of each. As a consequence, a primary diagnostic task in leadership practice is assessing which components of a challenge are amenable to authoritative action and which demand an adaptive mode of response. Transporting people safely to the moon and back, while enormously complex, consisted of a range of largely technical challenges solvable through applications of authoritative expertise, yet both the space program and the lunar missions also contained adaptive challenges requiring new ways of thinking and doing. The film *Apollo 13* powerfully illustrated adaptive work when the program director put a bunch of equipment on the table and asked engineers to figure out how to keep the crew alive while conserving enough resources to get them home.

The global pandemic, our ongoing economic crisis, and the legacies of racial inequity all consist of challenges with large adaptive components, demanding leadership beyond anyone's authoritative expertise and illustrating many of the common properties of adaptive work: the need for widespread experimentation; value-laden, conflictual learning processes; prolonged periods of "disequilibrium," that is, social strains of uncertainty, frustration, and divergence; the uneven distribution of losses; and the need for widespread leadership and responsibility-taking to produce local adaptations to local environments.

Likewise, the challenges at the center of this volume—how American states through their public university systems can provide more accessible, affordable, relevant, and high-quality postsecondary education to an increasingly diverse society—are not solvable through technical approaches alone. Rather, these challenges involve institutions, cultures, relationships, policies, and myriad other settings for adaptive work where there is not a linear road map or a single, clear authoritative solution.

One of the leaders seeking tools for adaptive leadership applied to public university systems is the editor of this volume. At the time he came to the Kennedy School, Jim Johnsen was chief of staff to the president of a university system that was experiencing declining enrollment, budget cuts from the state, and flagging public confidence. Our courses gave him the words and concepts to explain what he already knew from painful experience, and would experience later when he became president of the system, that a technical solution—even one with an inspiring vision, a strategic plan with goals and objectives tied to the state's needs and buttressed by survey data, objective third-party analysis, validation by an authoritative group of the state's leaders, and a media campaign—was not enough to meet the challenge.

That's because the problems were deeply nested in the culture of the university system and the state, and that instead of a radical restructuring, a more subtle strategy would be needed over time to both hold and prod various sets of relevant parties to answer three essential questions in a wide array of political, institutional, and public settings.

We know these three questions from evolutionary biology. Successful adaptations, from minor to transformative, are produced by "answering" them.

- What DNA should be conserved?
- What DNA should be discarded (i.e., re-regulated, suppressed, lost)?
- What innovations will enable us to take the best of our accumulated capacity and thrive in a changing, challenging world?

These processes in nature suggest a key insight for the practice of leadership in human systems: lasting, transformative change is highly conservative, and therefore talking only about change and innovation risks not only frightening people unnecessarily, generating overwhelming resistance, but also risks disrupting values, strategies, structures, processes, and cultural norms that should be conserved. Change needs to be given context in the cultural DNA that should endure.

Even when our primary aim is to preserve what's core to our organizations and publics—our missions and purposes, our orienting values—loss accompanies the territory of change. If leadership were all about creatively adding to what we do, fashioning positive-sum outcomes and distributing gains, it would be an easy job. Leadership is dangerous because we often are in the business of distributing losses. We all know the aphorism that "people resist change," but people do not generally resist change when they believe it's a good thing. (Nobody gives back a winning lottery ticket.) People resist change when it involves the risk or reality of loss.

Although contextualizing losses in the terms of conserving what remains precious and essential will nearly always be a wise strategy, staying alive in leadership also demands respect for the pains of change, facing potential the losses, assessing them with heart, and engaging the people who will have to sustain and accept those losses. A central strategic question becomes: Who needs to learn what—who are the relevant parties inside and outside the system, and what kinds of adaptive work will each need to do?

Leadership is an improvisational art. It involves patience, a practice of continuous experimentation, a profound humility in the face of challenges beyond one's know-how, and an imperative to distribute the work of leadership among the various sets of parties related to each component of the challenge, down to the "front line." Leading requires a stomach for failure, because even the best fail much of the time. And the quicker one can step back from the action, to "leave the dance floor and get up on the balcony" to debrief daily and weekly mistakes, and understand the situation through a broader lens, the faster one can take corrective action. So, a regular set of practices to aid reflection in action are essential life-saving devices, not expendable luxuries. We need quiet moments and sanctuaries, scheduled debriefings with colleagues and confidants, and regular routines outside of work. It's important for leaders, regardless of where they sit in a system, to pause and find a broader, more objective view, one that affords a clearer perspective of what's happening and one's role in it. Then they can reengage in the action with heightened awareness and a renewed sense of direction.

After Jim left the university presidency, he got up on the balcony and with colleagues at the National Association of System Heads, codeveloped an agenda for the nation's public university systems, and proposed this volume to Johns Hopkins University Press. These essays on the future of American public higher education systems provide a much-needed view from the balcony, undertaken by the right people at the right time, on a set of serious adaptive challenges facing our nation and its universities. The authors of these chapters reflect a broad and diverse set of experiences as scholars, university presidents, system heads, consultants, and policymakers. The topics they address reveal the complexity of the problem, and their insights have the benefit of experimentation, painful failure, and celebrated success. They have come together at a time in our nation's history when we are responding to a confluence of forces—including the effects of a global pandemic, a long history of racial injustice, a changing climate, and widening gaps in economic status. These problems challenge our higher education systems in ways that cannot be addressed solely as technical problems through the application of authoritative expertise. The sheer complexity of these challenges on their own, much less taken together, require people throughout our university systems to think carefully about what is so core to their purposes that they must be preserved, what is less critical and thus can be left behind, and how can they foster innovations to achieve new adaptations that build from their capacities, reflect their specific conditions, and advance their long-term purposes.

The essays in this volume share insights from scholarship and practice with those governors, legislators, regents, trustees, and university leaders who are seeking to realize the full potential of their public university systems. These systems include the largest American institutions of higher education, which are responsible for conducting much of the research and discovery that improves quality of life through advances in science, medicine, and technology; training skilled workers critical to economic development and prosperity; elevating the social and economic status of people from diverse backgrounds; and preparing engaged, thoughtful citizens who help sustain our democracy.

These systems and their institutions do so much, but as we see in the pages ahead, they sit at the confluence of invaluable opportunities to work the myriad challenges our country faces, creating ideas and capacities to realize a more just and prosperous democracy in the decades to come. The essays treat a wide variety of topics—from structure and accreditation to collective bargaining, governance, and innovation and technology—but common across them all is their recognition that there are no easy answers. Instead, there are insights, suggestions, ideas, stories, models, and recommendations for how leaders from the board room to the classroom can work together with humility, respect, and grace to exercise leadership that is adaptive to their own contexts. By doing so, they realize the promise of our public university systems to America's future.

—RONALD HEIFETZ

ACKNOWLEDGMENTS

This collection of essays on the future of public university systems is the fruit of many years of studying and leading systems. While little of the higher education literature or press pay much attention to them, these systems play a critical role in American higher education, and as the contributors to this volume all argue, by leveraging their scale, they could do even more.

This idea for this book was born in numerous conversations with system leaders Nancy Zimpher, Jason Lane, and Rebecca Martin as we developed the Power of Systems initiative at the National Association of System Heads (NASH). Their experience leading within and across systems has inspired a growing body of successful experiments in leveraging the scale of systems for student success. As a former member of the NASH board, I was aware of and supported NASH's numerous initiatives, but only during my time as a senior fellow did I realize the full impact of its work. I thank Nancy, Jason, Rebecca, and the NASH board for providing me an intellectual home and for NASH's financial support that made this book possible.

To the system leaders who contributed chapters to the book, my gratitude for their many and varied contributions to the field over the years both in scholarship and practice. I especially appreciate their willingness to explore what's possible for American higher education if university systems were more effectively utilized.

Thanks to the team at John Hopkins University Press: Greg Britton for sharing our passion for the subject and patience as we pulled it together, Ashleigh McKown for her careful editing, Charles Dibble for managing the book through production, and Kris Lykke for marketing the book to those leaders and policymakers in the position to bring our ideas to reality.

I also want to thank John Aubrey Douglass of the Center for Studies in Higher Education at the University of California, Berkeley, for his longtime friendship and support. I have treasured our conversations over the years at Berkeley, including memorable time spent with Clark Kerr and Marian Gade.

My lessons in university leadership have come as a student learning from superb teachers, as a team member supporting others as they led, and as a system head navigating between the rocks and whirlpools of a university system in crisis. My deepfelt thanks go to these leaders I admire and whose lessons I have sought—imperfectly—to put into practice: Leon Panetta, Theda Skocpol, Robert Meister, Richard Mather, Matt Hartley, Mark Hamilton, Ronald Heifetz, Cary Keller, Wendy Redman, Patty Kastelic, Jyostna Heckman, Mary K. Hughes, Terry MacTaggart, John Davies, Gloria O'Neill, Norman Phillips, Aaron Schutt, Anand Vadapalli, and numerous others, too many to name.

Thanks are also due to my colleagues at Greenwood Asher and Associates, who have kindly tolerated my waxing on about the unique leadership qualities needed for university systems.

And, finally, thanks to my parents—both models of lifelong learning and service—as well as to my life partner Mary and our adult children Greta and Jakob, who have been so generous over the years with their patience, humor, and love.

PUBLIC UNIVERSITY SYSTEMS

Introduction

JAMES R. JOHNSEN

THIS BOOK EXPLORES what is possible for American higher education if our public higher education systems fully realize their unique ability to create value greater than the sum of their institutional parts. The confluence of numerous political, demographic, economic, technological, and social forces exacerbated by the global COVID-19 pandemic helped prompt this exploration. First, our nation competes in an increasingly challenging global economy, one in which university-educated talent contributes to increasing productivity and prosperity. Second, the role of higher education in creating individual and societal goods is in question as alternative forms of certification are increasingly seen as more relevant, not to mention more convenient and more affordable, both to workers and employers. Third, the cost of paying for public higher education has increased and the burden has shifted from states to students, raising concerns about access and affordability. Fourth, the rise of online higher education courses, programs, and institutions has provided a wider range of options for students, and at the same time put pressure on those institutions that relied on face-to-face instruction. Fifth, the number of traditional-age college-going youth is declining, resulting in large regional enrollment declines in some regions of the country. This decline in enrollment is accompanied by a shift from traditionally prepared high school graduates to an increasing number of first-generation, low-income students from diverse racial backgrounds who may lack community support and good schools to prepare them for our currently configured curricular portals and co-curricular university support systems. Sixth, we have seen universities in general, and systems in particular, increasingly subject to partisan political intrusion in a variety of forms, from radical state funding cuts to curricular control, and hiring of leaders without backgrounds in academic leadership. Finally, all these factors have conjoined with increased societal recognition of racial inequities and have forced public higher education systems to rethink how they carry out their missions more effectively in this complex and rapidly changing environment.

It is time—past time—to rethink the role of public university systems, to "get up on the balcony," as leadership scholar Ronald Heifetz suggests in the foreword to this volume, to consider the tough adaptive leadership set of questions: What of the many things university systems do should we conserve, what should we shed, and how should we foster a culture of innovation to create the capacity to continue serving our core purposes, adaptive to every context in a fast-changing world? From the early work on public multicampus systems conducted under the auspices of the Carnegie Foundation led by iconic university system head Clark Kerr half a century ago up to the present Power of Systems: Advancing the Nation's Prosperity initiative developed by the National Association of System Heads (NASH), there has been recognition of the powerful role played by systems, but little scholarly attention. Certainly, the numerous studies conducted by the National Center for Higher Education Management Systems (NCHEMS) have provided practical solutions for system leaders and state policymakers over the years, contributing much to our understanding of the diversity of systems across the country as well as to their common features and best practices. But at the end of the day, compared to the literature on institutions, broad policy issues, and studies of functional areas such as finance and student affairs, systems have not received the attention they are due.

This study of America's public university systems is intended, in part, to remedy that dearth of knowledge about their contributions to American higher education and thereby to lift them up to policymakers, governing boards, and university leaders for what they are and can be. This book looks forward to what is possible for higher education in America if our public university systems were to take greater advantage of "systemness" by leveraging scale and innovation in ways not available to all but the largest institutions. The role of our college and university systems in serving their students and their states has never been more important, as they produce scientific discoveries and innovation, workforce and economic development, social mobility, health care, and so many other contributions to society.

The prevailing organizational model for public four-year colleges and universities in the United States is a system, established on a state-by-state basis, of separately accredited institutions, each with its own leadership governed by a single system board through a single chief executive. According to NASH, 44 states have established at least one system for providing and governing public higher education in their states either in the state's constitution or statute. Even in the remaining six states, while there is no system per se, multiple forms of formal and informal coordination have been established to capture at least some of the benefits of systemness.

While there are commonalities among the nation's systems, it is also true that there is significant variance based on history, culture, politics, economics, demographics, and other factors. Playing off a famous statement attributed to Ronald Reagan when running for governor of California in 1966—"when you have seen one redwood tree, you have seen them all"—the nationally recognized expert on systems Dennis Jones has observed that "when you have seen one system, you have seen one system."

Several states have a single system that includes all three traditional segments of higher education (community college, comprehensive, and doctoral/research). Examples are Alaska, Hawaii, New York, and Wisconsin. Other states have multiple systems, some based on similar missions (e.g., California and Minnesota), and others based on geography (e.g., Texas and Colorado).

In terms of their scale, fully 75 percent of the nation's public four-year college and university students are enrolled at an institution in one of these systems. They include the nation's land-grant universities with a long history of contribution to economic development and opportunity; research universities conducting pathbreaking discoveries; academic medical centers providing health care to millions; comprehensive universities preparing professionals for careers in a wide range of professions; institutions with the nation's highest economic mobility rates; community colleges training our technical workforce; and a large number of institutions whose primary mission is to serve students from diverse and minority backgrounds, providing a an additional set of portals to liberal arts and professional education.

In addition to scale, measured by the number of their students and impact of their missions, these public university systems bring several unique benefits of scale to their students and their states. Systems provide students access to programs and courses from campuses within a system and, in some cases, even across systems. This seamless access helps students progress at a faster rate and reduces the need for every campus in a system to replicate programs and courses already available elsewhere in the system. Systems provide accountability to their funders by delivering cost-effective and compliant administrative services and well-coordinated and defined academic missions and student services. Systems advocate for resources and public support with a unified voice. Systems ensure that the needs of the state—such as workforce preparation, research and economic development, food security, civic engagement, health care—are paramount in academic planning and decision-making. Systems support innovation and collaboration and then scale those benefits across the system and beyond.

Despite the prevalence and importance of systems, they have not received the attention they deserve. Systems are not included in the federal laws governing American higher education, they are largely left out of the accreditation process, they are often viewed as being more hinderances to change rather than accelerators of it, and they have received little scholarly attention over the past 50 years (with notable exceptions being Lee and Bowen, 1971, 1975; Gade, 1993; Gaither, 1999;

Richardson et al., 1999; Lane and Johnstone, 2013; Gagliardi and Lane, 2022; Martin et al., 2022).

As society seeks to address its many challenges in this increasingly volatile, uncertain, complex, and ambiguous world, the nation's higher education systems are being called on to do more, to bring their full weight—which system leaders and scholars have demonstrated is greater than the sum of their institutional parts—to the work. An example of this resurgence of interest in systems is the development and implementation of NASH's Power of Systems initiative. NASH has brought together hundreds of system leaders to develop a transformation agenda for the nation's systems that includes goals, imperatives, and measures. The agenda is being advanced along three complementary paths: (1) application of improvement science to key processes, such as transfer, by system innovation teams; (2) development of baseline data on systems, a tool kit for effective system policies and practices, and an annual report on system performance; and (3) a new partnership between the states and the federal government, initially focused on Afghan and Ukrainian refugee resettlement as well as funding to improve timely completion in support of social equity and workforce development goals. In addition, NASH has sponsored national convenings, partnered with higher education foundations and sister associations, and taken steps to contribute to scholarship on higher education systems. NASH's scholarship program includes contributions to academic journals such as *Change Magazine* (Martin et al., 2022) and extends to several chapters in this book.

The driving questions in the chapters that follow are: How are systems organized, and what functions do they perform? What are the major challenges faced by systems as they re-create themselves in order to provide even more value to society? What characteristics of systems make them especially well suited to address major societal challenges and goals? What is possible for university systems and the students and states they serve?

These and other questions are explored by a diverse set of contributors, all higher education experts on the topics they have chosen to explore. From the structure and functions of systems through to their leadership, this book offers not only substantive ideas for improvement but also new ways of thinking about what's possible. It is our sincere hope that the ideas and suggestions in this book support university system and campus leaders, board members, state and federal policymakers, and scholars of higher education as they take the opportunity to get up on the balcony to reassess how their systems may be of even greater impact for good in their states.

The book is organized into three parts. Part I looks at key structural and functional responsibilities of systems in relation to the institutions that comprise them. A broad overview of systems functions is followed by deeper dives into accreditation and quality assurance, collective bargaining, finance and affordability, and academic program prioritization. In part II, we examine alternative system models, with special attention to those that are student centric, lean, online, interstate, international, diverse, and coalitions. Part III explores what's possible for systems in terms of leadership, as Ronald Heifetz describes it, from various positions of authority—specifically, faculty governance, governing boards, system administrators, and system heads.

Part I

Part I begins with a chapter by preeminent scholars of systems and advisors to system leaders and policymakers, Aims C. McGuinness Jr. and Dennis P. Jones of the National Center for Higher Education Management Systems. One cannot have worked in or studied university systems without encountering the work of these experts. In chapter 1, they argue that systems, by virtue of their huge scale, have the power to guide the institutions within their purview to serve students, employers, and the state more effectively and efficiently. To exercise that power fully, however, systems must evolve from the roles and functions that justified their creation to roles that will justify their continued existence. That evolution lies not in radical restructuring of systems, but rather in changes in how key functions—administrative and academic—are performed and in a shift of focus in the culture from institutions to their clients.

Peter T. Ewell, also a former leader at NCHEMS and eminent scholar of higher education systems, examines in chapter 2 the role of multi-institutional higher education systems in the accreditation function, the principal mechanism for promoting and signifying quality in higher education in the United States. While Ewell recognizes that there are challenges associated with systems performing these tasks, he argues that multi-institutional systems have many advantages in discharging accountability and assessing student learning. They can speak with a single voice that commands public attention, use their central authority to gain efficiencies, coordinate the accreditation activities of constituent institutions, and, if appropriate, combine weak programs so that they are accreditable. Finally, looking forward, he identifies a range of likely developments, such as the rise of online instructional delivery, that will affect system operations with respect to assessment and accountability.

In many systems, employment relations with faculty, staff, and graduate students are conducted through collective bargaining. Daniel J. Julius, like others in this collection, is not only a widely published scholar but also a university leader. Julius's scholarship is especially renowned in the area of collective bargaining, a logical extension of his early career at the bargaining table. Chapter 3 explores the constraints and possibilities for institutional innovation and adaptation that could result from the collective bargaining process. Julius argues that modifications to the process cannot be imposed by one party or the other, but instead must be a joint undertaking. Julius suggests that such joint effort will require looking beyond the status quo to adopt practices that reinforce evidence-based decision-making, reflect best practices, and demand benchmark measures of success. Adoption of these practices, he argues, will benefit faculty, employees, and stakeholders, and better enable the university and systems to be responsive to students and society.

Another critical function in all organizations is finance, and in the context of public university systems, Paul E. Lingenfelter is widely recognized as an expert. In addition to his scholarship, Lingenfelter has served as a leader in state system offices as well as president of the State

Higher Education Executive Officers, a national organization that includes many state system heads and produces a highly regarded and widely used annual report on state higher education finance. In chapter 4, he takes on several challenging and perennial questions that face legislators, governors, and the leaders of public systems: How much should postsecondary education cost? What about student tuition and fees, and public, philanthropic, and investment capital in financing postsecondary education? What are the contributions and limitations of each source of funding? What about the financing of research and public service? Who should fund student aid? What public policies and institutional practices are needed to meet the needs of individuals and the broader society for effectiveness and efficiency in postsecondary education?

Resource reallocation is a key function of boards and system offices, especially in light of increasing downward pressure on revenue from government and declining enrollment and accompanying tuition revenue. Robert C. Dickeson—well-known former university president, higher education organization leader, consultant, and author—applies his model for prioritization of academic programs and services to the system level. While the model was developed primarily for application at the campus level, Dickeson explores the opportunities and risks of its application at the system level. He begins chapter 5 with a stark statement: "It is time for university systems to get serious about this fundamental reality: The most likely source for needed resources will come from reallocation of existing resources." In other words, cost reduction in some areas will be necessary to fund investment in others. He recognizes the difficulty of the task and how seldom it is taken on at the system level, and how even more seldom it includes academic programs and services. But if higher education systems are to control costs in order to invest in new programs that advance innovation, spur economic growth, respond to workforce demand, and pursue social goals, they must prioritize academic programs and services. The more politically expedient option of across-the board cuts is much more commonly used, but Dickeson argues it is based on the flawed assumption that all programs are equal. His model for system-led academic program review and prioritization should be of special interest to governing boards with a mandate to reallocate scarce resources wisely in service to their mission.

Part II

Part II explores new models for systems. Tristan Denley, now at the Louisiana Board of Regents, leads off in chapter 6 with a look into what a system would be like if it were truly student centric, if curriculum were redesigned to better meet student needs. Based on success in two state systems where Denley led academic innovation—Tennessee and Georgia—he poses challenging questions about how our own structures materially contribute to students' lack of success at scale, and what can be done about those failings. The Momentum Year strategies for system-wide curricular innovation in those two systems have resulted in marked improvement in student success. He argues that such a comprehensive integrated approach can make lasting progress in the quest for equitable outcomes.

Steven J. Patin is an expert in lean process improvement, with deep experience in its application in higher education, business, and the military. While lean principles have been applied widely and with great effect in manufacturing, health care, and service sectors, and in a limited way in higher education (primarily at the institutional level), there is little evidence that systems have applied lean principles and practices to their administrative, academic, and student service processes. In chapter 8, after a brief overview of lean—where customers define value, not producers; processes are continuously reviewed and improved; and waste of various sorts is identified and reduced, if not eliminated altogether—Patin explores its application to higher education and addresses what would be possible for students, research funding agencies, community partners, and other customers if systems implemented principles and practices of "lean" process improvement.

While online education is hardly a new model, its growth has primarily been at the institutional level, without the advantages that could be gained with system leadership. In chapter 8, Wallace E. Boston, former chief executive officer and chair of the American Public University System—a private, for-profit provider—examines the barriers and opportunities for systems in more effectively serving their mission through system-level coordination of online courses and programs delivered by their institutions. Boston identifies the numerous barriers to overcome, the challenging questions to be answered, and the many benefits to systems, institutions, and their stakeholders that can be realized through standardized student services, collaboratively developed curriculum, shared faculty and staff resources, revenue- and cost-sharing, and system-level leadership in building corporate partnerships. He also highlights the recent rise of a consortium of nearly 500 institutions, including an entire system, that uses a course-sharing platform that offers financial aid eligibility, transparent payment processes, ability to transfer grades and credits, and assurance that courses will be accepted and transcribed.

Two additional consortial models that deliver the added value of systemness to the higher education of a state, region, or segment of the population are the subject of chapters 9 and 10. Demarée K. Michelau, president of the Western Interstate Commission on Higher Education (WICHE), describes the financial and other benefits that have accrued to the 15 states, territories, and freely associated states that are part of the compact through WICHE's policy research and outreach to state governors and legislators, workforce needs assessments, training for boards and university leaders, tuition reciprocity programs for students, and support for interstate authorization reciprocity.

The Stakeholder Alignment Collaborative, itself a voluntary consortium, asserts that new combinations of social and technical systems typically define an era, while prior sets of social and technical systems do not disappear. In the current digital era, the challenge for public higher education systems is to lead, adapt, or fall behind as new institutional arrangements move to the foreground. Will public higher education systems help to define the current era, or will other organizational forms become definitional for education and research? In other words, how will US public higher education systems evolve in this digital age? The Collaborative describes how individual universities and public higher education systems are already deeply involved in the formation of smaller, more agile, and adaptive consortia, and suggests lessons from those consortia for higher education systems.

While not addressed to a significant degree in the literature about systems, according to system scholars Jason E. Lane and Jessica Schueller, systems are playing an increasing role in the internationalization of American higher education. In chapter 11, Lane and Schueller revisit prior work outlining the primary international functions of system offices in the United States and then explore the increasingly international approach of US systems in collaborating with systems abroad, with particular emphasis on two areas in which systemness is being applied to internationalization activities in other countries: the European Universities Initiative and Cross-National Regional Universities. With US systems increasingly facilitating system-wide internationalization initiatives and the trend of system-to-system international partnerships, this chapter sets the stage for understanding how systemness can be complementary to internationalization initiatives that bring together public higher education in two or more countries for the betterment of the student experience and broader societal aims.

In response to the need for increased coordination and effectiveness of diversity, equity, and inclusion (DEI) initiatives in higher education, experts Khaleel Seecharan and Darren Greeno suggest new models and best practices for system-level initiatives based on their review of two cases studies, one in Missouri and the other in California. They argue that even as higher education has become much more accessible to underrepresented segments of our population, education disparities persist. Now, with more than 75 percent of students enrolled in public colleges and universities that are part of multicampus systems, we have opportunities to address these education disparities at the system level, at scale, utilizing systemness. Chapter 12 is a reflection on the opportunity to utilize the unique power of systems to actualize a fundamentally inclusive and equitable framework in higher education.

Part II concludes with a chapter on cyber-resilient systems by Mark Hagerott, chancellor of the University of North Dakota System and globally recognized expert on cybersecurity. He observes that our economy, society, and higher education are moving from a period of relative equilibrium into a period of disequilibrium. Chapter 13 builds on the supposition that the emergence of artificial intelligence (AI) is the underlying driver of disruption that will reshape education, society, the economy, and government. State university systems will be challenged to thrive, or in some cases to even survive the disruption. But state systems have yet another calling: to help society navigate disruptive change. Hagerott recommends that system leaders build resilience in the human, the machine, and the cyberspace of software data while reliably meeting the day-to-day needs of students. As well, it suggests that cyber-insecurity may now exceed the response capabilities of individual campuses, and thus state university systems should play a key role helping those campuses, the states, and society at large navigate this digital security challenge. But for some systems and states, it is also possible that the scale of the problem may overwhelm state budgets and human capital resources, and that a larger effort on the part of state systems may be in order. Chapter 13 concludes with a sketch of such a possible new program.

Part III

In part III, we consider several aspects of the critical role leadership plays in re-creating university systems in and for the future. These include faculty governance, board leadership, change management, and system administration.

George Blumenthal explores the benefits of a single system-level faculty senate based on his own leadership roles in the University of California (UC) Faculty Senate, as a chancellor in the UC system, and as director of the Center for Studies in Higher Education at UC Berkeley. Chapter 14 reviews the role of faculty senates in general, the reasons for a system-wide senate, and the added resilience and capacity for evolution and adaptation when faculty voices are "at the table" with the system governing board and administrative leaders.

Kevin P. Reilly, president emeritus of the University of Wisconsin system, discusses the critical role played by governing boards in chapter 15. Assuming they will continue to operate in one form or another, he describes three accelerating trends affecting the future of American higher education and then suggests tools, initiatives, and incentives that university system governing bodies might uniquely—or more effectively in comparison with single-institution boards—do to help shape those trends for the public good going forward.

Managing change processes so that systems increase the likelihood of implementing lasting improvement is the subject of chapter 16, by Allison M. Vaillancourt. Based on her own scholarship and experience as an administrator and consultant to universities, Vaillancourt reviews the major pressures on higher education and barriers to change, common mistakes made by leaders trying to implement change, and best practices from both her experience and the academic literature. She concludes with a practical checklist for leaders seeking change and organizational improvement.

The final chapter, written by Nancy Zimpher, president emeritus of the State University of New York system, and former NASH executive director Rebecca Martin, addresses the many challenges higher education system leaders face. Zimpher and Martin argue that system leaders possess unique capabilities to unleash innovation, advance social and economic mobility, and improve our quality of life. To realize their full potential, the future roles and functions of higher education systems need to be reshaped, requiring leadership from system leaders. Zimpher and Martin provide a detailed overview of the several strategies developed by NASH hand in hand with system leaders from across the country under the auspices of its ambitious Power of Systems project, offer a compelling vision for systems of the future, and call for strong yet adaptive leadership to realize that vision through adoption of compelling goals and measures along with the use of scalable initiatives within and across systems.

Finally, I conclude the book by building on the contributions of these and other scholars and leaders in American higher education to directly address Ronald Heifetz's set of questions referenced above: What of the many things that university systems do should we conserve, what should we shed, and how should we foster a culture of innovation to create the capacity to continue serving our core purposes adaptive to each of our contexts in a fast-changing world? It is my sincere hope that after reading the book, university leaders—from the governor's office to the legislative halls, and from system board rooms to classrooms—gain not only ideas, but also tangible strategies for advancing higher education where they live and lead.

References

Gade, Marian. *Four Multicampus Systems: Some Policies and Practices That Work.* Washington, DC: Association of Governing Boards, 1993.

Gagliardi, Jonathan, and J. E. Lane, eds. *Higher Education Systems Redesigned: From Perpetuation to Innovation to Student Success.* Albany: State University of New York Press, 2022.

Gaither, Gerald, ed. *The Multicampus System: Perspectives on Practice and Prospects.* Sterling, WV: Stylus Press, 1999.

Lane, Jason, and D. B. Johnstone, eds. *Higher Education Systems 3.0: Harnessing Systemness. Delivering Performance.* Albany: State University of New York Press, 2013.

Lee, Eugene, and F. M. Bowen. *The Multicampus University: A Study of Academic Governance.* New York: McGraw-Hill, 1971.

Lee, Eugene, and F. M. Bowen. *Managing Multicampus Systems: Effective Administration in an Unsteady State.* San Francisco: Jossey-Bass, 1975.

Martin, Rebecca, N. Zimpher, J. Lane, and J. Johnsen. "Leveraging the Power of Systemness to Improve the Success of Students and Society." *Change: The Magazine of Higher Learning* 54, no. 4 (2022): 38–44.

Richardson, Frank, K. Bracco, P. Callan, and J. Finney. *Designing State Higher Education Systems for a New Century.* Phoenix: Oryx Press, 1999.

Part I

STRUCTURE AND FUNCTIONS

1

Structure and Functions

AIMS C. MCGUINNESS JR. AND DENNIS P. JONES

SYSTEMS ARE A FACT OF LIFE regarding higher education governance. If one defines a "system" as several institutions or campuses under a single governing and leadership structure, such entities enroll more than 60 percent of all students enrolled in US higher education institutions. More than 80 percent of students enrolled in public colleges and universities (52 percent in public universities and 28 percent in community colleges) are attending campuses within systems. Because of their large footprint, systems have the power to play a major role in ensuring that the institutions within their purview serve students, employers, and the state effectively and efficiently. To exercise that power fully, however, systems must evolve from the roles that justified their creation to roles that will justify their continued existence.

Early Systems

Rationale for Early Systems

Many of the systems of public colleges and universities were created during the 1960s and 1970s, when college enrollments were exploding and new institutions were being built to respond to this increasing demand. Some systems evolved as the state's land-grant university extended campuses to growing urban areas. States established other systems by consolidating previously separate institutions or sectors within a single structure. State leaders saw systems as a means to address multiple problems. While the specific issues varied among states, the creation of systems shared common rationales:

- To provide a single point of accountability to the governor and state legislature for efficient and effective governance and administration of multiple public campuses.
- To mitigate regional competition and conflicts regarding the location of new institutions and high-cost programs (e.g., engineering and health sciences and doctoral programs) and remove these decisions from the political process.
- To reduce or prevent unnecessary duplication of programs and gain efficiencies in the delivery of programs and the provision of back-office operations.

Traditional Functions

The early systems' governing boards and executive offices carried out basic governance and administrative functions like those performed by the leadership of standalone public institutions. In most early systems, the constituent institutions operated with considerable academic independence (e.g., academic programs, faculty governance, student affairs policies) with limited, if any, collaboration between and among campuses. Branch campuses of land-grant universities were an exception to this pattern; however, many of these branches evolved into independently accredited campuses with operational independence of the institutions from which they evolved.

Common system office responsibilities included administrative and regulatory functions as well as supporting the governing board's decision-making in key areas:

- Appointing, evaluating, and holding accountable the system and institutional chief executive officers (CEOs)

- Reviewing and approving requests for new campuses and academic programs
- Developing and approving operating and capital funding requests submitted to the governor and state legislature
- Approving tuition and fee policies
- Advocating for funding of constituent campuses before the governor and state legislature
- Developing and approving operating and capital budgets, including ensuring equitable allocation of funds among constituent institutions
- Allocating appropriated funds to constituent institutions
- Approving institutional budgets
- Serving as the fiduciary agent and employer of record for the system institutions
- Approving policies and regulations, especially those regarding faculty personnel policies and tenure

Other system functions included legal affairs, comptroller (fund accounting and control), communications, and government relations. Many systems also carried out functions designed to achieve efficiencies in such areas as procurement and construction management.

The specific functions of systems varied from state to state depending on the diversity of missions and differences in the scale of constituent institutions. Also important were differences in the role of state government in finance/budget policy (e.g., control of capital facilities financing) and personnel.

In early years, state and higher education institutional leaders viewed systems primarily as bureaucratic structures formed to carry out administrative, oversight, and regulatory functions. The perceived role of the system was primarily internal—that is, functions of governance, finance, and administration in support of the constituent institutions. Few saw system offices as entities with an overarching educational mission distinct from and complementary to the educational mission of the campuses. To the extent that the focus was external, it was to advocate for the interests of constituent campuses, not necessarily for a

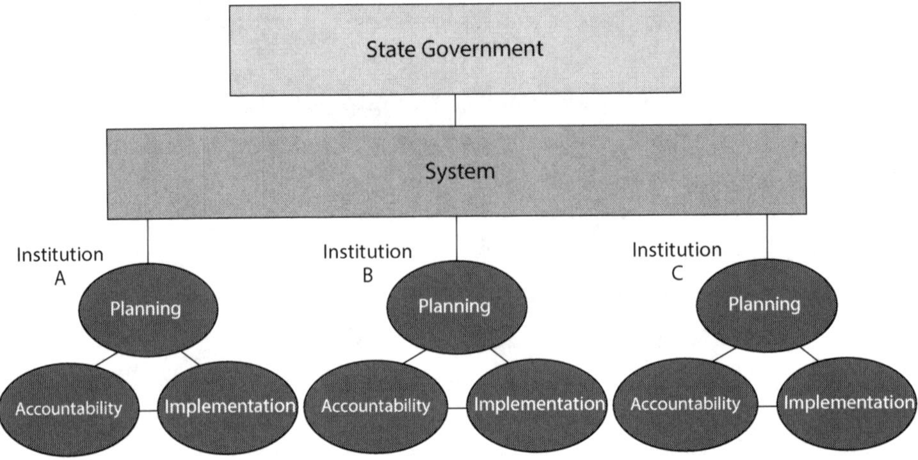

Figure 1.1 The structure of early systems.

broader public interest that might transcend those internal priorities. Figure 1.1 depicts the relationships among the system (the governing board and executive office), the constituent campuses, and state government in early systems.

Evolution of System Functions

Over the past two decades, the functions of some systems have evolved to perform distinct "system" functions in response to changes in the political and economic environment and changes within higher education. Important new functions include:

- Strategic or master planning for the system, setting forth goals that link the system as a whole, not just the independent components, to public priorities such as access, affordability, completion, and workforce and economic development.
- Ensuring that each campus has a strategic plan (with associated performance metrics) in place. These plans are typically required to reflect the unique characteristics (and aspirations) of each campus while at the same time aligning with the priority goals of the system.

- Holding institutions accountable for making progress toward achieving their goals and contributing to system goals—monitoring progress and working with institutions that are falling short of expectations to improve their performance.
- Moving from operational budgeting to strategic budgeting—linking the budget to the strategic plans at the state and institutional levels—along with maintaining databases and conducting institutional research to support strategic decision-making.
- Achieving economies of scale in areas such as information technology, procurement, and human resources.
- Holding institutions accountable for adherence to approved budgets and providing technical assistance to institutions that are failing to operate within their approved budgets.
- Providing information on best practices that have proven to be effective in improving student retention and completion.

Many systems, which serve as the single point of legal authority for human resources—as the employer of record—also assumed greater responsibilities for collective bargaining with faculty and staff unions. One effect of this development was to draw some systems deeply into matters which heretofore had been primarily institutional-level matters, for example, defining faculty conditions of employment, faculty workloads, promotion and tenure processes, grievance procedures, and details of compensation agreements. This development has added to the politicization of systems inasmuch as collective bargaining is regulated by state government, which in numerous states is subject to strong influence from public employee unions.

Changes in System Roles

This set of functions provides the baseline for system activity. They are primarily "inward facing"; that is, they focus on relationships with institutions within the system. The main "outward facing" functions were governmental relations and advocating on behalf of institutions to state government and the public. Systems will continue to perform these baseline functions. It is the functions they perform in addition to this list that will determine the effectiveness and even continued existence of systems going forward.

The conditions that prompted the formation of early systems no longer apply—for example, higher education institutions are now scrambling to fill the seats they were once struggling to create. But most systems continue to focus on the roles they were created to fulfill; they have not adapted to new realities. There is a growing gap between the roles they are playing and the roles they need to play. In the future, systems will need to lead and manage the shift, as described in table 1.1.

Table 1.1 The past and future roles of higher education systems

From	To
Overseeing expansion	Overseeing realignment, contraction, and consolidation
Reliance on the state as the principal source of core funding	Students as the primary source of revenues
A subsidized entity	A multiunit, market-driven enterprise in which the individual units compete for enrollments and revenues from tuition and other nonstate sources
A political environment that promotes expansion of access	A political environment that emphasizes student success/completion and often questions the performance and value of the enterprise
A tradition of students going to the source of instruction	A new requirement that instruction be delivered to students wherever they may be
A traditional degree structure	A world experiencing a proliferation of credentials—certificates, badges, etc.
A hands-off approach to academic affairs	Systemwide involvement to eliminate barriers to transfer and students' ability to draw on assets of all system institutions
Expecting individual constituent institutions to respond to state priorities	Orchestrating the collective system response to those priorities
Evaluating campus leaders' performance	Complementing evaluation with providing professional development to ensure campus leaders' effectiveness
Relying on institutions to adopt good practices with regard to student success initiatives	Identifying such initiatives and ensuring that they are taken to scale through adoption by all constituent institutions

The future will require that systems foster collaboration among their constituent institutions to ensure that students in all parts of the state receive seamless access to the full range of educational assets of the system. It will also require that these collective assets be brought to bear on the priority needs of the state and regions within the state.

Two major changes in practices will be required if systems are to add value in the future. The first involves the nature of the inward facing relationships between the system office and the constituent campuses. The second involves the outward facing relationships between the system office and external entities.

Changes in Inward Facing Relationships

The inward facing relationships have historically been individual ties between the system office and each constituent campus, as shown in figure 1.1. In the future, these relationships will have to be expanded to include those among the system office and constituent campuses, all working in collaboration with each other. Figure 1.2 depicts the nature of these more deeply integrated relationships.

Figure 1.2 reflects the reality that systems operate in an increasingly complex environment in which states, systems, and institutions all have their own priorities, different approaches to achieving their goals, separate identities, varying capabilities, and different metrics for monitoring progress toward goal achievement. The task for the system office is to ensure that these state, system, and institutional goals are brought into alignment as appropriate while ensuring institutions have the flexibility to pursue these goals in ways that fit their mission and culture. The key is clarity of goals at all levels and agreement on the metrics to be used in measuring progress toward achieving those goals.

Changes in Outward Facing Relationships

The second major required change is in the outward facing role: that between the system office and external entities. This change will re-

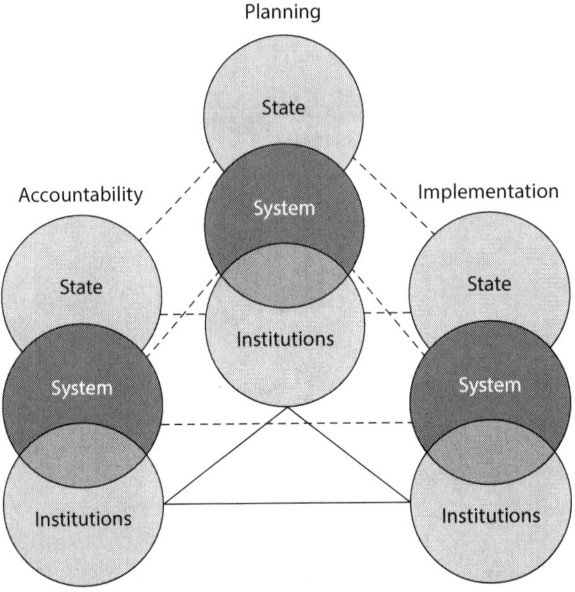

Figure 1.2 The relationships of system offices to institutions and the state.

quire expanding those relationships beyond state government to include partners that can help address the priority problems of the state or regions within the state and to capitalize on the opportunities these problems provide. The partners could be K–12 education, other post-secondary institutions (including private sector institutions), health care providers, state and local economic and workforce development agencies, and more. In this scenario, systems identify state or regional problems requiring attention, seek the involvement of other parties that can make contributions to solutions, and ensure that the assets of their constituent institutions are brought to bear on addressing the problems. Combining the inward and outward looking perspectives of the future system results in the depiction presented in figure 1.3.

In order to perform the roles indicated in figure 1.3, system offices will need to change both their functions and, in some cases, their structures. These required changes are described in the following sections of this chapter.

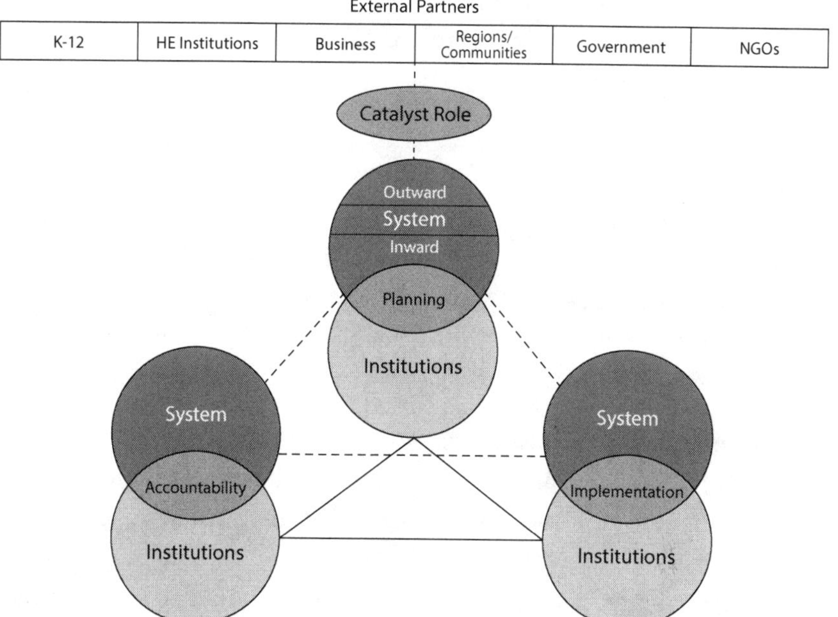

Figure 1.3 The relationships of the future.

Changes in System Functions

In the future, systems will need to become much more adept at performing functions that involve increasing the level of collaboration among institutions to both improve efficiency and enhance provision of services.

Improving Efficiency by Promoting Collaboration and Sharing of Resources

Collaboration in pursuit of efficiencies most often involves centralizing services, frequently in the system office but occasionally at one of the constituent campuses. This is not new territory for most systems; they already centralize some key functions such as legal services and government relations. The question is, What other functions might be considered for operating as shared services?

Functions to Consider for Improved Efficiency

Numerous changes will be required to transform the conception of a campus from a full-service entity to one in which the campus is a point of delivery for services that draw on all instructional and support capacities of the system. As an aside, the changes suggested by such a transformation have major implications for the accreditation process.

The following list provides a starting point for discussion about additional functions that might be considered for performance as a shared service:

1. Institutional leadership/cabinet functions. Most such functions are difficult to consolidate because the demands of community and internal institutional constituents require a single institution focus, though in a select few cases, leadership positions of the system office and a campus can be combined. Exceptions are the functions performed by the chief financial officer (CFO), the institutional research/planning office, and the budget office.
2. Student service and institutional support functions associated with:
   a. Student academic records
   b. Student financial aid processing
   c. Student advising for intercampus opportunities
3. Accounting
4. Internal audit
5. Human resources
6. Construction management
7. Risk management
8. Administrative support for information technology (IT)
9. Institutional research
10. Grants and contracts administration
11. Research compliance
12. Fundraising. This one is tricky because most donors have a connection to a specific campus, not the system. Yet system officials can seek support for system-wide initiatives from some

donors. A useful function at the system level is to coordinate the approaches to donors to ensure that they are not being bombarded by multiple campuses.

13. Academic support functions
    a. Academic IT support
    b. Acquisition and sharing of library materials and other information resources

All these functions require specialized expertise, the kinds of expertise that need not be replicated at every campus in the system if appropriate sharing mechanisms are put in place. To be sure, generalists in the field may be needed on each campus, but many costs can be avoided if individuals with the most expertise and the highest salaries can be shared among multiple institutions.

Role of the System Office

A key role for the system office is to set the agenda for change—to make the case for necessary change and to create the conditions in which institutional leaders, faculty, and staff embrace change and work diligently to achieve it. Central to this change agenda is the need to work collaboratively in meeting the needs of students, communities, and the state. The role of the system office in promoting collaboration and sharing resources is to create an environment in which their institutions see it as in their best interest to work together in pursuit of cost savings and improved services to students and other clients. At heart, this is an exercise in managing culture, specifically a change from a culture of institutional competition to one of institutional collaboration. Two practices are particularly important in this regard. The first is the use of data to ascertain the benefits of any changes. In the case of collaborating on consolidating any of the functions listed above, the data of most importance are those showing the benefits of joint action, both economic and regarding service levels. The data may show that some consolidations will not yield the intended benefits. In such instances, it is wise to back away from consolidation and not move in this direction in pursuit of organizational symmetry—an attitude of making collaboration an all-or-nothing proposition. Not all functions that possibly can be shared necessarily should be, and not all institutions need be part of the shared services arrangement. The benefits for some institutions simply may not be evident from the analyses.

The second important practice is to communicate the reasons for consolidation and the supporting data widely and consistently within the institutions involved. It is equally important to communicate the reasons for not consolidating functions in those instances in which the data do not support such actions. Transparency and openness are critical. Part of the communication should include a description of how the consolidation of processes will affect users at the campus level. Users need to be convinced that the new processes will be easier to use, yield better results, and be supported at the campus level. Perhaps more important than communication about resulting cost savings are conversations about how those savings will be utilized—how savings will be invested in things that are important to the campus community. Cost savings alone seldom win the day.

Collaboration in Sharing of Academic Programs

The discussion thus far has focused on largely administrative functions. But it is in the sharing of academic programs that major benefits to students can accrue. Declining enrollments and the associated reductions in tuition revenues are financially stressing institutions in many systems. The reaction has been to cut programs and student support services (much easier to do than reducing tenured faculty lines); at the extreme are campus closures. Neither of these responses are recipes for enhancing services to students. Systems have a role to play in brokering program-sharing relationships between and among institutions—relationships that allow either the joint delivery of programs or the delivery of full programs from an institution with a critical mass of students and faculty to an institution that has determined it must discontinue its own program. The system role is first to bring the parties together and foster the conversation, and second to create a funding mechanism that offers incentives for the institutions to share programs.

Eliminating Barriers to Transfer

Brokering bilateral institutional arrangements is the least complicated role systems can play in promoting academic collaboration among constituent institutions. There are several more expansive roles that can be played. One of those roles involves eliminating barriers to transfer and the loss of credits in the transfer process. This is a problem that bedevils most systems and provides fodder for legislators looking for issues they can use to criticize system and institutional leadership. Constituent complaints concerning loss of credits in the transfer process is high on the list of topics in many legislative oversight hearings. The ideal system response starts with creating a committee of faculty and charging them with developing a common general education curriculum, one that is designed to be used by all institutions in the system. This step alleviates most of the loss of credit during transfer and is especially important in systems that have community colleges among the members. The role of the system in the process is to convene the participants, set the expectations (there *will* be a Common Core curriculum), and ensure that the process continues to move forward. A "hung jury" is not an option. The system role can be extended to ensure that there is no loss of credit in transfer of credits in the basic courses in most popular majors. Too frequently, academic "snobbism" gets in the way of transferring courses and having them count as credit toward a degree in the major, not as elective credit. This issue is most prevalent when the basic courses in the major are taught at a community college and students seek to transfer those credits to a university. The objective from the system perspective should be to minimize, if not eliminate, any loss of credit in the process of transfer among the system institutions.

Granting Credit for Prior Learning

A second role that can be played by systems to help students complete their programs of study in a timely fashion is to allow the granting of credit for prior learning. This role can be played out in numerous ways. First, the system can act to remove any fiscal disincentives for campuses to accept credit for prior learning. One way to accomplish this is to treat all prior credits as if they were taught in the classroom by campus faculty in the system calculations for allocation of resources. Acceptance of such credits can be further incentivized by providing a bonus in the resource allocation model, in much the same way that bonuses are granted for credits earned by identified high-priority populations. A more aggressive approach is to establish a system-wide approach to prior learning assessments (PLAs). This requires that the system office work with campuses to identify faculty assessors in the different disciplines and train those faculty in the nuances of assessing prior learning. This specially trained cadre of faculty assesses all requests for granting of credit for prior learning, not just requests that arise from students enrolled at the faculty member's home campus. Once a judgment is made, all institutions in the system are bound to accept the decision.

Leadership that results in a system-wide approach to assessments of prior learning benefits students in multiple ways. It allows them to complete their programs of study with less wasted time and at less cost. Equally important, it keeps students moving forward rather than treading water (and resenting the fact that they are having to spend time and money repeating content they already know). Having the assessments apply to all institutions in the system also eliminates problems in transferring credits earned through PLA, especially when the credits were initially assessed at a less prestigious institution and transferred to an institution higher in the academic pecking order.

Improving Student Experience and Student Success

Steps that improve the student experience and enhance the likelihood of student success through actions that apply to all institutions in a system can only be accomplished with leadership from a system office; voluntary actions of institutions will not yield the same results. These improvements are examples of the ways in which systems add value to the benefits provided by their campuses. Implementing such changes requires skillful change management on the part of system leaders. These steps deal with topics that are the purview of faculty, and faculty must both buy into these efforts and actively participate in their implementation. System leaders can orchestrate the process needed to put these processes in place, but they cannot substitute their judgments for those of academics who have the disciplinary expertise needed to legitimize the decisions made.

Monitoring Results

The functions performed at the system level must extend beyond putting processes in place to also include regular monitoring of the results. Agreements reached among institutions can quickly erode—new course requirements for degrees get approved at the campus level, and general education requirements that were agreed upon by all system institutions get picked apart piece by piece, with institutions either substituting requirements or adding them. While the monitoring function can be performed by imposition of detailed reporting requirements that accompany any campus-level changes, there are less obtrusive ways of assessing whether the agreements reached are being abrogated. Such changes will inevitably result in students taking additional courses to graduate. Calculating trends in credit hours accumulated by program completers—and comparing these trends for students who transfer vis-à-vis those who complete their programs at a single institution—will provide all the information needed to determine whether discussions about the agreements need to be reopened.

Adopting a Systemic Approach to Student Access and Success

The steps described above are actions that can improve student access and success, but systems can—if they adopt a true systems approach—

do much more in this regard. The system objective should be to serve clients (students, employers, communities, and the state) in all parts of the state as efficiently and effectively as possible. Serving effectively means providing services where they are needed and when they are needed. Serving efficiently means using available system educational assets—including faculty, staff, budget, and facilities—not creating new ones whenever and wherever new demands arise. This translates into institutions with the needed programs being willing to deliver those programs wherever in the state there is a minimum level of demand, often through use of technology-enabled delivery mechanisms.

Creating the Environment and Incentives for Implementation

The function of the system in this set of circumstances is to create the environment and incentives to promote sharing of educational resources among institutions and to ensure that the technological infrastructure necessary for such sharing is in place. Creating the environment requires a concerted effort to alter campus cultures, changing from institution-centric to client-centric and from competitive to collaborative. Culture change requires a clear, and frequently repeated, rationale, and the use of the normal system processes—resource allocation, hiring and personnel evaluations, campus leadership, the award of tenure, and accountability reports—to reinforce the focus on delivery of service to wherever it is needed from wherever it is available. System actions include:

- Articulating a clear vision for the ways in which an effective twenty-first-century system, particularly a system supported by public funds, should serve its multiple stakeholders. Such a vision statement sets the tone for all the decisions that follow.
- Allocating resources in ways that reward collaboration and pays for the infrastructure needed to support faculty development and the development of courses and programs specifically designed for online delivery.
- Hiring campus leaders with a track record of, and ongoing

commitment to, collaboration in the delivery of services, and regularly evaluating and retaining those leaders on their demonstration of those qualities.

- Modifying promotion and tenure policies to remove disincentives for acting as good system citizens—not just discipline experts and participants in campus service—and to include expectations for collaborative activities in the criteria. This is not to suggest that existing criteria for excellence in the classroom and contributions to the discipline's body of knowledge should be dismissed, but rather that the fuzzy definition of the "public service" portion of most tenure and promotion criteria be honed to reflect service to a broader set of stakeholders than those found inside the academy. This may be accomplished, in part, through linking promotion and tenure criteria to an expectation that faculty research or public service work links the content of the discipline to the needs of the external constituents (agriculture extension is a classic example of public service carried out in a way intended by this definition).
- Changing the annual system accountability report. Doing so requires little more than the addition of one or two additional metrics that show progress on various collaboration initiatives and the numbers of clients that have benefitted from these initiatives. Perhaps more important, it requires ensuring that the metrics reflect a system-wide perspective—for example, system-wide data on access, completion, and success—not institution by institution, and that populations that are underserved (by income, race, geography, etc.) are presented as a way of both showing improvements and drawing attention to areas needing more focus. Important to the culture change agenda is ensuring that collaborative initiatives are highlighted in the narrative.

Outward Facing Functions

The discussion about system roles presented above has focused on the inward facing roles of system offices, those that deal with ensuring that institutions are effective and that they work together to enhance delivery of services and achievement of efficiencies. Outward facing activities have most often confined to those involving advocacy and government relations. In the future, it will be in the best interests of the system, and higher education generally, to demonstrate contributions to a broader array of stakeholders. With numbers of high school graduates declining in most states, systems and constituent institutions will have to increasingly justify their requests for state funds by proving their worth to other beneficiaries. A slight adjustment in focus would have them serve more adults, especially those whose employers require them to acquire updated or different sets of skills. These adjustments will be hard to implement in institutions steeped in a culture of serving recent high school graduates; system leadership and assistance to institutions will be crucial. New methods of delivery, programs subdivided into stackable credentials, each of which has value in the marketplace, and provision of different kinds of student support services will all be required. But they will be important to the financial viability of systems in the future, and system offices can play key roles in helping their institutions acquire the capacities and abilities that will be necessary to play those roles.

But serving new audiences with essentially the same programs minimally repackaged, even if done exceedingly well, will underplay the value that can be added by systems. Even if systems do not have land-grant institutions established by the Morrill Acts of 1862 and 1890 among their members, they would do well to adopt some of the cultural values of those types of institutions and emulate some of the behaviors of the best of them. These institutions bring their knowledge to practitioners in many different fields and in the process help not only the individuals but also their communities and the state. At the core has been helping practitioners in the agriculture industry, and these institutions established outreach centers in every county in their states. These extension centers have evolved to incorporate urban agriculture, horticulture, and all manner of other topics centered on helping people grow things successfully. They represent the epitome of service to a specified audience. There is no reason that those basic principles cannot be elevated from the campus to the system level and applied to a much broader set of industries—health care, education, energy, manufacturing, transportation, energy, housing, the environment—and, for many communities, to assist entrepreneurs regardless of industry. To implement this vision of public education in service to the state requires that systems play several roles that are outside their typical repertoire:

- *Assessing needs*. Systems may have analytic staff that can develop "social indicators" and environmental scan reports for the state and pinpoint the different needs in different parts of the state. These analyses can provide direction for actionable initiatives—not just health care needs, for example, but the more specific issues of obesity and diabetes in one part of the state and neonatal care in another.
- *Convening partners*. None of the problems identified can be addressed by systems or their member institutions acting alone. Depending on the issue to be addressed, the capacities of a variety of partners may need to be tapped. These partners can include community organizations, state agencies (workforce/economic development), K–12 districts, other higher education institutions (including private colleges), health care organizations and agencies, and business groups. The university system need not do all the work—or even lead the work—but it must ensure that the right players are at the table, that a plan of action is developed, and that the functions assigned to the system and its constituent institutions are implemented.
- *Marshalling system resources as appropriate*. University systems and their campuses have a wide array of assets that can be deployed to address a wide range of problems. The obvious assets are the instructional and research capacities embodied in faculty. But they also have students seeking community service projects, legal and human resources expertise, technology infrastructure and associated management capabilities, and a host of other, often unique in the state, resources. The role of systems is to connect these resources to the problems identified and to create

environments in which individuals with the skills and knowledge to be helpful want to be part of the solution. A recent example of this role played by systems across the country was in leading various responses to the COVID-19 pandemic. Specific system contributions included clearing the way with state credentialing bodies for nursing students to graduate early so they could meet the increased demand for patient care, tapping into state epidemiological expertise and sharing it across the system, negotiating favorable contracts with Internet service providers in support of the shift to online education, and helping to clear regulatory barriers to converting laboratory facilities to testing centers.

- *Taking the heat.* Much of what is being proposed in this chapter will go against long-practiced traditions and deeply held beliefs. This can make managing change difficult, sometimes politically perilous work. System leaders can make this work easier for campus executives by openly stating specific priorities or changes, thereby providing cover for campus leaders who are making necessary but unpopular decisions or calling for particular changes. This system role is increasing in importance in states where the imperatives of demography and workforce needs sharply conflict with social policy initiatives of state policymakers. In many states, workforce needs cannot be met without increasing the number of underrepresented minorities who successfully complete postsecondary education programs. This reality runs headlong into political debate over diversity, equity, and inclusion (DEI) initiatives in those same states. System leaders can play a crucial role in developing strategies for bridging this chasm, taking the political heat for these strategies and helping institutions navigate turbulent waters.

Proactive System Leadership Roles for the Future

All the above suggests that, in the future, systems will have to take a more proactive approach to their leadership roles. This means that system leaders might take the lead in identifying additional programs needed in the system and choosing the institution(s) in which those programs could best be housed. The less desirable approach is waiting for one of their institutions to seek approval to offer the program. Similarly, system leadership will have to be more aggressive in identifying social, political, and economic issues to be addressed and in linking system resources to those problems. As well, system leaders will need to strike a fine balance between leading changes within the system in response to external demands and, at the same time, providing some degree of insulation from certain external forces that would undermine institutional effectiveness. In short, system leaders will need to expend less of their effort in managing their institutions and spend more time ensuring that external stakeholders are served.

Structure

Following the maxim that form should follow function, changing the roles of system offices implies the need to modify system structures accordingly. This is not to suggest wholesale change; some departments within system offices will continue to operate very much as usual. The functioning of some departments will necessarily change, however, and some new units and functions will need to be added.

Functions Requiring Limited Structural Change

The structure of some functions will require little or no change. For example, there will be little need to change the structure of the system's government relations office. While the specifics of advocacy may change, there will be no cause to change the general organization of the office. The same holds true for the offices of the general counsel and the system's chief diversity officer. There will continue to be need for a chief financial officer; the functions of this office will likely continue substantially as before.

Structure of Academic Functions

In contrast, significant changes may be required in the chief academic office. Historically, the primary functions of a system academic office have been to act on institutional requests for new programs (recommended approval or denial) and to create venues for the sharing of good educational practices among campus chief academic officers. In some systems, that role has expanded to include leadership of articulation and transfer initiatives within the system. In the future vision for system leadership, however, the roles of this office will have to change even more. First, these offices will have to become more proactive in their inward looking academic planning activities and view the shaping of system educational assets as a primary objective. As systems seek to serve a broader set of stakeholders outside academe, they will have to align their educational and other assets with the needs of those stakeholders. Instead of only responding to institutional initiatives regarding establishment of new programs, the most effective systems will identify additional programs needed somewhere in the system and identify the institutions best situated to deliver those programs. This forward looking stance extends beyond academic programs to include assets such as technology infrastructure.

The question for system-level planners is, What changes to system infrastructure would have to be made to allow the system, as a collective, to serve high-priority needs of other stakeholders, for example, to provide telemedicine to parts of the state underserved by health care providers?

Structure of Back-Office Operations

Many systems are seeking cost savings and provision of better service to their campuses by consolidating a variety of operations. In the main, these are back-office operations, but there are opportunities to extend this consolidation to include online programs, advising services, and the like. They pursue consolidation for all the right reasons, but then must consider how best to organize the offices that conduct these activities. One option is no change—keep the relevant system offices intact and expand their roles to include providing services for all (or some) of the constituent institutions. The alternative is to organize these functions under the auspices of a spin-off "services corporation" and remove them from the daily functioning of the system office. There are several good reasons for considering this step:

- It separates the tactical, operational functions of the system office from the broader strategic functions that should be the primary focus of that office. Experience indicates that the immediacy of operational issues will take precedence over attention to the strategic functions, leaving the most important work of the system office without appropriate consideration. Protecting the scarce resource of executive time and attention from the demands of secondary issues is a worthy objective.
- It creates a circumstance in which the centralized functions can be managed by individuals who have specific program management skills. Their only job would be to provide effective and efficient services in a prescribed set of areas. This structure allows these individuals to focus only on operational issues and not be distracted by unhelpful conversations about the strategic issues facing the system.
- It protects the system office from charges of administrative bloat. Performing centralized functions requires a staff large enough to get the job done. If this staff is integrated into the system office, the count of system office employees will balloon, inevitably leading to charges from faculty and others at the campus level that the system is growing at the expense of the campuses. No amount of accurate data and explanation of benefits to the campuses is likely to persuade those who want to make an issue of system overreach. Housing these functions in a related, but separate, organization provides a level of protection to the system office.
- It creates business opportunities for the service corporation. Providing services to institutions outside the system is difficult if managed by a unit inside the system office. There are fewer

restrictions on creating fee-for-service business opportunities if those services are provided by a separate organization. If nothing else, the possibility of such money-making opportunities will serve to keep the service corporation competitively priced.

Structure of Outward Facing Functions

All the functions described above can be performed by units within the system office without a change of structure. But there are some outward facing functions that will require changing the internal structure of the system office. Most system offices have no unit devoted exclusively to identifying state and regional problems that must be solved if the citizens of the state are to have economic opportunity and a high quality of life. The work of this unit must also extend to developing partnerships that can collaborate to address these problems. Most systems have institutional research units that almost exclusively analyze the factors that affect institutions within the system. There is a need for these units to expand the scope of their analyses to include creating social indicators that describe the "state of the state" with regard to key factors—including social and economic mobility—and to analyze regional data with an eye to identifying the most important problems facing the region. While the analyses of these data will require an expansion of role, the unit conducting these analyses will not necessarily require structural reform. There remains, however, the need to use the data as a basis for forming partnerships that can address the identified problems. This is a function outside that typically performed by any unit within system offices: it will require a new unit with the explicit assignment of identifying and creating conditions for addressing priority problems at the state and regional levels.

Changes in Structure: Not the First Option

It is clear from our discussion of roles and structure that the primary changes required are those involving functions, not structure. The kinds of changes needed to make systems more effective in the future will not require major organizational upheaval. They will require purposive actions by existing organizational units, with the express intent of serving a broader array of stakeholders. The fact that wholesale structural changes will not be required reduces the extent of internal pushback to the kinds of changes being suggested in this chapter. But there will be pushback, primarily from internal constituents who resent system leadership time and money being devoted to any entity or cause outside system institutions.

When changes to systems are proposed to improve the efficiency and effectiveness of institutions within the system, the focus is almost always on making structural changes. With the exception perhaps of a severe funding crisis or loss of accreditation, the above discussion indicates that restructuring is less important than modifying the functions performed by units within the existing structure. A focus on function rather than structure has numerous benefits. It keeps the change process under the control of the system rather than letting it fall victim to the whims of a state-level political process. This allows those functions that do not need to change to continue without disruption. It also allows changes that do need to be made to occur in a measured and targeted way—the application of the scalpel rather than the cleaver over the extended period required to make changes thoughtfully. The most important change of all is a change in culture, from institution-centric to client-centric. No change in structure will yield culture change. Change in function is an enabling tool; done wisely, it promotes the broader culture change that will allow systems to demonstrate their value to both policymakers and the citizens of the state.

Failure to adapt in the ways outlined in this chapter will be to the detriment of both students and the broader state and society. Students who are part of states' changing demographics will be deprived of access and opportunities. Employers will not get ready access to the skilled workforces they need. And the state will squander opportunities to draw on its major intellectual asset to help address major societal problems. Adaptation in the ways we suggest will benefit individuals and the larger society and redound to the benefit of the system and its component institutions.

Higher Education Systems

Higher education systems can be defined as groups of institutions that are organized in some manner to accomplish common purposes and pursue common goals. By far the predominant form of higher education system in the United States is one in which several public universities fall under the legal authority of a single board (commonly a board of trustees or board of regents). These systems are identified in the chart below. In a book about higher education systems, however, it is important to recognize the other kinds of systems that exist in the higher education ecosystem. Principal examples include:

- Local community college districts that are organized as systems with central leadership but separately established campuses—"systems" such as the Los Angeles Community College District, Maricopa Community College District, and Miami-Dade College. These systems exist within broader statewide systems or coordinating agencies.
- Voluntary systems of institutions that join for common purposes (e.g., shared academic programs, library resources, administrative services) but do so without ceding their independent governance structures. Examples include the Associated Colleges of the Midwest, the Claremont Colleges, and the Big 10 Academic Alliance.
- Systems of independent institutions such as Antioch University, Webster University and its international campuses, and Carlos Albizu University.

While not the explicit focus of this book, these kinds of systems play many of the same roles as their public higher education system counterparts. As higher education moves into the future, this broader view of systems must be embraced. Table 1.2 gives a list of higher education systems by state, including public university and college systems, universities with multiple branches, statewide community and technical college systems, statewide coordinating/regulatory entities, and statewide college and university associations.

Table 1.2 State-by-state listing of higher education systems

State	Public University Systems with Multiple Colleges and Universities	Universities with Multiple Branch Campuses Linked to Main Campus[1]	Statewide Community and/or Technical College Systems[2]	Statewide Coordinating Boards/State Higher Education Agencies[3]	Statewide Voluntary (Nongovernmental) Associations of Colleges and Universities[4]
Alabama	University of Alabama System		Alabama Community College System (C)	Alabama Commission for Higher Education	
Alaska	University of Alaska System			Alaska Postsecondary Education Commission	
Arkansas	Arkansas State University System, University of Arkansas System			Arkansas Division of Higher Education	
California	California State University System, University of California System		California Community College System (C)		
Colorado	Colorado State University System, University of Colorado System		Colorado Community College System (G, C)	Colorado Commission on Higher Education/ Department of Higher Education	
Connecticut	Connecticut State College and University System	University of Connecticut		Connecticut Office of Higher Education	
District of Columbia	University of District of Columbia			Office of the State Superintendent of Education Government of the District of Columbia	Consortium of Universities in the Washington Metropolitan Area

(continued)

Table 1.2 Continued

State	Public University Systems with Multiple Colleges and Universities	Universities with Multiple Branch Campuses Linked to Main Campus[1]	Statewide Community and/or Technical College Systems[2]	Statewide Coordinating Boards/State Higher Education Agencies[3]	Statewide Voluntary (Nongovernmental) Associations of Colleges and Universities[4]
Florida	State University System of Florida		Florida College System, Florida Department of Education (C)		
Georgia	University System of Georgia		Georgia Technical College System (G)		
Hawaii	University of Hawaii System				
Idaho	Idaho State Board of Education				
Illinois	University of Illinois System, Southern Illinois System		Illinois Community College System (C)	Illinois Board of Higher Education	
Indiana		Indiana University, Purdue University	IV Tech Community College System (G)	Indiana Commission on Higher Education	
Iowa	Iowa Board of Regents				
Kansas	Kansas Board of Regents				
Kentucky			Kentucky Community and Technical College System (G)	Kentucky Council on Postsecondary Education	

Louisiana	Louisiana State University System, Southern University System, University of Louisiana System		Louisiana Community and Technical College System (G)	Louisiana Board of Regents	
Maine	University of Maine System		Maine Community College System (G)		
Maryland	University System of Maryland			Maryland Higher Education Commission	Maryland Association of Community Colleges
Massachusetts	University of Massachusetts			Massachusetts Board of Higher Education, Department of Higher Education	Massachusetts Association of Community Colleges
Michigan					Michigan Association of≈State Universities, Academically Michigan Community College Association
Minnesota	Minnesota State University	University of Minnesota			
Mississippi	Mississippi Board of Institutions of Higher Learning		Mississippi Community College Board (C)		
Missouri	University of Missouri System			Missouri Department of Higher Education and Workforce Development	Missouri Community College Association

(continued)

Table 1.2 Continued

State	Public University Systems with Multiple Colleges and Universities	Universities with Multiple Branch Campuses Linked to Main Campus[1]	Statewide Community and/or Technical College Systems[2]	Statewide Coordinating Boards/State Higher Education Agencies[3]	Statewide Voluntary (Nongovernmental) Associations of Colleges and Universities[4]
Montana	Montana State University System				
Nebraska	University of Nebraska System, Nebraska State College System			Nebraska Coordinating Commission for Postsecondary Education	Nebraska Community College Association
Nevada	Nevada System of Higher Education				
New Hampshire	State University System of New Hampshire		New Hampshire Community and Technical College System	New Hampshire Department of Education, Division of Educator Support and Higher Education, Higher Education Commission	
New Jersey		Rutgers University		New Jersey Office of the Secretary of Higher Education	New Jersey Association of State Colleges, Universities New Jersey, Council of County Colleges, New Jersey Presidents' Council
New Mexico	New Mexico State University	University of New Mexico			New Mexico Association of Community Colleges

New York	State University of New York, City University of New York			New York State Education Department, Office of Higher Education	
North Carolina	University of North Carolina System		North Carolina Community College System (G)		
North Dakota	North Dakota University System				
Ohio		Ohio State University, Ohio University, Kent State University, Bowling Green State University, Miami University, University of Akron, Wright State University		Ohio Department of Higher Education	Ohio Association of Community Colleges
Oklahoma				Oklahoma Board of Regents	
Oregon				Oregon Higher Education Coordinating Board	Oregon Community College Association
Pennsylvania	Pennsylvania State System of Higher Education	Pennsylvania State University, University of Pittsburgh, Temple University		Pennsylvania Department of Education, Office of Postsecondary and Higher Education	Pennsylvania Community College Association
Rhode Island	Rhode Island Council on Postsecondary Education, Office of Postsecondary Education Commissioner				

(*continued*)

Table 1.2 Continued

State	Public University Systems with Multiple Colleges and Universities	Universities with Multiple Branch Campuses Linked to Main Campus[1]	Statewide Community and/or Technical College Systems[2]	Statewide Coordinating Boards/State Higher Education Agencies[3]	Statewide Voluntary (Nongovernmental) Associations of Colleges and Universities[4]
South Carolina		University of South Carolina	South Carolina Technical College System (G)	South Carolina Commission on Higher Education	
South Dakota	South Dakota Board of Regents		South Dakota Board of Technical Education (G)		
Tennessee	University of Tennessee System		Tennessee Board of Regents: Community College System and Tennessee Colleges of Technology (G)	Tennessee Higher Education Commission	
Texas	Texas A & M System, Texas State University System, Texas Tech University System, University of Houston System, University of Texas System	Texas Women's University University of North Texas System		Texas Higher Education Coordinating Board	Texas Association of Community Colleges
Utah	Utah State System of Higher Education				

Vermont	Vermont State College System			
Virginia			Virginia Community College System (G)	State Council for Higher Education in Virginia
Washington	University of Washington, Washington State University		Washington State Board of Community and Technical Colleges (C)	Washington Student Achievement Council
West Virginia		West Virginia University	West Virginia Community and Technical College System (C)	West Virginia Higher Education Policy Commission
Wisconsin	University of Wisconsin System		Wisconsin Technical College System (C)	
Wyoming			Wyoming Community College Commission (C)	

1. Included in this list are primarily universities with more than one branch campus.

2. C, coordinating entities for locally governed institutions; G, statewide governing entities.

3. Coordinating entities do not have legal authority govern public universities. Common system functions include statewide strategic planning, promoting student transfer and articulation among the state institutions, promoting collaboration and sharing of resources among institutions, making recommendations to the governor and state legislature on higher education budgets and finance policy, administering state student financial programs, and licensure/authorization of nonpublic institutions and out-of-state providers in line with state and federal requirements.

4. Included in the listing of statewide associations are voluntary/nongovernmental entities that play a significant "system" coordinating role for locally governed colleges and universities.

2 | Accreditation and Quality

System Perspectives

PETER T. EWELL

THIS CHAPTER EXAMINES the role of multi-institutional higher education systems in promoting academic and institutional quality. More particularly, it covers the role of such systems in accomplishing accreditation—the principal US mechanism for promoting and signifying quality. While focused primarily on public institutions, it addresses and provides examples drawn from all institutional types at both the four- and two-year levels.

Introduction: Why Should Systems Address These Issues?

A first important question is why multi-institutional systems should examine quality and get involved in accreditation at all. There are several reasons to justify this approach.

First, they can represent public stakeholder views and interests better than individual institutions acting independently. This is consistent with lately popular arguments about the "public" as opposed to instrumental purposes of higher education (Brenneman et al., 2010).

Second, the central coordination provided by a system usually means greater efficiencies with respect to data collection approaches and tools.

For example, common instruments like assessments and surveys can be provided together with data extraction techniques applicable to the common course management systems that many systems employ. "System accreditation," if applicable, moreover involves a single report generation and review process rather than preparation of duplicative and costly responses by individual institutions.

Third, approaching quality review as a system can address the complex issue of assessing student progress and completion for students who attend several institutions in the system sequentially or simultaneously, which is increasingly the case. Most systems have centrally administered unit record databases that contain records for all students enrolled, regardless of which institution they attend, which makes longitudinal tracking of this kind straightforward.

Finally, because system administration is centralized, systems can speak with a single voice that is considerably more authoritative with respect to the provision of public information, interaction with major employers, and advocacy for state and federal funding.

Different Approaches (with Selected Examples)

Once a multi-institutional system decides to get involved with accountability for student learning and success, there are many approaches to choose from, virtually all of which have been tried somewhere. Here we discuss some of the most common approaches.

Systems can first establish common requirements for all institutions to administer the same data collection instruments on a regular basis. These can include cognitive assessments such as the University of Texas system's use of the Collegiate Learning Assessment (CLA) under board direction.[1] Or they can include common student surveys such as those administered by the University of North Carolina and the North Carolina Community College System (NCCCS).

1. All examples in this chapter, unless otherwise noted, are drawn from the author's 35 years of experience in consulting with the named systems while employed by the National Center for Higher Education Management Systems. Descriptions can also be found on agency websites, but these are not individually cited to avoid redundancy.

One version of this is performance funding that is allocated to member institutions on the basis of desired outcomes, which may include performance on designated common examinations or surveys. Tennessee engaged in this strategy for many years, using scores on the ACT COMP Assessment (and later the CLA) as well as common surveys to measure institutional performance. This applied to both the state's public systems, the University of Tennessee and the Tennessee Board of Regents.

Another approach is to establish a system-wide reporting requirement with the choice of data collection method left up to participating institutions. For example, the Virginia Community College System has required all institutions in the system to report outcomes under several common headings using a set of assessments from which the institution can choose.

As a final approach, systems can provide member institutions with technical assistance to develop their own assessment approaches, with results periodically reported to system authorities under established guidelines. The North Carolina Community College System has provided such assistance for several years.

Challenges and Issues

As they undertake these activities, multi-institutional systems face several challenges and issues. These are not uncommon in other settings, but the system context renders them more salient.

One of the most common challenges can be termed the "unit of analysis" problem. This arises whenever dissimilar entities (e.g., institutions in a system) are lumped together for assessing quality or to seek accreditation. It can occur at any level (e.g., departments in an institution as well as institutions in a system), and it becomes particularly relevant in accreditation, when systems seek a "system accreditation" under which all institutions in the system would be recognized under a single accreditation. Recent examples include Maine and Connecticut, which are now recognized as a single system entity by the New England Association of Schools and Colleges (NEASC) and the Pennsylvania State

System of Higher Education (PASSHE), which is (as of this writing) engaged in a process directed toward single recognition by the Middle States Commission on Higher Education (MSCHE). This approach, while efficient, may be problematic if it involves lumping together institutions with different missions and contexts, and most institutional accreditors have so far resisted it. One creative, though uncommon, approach to dealing with appropriate differences in context is to proactively adjust for them through a formula of some kind. For example, in assessing and reporting student progress (retention and graduation), the Oklahoma State System of Higher Education calculates "predicted" performances for each institution based on a regression model using national data, then compares these predicted statistics with actual historical performance; institutions are rewarded if their actual performance exceeds their predicted performance.

A second challenge centers on students attending multiple institutions in the system, either sequentially or simultaneously. An example is the California Community College System in the Los Angeles area, where students frequently behave in this fashion to seek out the courses they need or for scheduling reasons. The principal challenge here is how to assess the differential contributions of each institution to student success and observed learning outcomes, and to attribute cause or responsibility for purposes of accountability or accreditation. This could be addressed by treating all affected institutions as part of a single entity, but doing so runs into the "unit of analysis" problem described above.

A third challenge is about balance of authority, in particular, how much system authorities should dictate and how much they should allow individual institutional voices to determine how to move forward. Systems differ in the extent to which they are centralized and therefore in the latitude they allow constituent institutions to act on their own. Systems composed of major research universities, like the University of California or the University of North Carolina, allow constituent institutions considerable latitude of this kind compared to systems comprising less selective institutions, such as the California State University System. Systems comprising a wide variety of institutional types, like the State University of New York (SUNY) or the University of Georgia system, meanwhile, allow a wide range of discretion because they must deal with so many different types of schools.

A related challenge is appropriate division of labor between system authorities and individual institutions. Systems are better or more efficient at certain components of quality review, for example, the adoption of common procedures, technical assistance, and the procurement or production of common instruments like examinations or surveys. As noted above, this applies to surveys and performance indicators for systems like the North Carolina Community College System or for performance funding for the two systems in Tennessee. Individual institutions, in turn, are better at other components of quality review, like using nonstandardized "authentic" assessment approaches, developing assessments that reflect distinctive programmatic structures, and adjusting for different campus/departmental contexts that may affect the outcome of an assessment. As a result, system leaders need to carefully determine and balance which tasks to assume centrally and which to allow institutions discretion to gain the advantages of each.

When institutional accreditation yields different conclusions than—or directly contradicts—state or system policy, that poses a challenge for systems. All accreditors, for instance, have standards on governance emphasizing that board members should be unfettered by policies that would threaten their independent authority. But this may conflict with system policies that regulate similar matters directly. For example, the University of Alaska System—established in the state's constitution and governed by the Board of Regents—was recently challenged by the Northwest Commission on Colleges and Universities about governance when the responsibility for governance decisions at both system and institutional levels is clearly in the realm of the University's Board of Regents.[2] In such cases, system policies should dominate because it is the system that ultimately "owns" the actions of constituent institutions. Yet contradictory accreditation actions (or allegations) can cause a good deal of mischief until things can get sorted out.

2. Personal communication from the system's president.

A sixth challenge is how to handle small and redundant programs scattered across multiple institutions in a system or even, occasionally, within institutions themselves. This causes problems because small programs with few faculty are expensive and may be of questionable quality because they lack critical mass. The latter clearly affects their potential accreditation status. To address the issue of quality and to enable accreditation, systems may combine programs to increase numbers of faculty to viable levels. Doing so also maintains geographic presence across multiple campuses for a given program area. Another approach is to designate specific campuses as "lead institutions" for a particular programmatic emphasis, which allows each designated institution to invest sufficiently in this programmatic area while avoiding duplication. This was accomplished some years ago with the SUNY Agricultural and Technical Colleges under the direction of the system.

A final issue is how to handle programmatic or specialized accreditation for programs offered by member institutions. The most straightforward solution here is to use system resources to provide coordinated and centralized support for all affected programs. This generates efficiencies because system-level support can be provided using common approaches and data resources. More radically, redundant programs can be combined so that they only require one programmatic accreditation. This solution, of course, is itself subject to the "unit of analysis" challenge addressed above. If they have established system-wide approaches to program review, moreover, specialized accreditation can be undertaken under these auspices through the provision of simultaneous joint reviews by accrediting representatives and system-supplied program review authorities.

There are undoubtedly additional challenges not covered by this list, but the ones noted here can certainly keep system leaders and constituent institutions well occupied for a long time.

Future Developments and Their Impact

Several highly probable future developments will have notable impact on systems and how they conduct their business with respect to accountability and accreditation. Probably the most important future development will be the continuing growth of online instructional provision. The growth of remote instruction is partly attributable to COVID-19, but it is an independent phenomenon as well, one that was present and growing well before the pandemic. According to US Department of Education surveys for the fall of 2019, almost 18 percent of postsecondary students enrolled were fully online, with a further 38 percent enrolling in courses having some online components, including supplementary instruction or electronic access to content and the submission of student work (National Center for Education Statistics, 2020). Paradoxically, this situation makes the assessment of student learning both harder and easier. It is harder because traditional in-class assessment methods like examinations and assignments are either unmanageable or inappropriate. At the same time, assessment is easier because examinations or assignments must be designed much more intentionally, and student learning outcomes must be much more precisely defined from the outset.

A second important future development is the growing prominence of competency-based instructional provision as opposed to time-based or seat-time approaches. While statistics on this growth are harder to find than instances of online provision, a 2020 survey by the American Institutes of Research (AIR) reports that 13 percent of participating institutions had established competency-based programs, and an additional 47 percent were in the process of implementing them (AIR, 2020). Adopting such an approach enables student outcomes assessment to be tied to competency attainment directly because measurements of student learning are the basic structure for accounting for student progress. The primary example of this approach is Western Governors University, established in 1997. After just 25 years of operation, it has an enrollment topping 136,000.

A third important future development is increasing pressure for cost-effectiveness from government officials. For state policymakers, this is visible in accountability demands to show evidence of productivity, as revealed in student success rates (retention and graduation). This is matched at the federal level because of the sheer size of federal investment and rising concerns regarding student debt. Neither of these points explicitly toward evidence of student learning, but providing such evidence is part of a growing culture of accountability. Institutional accreditors, meanwhile, are also responding to this pressure so that evidence of student success is now prominent in the evidential requirements of all seven regional commissions.

A final future development centers on new and emerging approaches to institutional accreditation review. Established approaches rely on the familiar rhythm of self-study, followed by a multiday site visit by a review team, which in turn yields a commission or panel recommendation of continued affirmation or a change in accreditation status. For the future, new technologies can enable "virtual visits" where all reviewers conduct their business electronically from a distance. This can be enhanced by no-notice sampling of student work and faculty/staff behavior observed directly and unobtrusively by members of the review team. This refocusing, if done properly, provides the opportunity to emphasize student learning and success, with less emphasis on issues like the adequacy of available resources and physical/structural infrastructure. Most accreditors are already moving in this direction, but going virtual will probably accelerate this trend.

These future developments will probably occur gradually, with no immediate or abrupt impact on institutional or system practice. But their likely inevitability will mean that system leaders should plan for them and take appropriate steps as noted to mitigate their impact.

Conclusion

In sum, multi-institutional systems have many advantages in discharging accountability and assessing student learning. They can speak with a single voice that commands public attention, and they can use their central authority to gain efficiencies in generating common data and procuring assessment instruments. On the accreditation front, they can coordinate the activities of constituent institutions and, if appropriate, combine weak programs so that they are accreditable. System approaches to this task, meanwhile, can range from centralized administration of common instruments to the provision of coordinated technical assistance to constituent institutions. Predominant challenges associated with performing these tasks include selecting the proper unit of analysis (system or institution), dealing with students attending multiple institutions, establishing an appropriate division of labor and balance of authority between institutions and system leadership, and determining how to handle small and redundant programs scattered across institutions in a system. For the future, finally, a range of likely developments, including increased use of online instructional delivery, will certainly affect system operations with respect to assessment and accountability.

References

AIR. American Institutes of Research. *State of the Field: Findings from the 2020 Survey of Postsecondary Competency-Based Education*. Washington, DC: Postsecondary Competency-Based Education Research, 2020.

Brenneman, Megan Wilson, Patrick M. Callan, Peter T. Ewell, Joni E. Finney, Dennis P. Jones, and Stacey Zis. *Good Policy Good Practice II*. San Jose, CA: National Center for Public Policy and Higher Education, 2010.

National Center for Education Statistics. "Fast Facts." Retrieved July 20, 2023, https://nces.ed.gov/fastfacts/display.asp?id=80.

3 |

Is Responsive and Adaptive Collective Bargaining Possible, or Is This Déjà Vu All Over Again?

DANIEL J. JULIUS

Collective Bargaining Challenges

THIS CHAPTER EXPLORES TWO IDEAS: first, how university systems might become more responsive to external constituents, faculty, staff, and students through collective bargaining, and second, whether the labor relations process can be managed in a way to make it more rational, adaptive, and efficient. I write from the perspective of someone who has spent 45 years representing public and private institutions and systems at the bargaining table, including some of the largest systems in the nation, serving as an arbitrator, mediator, and past president of two higher education national associations in human resources: the College and University Personnel and Human Resources Association (CUPA-HR) and the Academy of Academic Personnel Administrators (AAPA). I have also supervised labor management relations as the chief academic officer.

At the outset, I acknowledge the difficulties in making recommendations about labor relations, responsiveness, rationality, and adaptation. Many observers are convinced collective bargaining is inherently a conservative process, designed to preserve the status quo, one that rarely encourages change or other adaptive processes widely perceived to be necessary, particularly in large university systems. After all, the world of collective bargaining is built on the dichotomous reality that two sides (parties) have different interests, political pressures, and outlooks on key issues. In university settings, negotiation processes leave out too many internal and external constituencies who, because they are absent from the table, are less able to shape or influence outcomes. Some believe unions present significant obstacles to the ability to follow through on meaningful change. While this may be true in some cases, in my experience, it is attributed more to the unions' desire to protect hard-earned benefits and rights in the face of administrative (what are often viewed as superficial or politically expedient) interests in changes to funding formulas, governance, or compensation. I will have more to say on this point later in the chapter.

Unions in Higher Education

The Public Sector

Readers might be surprised to learn that collective bargaining in higher education stretches back over 100 years. The *Daily Illini* contains news of a union action by custodians at the University of Illinois in October 1917 (asking for an increase of six cents an hour in wages). Faculty locals (legally unrecognized) existed in Montana, South Dakota, and other states in the Pacific Northwest in the 1920s. Following more favorable federal legislative and judicial treatment of private sector unionization in the 1930s and 1940s, early craft unions appeared in the Ivy League (painters at Columbia in 1938), and faculty at Howard University, Hampton Institute, and the New School for Social Research organized and received recognition in the late 1940s.

It was not until the mid to late 1960s, however, following passage of public sector labor legislation in several states (and significant social upheaval on campus coincident with social justice issues, many echoes of which we hear today), that unions gained a foothold in academia, commencing in New Jersey, New York, Michigan, and Wisconsin. It may also come as a surprise that higher education is now one of the most unionized sectors in the United States, where close to 40 percent of full-time faculty and staff are represented for purposes of collective bargaining—a majority in large public systems such as the State University of New York (SUNY), the City University of New York, the California State University system, the University of California (UC), and Massachusetts and Pennsylvania State Colleges, for example, where, with the exception of the University of California, the employer is the system rather than the campuses. The lion's share of faculty, graduate students and academically related employees in public systems are unionized in approximately 15 states and include graduate students (in some cases undergraduate students at institutions in these states) and teaching assistants. One of the earliest strikes by graduate students took place in Wisconsin in 1971. In these locales, enabling labor legislation and accompanying administrative agencies (labor boards) initially facilitated unionization.

The Private Sector

In the private sector, following a ruling by the US Supreme Court in *NLRB v. Yeshiva Univ* (1980), bargaining was curtailed for newer faculty units attempting to gain recognition or negotiate a first-time contract. The court found that full-time faculty at private schools (but not graduate assistants/students, adjuncts, or clerical groups) were generally excluded from coverage of the National Labor Relations Act and hence unable to claim "employee" status required by law to bargain collectively because they exercised discretion over so many work-related matters. Ironically, the decision had a negligible impact on previously established units in the private sector, and for many reasons, most continue to exist today. Unionization of employees at private schools (for other than full-time faculty) has doubled since the *Yeshiva* decision, and coupled with a union-friendly NLRB, which has determined that both undergraduate and graduate students may be eligible to organize as employees, recent efforts to organize adjunct faculty, graduate and undergraduate students, and teaching assistants have accelerated, particularly in the elite private sector, such as at Brown, Columbia, Georgetown, Harvard, the Massachusetts Institute of Technology, New York

University, and Yale. The public sector remains by far the most robust, however, both before and after the *Yeshiva* Decision.

Understanding the Forces and Variables That Shape Collective Bargaining in Higher Education

A great deal has been written about unions in academe, the reasons for their existence, the causes and consequences. The following information about collective bargaining in higher education is pertinent.

Institutional and demographic factors shape and influence outcomes. For example, bargaining with academic-related personnel and faculty is associated with larger institutions and public two- and four-year systems in the East and Midwest and several union-friendly states (with enabling labor legislation) in the far West and Florida. Institutional prestige tends to be inversely related to the presence of unions with respect to four-year faculty (this is not the case for graduate students or assistants or adjunct/part-time faculty, where the elite private sector has become fertile ground for organizing campaigns). Parenthetically, when speaking about full-time faculty, it may not be institutional prestige per se, but individual and departmental autonomy, lighter workloads, and greater voice in institutional affairs that faculty in higher-prestige institutions possess, all of which mitigate the need for a union. Such is not the case for faculty in many comprehensive state systems or two-year schools where decisions regarding mission, finances, course delivery, and the like are made off campus, at the system level or by the governor's staff. To illustrate this point, consider that full-time faculty bargaining units exist in only six member institutions of the Association of American Universities (AAU), a higher education association considered the most exclusive. Even here the demographics are interesting. Of the six, two (SUNY Buffalo and Stony Brook) are in the huge New York (SUNY) public university system, one (UC Santa Cruz) is in the University of California system, and the fourth, the University of Florida, is in the State University System of Florida. The University of Oregon, also unionized, was (but is no longer) part of a large state system. Rutgers University, the other AAU member, is situated in a state with accommodating labor legislation and where all public sector colleges and universities (and most public sector employees) are unionized. The same institutional demographics are associated with a smaller group of unionized schools where full-time faculty bargain collectively and, although not members of the AAU, are nonetheless excellent universities, such as the Universities of Connecticut, Massachusetts, and New Hampshire and Wayne State University. Nonetheless, the overwhelming majority of unionized public sector faculty can be found in comprehensive state and university systems in locales where favorable legislation supporting unionization exists or existed, where the majority of faculty have few opportunities for mobility to other institutional sectors, and where the unions wield substantial political influence in state legislatures and offices of the governor.

Faculty unionization reflected, from its earliest inception, the desire to safeguard jurisdiction over decision-making in academic matters: in shared governance, the curriculum, and reappointment, promotion, and tenure. In the 1960s and 1970s, the union movement in academe may have been energized by opposition to the Vietnam War, changing mores in society, permissive attitudes, and the like. But preserving hard-won gains in shared governance and professional autonomy, which included promotion and tenure processes, were the primary factors driving expansion of collective bargaining. During this era, a rise in student power and student rights sometimes intersected with the rise of faculty unions and at other times did not. Whether these two movements reinforced or negated each other is at best speculative. No doubt the reaction to what was perceived as arbitrary decision-making and heavy-handed management by university leaders over teaching schedules and workload, research, and other funding priorities spurred organizing activities. Educational unions like the American Federation of Teachers (AFT) and the National Education Association (NEA), which had robust and longtime organizational experience in the K–12 sector, eagerly sought to expand membership and negotiate on behalf of college and university faculty in states where they already represented public school teachers. Interestingly, in the early years, many faculty sought to be represented by the American Association of University

Professors (AAUP), an association with a long and distinguished record of defending faculty rights. But leaders of the AAUP were, at that time, far more conflicted about representing faculty for the purposes of collective bargaining, and the AAUP endeavored to retain status as both a union and association for some time. These trends emanated, in the eyes of organized labor and many faculty, from the corporatization of academe, the nexus of the academic and the military industrial complex, and later a decline in state and federal support, leading to the need for alternative revenue sources, downsizing, and the like in response to fiscal and enrollment-related factors. This was not the prevailing view of those leading institutions; their reality was and remains different, shaped by enrollment, student demand, funding, and external political factors. It was also soon evident that faculty in many public systems found they were one of the few groups at state capitols that lacked union representation. For this reason, they were without the concomitant leverage needed to pressure state legislators and other elected officials to allocate more resources to postsecondary education and protect faculty rights. Deliberative processes associated with senates and shared governance in general (some of which did not operate in the summer) were not initially able to accommodate themselves to the realities of decision-making environments, as internal and external forces buffeted the academy in the 1960s and 1970s. Unions represented a more effective way to assert their voice. Preserving professional autonomy, sharing decision-making, and safeguarding the status quo were more salient than economic concerns for faculty who sought to unionize in these years. After all, in comparison to many in the labor movement, full-time faculty continue to have exceptional working conditions, salaries, and benefit packages compared to (with a few notable exceptions in arts, entertainment, and professional sports) other unionized workers.

The academic union movement commencing in the 1960s was largely non-ideological and focused on "boiler plate" contract matters. This included recognition of bargaining agents, preservation of craft-like or professional authority over entrance into and promotion through academic ranks as well as academic freedom, workload, grievance and arbitration provisions, and layoff clauses. What occurred in academe from a labor relations perspective did not quite mirror collective bargaining in numerous other industries. There remain unique aspects of labor agreements, for example, the preservation of academic freedom and "academic judgment," which is normally withheld from arbitral review. Non-ideological approaches prevailed in more established relationships; for example, unions representing faculty frequently partner, and in some cases merge, with other bargaining agents regardless of organizational differences or ideology. As of today, greater numbers of full-time faculty are represented by joint affiliations of the AFT, NEA, and AAUP than are represented by a single bargaining agent. This has not been the case with graduate students, clerical, or adjunct/part-time employees. Here, some of the more established academic unions appeared to be reluctant, for a variety of reasons, to represent units composed solely of graduate students or assistants, particularly at elite private schools (where faculty were not represented) or in larger state systems. While there are exceptions, bargaining representatives for nonfaculty groups, whose status as "employees" is often contested, tend to be characterized as "industrial unions"—United Auto Workers (UAW), Communication Workers of America (CWA), United Electrical, Radio and Machine Workers of America (UE)—or unions representing municipal and state service workers, such as Service Employees International Union (SEIU) or the American Federation of State, County and Municipal Employees (AFSCME), many in search of new dues-paying members and the associated political clout union membership brings. Perhaps "industrial" or "public sector" unions were approached by employees in need of representation after more traditional academic unions failed or were reluctant to accommodate certain groups. Unions like SEIU are well organized at the ground level and willing to use a city-based or multi-city approach, not unlike the labor market strategy used for organizing janitors in California. Interesting, however, that despite a great deal of rhetoric to the contrary, claims by one bargaining agent to be more effective than another agent in advancing the rights and benefits of one or another employee group are suspect, and few if any scholarly or objective studies demonstrate this to be the case.

Can Labor and Management Innovate?

During the past century, a great deal has changed in postsecondary education and in labor management relations. While the legal, political, and organizational environments shaping collective bargaining have evolved, unions now represent a relatively small portion (6.5 percent) of private sector workers in select industries, and a much larger proportion (nearly 40 percent) of public employees in select states. The parties to labor agreements, by and large, still view the other through an adversarial or "win-lose" lens, particularly in negotiations involving newer employee groups. The above notwithstanding, labor history in general reflects instances where employers and employee representatives were able to adopt significant changes for the betterment of constituents, clients, and customers, in textiles, heavy manufacturing, shipping, and mining. Such changes often came about because of a gut-wrenching tragedy (after the Triangle Shirtwaist Fire in the early 1900s) or sustained labor conflict (strikes and violence involving workers in mining camps or the manufacture of Pullman railroad cars), followed by legal or legislative intervention. Innovation also resulted from significant financial, legal, or competitive threats to a particular industry, and in these cases, adaptation generally proved preferable to extinction. Most established industries, and higher education is no exception, are anything but nimble by design or heritage and struggle with efficient and adaptive capacities effectuated through collective bargaining. Unionized colleges and universities have by and large become more bureaucratic, with formalized contracts and the entrance of "third parties" (state administrative agencies, courts, arbitrators, and the like) who oversee labor management relations. Collective bargaining is a multidimensional process, with myriad internal and external constituencies, and is not predisposed to rationality, adaptation, or efficiency. But the postsecondary landscape is changing in response to new technologies, a decline in enrollment, particularly among men, and funding and political issues. Save for a small group of elite institutions who remain largely insulated from current trends owing to a variety of factors associated with wealth, prestige, high quality of instruction, and mobility for graduates, transformation and disruption may be around the corner, which may encourage cooperation and adaptation.

Can higher education and union leaders adapt new modalities through collective bargaining? Can they arrive at a point where collective bargaining processes are more rational, productive, and designed to serve a wider group of constituencies? I believe the above is possible and necessary given the politicization and accompanying paralysis in which we find ourselves today.

What the Pandemic Has Wrought

The COVID-19 pandemic accelerated many vulnerabilities (and possibilities) in governance, instruction, and decision-making in higher education. One of the most salient impacts resulted in changes in the delivery of courses, the teaching/learning environment, and management of faculty, staff, and students. Major considerations at the campus, system, state, and federal levels concerning responses to the pandemic, reimbursements, costs, and safety have caused a reexamination of health benefits and working hours, remote work, who is essential and who is not, mask mandates, testing, vaccinations, furloughs, and the like. In cases where employees are unionized, many of these changes in wages, hours, and working conditions must by law be negotiated.

Based on observation and communications with numerous labor relations practitioners, between the start and the messy conclusion of the pandemic, many employer and employee representatives agreed to extend current contracts and resolve pressing issues "down the road," when it is hoped more funding, guidance, and support (on many of the matters listed above) from executive offices and federal or state governments will be forthcoming. Complicating matters, leaders at unionized public institutions in "red" states (e.g., Alaska and Florida), where there is generally more opposition to mask and testing mandates, have tried to stay under the radar in order not to find themselves crosswise with policies supported by the governor's office, which in many states appoints university regents or trustees and has the legal right to approve or veto changes in monetary terms of labor contracts. Many are hoping for a "return to normal," which may never return, particularly as political candidates in some states desire to appease or win over voters by waging culture wars and attacking cultural, recreational, or postsecondary education as too "woke." Labor management relations are cyclical and political, and sooner or later, difficult issues, temporarily postponed, must be addressed. The luxury of waiting for more guidance or funding may not assuage those who feel they have sacrificed enough. Already there are calls for a return to more inclusive shared decision-making, and as the current round of extended agreements expire, new demands will be brought forward by all parties. Given the changes necessitated by responses to the COVID pandemic and accompanying political polarization and paralysis, it would be prudent to refocus attention on labor management relations.

Is Change Possible?

Change is possible when external realities force a reconsideration of "business as usual," and administrative and faculty leaders are encouraged to conceptualize and implement labor management relations in alignment with strategic plans, shared governance, assessment, reward systems, and communication practices. There is a tipping point when administrative and faculty attitudes, perceptions, and behaviors shift to consider new possibilities, which may be approaching at this time. It may be possible to offer a set of recommendations that, if adopted, will make bargaining more rational, efficient, and responsive. Alignment in communication, involvement of many groups surfacing different points of view, the way policies and practices are implemented, and trust between the parties are core issues to address.

This is certainly not the first time such matters have been considered. Over the years, much has been written about more effective approaches to labor management relations in higher education. A considerable body of literature and experience has grown up, for example, around alternative dispute resolution processes including interest-based bargaining (IBB), with the often-repeated criticism it is too time consuming. In my experience, if an administration and union had successful experiences with IBB, they will have developed a foundational relationship that can enhance efficient and responsive outcomes under certain circumstances, provided the union's interests as an organizational entity are not compromised. IBB, to be successful, requires sustained cooperation, stable and committed leadership on both sides of the table, the requisite authority given to chief negotiators, supportive external administrative agencies, and shared past experiences where many remember how dysfunctional more traditional collective bargaining may have been. In the unfortunate absence of many of these conditions, IBB is difficult to effectuate in practice, and therefore not frequently used in postsecondary jurisdictions.

Permit me two additional observations that make it difficult if not impossible to bring to fruition the ideas set forth in this chapter. The first involves a scenario where the faculty union has been taken over by those who cannot get beyond seeing the "administration" as the enemy (capitalist employer). These faculty, expert at nursing insults and grudges, are ideologically predisposed to grieve or disdain anyone who endeavors to change the status quo, particularly around assessment, measures of meaningful educational outcomes, or programs more responsive to environmental pressures, most often if they sense institutional responses may result in an increase in workload. They cloak themselves as defenders of the "original" mission of the university. Such faculty are often mediocre scholars who may have been administrators at one time (and failed), and who joined the union to take it over for protection against more discerning faculty (the old guard) who may have been decidedly unsympathetic to their adversarial attitudes, mediocre credentials, and scholarly output. They are often characterized as having a militant verbiage and affected working-class demeanors, both of which hide thoroughly middle-class orientations. They speak triumphantly in the name of students, particularly the marginalized, but they care far more about job security, compensation, and opposition to innovation or progress.

The second instance occurs when senior leaders, normally the president or members of the governing board, care more about holding on to their jobs and avoiding any actions or plans that could potentially result in putting their hard-won prestige and compensation at risk. These types normally ascend to leadership positions through a crisis, by doing the bidding of those really calling the shots, or simply by being the last person to remain when others had the good sense or ability to leave the organization. They, too, often have mediocre credentials, in some cases no scholarly accomplishments whatsoever. They tend to be legal, financial, or fundraising types, politically connected, blithely unencumbered by any desire to engage in self-criticism, and possess the unflinching ability to cut budgets and hire or promote sycophants who publicly acclaim their "wisdom and leadership." They focus on and seek to assuage any individual or constituency with whom they need peace and support to survive. In such cases, union leaders like those described above often enter pacts with the president or other senior administrators and board members to feather their own nests and settle old scores, all in the name of being responsive to environmental pressures and student concerns. Those reading this chapter will unfortunately recognize when these two situations are present on campus or in the system. In such cases, it can take years to dislodge such individuals from positions of power.

Recommendations for Improved Collective Bargaining in Higher Education

Based on my experience, let's imagine for a moment what might be possible for the nation's postsecondary sector—and university systems in particular—if more favorable conditions were present. What if IBB were the prevalent bargaining model? What if the parties had stronger relationships and shared understanding (and control over) of internal and external factors shaping their relationship? What if the representatives at the table were better trained and had greater autonomy? What if collective bargaining processes were more aligned with other key decision-making processes? What if the parties approached the table with shared perspectives? Here are several modest and practical suggestions (not listed in priority order) to improve bargaining relationships, particularly with negotiations involving employee groups newer to unionization. These are offered knowing that collective bargaining remains a complex, interactive, politicized, and multidimensional process, shaped by legal and legislative precedent as well as political pressures. At its core, it is a process that reflects the use of power and influence, leverage, and counter-leverage. The above notwithstanding, processes and outcomes can be improved for the benefit of many.

Enhance the Role of Chief Negotiator

Collective bargaining would benefit if chief negotiators had greater access to senior leaders and decision-makers for extended conversations (without fearing repercussions from supervisors or others at the same level in the organization), asking about ways to make bargaining processes more rational and proactive. Over the past half century, legally sanctioned collective bargaining has moved from being personality driven to "institutionalized" in the public sector, and to a lesser extent in private schools where negotiations are more commonly done by outside counsel. What institutionalization has meant in practice is that those managing these processes are now located further down in the administrative hierarchy than in the 1960s and 1970s, or collective bargaining is contracted out to outside counsel. Negotiators lower in the administrative hierarchy or contracted out often lack access to senior academic or government leaders, who themselves may be unfamiliar with the intricacies and unique issues of collective bargaining in higher education. In fact, it is more and more the case that those responsible for negotiating contracts are essentially told what to negotiate, often with little guidance and limited access or opportunity to converse with institutional or political leaders, let alone deans and others, about the potential impact or long-term outcomes of contract language. Over time, these positions can become populated with individuals who may be expert negotiators (or expert outside counsel) but are relatively unfamiliar with major academic issues and concerns, let alone given the opportunity to utilize the labor management relationship in a proactive way to further institutional goals. In select state systems, a governor's representative (sometimes a political appointee) negotiates on behalf of the system and often responds to political interests of the governor, not necessarily those of the university or its employees or students.

Adopting this recommendation may necessitate developing expertise beyond negotiation and contract administration skills. While such skills are essential, a willingness to utilize the collective bargaining process proactively may require additional attributes and certainly will require more job security and higher compensation for negotiators, many of whom are, in my experience, scapegoated when negotiations falter.

Even with increased access to leaders and enhanced skill sets, those who manage labor relations processes may face significant hurdles trying to be proactive, and such recommendations may require several years to come to fruition. For example, in "blue" states, government leaders may covet union support, which may result in a reluctance to make significant changes to contracts to improve cost-effectiveness or other university priorities. In these locales, university leaders themselves may lack real influence over the chief negotiator or important negotiation issues (e.g., finance, compensation). In systems, collective bargaining processes are filtered to campus executives through one or two individuals, often with their own interests to safeguard, and summaries from the bargaining table are made through multiple intermediaries. Nuanced comments from the chief negotiator may not survive multiple interpretations, and constituencies on campus are left to fill in the blanks. In large systems, organizational hierarchies impede progress, and decision-makers are far from the table. It is up to negotiators to somehow deduce what will work and what will not. Changing these dynamics will take time.

More Conversation around Bargaining Issues

Executives should meet regularly with representatives from academic and administrative units to discuss collective bargaining topics and general goals. This recommendation also goes to the wider issue of transparency and trust, building a culture that incentivizes shared interests over divergent ones. In my experience, these meetings rarely happen unless there is a crisis, and I write this knowing the logistical challenges associated with this recommendation, particularly in large organizations. Added to the challenge is the reluctance of some senior campus leaders to involve themselves with labor relations. I personally believe that having faculty labor relations in colleges and universities where faculty are unionized report to legal affairs or human resources is a mistake. In my experience, many academic leaders in general are a risk-averse lot, staying as far away from the bargaining process as they possible can. Some do not know, or care to know, the basic parameters governing collective bargaining. One result is that their voices are not listened to when addressing important institutional matters that are invariably discussed in labor agreements. I am not suggesting leaders be at the table (normally unwise for many reasons), nor am I suggesting those unfamiliar with bargaining processes dictate strategy to people at the table. In my opinion, however, negotiators and senior administrators across units would benefit from sustained communication, and once strategies and positions are explained, my experience has been that ideas for compromise or innovation around the thorniest issues are more easily generated and entertained. To those who argue all conversations must be highly confidential, or worry over the potential for an unfair labor practice (ULP), my response is that little is truly confidential in public universities, and it might be of value to quell the rumor mill with facts rather than speculative theories. There are instances where the union and the faculty do have legitimate and divergent interests. But when parties to collective bargaining feel they are making progress and there is a developing sense of trust and respect, ULPs are rarely filed.

Different Approaches to the Development of Bargaining Parameters

Negotiation goals and objectives should be formed using a process that is more inclusive, involving many individuals at the university and, in the case of graduate student negotiations, faculty. What is being suggested here will not be easy to do (nor of interest to some) but is essential if institutions and systems hope to be more proactive. The process of developing collective bargaining parameters or what are known colloquially as "bottom lines" might be reconsidered. Skilled negotiators would be reluctant to negotiate without knowing the parameters of what may or may not be acceptable to the principals. To engage in bargaining without clear parameters could result in legal and political difficulties. All of this becomes problematic when negotiation parameters, strategy, and long-term considerations may be developed in a vacuum or outside the purview of major university constituencies to discuss and comment upon. Take the seemingly small matter of who gets invited to what meeting. Universities are political entities, and there are occasions when those with titles of director, associate director, department chair, or associate dean may not be invited to meetings where their comments and observations could be helpful. Such distinctions and "prestige" hierarchies can impede progress at the bargaining table.

Negotiation parameters can be arrived at through inclusive processes involving a wide range of individuals and groups and utilized in the vein of "appreciative inquiry" in order to bring to the surface and address constituent concerns and larger organizational problems. Surveys are also a useful tool. Recommendations could be moved forward to senior executives. Unfortunately, too often there is fear that essential and confidential information will be leaked and impede negotiations in some manner or prolong collective bargaining. One result of not adopting this approach is that collective bargaining becomes largely reactive, takes longer, and generates more conflict.

Where outside counsel is used, particularly in negotiations involving employee groups new to unionization, these individuals (with some notable exceptions) come from law firms with less experience dealing with the realities of university life. In too many cases, those representing the "employer" may not appreciate that the "employees" who they are representing at the table are union members but also colleagues or students in meetings, often that same afternoon, and in completely different roles necessary for research administration or peer review.

Identities, roles, and responsibilities are fluid, which makes collective bargaining more challenging in large systems. Negotiators representing larger unions organizations face similar challenges. Candidly, the management of the development of bargaining parameters is, in many locales, in need of reconsideration if the challenges and vulnerabilities brought about by the COVID-19 pandemic or other major issues confronting postsecondary education are to be addressed in more efficient and rational ways.

Seek Agreement on Definitions of Terms Used during Bargaining

Coming to agreement about the scope and topics of negotiations—particularly criteria for decision-making and definitions for terms, and how such terms and decisions could be applied contractually—may go a long way toward enhancing the process. As anyone who has ever negotiated a contract knows, if an issue is really a problem to a large constituency, whether it is mandatory or permissive subject of bargaining, invariably it will end up in the agreement (or litigated) in some form. While it is no doubt the case that expansion of arbitral review for nonmandatory subjects of bargaining may dissuade conversation on matters that appear basic and directly relevant to unions, particularly those with "social unionism" orientations, preliminary conversations, however time consuming, will be of value. Seasoned negotiators on both sides of the table know this well, in addition to the patience required to go through the process. Proposals that seem straightforward to union negotiators may be interpreted as so far out of scope to employer representatives they may be reluctant, for a variety of legal and political reasons, to discuss them. For example, demands to demilitarize or defund campus police departments may be offered and no doubt reflect broader societal concerns with police and the rights of marginalized populations. Proposals that may seem morally or ethically sound to one party may be viewed with extreme skepticism by the other, thought to be beyond the scope of bargaining, even the control of one party to address, regardless of what is negotiated. Arriving at shared definitions and criteria around the scope or topics of bargaining and implementation of contract clauses may enable the parties to identify approaches other than collective bargaining needed to satisfy constituencies who shape bargaining from afar and, more importantly, whose support is necessary to ratify agreements.

Methodologies to Cost-Out Proposals: Obtain Meaningful Institutional Comparators

Prior agreement on acceptable methodologies to "cost-out" union or management proposals and appropriate institutional or area "comparators" for purposes of utilizing benchmarks and best practices is important. Agreement on comparators and costing methodologies can result in minimizing disputes, allowing parties to transcend individual institutional concerns and focus on universal best practices. Take the seemingly straightforward issue of a "living wage," which is often predicated on factors associated with the cost of living (COL) in a particular locale. Agreement on a COL cost methodology could advance negotiations and arguments on whether the COL is similar or different in Albany, Atlanta, Berkeley, or Minneapolis. In fact, such arguments over the COL can and have delayed negotiations for months, to the detriment of all concerned.

Another example is health benefit coverage for transgender operations. What might seem like a negligible cost to a bargaining agent may in fact appear overwhelmingly costly to an employer. Such procedures, which may be considered by some to be a human right and included more broadly in benefit packages, may be a low expense if applied only to employees in one bargaining unit. Should the parties agree to provide coverage, however, institutions may be legally obligated to provide such benefits to all employee groups, and costs consequently assume a different proportion. Understanding the full costs of proposals will undoubtedly allow the parties to understand each other's perspective (and while this may not speed agreement, it may curtail acrimony).

Changing institutional budget and resource priorities in a post-COVID era, when unionized universities will become more, not less, dependent on state and federal support (and as elected officials will be more concerned with the economy in general), is fraught with pitfalls. It may require agreement of important external constituencies and reconsideration of tuition (not always under the control of university officials), revenue streams, deferred maintenance, operating expenditures, and the like. Agreement for determining costs, the ability to fund proposals, or plans and practices used in other locales will encourage a more nuanced and sophisticated approach to collective bargaining and, in my experience, lay the groundwork for compromise.

The Fundamentals of Collective Bargaining

Educating all parties on the fundamentals of collective bargaining and established best negotiation practices would enhance the process, particularly with employee groups newer to collective bargaining. Graduate student spokespersons, for example, often appear to lack a firm grasp on, or choose to ignore for whatever reasons, many of the essential basics of negotiations working in similar locales and in place for nearly a century. Those in elite private schools where graduate students are currently organizing might consider that the same groups have been organized in elite public universities for 50 years. Certainly, there are some lessons to be learned or notions about the impact of bargaining that may not be true or realistic. Why reinvent the wheel? Another case in point concerns the conduct of negotiations. For example, appointing "team coordinators" or "revolving negotiators" as chief spokespersons may seem reasonable to some union advocates yet ridiculous and nonproductive to experienced employer representatives. Better understanding of what constitutes an "unfair labor practice" or an "end run," and how such tactics derail negotiations and destroy trust between the parties (the latter almost always essential for final settlement), will advance discussions. The value of arriving at a "tentative agreement" (and knowing what that means in the bargaining context) is important if bargaining is to be more responsive and rational. It is important to establish and adhere to "ground rules," such as not tweeting about or taping bargaining sessions. It is also unhelpful to view compromise as capitulation, as it often leads to nonproductive outcomes. Negotiations will not conclude effectively if viewed as political theater, but they do operate well under long-standing procedures and guidelines. For example, employing "side bar" discussions or creating union management committees (which have a defined scope, time line, and which meet away from the table, making recommendations to the parties) constitute effective approaches used successfully for the past 75 years to resolve contract disputes. The legal environment for labor management relations for some groups (graduate students in the private sector) is still evolving, giving additional reasons to ensure parties are cognizant of time-tested methods to resolve disputes.

Planning for Social Media

Parties to collective bargaining should prepare for wider uses of social media (and soon artificial intelligence) that inevitably accompany negotiations. Employer side bargainers, particularly in larger institutions, may be challenged keeping senior leaders (several administrative levels above them) informed of the potential liabilities of social media campaigns. Union leaders are sometimes unfamiliar with postsecondary education cultures and are therefore reluctant or unable to exercise authority over the use of social media by table participants, which can, and has, derailed negotiations. The use of social media has changed dramatically over the past 20 years. Today it undoubtedly influences our political culture as well as professional and personal behavior in a variety of spheres.

Negotiating with groups that are adept in the use of social media often confounds those who are not as conversant with communications and organizing strategies. For example, those representing graduate students or teaching assistants may be less sophisticated (or influential) in reaching settlement at the bargaining table but more effective using social media for leverage, political disruption, or continuation of the organizing process. Bargaining reflects the exercise of power and influence, and pitfalls exist for professionals who fail to grasp relationships between the exercise of influence and social media. A skilled negotiator may not take seriously the political theater unfolding at the table or on campus. Presidents and provosts, however, may be sensitive to legislators and board members who hear about and want to know why "disruption" is occurring. Those in power always have adversaries and competitors who skillfully use such scenarios to demonstrate why a particular leader in charge cannot manage the situation (and therefore should not be in charge). University leaders may not be familiar with (or may not have time) to study the give-and-take at the table, the details of proposals and counterproposals, or legal challenges winding their way through labor boards or courts. At the table, what may seem like nonsensical or ineffective social media tactics to professionals may be taken in a very different light by others away from the table.

One result, in my experience, in the failure to plan for uses of social media during bargaining is less leverage in discussions for those representing either party. To compound matters, university and union leaders are invariably told by well-meaning experts that "ground rules" to prevent disruptive social media campaigns or such "theatrics" at the table have no merit. While the above may be true in some cases, people in charge get concerned when students, alumni, legislators, or full-time faculty are influenced by social media, especially when they receive communication about ongoing conflict. Administrators or union leaders may be vulnerable if they appear unable to resolve conflict exacerbated by social media without communicating why.

Conclusion

Effectuating more rational, efficient, and adaptive collective bargaining, with the goal of incentivizing institutions or systems and unions to be more responsive to constituencies they serve, cannot be imposed by one party or the other. Such must be a joint undertaking. It is time, I believe, for all involved to work harder toward arriving at shared interests. This will necessitate a willingness to look beyond the status quo and consider approaches to negotiations and the maintenance of relationships that reinforce evidence-based decision-making, reflect best practices, and demand benchmark measure of success. Engaging in these kinds of activities will benefit faculty, employees, and stakeholders, and better enable the university and systems to be responsive to students and society. Although this may sound simple and direct, it is a complex task, and like other transformations, success will not be evident until long after the ideas set forth here are put into practice.

4 | Public Systems and the Financing of Postsecondary Education

PAUL E. LINGENFELTER

IN THE 1970S, the chair of the Proprietary Advisory Committee of the Illinois Board of Higher Education said these words at every board meeting: "The capital basis of an institution, whether it be public capital, philanthropic capital, or investment capital, should have no bearing on the eligibility of its students for state financial aid."

His memorable and eventually persuasive argument implied, but did not engage, deeper questions that face legislators, governors, and the board and leaders of public systems: How *much* should postsecondary education cost? What are the appropriate roles of student tuition and fees, and of public, philanthropic, and investment capital in financing postsecondary education? What are the contributions and limitations of each source of funding? What about the financing of research and public service? What should govern student aid? What public policies and what institutional practices are needed to meet the needs of individuals and the broader society for effectiveness and efficiency in postsecondary education? This chapter will not settle these questions, but it will address them, drawing on the accumulated experience of postsecondary education in the United States and around the world.

How Much Is Enough?

Expenditures per student among postsecondary institutions vary enormously. And for many years, the prices charged to students have increased faster than inflation. Although the law of supply and demand and its effects on prices and quantities available for purchase apply to postsecondary education, the complexities of postsecondary education make its effects far from simple. Both the variation in costs and their upward trajectory are driven by several interrelated factors.

According to Howard Bowen's (1980) "revenue theory of costs," every institution, whether for profit or nonprofit, public or private, will raise and spend all the revenue it can. Nonprofit institutions maximize prestige-enhancing activities rather than profit-maximizing ones. Both prestige and their missions—the advancement, transmission, and utilization of knowledge—know no bounds. For-profit institutions act as traditional profit-maximizing firms, pursuing all the marginally productive dollars the market will provide and spending them on programs that yield higher returns for the shareholders.

From the perspective of Bowen's theory, the only restraint on postsecondary spending is what the market of buyers is willing to provide through tuition and fees and public, philanthropic, or investment capital. That hasn't been much of a restraint. The growing value of education in the global knowledge economy has yielded steadily expanding revenues to the industry. Although resistance to spiraling prices is increasing, students from prosperous families remain willing to pay high prices for an education at prestigious institutions.

The ability to raise revenues is not, of course, the only factor driving increases in costs and prices. Other factors play important roles. First, the economic benefits of being well-educated translate into higher costs for both students and all employers of well-educated people. Colleges and universities compete with each other and with the private sector for talent. The "market rate" for people with advanced degrees has increased steadily for more than 50 years, driving up the cost of postsecondary education as well as its value.

Second, although technological change generally improves productivity, it also imposes costs in postsecondary education. Compared to 50 years ago, colleges and universities currently employ few clerical workers but substantially more information technology professionals. Postsecondary education must stay current with and lead technological change; it cannot fall behind. This imperative tends to increase its cost.

Third, the "customers" of postsecondary education are demanding shoppers. As the general quality of life has improved, students increasingly value expensive amenities (good food, roomy accommodations, and recreational opportunities and facilities), they care about the personal attention made possible through low student-to-faculty ratios, and they are attentive to prestige and convenience. All these demands tend to increase cost and price. Although not every student can afford high-cost amenities, those who can set expectations for the industry that drive up cost and price.

Fourth, institutional viability and prosperity depend on enrollments. Marketing and recruiting expenses, both direct and indirect, are an important cost center in most institutions. For example, even small institutions that struggle to meet enrollment targets provide significant subsidies for intercollegiate athletics. Elaborate "enrollment management" strategies have been devised to enhance enrollment levels, revenues, and institutional attractiveness.

Fifth, nonprofit postsecondary institutions have traditionally "bundled" activities and services with costs that vary substantially. The cost of lower-division instruction courses tends to be less than upper division or graduate courses because of class size. The cost of laboratory courses and courses requiring clinical practice and supervision is higher than for courses that primarily employ lecturing and independent study. High-demand areas (business courses, for example) permit larger class sizes and tend to be less expensive than courses with lower enrollments, such as foreign languages, philosophy, or physics. And institutions that support research and public service as well as instruction will have costs that are not borne by institutions that focus only or primarily on instruction.

Finally, an elaborate system of publicly and privately funded grants and loans has been constructed to enable students to pay the price of higher education and to influence their choices of institution. The availability of financial assistance reduces the price of postsecondary education for many students, increases the number who enroll, and influences the decisions they make about where to enroll. Such third-party payments likely add to the cost of postsecondary education because they reduce the sensitivity of students to price and enable institutions to offer higher-cost services. In this respect, financial aid functions much like sale prices and other incentives provided to build market share or to encourage the production or consumption of services. In education, this is justified by its broad social benefits.

Actual prices and spending per student vary substantially among sectors and within sectors of postsecondary education. According to the National Center for Education Statistics, in 2018–19, average per student revenues from tuition and fees were $8,000 for public institutions, $22,700 for private nonprofit institutions, and $17,400 for private for-profit institutions. Appropriations to public institutions mean the average spending for instruction in public institution is approximately $16,000.

Within each sector, per student revenues and spending vary substantially by type of institution. The Delta Cost Project (2016) found that in 2013, per student educational spending in the public sector ranged from $10,804 in community colleges to $17,252 in research universities. In the private sector, on average, bachelors' institutions spent $23,138 per student, and research universities spent $37,812 per student. Individual institutions in each sector have costs well below and well above these averages.

Clearly, there is no "standard" for the cost or price of postsecondary education. Costs and prices vary widely. The value and quality of different programs vary as well. Although a positive relationship surely exists between cost and quality, both good value and poor value for money paid are likely at both higher- and lower-cost institutions.

Who Benefits, Who Pays, Who Should Pay?

As America responded to Russia's launching of Sputnik in 1957 and the baby boomer generation entered adolescence, postsecondary education saw enormous expansion in the 1960s. In turn came a vigorous debate on the questions of benefit and responsibility to pay the cost. Some argued that the broad public benefits of postsecondary education justify low or no tuition in public institutions for all students. Others argued that low tuition is a regressive tax—students from more prosperous families disproportionately enroll, while taxes from lower-income, nonparticipating families subsidize their education.

At that time, after consulting with several leading economists, the Carnegie Commission concluded, "No precise—or even imprecise—methods exist to assess the individual and societal benefits as against the private and public costs." The commission's analysis suggested that for public institutions, students and parents were paying approximately one-third and the public was paying two-thirds of the direct monetary outlays for higher education and living expenses during study. When the opportunity cost of not working while enrolled was added, students and parents were paying two-thirds of the total direct and indirect costs.

Believing that the public interest required broad postsecondary participation, the commission offered modest policy proposals to address these issues: providing need-based assistance to lower-income families; charging less for the first two years of higher education and more for advanced undergraduate and graduate study; narrowing the gap between the tuition fees in public and private institutions; and developing more progressive tax systems (Carnegie Commission on Higher Education, 1973). (Some countries have addressed this problem by providing large, income-contingent loans to postsecondary students. Students who reap substantial economic benefits eventually pay the full cost of their education; those who choose or involuntarily find themselves in lower-paying employment will receive a public subsidy.)

Although the commission's recommendations influenced state and national policies, they did not lead to uniformity. Substantial differences exist among the states in the level of tuition and fees, in the amounts and forms of student aid provided, and in the relative size of their direct and indirect support of public, private nonprofit, and for-profit institutions.

Despite differences among the states, for a while, low or moderate tuition in public institutions became the norm. From 1970 to 2000, tuition and fees at public institutions on average financed between one-quarter to one-third of instructional cost. In varying amounts, states also provided financial aid and other grants to help students choosing to attend private institutions. A surge in enrollments at the beginning of the twenty-first century, accompanied by recessions in 2001 and 2008 and growing health care and retirement costs, resulted in states shifting the cost burden dramatically to students and their families. By 2020, tuition and fees covered an average of 44 percent of instructional costs in public institutions. The student share was more than 50 percent in half the states (SHEEO, 2021).

The Strengths and Limitations of Difference Sources of Funding

Student Tuition and Fees and Financial Assistance

Students benefit economically and in many other ways from the knowledge and skills they gain in postsecondary education. "Traditional students" also may benefit from an enjoyable transition from living with parents to becoming an independent adult. Beyond these personal benefits, competition for students also tends to improve the quality and diversity of institutional offerings. Accordingly, student payments are a legitimate and appropriate source of funding postsecondary education.

Despite these advantages, only a few students come from families who can afford the price of the most expensive institutions, most students have some difficulty affording the average price, and many potential students cannot afford even the least expensive postsecondary opportunities. Without student aid and/or public subsidies, only a small fraction of the population would obtain a postsecondary credential.

With mixed success over the past 50 years, student financial aid has significantly undergirded the role of tuition and fees in financing the enterprise. More than 85 percent of full-time undergraduate students receive financial aid of some kind (National Center for Education Statistics, 2023).

The provision of public financial aid generally has been guided by two goals.

1. Assisting students who cannot afford the price, or need-based aid.
2. Assisting students who demonstrate higher levels of academic ability, or merit-based aid.

Such programs have become increasingly complex as they address different levels of financial need, the widely varying costs at different institutions, differences in academic ability and effort, and the interests of all families in lower-cost postsecondary education. Need-based programs have been criticized for using too-low standards of students' ability to benefit or inadequate requirements for student effort and achievement once enrolled. Merit-based programs have been criticized for subsidizing students who would enroll and succeed without financial assistance, a waste of public resources.

Financial aid from institutions supplements public programs, and it is based on an array of criteria—need, academic ability, and other factors, ranging from athletic ability to giving preference to the children of alumni. Meeting enrollment targets through tuition discounts is frequently an overarching goal of institutional aid.

Philanthropic Contributions

Philanthropy has always played an important role in the financing of postsecondary education in the United States. The names of donors appear on many campus buildings and on a few institutions. Annual giving and endowment returns provide a significant fraction of the budget at many, but far from most, colleges and universities. Philanthropic income is most significant at private, nonprofit institutions and at the more selective institutions, both public and private.

Although philanthropy has added to the scope and quality of programs at traditional colleges and universities, its benefits are unevenly distributed. Both personal priorities and an affiliation with the institution tend to be important motivations for donors. Institutional prestige is the most visible priority, as evidenced by the plea at an alumni event I attended: "Give so the university can attract the best students and faculty in the world."

The interests of donors also shape the impact of philanthropy. Some donors will focus on specific areas of research or instruction, some are looking for a building project to memorialize the family name, and others will support intercollegiate athletics. Although institutions work to attract philanthropy to institutional priorities, donor priorities greatly shape institutional behavior.

In short, philanthropy contributes to the quality and the level of spending at the highest-cost institutions and to wide variation in the quality of the student experience among institutions. It adds both value and complexity to postsecondary education.

Private Investment Capital

During the deliberations of Secretary of Education Margaret Spellings' Commission on the Future of Higher Education, a prominent business leader told me that the best way to address the nation's educational problems was to get more private capital involved. His belief, I surmised, was based on both an ample supply of private capital and a conviction that investment capital would be more efficient and innovative than public or philanthropic sources of funding. The record of for-profit postsecondary education in the United States provides some support for this view.

Proprietary apprenticeships and schools have trained practitioners in business and in trades and service occupations (initially including law and medicine) for much of US history. Traditional educational institutions initially avoided these "nonacademic" areas of study. The demarcation between "practical" and "academic" education began to blur with the passage of the Morrill Act in 1862, and by the mid-twentieth century, academic knowledge had become vital to the training in many practical professions. Consequently, "traditional" institutions expanded their curricula to include practical education in a wide range of fields. With growing demand for postsecondary education over the past 40 years, entrepreneurs saw opportunities for profit by competing with programs offered by public and nonprofit colleges and universities.

First, academic institutions tended to structure their offerings according to the habits and preferences of faculty and full-time, traditional students aged 18–24. Proprietary institutions met the needs of working adults by offering more flexible options—evening and weekend classes, credit for prior learning, and innovative approaches for distance learning. Second, proprietary institutions tended to focus on vocational programs with high student demand (business, education, computer technology, etc.), combined with little, or substantially less intensive, instruction in general education. Third, proprietary institutions avoided investing in research or public service, focusing entirely on instruction. And, finally, proprietary institutions largely standardized the curriculum and instructional practices. Courses designed by a small core of full-time faculty are typically taught by part-time faculty who may have other full-time jobs or for other reasons are willing to work for lower pay.

These practices enabled for-profit institutions to secure an ample profit margin by reducing the actual cost of instruction while charging prices that were competitive with the price at nonprofit private institutions. Although investment capital "seeded" for-profit institutions, public capital was key to the business model because students in for-profit institutions disproportionally rely on publicly funded grants and loans to pay for their education. Data from 2018–19 demonstrate the significant role of federal grants and loans in financing for-profit institutions. Table 4.1 shows the percentage of students who receive financial aid along with average award amounts.

While the profit motive has been beneficial in fostering innovation and reducing the cost of instruction, it has been much less successful in meeting the postsecondary goals of students and society. A common for-profit business strategy has emphasized recruiting and enrolling,

Table 4.1 Percentage of students with financial aid and the average award

Sector	Percentage with Federal Grants	Average Federal Grant	Percentage with Institutional Grants	Average Institutional Grant	Percentage with Loans	Average Loan
Public	42.1	$5,054	40.3	$5,666	35.6	$6,639
Private Nonprofit	35.4	$5,385	78.8	$21,794	59.3	$8,224
Private For-Profit	68.5	$4,689	19.2	$4,099	72.4	$7,553

rather than retention and graduation. In some cases, deceptive or fraudulent recruitment practices have been employed, and students have received inadequate support to foster their success. As a consequence, private, for-profit institutions have had the most disappointing rates of student failure to complete and student loan defaults among all postsecondary sectors.

With mixed success, accreditors and the US Department of Education have employed various regulatory strategies to address such issues. Although many for-profit institutions have provided instructional opportunities that have benefited students and society, the tension between maximizing profitability and providing quality education has eroded those contributions. Figures 4.1 and 4.2 show the rates of stop-out among full- and part-time students, respectively, while figure 4.3 depicts student loan default rates.

Public Capital

In theory and in practice, the most appropriate use of public capital is to achieve public purposes that other sources of money will not or cannot achieve. In the United States, public funding has shaped the character and scale of postsecondary education much more than student payments, philanthropic donations, or investment capital.

At the nation's founding, public funding provided "seed capital" for the Ivy League and early public universities in order to educate community leaders. In the nineteenth century, when elementary and secondary education became a priority, public funding created "normal" schools

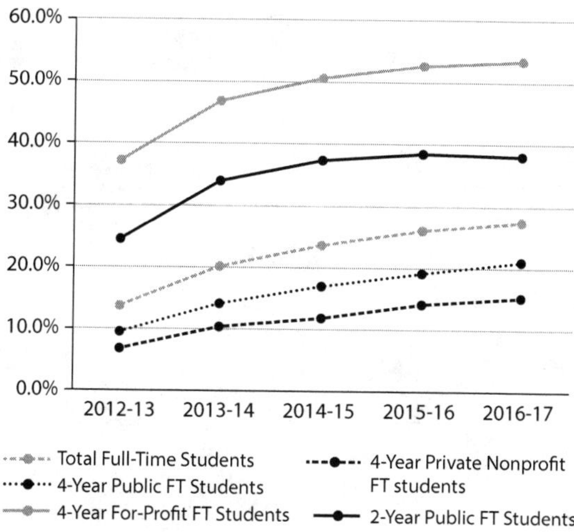

Figure 4.1 Attrition of full-time (FT) students by sector. Attrition is highest for for-profit institutions and two-year public institutions. *Source:* National Student Clearinghouse Research Center

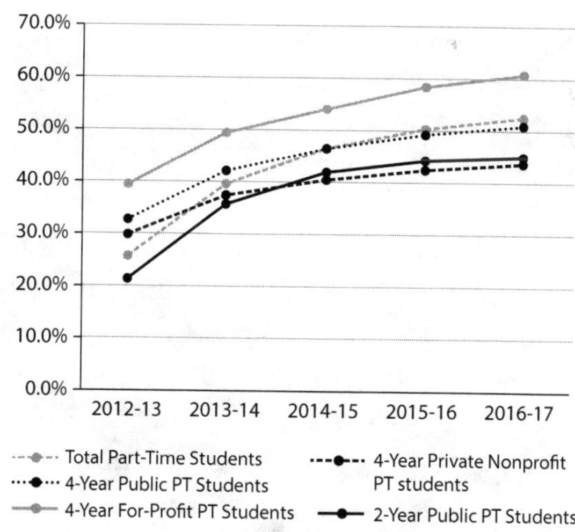

Figure 4.2 Attrition of part-time students by sector. Attrition is highest for for-profit institutions and two-year public institutions. *Source:* National Student Clearinghouse Research Center

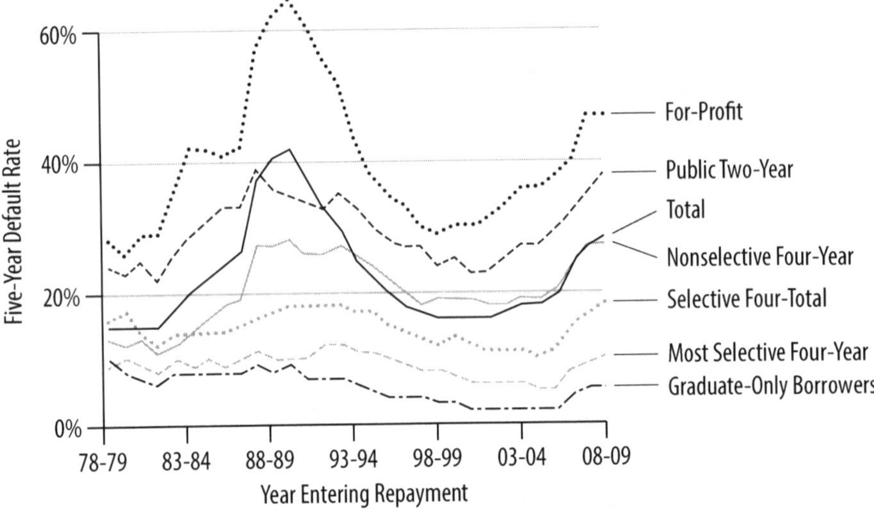

Figure 4.3 Student loan default rates after five years, 1978–2009. Default rates were highest for for-profit institutions and two-year publics. The lowest default rates were for graduate borrowers and most selective four-year institutions. The median loan amount was highest for graduate borrowers and the most selective institutions. *Source:* College Board

to prepare teachers. When research and education in engineering and agriculture became a higher priority, the federal Morrill Act expanded the scope and focus of postsecondary education.

In the mid-twentieth century, public dollars financed the GI Bill, which slowed the reentry of veterans into the job market and dramatically increased the educational attainment and productive capabilities of the workforce. Concomitantly, following World War II, the federal government supported major investments in research and development, perhaps motivated primarily as means of national defense but with side benefits that advanced both scientific knowledge and economic progress. In response to the space race with Russia, public money financed the National Defense in Education Act, upgrading instruction in science, math, and languages and expanding student financial aid and support for counselors and teachers. Simultaneously, at the state level, public funding provided capital investments and operating funding for a massive expansion of postsecondary education, which for the remainder of the twentieth century made the United States the world leader in educational attainment.

Today, federally funded research and development (R&D) that emphasizes (although is not exclusive to) the physical and life sciences is a major function of public and private nonprofit universities. Basic research in universities and other laboratories is predominantly funded by government and nonprofit sources (70 percent of all spending in the United States). Applied research is funded almost equally by investment capital (55 percent) and government/nonprofit sources (45 percent), and it occurs in both academic and nonacademic settings. Private investment in R&D emphasizes the development of particular products (85 percent of all spending) and occurs largely outside the academy (Sargent, 2022).

The federal Higher Education Act of 1965 (reauthorized in 1968, 1972, 1976, 1980, 1986, 1992, 1998, and 2008) is a major source of student financial assistance for all sectors of postsecondary education. It provides access for students who cannot pay the cost of tuition, fees, and other expenses, and to a significant extent it enables students to have freedom of choice among institutional options.

These contributions of public spending in postsecondary education are evidence of its capabilities. Public investment has enabled lower-income students to enroll in postsecondary education, supported research unable to attract sufficient philanthropic or investment capital, and materially advanced human knowledge and well-being. With such benefits, some suggest there is no downside to public investment in postsecondary education. But there are many other public purposes and demands on resources. Limited resources, the complex nature of postsecondary education, and the interactions among public and nonpublic sources of revenue make the stewardship of public revenues a challenging task.

The Pursuit of Public Purposes

What objectives justify public investment? For instruction, they might be: (1) to produce a capable workforce, enough people who have the knowledge and skills necessary for widespread economic prosperity; (2) to develop well-educated citizens to strengthen and preserve democratic government; and (3) to provide equal educational opportunities so all people can realize their potential to lead productive, fulfilling lives. Although all three of these objectives are widely accepted, people differ about the substance of "well educated" for work and citizenship, and some question the existence or the extent of society's obligation to provide equal opportunities.

Public investment also supports research and service to advance knowledge, address human problems through the application of knowledge, and enrich the cultural life of society. As for instructional objectives, these objectives are widely accepted, but different views exist on questions of substance, sufficiency, and financing strategy.

Each of the four sources of revenue—student payments, philanthropy, private investment capital, and public investments—has contributed to the achievement of these purposes. The nonpublic sources of revenue, distributed according to the preferences and choices of individuals, have the advantages of market discipline. But the market fails to meet public educational objectives when individuals lack resources to pay. It also fails to achieve other purposes that benefit individuals only indirectly. Both public investment and public regulation of postsecondary education should be driven by wise and deliberate decisions about where public resources should be deployed, how they should be allocated, and how much is required.

Where Is Public Investment Required?

Although dissent can never be entirely ruled out, it has been fairly easy to achieve a working consensus on the need for tax-supported spending and governmental leadership for some purposes. Such purposes include national defense, public safety, and establishing necessary conditions for the rule of law. For other purposes, such as transportation, food production and security, education, energy production, public utilities, and health care, the United States and other nations have employed a mixture of governmental funding, incentives, and regulations that shape the choices and spending decisions of individuals and organizations in the marketplace.

The classic book *Politics, Economics, and Welfare* by Robert A. Dahl and Charles E. Lindblom (1953) comprehensively considers the capabilities and limitations of four social mechanisms—the price system (markets), bureaucracy, hierarchy, and bargaining—for allocating resources purposefully. Polyarchy, the democratic control of leaders by the people, is the means through which public purposes and the means of pursuing them are determined in a democracy. To different degrees, the price system, hierarchy, bureaucracy, and bargaining dominate resource allocation in different countries or situations, but all of them tend to be in play everywhere. Likewise, the degree of democratic influence over leaders varies among nations.

Assessing the need for public investment in postsecondary education requires considering public objectives, examining the status quo in terms of those objectives, and then considering what is required and what mechanisms should be employed to meet those objectives. This is the subject of an ongoing conversation among citizens and political and educational leaders. The remainder of this chapter is a contribution to that conversation.

Postsecondary Objectives Requiring Attention in the United States

Workforce Capability

In the last half of the twentieth century, the United States led the world in postsecondary degree attainment, a key indicator of workforce capability. For adults 55 to 64 years old, the United States still ranks high, with 43 percent postsecondary attainment, exceeded only by Canada at 48 percent, and tied with Japan. According to the Organisation for Economic Co-Operation and Development (OECD) the average postsecondary attainment rate for older adults is 27 percent, substantially lower than the US figure.

For younger adults, aged 25 to 34 years old, the United States has lagged progress elsewhere in the world. The US postsecondary attainment rate for younger adults is 49 percent, just a bit above the OECD average of 44 percent, one of a cluster of 12 countries with attainment rates between 45 and 51 percent. Six countries, led by Korea (70 percent) and Canada (62 percent), have attainment rates of 55 percent or higher (National Center for Education Statistics, 2020). For this age group, the United States falls in the middle of 18 countries whose postsecondary attainment is higher than the OECD average.

For those who *do* receive a postsecondary credential, AAC&U periodic surveys of business leaders generally have found both a reasonable degree of satisfaction with the capabilities of college graduates and room for improvement. From the perspective of business leaders, the most notable areas for improvement are in oral and written communication skills as well as the higher-level skills (real-world problem-solving and critical thinking/analytical reasoning) required for advancement above entry-level positions.

Improving workforce capability clearly requires increased and continuing attention in the United States. The evidence provides no justification for complacency about either the numbers of citizens completing postsecondary education or the quality of the education they receive.

Education for Citizenship

Poor education is a treacherous foundation for government by the people. Among the nation's founders, both Thomas Jefferson and John Adams valued education as an essential foundation for viable democratic government. But their agreement on the importance of education didn't preclude significant differences of opinion between them or severe, sometimes violent conflict over political questions among their followers.

Education does not prevent disagreement; it frequently fosters it. In the twenty-first century, well-educated leaders differ sharply on political and policy questions, just as they did as when the nation was founded. Although contentiousness is more common than consensus in American history, the nation's greatest achievements have occurred when there was a sense of common purpose that transcended difference. Perhaps the proper role of education is to help people inform contention, understand different perspectives, and discover common purpose.

Effective citizenship requires skill in critical thinking and the evaluation of information. It also requires knowledge of history and of different people, cultures, and perspectives. Such differences need not be destructive; they can be productive when tempered by respect, understanding, and civil dialogue. Education needs to strengthen democracy by fostering understanding and the ability to bridge differences for mutual benefit.

Intolerance for difference, emerging from divergent interests and perspectives and passionate competition within the marketplace of ideas, can be found everywhere, including in the academy. Precisely because of diversity, freedom of inquiry, thought, and expression—core educational values—should be sacrosanct in postsecondary education. Some ideas will prosper, and some will be marginalized in the marketplace, but none should be denied a hearing. Publicly supported institutions should be exemplars of these values and effective education for citizenship.

Education for Opportunity

The GI Bill after World War II became an engine for upward social and economic mobility. By the time the postwar baby boomers were in high school, the expansion of community colleges, state universities, independent colleges (at a smaller but significant rate), and federal aid to education shifted the engine of upward mobility into overdrive. Both the capabilities of the US workforce and the prosperity of its workers grew substantially.

During the ensuing half century from 1970 to the present, the rewards of postsecondary attainment and the penalties of non-attainment have grown steadily. Adults with a high school education or less have experienced dramatic losses of earning power and difficulty in finding and keeping employment. People with postsecondary education earn more, live longer, and have better health, lower rates of incarceration, and more stable families. Although the economic returns of postsecondary education vary substantially by field of study, all these positive outcomes tend to be higher with greater levels of educational attainment.

While these benefits have led an increasing number of people to seek postsecondary education, the upward mobility engine has stalled. Students from families with higher incomes and levels of educational attainment (socioeconomic status, or SES) enroll and complete postsecondary education at high rates, even high-SES students with average or below-average academic potential. Students from lower-SES strata with comparably measured academic potential enroll and complete degrees at substantially lower rates.

High-SES families have both the financial resources and the experience/information required to give their children the best possible opportunity to realize their potential. They work to ensure that their children are well prepared to succeed academically in postsecondary education. Even the most able students from lower-SES strata lack parental financial support and know-how and frequently also suffer the disadvantage of inadequate preparation in elementary and secondary education.

The world-leading educational attainment the United States achieved for the baby boom generation has not been sustained for the succeeding generation, those who are age 25–34 today. The health care and retirement costs generated by the baby boom generation, combined with its resistance to both tax increases and entitlement decreases, appears to be largely responsible for lower state appropriations, higher public tuitions, and inadequate support for student aid.

Students from lower-SES families who enroll in postsecondary education have lower completion rates and higher student loan debts, and they have been most likely to be harmed by the aggressive recruitment practices and poor supports of many for-profit institutions. Both the capabilities of the US workforce and opportunities for social and economic mobility must be renewed as public priorities.

Discovery and the Application of Knowledge

The vital role of universities in research and development is well established and widely accepted. That said, there is much debate over the extent to which R&D should be supported and the means by which resources should be allocated.

A half truth about the relationship between instruction and research—

the assertion that competence in research is essential for excellent instruction—is a factor in driving up the cost of postsecondary education. This assertion is true to the extent that each instructor should understand research methods, be familiar with current developments in their field, and be able to support the early development of students who have the potential of becoming skilled researchers. Also, some great teachers are also accomplished researchers. But it is not true that excellent instruction can be delivered only by an active, competent researcher.

The legitimate connection between research and instruction, the importance of advancing knowledge, and the difficulty of predicting the returns from research have been used to justify substantial allocations of faculty time to research in public and nonprofit institutions of higher education. Although rigorous, wise decision-making about investing in research is difficult, it is not impossible to make good judgments about priorities and the likely return on investments in research.

As other nations increasingly emulate the achievements of the US research universities, more attention should be paid to increasing the development of American researchers and the continued attractiveness of our research institutions to international talent. Also, a broader conception of scholarship, as advocated by Earnest Boyer, would help improve both instruction and research productivity everywhere, especially at institutions where teaching is the primary mission (National Commission on Higher Education, 2005, 28).

The Roles and Responsibilities of Public Systems

Although student payments, philanthropic support, and private investment capital are important sources of revenue for postsecondary education, they lack focus on public purposes and consequently are less effective in addressing public needs. Federal funding for student assistance is focused on public purposes, but the federal government needs partners. It lacks the flexibility and control over institutional instructional practices necessary to achieve public purposes. Federal regulation and voluntary accreditation have proved to be only partially effective in ensuring quality and continuous improvement in postsecondary education. Although the peer review system gives federal funding for research a meaningful degree of quality control, the effectiveness of federal research is deeply dependent on the graduate programs and research infrastructure of public and private research institutions.

As they have throughout history, state-financed postsecondary systems must continue to play a leadership role in addressing public needs in the United States. To meet the needs evolving in the twenty-first century, states and the leaders of public systems must become a more effective force for:

- increasing successful participation in postsecondary education;
- improving the cost-effectiveness of instruction, research, and public service; and
- raising the quality of postsecondary education.

Increasing Successful Participation

More widespread educational attainment in the United States is essential for the global competitiveness of its workforce, for providing opportunity for and the means of social mobility to its citizens, and for strengthening democracy. Public systems must address the barriers to attainment facing both young people and older adults.

Those barriers and the means of surmounting them are well known. *More Student Success: A Systemic Solution* (SHEEO, 2007) outlines six essential strategies for increasing the attainment of students moving through the educational system.

1. Early outreach in elementary school and junior high school to encourage parents and students to have high aspirations, to learn what is required for postsecondary success, and to be confident about their ability to attain it.
2. Curriculum and assessment systems that make clear the knowledge and skills that students need to acquire.

3. Effective teaching at every level to engage students and enable their academic achievement.
4. Adequate, reliable, and clearly understood financial assistance to remove real and perceived financial barriers to postsecondary enrollment and completion.
5. Data and accountability systems to monitor progress, identify issues requiring attention, and provide guidance for continuous improvement.
6. Postsecondary policies, programs, and practices intentionally designed to increase attainment.

The last of these strategies includes "high-impact" instructional practices to increase student engagement (Kuh, 2008), counseling support to help students cope with life challenges, and flexible scheduling and means of instruction to meet the needs of adult students, including many of the innovations emerging from the for-profit sector.

Because they educate teachers and school leaders and establish expectations for postsecondary readiness, public postsecondary systems play a critical role in all of these strategies, including those focused on K–12 education. The "school reform" initiatives of the past 20 years have produced both instructive failures and many good ideas for increasing education attainment. The good ideas include Common Core standards and assessments; strategies for improving the recruitment, preparation, and retention of teachers and school leaders; and the continuous improvement strategies developed by the Carnegie Foundation. Public systems should contribute to more widespread implementation of such effective practices.

Improving Cost-Effectiveness

The perception and the reality of inefficiency in postsecondary education are obstacles to more widespread attainment and the acquisition of essential, reliable public support. Effective postsecondary education is inherently costly, but it must be affordable to both students and society. Public systems can be and should be leaders in demonstrating productivity gains in postsecondary education.

An obvious strategy, increasingly being employed, is the effective use of technology for delivering instruction and improving administrative efficiency. Some have imagined that super-efficient, robotic professors could be cheaper, easier to manage, and more effective than human professors. Experience suggests otherwise. Personal involvement remains critically important to effective instruction, but employing technology can substantially increase both quality and cost-effectiveness.

The more extensive use of technology is often accompanied by collaborative faculty efforts and a division of labor in course design and delivery. These can yield both cost savings and quality improvements if carefully managed to draw on the strengths of different faculty while providing flexibility for individual instructors to add innovative, personal contributions.

A more difficult challenge for public systems is mitigating the cost-escalating effects of competition among institutions. Institutions naturally pursue prestige, market position, and market share. Competition plays a useful role in education, but it needs to be buffered by other values, the broader public interest, and the welfare of the educational enterprise as a whole.

Public systems, more than any other part of American postsecondary education, are able to temper the perverse effects of excessive competition. It is their responsibility to take advantage of their "systemness" to share resources and allocate programs among institutions for greater cost effectiveness. They should also continue efforts to moderate excessive expenditures for intercollegiate athletics as a means of advancing student recruitment and institutional prestige.

Another opportunity to increase cost-effectiveness is to "unbundle" instruction, research, and public service where comingling these functions increases cost and reduces accountability for effectiveness. All three functions are integral, somewhat interrelated parts of the mission of public systems. But their interconnections in the work of individual faculty often have obscured clarity about the allocation of resources to and the effectiveness of each function. Is the faculty time allocated to research and service generating scholarship and contributions of commensurate quality and value? Is the time and talent allocated to instruction sufficient to meet student needs and goals? Both quality and cost-effectiveness could be enhanced by more transparent expectations and appropriate divisions of labor according to the different capabilities of faculty members.

Finally, cost-effectiveness will improve only when it receives continuous attention. Inertia is the enemy of efficiency and effectiveness in every organization. Public systems can improve both their cost-effectiveness and public support by visibly and continuously reallocating resources based on priorities and opportunities to improve quality.

Improving Quality in Postsecondary Education

More educational attainment and more efficient operations in postsecondary education are false progress if quality declines or fails to improve. Although the size of the nation's investment in postsecondary education is fundamentally important, the use of available resources and their effectiveness in meeting the goals of students and society is even more important.

The metaphor of an "iron triangle" with the points Access, Cost, and Quality has been used to describe difficult trade-offs in health care and higher education. The theory holds that it is difficult to achieve desirable improvement in all three simultaneously. Expanding access, for example, tends to lead to higher costs and lower quality. Improving quality tends to require higher costs and less access. Lower costs can be achieved only by reducing access and quality.

These interrelationships are real, but the trade-offs are not ironclad. In postsecondary education, access and success can be improved without diminishing quality *if* student preparation and instruction are improved. Costs can be reduced without impairing access or quality if unproductive resources are reallocated to productive use. Quality can be improved by employing the techniques of continuous improvement within existing resources.

For much of the twenty-first century, public investment in postsecondary education has not kept pace with enrollment growth and inflation. To the extent that spending per student *has* kept pace with inflation, students and their families have borne the cost. This fact is an argument for increased public spending, but only if greater public support leads to higher levels of participation and attainment for students for whom the cost has become unbearably burdensome.

Some "solutions" for controlling or reducing the cost of postsecondary education essentially propose to reduce the definition of acceptable quality to the acquisition of temporarily marketable workforce skills. Workforce skills are essential, but the most valuable workforce skills are the ability to learn, the ability to solve problems, and the ability to adapt to changing conditions. The essential learning outcomes identified by AAC&U and the closely related Degree Qualifications Profile provide a framework to guide the pursuit of quality in postsecondary education. Achieving these outcomes for students and improving the quality and value of research and public service are worthy objectives for those who finance and lead public postsecondary systems.

References

Bowen, H. R. *The Costs of Higher Education*. San Francisco: Jossey-Bass, 1980.

Carnegie Commission on Higher Education. *Higher Education: Who Pays? Who Benefits? Who Should Pay? A Report and Recommendations*. New York: McGraw-Hill, 1973.

Dahl, Robert A., and Charles E. Lindblom. *Politics, Economics, and Welfare*. New York: Harper and Row, 1953.

Delta Cost Project. *Trends in College Spending, 2003–2013: Where Does the Money Come From? Where Does It Go? What Does It Buy?* Arlington, VA: American Institutes for Research, 2016.

Kuh, George D. *High-Impact Educational Practices: What They Are, Who Has Access to Them, and Why They Matter*. Washington, DC: American Association of Colleges and Universities, 2008.

National Center for Education Statistics. *The Condition of Education 2020*. Washington, DC: National Center for Education Statistics, 2020. https://nces.ed.gov/pubsearch/pubsinfo.asp?pubid=2020144.

National Center for Education Statistics. "Fast Facts: Financial Aid." Retrieved August 30, 2023, https://nces.ed.gov/fastfacts/display.asp?id=31.

National Commission on Higher Education. *Accountability for Better Results: A National Imperative for Higher Education*. Boulder, CO: SHEEO, 2005.

Sargent, John F. Jr. *U.S. Research and Development Funding and Performance: Fact*

Sheet. CRS Report R44307. Washington, DC: Congressional Research Service, 2022.

SHEEO. State Higher Education Executive Officers Association. *More Student Success: A Systemic Solution*. Boulder, CO: SHEEO, 2007.

SHEEO. State Higher Education Executive Officers Association. *SHEF: State Higher Education Finance* 2020. Boulder, CO: SHEEO, 2021. https://shef.sheeo.org/wp-content/uploads/2021/05/SHEEO_SHEF_FY20_Report.pdf.

5 | Reallocating Resources

ROBERT C. DICKESON

Introduction

IT IS TIME for university systems to get serious about this fundamental reality: The most likely source for needed resources will come from reallocation of existing resources.

American systems of higher education have grown significantly over the years, to the point where many millions of dollars are expended annually to accomplish the teaching, research, and service functions attendant to this burgeoning—and essential—enterprise. Yet the need for more resources—fiscal, human, space, technology—continues unabated as institutions confront various and often competing expectations:

- To enhance revenues at a time when economic realities are uncertain at best.
- To reduce expenses when some expenditure categories are beyond institutional control.
- To improve quality as the nation demands world-class results in the escalating global competition.
- To enhance reputation when the vagaries of social marketing require institutions and their systems to compete for students, research grants, and donors in an uncharted world.

Controlling costs in colleges and universities is hampered by the failure of governing boards to focus on academic programs. Some systems may have the impression that tackling academic issues is like touching the third rail of higher education. All too often, as a result, past attempts to reduce expenses have concentrated on the administrative side of the budget. Across-the-board cuts, where all programs, academic and non-academic, suffer equally is politically expedient but academically repugnant for the following reason: Not all programs are equal.

- *Some programs are more efficient*. They can be delivered with optimal cost/benefit ratios.
- *Some programs are more effective*. They demonstrate a higher degree of goal achievement, and often their results are sources of approbation for the institution and the system. Among the less effective programs are those that are so small as to beg the question about quality.
- *Some programs are more central to the mission of an individual institution*. A few such programs are seen as more essential to the achievement a unique reason for the institution's existence.

And yet insufficient effort at the system level has gone into forthrightly addressing and acting on the efficiency, effectiveness, and essentiality of programs, particularly academic programs.

Reallocating resources—from lower to higher priorities—thus requires a prioritization process to accomplish tangible results. The perceived barriers to undertaking prioritization are daunting. The institutions' own marketing efforts to induce students to enroll have driven the accretion of academic offerings; academic programs also burgeon because of the specialized interests of the faculty; *curriculum creep* leads to *program creep*, which often results in *mission creep* as institutions take on more and more demands; the mission may have veered off course owing to narrow requests of well-meaning donors or political interests; strategic plans are rarely connected to fiscal realities, particularly through reallocating resources; and reform is often impeded as a result of anticipated resistance from the faculty and community leaders.

Despite the obstacles, reallocation must occur. Colleges and universities have evolved to the point where the bloated curriculum receives inadequate resources to accomplish its purposes. No program director, dean, or department head feels their program resources are currently sufficient. Most academic programs are seriously undernourished. Keeping up with qualified faculty and adequate support staff is difficult. It is nearly impossible to provide equipment necessary to mount programs in a respectable way, especially in an age of rapid technological transformation. Conducting programs in facilities that are in their worst shape in American history is ludicrous. The *price for academic program bloat for all is impoverishment of each*. In business, the process of measuring, analyzing, and prioritizing a company's products and services is accomplished by looking at two factors: market growth and market share. Higher education does not have it as easy. The criteria required to measure a program's efficacy (in my 2010 book, I suggest that there are 10 such criteria) are more complex, and identifying the bottom line is fuzzier. To the extent that the reallocation of resources requires program prioritization, campuses will need to follow a process that accommodates its unique needs and culture as it undertakes this important analysis. Based on numerous professional engagements and research in multiple campus settings, a system should approach reallocation by confronting several key issues (Dickeson, 2010, 2013, 2014, 2015).

Key Issues in Reallocation

Understanding the Need for Reallocation

To what extent are the governing board, key external stakeholders, and the campuses of the system aware of the resources problem, the need to address overprogramming, and the likelihood that new resources will mostly come from reallocation of existing resources? Part of securing commitment is building awareness of the overall vision for the system. The noble goals of any vision cannot be attained without the people, money, and other resources committed in more focused ways. Understanding the need for reallocation is therefore required for commitment to reallocate.

Identifying Responsible Leadership

How committed and visible are the campus presidents/chancellors and their executive team members? What is the state of the system's board member readiness? Has appropriate leadership been empowered throughout the system to champion the coming process? Has the case been made in a compelling way sufficient to achieve the task ahead? Will the needs of the institution and the system to which it belongs transcend its personalities?

Reaffirming Institutional Missions

Since the mission of an individual institution is the grid against which all subsequent program decisions are to be made, serious questions must be addressed: Is the campus of high consensus about its role and scope? Is there a common sense of who it serves, what it does, and how well it performs? Do stakeholders recognize that it can no longer afford to be what it has become?

Defining What Constitutes a Program

The reallocation process to follow should be disciplined by a common program definition. Have *all* resources of the institution been arrayed into discrete program components? Is the distinction between a program and the administrative entity that shelters it made clear?

Selecting Appropriate Criteria

Are sufficient data likely to be available to support all chosen criteria? Will the criteria selected, once sustained by information, yield the results expected from this process? Since these decisions may be challenged in numerous ways—possibly in the courts—has careful thought been given to the academically sound reasons for choosing criteria and assigning weights to them? Once these critical elements are in place, the system is adequately prepared to undertake program prioritization that can lead to effective reallocation.

Academic program prioritization is serious business. And its careful facilitation requires both an atmosphere conducive to the best interests of the institution and the interests it serves, and a commitment to see through to completion the decisions that the process will generate. Governing boards may initiate change in some instances, but in *all* instances, they will be required to act with the finality that only their authority permits.

It is one thing to initiate change; it is quite another to complete it. Before a system seriously considers undergoing a comprehensive prioritization of academic programs, an old-fashioned gut check is necessary: Do we have the leadership, the courage, and the will to see through to completion this important task? Are the leaders, particularly the board members/presidents/chancellors/faculty governance, willing to invest political capital in meaningful reform? This review of an institutional "profile in courage" is necessary in the light of the examples where the will was found wanting and the process failed.

Decision-making in a university system is often political. As in all other legislative arenas, interests collide, and dominant interests—or coalitions of views requisite to securing approval—win out. What is more, the interests do not usually go away after a decision is made. In a legislature, a proposed change in a law will surface the attention of those who are for or against the change. The forces that create a political equilibrium must be reckoned with in planning for change.

I have worked with governing boards where there was unanimity at the outset about the need for making difficult decisions associated with resource reallocation. But when the going got tough and the lobbying got tougher still, board members abandoned both their principles and their executive leader. In still other instances, boards have split into opposing camps, forcing the administration to negotiate a settlement on issues of academic importance to the institution. As a consultant at one private university, I was forced to meet separately with two board factions—one at a downtown restaurant, the other on the campus—in an attempt to foster communication.

Prior to undertaking academic reform, the board should reveal and discuss a clear understanding of its likely controversy. Legal, financial, and reputational issues will be at stake, as well as academic and management ones. Campuses that own programs do not readily give them up without a fight. Tactics often include end-runs around executive leaders to the board. To the degree that the board has permitted—even encouraged—ex parte communication with faculty, the role and success of the executive leaders are jeopardized.

Any number of reform efforts are delayed because the chief executive officer may be undergoing a performance evaluation by the board. Such leaders typically are politically astute. They know that a fractious faculty, upset over program reform, will not likely grade presidential performance favorably. Presidents thus have to strike a balance between their convictions to do what's right and their survivability, without which they get to do nothing at all. "I'm not sure the board will back me" has forestalled more serious reforms than any other single factor.

The system board has an anomalous situation to confront in this matter. On the one hand, it is pledged to support the chief executive and their administrative teams. After all, the primary duty of the board is the selection, support, or removal of the presidents/chancellors. On the other hand, a good board member wants to know what's really going on at the institutions. It is the fiduciary duty of the board to protect the institutions from leaders who may be leading them in the wrong direction, for example. It's the *system*, after all, to which the duty is owed, not any particular person in it. But how a board reconciles this anomaly is critical. An appropriate balance between enthusiastic support and healthy skepticism is required.

Resource reallocation also requires joint board-administrative planning about anticipating process issues (participation, communication, fiscal goals to be achieved, relationship to internal governance) and implementing program decisions.

Decisions—about program enrichment, consolidation, reduction, or elimination—are recommended by the campus heads after undergoing the prioritization process but can be made only by the governing board.

Only the board should have the authority to close programs, and this authority should not be delegated.

By simultaneously evaluating all programs against solid criteria and through an academically defensible process, resource reallocation decisions can be strengthened. The board's ultimate goal is to place the institutions in its system in the best possible position, ready and capable of responding effectively to new contingencies at the same time that it goes about shaping its future.

Basics

This chapter focuses systems thinking on seven basic elements of higher education funding and budgeting.

1. Academic programs (such as degrees offered) are not only the heart of the collegiate institution; they also constitute the real drivers of cost for the entire enterprise, academic and nonacademic.
2. Academic programs have been permitted to grow, and in some cases calcify, on the institutional body without critical regard to their relative worth.
3. Most institutions are unrealistically striving to be all things to all people in their quest for students, reputation, and support rather than focusing their resources on the mission and programs that they can accomplish with distinction.
4. There is growing incongruence between the academic programs offered and the resources required to mount them with quality, and most institutions are thus overprogrammed for their available resources.
5. Traditional approaches, like across-the-board cuts, tend to mediocrity for all programs.
6. The most likely source for needed resources is reallocation of existing resources, from weakest to strongest programs.
7. Reallocation cannot be appropriately accomplished without rigorous, effective, and academically responsible prioritization.

Reasons to Reallocate

Based on a survey of 300 institutions, some 11 different reasons to undertake prioritization emerge. Most institutions list two or more reasons. It is helpful, for communication and re-communication purposes, to identify the specific reasons the system needs to prioritize in order to achieve reallocation, and to refer to them constantly throughout the process.

Reasons Institutions Undertake Prioritization

1. To *balance the budget*. The yield from the process ranges from 2 to 10 percent, over a one- to two-year period.
2. To *inform future budget decisions*. Some systems, reluctant to cut faculty, have used the process to yield the same effect by slowly reducing budget allocations to a particular program.
3. To *improve overall efficiency and effectiveness*. The process often yields unexpected returns in streamlining internal processes, for example.
4. To *respond to accreditation demands*. Any number of regional accreditation bodies have criticized institutions for being "over-programmed for its resources."
5. To *dovetail with strategic planning efforts*.
6. To *respond to demands from public entities*.
7. To *achieve strategic initiatives*. Many institutional plans are merely wish lists and do not include where the needed resources are going to come from.
8. To *tackle specific shortfalls*. These shortfalls may include unfunded liabilities (such as pension plans), deferred maintenance, and other fiscal decisions.
9. To *reinvest in new programs to strengthen the institution for the future*.
10. To *create a contingency and reserve fund*.
11. To *create a database that can be used as a management tool for the future*.

A Reallocation Typology

Although most prioritization and reallocation projects are undertaken by individual institutions, over the past few years, I have consulted with nine different higher education systems about reallocation of resources. While each such project was unique to that particular system, certain patterns of similarities emerged, permitting a typology that might prove helpful in understanding how systems go about this issue.

Based on this sample, there are four types of system approaches.

1. *Providing information.* The system makes available information about reallocation to its member institutions, usually through a system-wide conference meeting or workshop. Some such assemblies included presidents or chancellors only in attendance; other examples included campus provosts, deans, and in one case faculty leaders who participated. The assumption behind this approach is that the individual institutions will undertake a project and report back to the system what results it may uncover.

2. *Providing centralized assistance.* The system provides information, as above, but also makes available to member institutions such services as consultative help, central data sharing, and in one case a system-wide 10-point data dictionary and data sources inventory.

3. *Recommending member action.* The system strongly encourages, but does not require, individual member institutions to complete a reallocation project. Periodic progress reports are shared with the system. Experience reveals that results from this approach are uneven, as institutional resistance prevails over system expectations.

4. *Requiring member action.* The system requires individual institutions to undertake reallocation of resources, establishes target goals for budget reallocation purposes, and monitors results on a regular basis. Presidents and chancellors are held accountable for achievement of system goals and objectives.

A few systems have proceeded through more than one of the above approaches. One system, for example, provided information at two separate workshops five years apart, and then moved to require reallocation a year later.

In sum, higher education systems undertake reallocation in ways that are as diverse as the systems in our country. There probably is no one best way. Each system will develop such an approach to the importance of reallocating its resources as will comport with its culture, its people, and its expectations.

It may be that a system-led review would help to buffer or alleviate some of the institution-led roadblocks that prevent full fruition of the benefits of resource reallocation. In any case, certain tenets can prove helpful in going forward.

Reallocation Going Forward

As higher education systems consider moving forward with projects to reallocate their resources more effectively, the wisdom and experience of past efforts suggest several tenets to be followed. These elements could be labeled "pitfalls to avoid" or "lessons learned," but in any case they are shared here to ensure a greater likelihood of success.

1. The process should be undergirded by establishing the values by which it is to be undertaken. As an example, in a recent process, the chief executive officer declared that "The process shall be fair, honest, forthright and responsible . . . [it] shall be open and transparent, with no a priori decisions having been made, and with decisions made based on the published criteria." Further, the CEO required that "In order to set realistic priorities, it will be necessary to rank all programs, academic and nonacademic, by quintiles . . . [and that there will be] opportunity for enrichment of some programs, as well as the possibility of diminution." Finally, the declaration noted that "While retaining our long-held culture of collegiality, we must also embrace a culture of evidence, one that ensures that program decisions, now and in the future, will be data-driven."

2. There is a difference between necessary duplication and unnecessary duplication. From a system-wide point of view, any form of redundancy is to be avoided. The whole idea of systems of institutions is that efficiencies and other benefits can be obtained by our collective action. Yet when it comes to a responsible curriculum, redundancy is required in some instances. For example, it would be absurd to limit only one English program in a system, when the individual institutions all require it as a condition of graduation. The challenge for systems is to honor the needs of institutional missions while simultaneously monitoring duplication that cannot be justified academically or financially. This monitoring will occur most prominently in assessing the relative value of graduate and professional programs.

3. Decisions must be data based. To ensure that a "culture of evidence" replaces politics-as-usual on campus decisions, the process requires that programs are assessed using data to justify actions. Data come in all kinds and sizes. We usually think of data as quantitative, for such things as program demand, costs, revenues, size, and productivity. But a good process will also cherish qualitative data for such criteria as quality, impact, overall justification, opportunity analysis, and measuring expectations. Academic programs especially are complex and should be analyzed with both quantitative and qualitative measures.

4. All programs should be judged in a way that assures reliability. Decisions that emerge from the reallocation process will likely have to be defended for academic and possibly legal reasons. For example, decisions that can be backed up by statistically relevant practice are stronger than those that are based on invidious discrimination. The best approach for a task force that is evaluating a program is to ensure a higher degree of inter-rater reliability by using a scoring rubric. In using a scoring rubric, task force members should rate programs and services, based on the data provided by offering departments, along the following three-score scheme. The scores—1, 3, and 9—are intended to force greater differentiation among program assessment results. Table 5.1 is an example of a scoring rubric used by an institu-

Table 5.1 Sample scoring rubric for assessing academic and administrative programs

Criterion	1: Minimal/Limited	3: Moderate	9: Exceptional/Significant
History, development, and expectations	The program or service meets the original expectations of the university.	The program or service meets the original expectations of the university and has demonstrated the ability to adapt to the changing needs of the university and its internal and external stakeholders.	The program or service meets the original expectations of the university and has demonstrated the ability to adapt to the changing needs of the university and its internal and external stakeholders, and demonstrates exceptional ability to anticipate change and build for the future.
External demand	Participation in the program/service is limited, its trend line is flat or declining, and raises questions about its efficacy.	Participation in the program/service is moderate.	Participation in the program/service is exceptional; it enjoys a positive trend line; it meets a variety of external policy expectations, and is seen as central to the university's future.
Internal demand	The program/service provides minimal or no service to other programs and services.	The program/service provides moderate service to other university programs and services.	The program/service provides exceptional service to other programs and/or services; such programs and services could not flourish without the service provided by this program.
Quality inputs	The overall quality of resources dedicated to this program is minimal and may be insufficient to mount the program with quality.	The overall quality of resources dedicated to this program is sufficient to mount the program with quality.	The overall quality of resources dedicated to this program is truly exceptional and stands among the very highest standards in the nation.
Quality outcomes	Measures of quality outcomes are limited, and the program/service does not achieve the standard for "exemplary."	Measures of quality outcomes are sufficient to be seen as "exemplary," but more work is needed to achieve consistency in performance.	Measures of quality outcomes are truly exceptional; external validation of the quality of the program is unassailable and serves as a model for other programs and services of the university.
Size, scope, and productivity	The program/service serves few people or entities, is limited in the range of its content, and does not demonstrate a positive return of outputs vs. inputs.	The program/service serves a moderate number of people or entities, facilitates a moderate range of content, and demonstrates a neutral return of outputs vs. inputs.	The program/service serves an exceptional number of people or entities, facilitates a comprehensive range of content, and demonstrates a positive return of outputs vs. inputs.

(*continued*)

Table 5.1 Sample scoring, continued

Criterion	1: Minimal/Limited	3: Moderate	9: Exceptional/Significant
Revenue	Program/service generates little or no revenue on its own. [Less than $______]	Program/service generates moderate revenue on its own. [From $_____ to $_____]	Program/service generates exceptional revenue, sufficient to sustain the program without draining other resources of the university.
Costs	Program/service costs exceed the norms for similar programs at other universities.	Program/service costs are in line with norms for similar programs at other universities.	Program/service costs are substantially lower than the norms for similar programs at other universities.
Impact	There is minimal evidence that the program or service is mission-critical.	There is moderate evidence that the program or service is mission-critical.	The evidence suggests that there is an exceptional relationship between the program/service to the university's mission. The program is integral to the university's future.
Opportunity analysis	Projections for the future of this program are unknown or tenuous; additional resources may be needed to maintain this program.	Projections for the future of this program indicate a moderate potential for improvement and enhancement of the university's overall portfolio.	Projections for the future of this program are exciting and hold great promise.

tion for assessing both academic and administrative programs. Most institutions use rubrics for each type of program category.

5. Boards should avoid external intervention. The history of American higher education is replete with examples of political and other types of influence being inappropriately foisted upon an institution's teaching, research, or service functioning. Governments, public policymakers, religious forces, and other social arbiters try to silence faculty members' pursuit of the truth, especially when that pursuit yields unpopular or unconventional conclusions that do not hold current sway. Academic freedom of this sort is a critical and essential characteristic of higher education and must be protected by the system.

6. Remember that higher education is a balancing act:
   - between offering a major and offering only courses needed for general education and service
   - between the liberal arts and sciences and the professional program offerings
   - between the "cash cows" and the costlier programs
   - between high-enrollment programs and high-cost programs
   - between undergraduate and graduate/professional programs
   - between academic and nonacademic programs
   - between institutional reputation and fiscal reality.

   And systems must strike the right balance among institutions and institution types. In the final analysis, you will be rebuilding the system and focusing on its future. This is terribly important work, and that's why judgment—based on data—must enter in.

Other Related Issues

When a priority-setting reallocation project takes place, it may uncover and address certain policies, procedures, and practices that simply don't make sense anymore. Often, these practices are continued "because we've always done it that way." These matters, formal or informal, may cost institutions significant resources. During the process, it's a good idea to identify these issues and confront them in a timely way.

Among the most common of such issues:

1. The *minimum number of faculty members that constitutes a "department."* Institutions often confuse an academic "discipline" with a "department." A department is an administrative unit of the organization and does not have to be populated exclusively by one academic discipline. Separate departments can be costly: administrative support, space, printed materials, and other expenses can add up. One- or two-person departments can hardly be justified in times of scarce resources. Many institutions across the country combine two or more academic disciplines into one department.

2. The *minimum number of graduates to sustain a major*. Institutions often list in their catalog offerings a wide range of academic majors for marketing purposes. There is little justification for some of these listings. A candid review of actual program graduates will reveal that the institution is keeping on its books certain major offerings with few or no participants. This practice is costly: maintaining faculty, space, equipment, and library holdings to sustain a shaky program diverts precious resources away from more viable programs that are key to the institution's future. A reasonable minimum standard would be that, to be sustained, an academic major should produce no fewer than five graduates over a three-year period. Similar standards should be established for graduate and professional programs, as well.
3. The *number of credit hours for a major, for general education, and for electives*. In a time of scarce resources, offering departments will often inflate the number of hours required for a major in order to attract more credit hours generated, thus "justifying" the number of faculty positions required to be sustained. Such departments often use supposedly "academic" arguments to support these ploys. With the exceptions of accountancy and engineering, there is no academic justification for extending the baccalaureate into a fifth year. A review of college catalogs nationally will reveal the politically successful programs, where "major creep" has expanded to approximately half of a four-year degree program. The baccalaureate degree program typically is constituted of one-third major and one-third general education, leaving one-third for a minor and electives.
4. *Abuse of released time*. In general, for all types of institutions, faculty teaching loads have diminished over the years. When we calculate a "full-time-equivalent," or FTE, student, we count students taking 15 credits per semester (or the proportionate numbers on a quarter system). The same approach is used for calculating an FTE faculty member, that is, one who teaches 15 credits per semester. In the past, most teaching faculty indeed

taught that amount per semester, and 15 credits was considered the standard "faculty load." Over the years, for a variety of reasons, the concept of "released time" was instituted: the practice of reducing the teaching load of an individual faculty member in order to be released to perform other institutional duties. Colleges and universities negotiate and then grant released time to faculty members for such things as:

- advising students and student organizations
- planning curriculum projects, such as new courses or new programs
- conducting research
- performing a role with the faculty union
- taking on administrative duties, such as chairing a department or chairing the faculty senate, or other projects and duties that can be negotiated.

By so doing, faculty teaching loads are reduced to 12, or 9, or 6, or, in some cases, 3 or even 0 credit-hour responsibilities. The widespread phenomenon of released time has led to situations on many campuses that are indeed costly. In all cases, the use of released time results in: (a) larger class sizes for students, (b) increased costs to the institution, and (c) identification of teaching as a lower institutional priority, something to be "released from." The cumulative released time on any campus would equate to a significant number of FTE faculty positions, adding up to a sizable cost.

5. The *proportion of faculty who are tenured or are on the tenure track*. In many cases, institutions have limited their flexibility to manage effectively by offering tenure or tenure-track positions to such an extent that whole programs are "tenured-up." The time-honored practice of tenure is costly. Originally conceived as a means to protect academic freedom, tenure has evolved into a system to protect job security. A combination of institutional practice and emerging case law has resulted in a situation where institutional flexibility is reduced in two key ways. First, if student demand for academic programs shifts,

faculty capacity to deliver it cannot. Tenured faculty members are not interchangeable parts (a physics professor can't usually teach journalism, and vice versa). Second, it has become increasingly difficult for college administrators to remove a tenured faculty member who is no longer effective. Thus the decision to tenure has an accompanying long-term price tag that easily exceeds $1 million per person. Institutions should establish policies that limit tenure/tenure-track positions to a fixed proportion, say 60 to 80 percent within a program.

6. The *ratio of full-time to part-time faculty members*. Not every position needs to be filled with a full-time faculty member. Campuses should evaluate their ratios of full-time to part-time faculty members, balancing the multiple factors of quality, student demand, and efficiency.
7. *Redundancy of courses offered in competing programs*. Thorough program review across the institution may reveal several redundancies in course offerings. Typical examples include writing or mathematics courses offered in departments outside English or mathematics. The reasoning behind these redundancies is often more historical/political than logical and results in unnecessary costs. Institutions should review the incidence of unjustified redundancies and eliminate this practice.
8. *Human resources classification rules*. In order to give a raise to an employee, rigid personnel systems may require a reclassification of the position the employee holds. Most classification systems reward the position if it is supervisory. Thus a costly restructuring takes place, where one person now supervises one or two people in order to justify a higher-level position. This practice is costly, results in middle- management bulge, and cannot be justified. Classification systems ought to reward additional duties or performance on an ad hoc basis, and not overvalue supervision as an element.
9. *Additional duties*. All positions are growth positions. All jobs have duties added to them. It is probable that any position would have a growth-of-duties factor that approaches 5 to

10 percent per year. The key is not to hire additional people because of this natural phenomenon; the key is to eliminate some duties that are no longer needed or are of a lesser priority. Position-by-position analysis is required on a periodic basis in order to right-size position duties.

10. *New requirements*. Every institution faces the same problem: mandates without money. These mandates may include new reporting requirements or new services required to be provided. Unfortunately, the practice of many colleges and universities is to add new positions to meet the new expectations. Many of the new requirements do not require a full-time position. Better alternatives are to (a) assign the new requirements to one or more existing staff members, remembering to prioritize their duties accordingly; (b) consider employing personnel to meet the new requirements on a part-time basis; or (c) outsourcing the functions when it proves to be cost-effective.
11. *Workarounds*. Many institutions, rather than confront a personnel issue head-on, go through elaborate restructuring, creating positions and in some cases whole units in which to place the recalcitrant employee. This avoidance technique is as costly as it is absurd. Conflicts and problems among personnel are normal; they should be resolved directly, without resorting to the workaround technique.
12. *Role in retention*. All institutions are becoming increasingly dependent upon tuition revenue. The best investment in enrollment management is student retention. Dollars wisely spent on retention have a much greater return on investment than dollars spent on recruitment. The key to look for is the direct, provable result that the service in question indeed contributed to improved student retention. If two services or programs are up for analysis and—all other things being equal—one is a direct contributor to improved retention, it should score higher in the analysis.
13. *Adjusting the reward system to meet current expectations*. One of the most valuable practices in thoughtful course delivery is to

team-teach a course or to offer interdisciplinary courses that span two or more disciplines. Years ago, seven of my colleagues and I—from seven different disciplines—taught an interdisciplinary course, "Dynamics of Culture and Creativity in the Renaissance." But the practice at most institutions is to discourage such interdisciplinary efforts—so valuable to students in making needed intellectual connections—by not counting such work in the calculation of credit for promotion and tenure purposes. It is an artifact of the "tyranny of the discipline" that only work taken under the aegis of a department counts in the reward system. A forward thinking system would upend this myopia as a part of its efforts to reform things.

Conclusion

The work of American higher education has never been more important to the future of our nation. Human and fiscal resources are required to achieve the great purposes for which our colleges and universities were formed. Since the most likely source of needed resources is the reallocation of existing resources, our higher education systems are in a pivotal position to ensure that such a reallocation is both responsible and effective.

References

Dickeson, R. C. *Prioritizing Academic Programs and Services: Reallocating Resources to Achieve Strategic Balance*. New York: Jossey-Bass, 1999, 2010.

Dickeson, R. C. "Understanding the Issue of Productivity." *Planning for Higher Education* 41, no. 2 (January 2013).

Dickeson, R. C. *How to Engage Faculty in Academic Program Prioritization*. Greenwood Village, CO: Academic Impressions, 2014.

Dickeson, R. C. "Placing Academics at the Heart of Higher Education Planning." *Planning for Higher Education* 43, no. 2 (January 2015).

Part II

NEW MODELS

6 |

Student-Centric Systems

TRISTAN DENLEY

I REMEMBER A CONVERSATION with a group of provosts not but a few years ago. I asked my colleagues what was needed to truly help more students to be successful in college and close equity gaps. I got a resounding consensus. They all told me that we needed different students.

My experience as a provost at Austin Peay State University and then as the chief academic officer of two public university systems has convinced me that they were wrong. Instead, I believe that to make profound impact on student success at scale, we need to study what works and what doesn't in systems of higher education, determine what the root causes of inequity in higher education are and how they can be removed, eliminate the barriers to our students' successes, and identify ways to support their journey to new heights. In this chapter, I explore how this task has already begun in two state systems and the impact that that work has had. But I also want to look to the future and what is yet to be achieved.

Much of the story that I will tell is based around work done while I was vice chancellor for academic affairs at the Tennessee Board of Regents (2013–17) and executive vice chancellor for academic affairs at the University System of Georgia (2017–21). The faculty, staff, and administrators in the 45 institutions within those two systems made Herculean efforts to make real change for student success. Their innovation, efforts, and results have not only affected the lives of hundreds of thousands of students, but also they have brought enormous insight into what can be achieved by a higher education system focused on this work.

The Evidence of Structural Barriers at a System Scale

You may be skeptical and rightly ask what evidence there is of barriers to student success across a whole system of institutions. Furthermore, even if we establish that evidence, what might be done? This part of the story begins with the student's most fundamental choice about college education: what to study.

Nationally, more than 33 percent of first-generation students begin college without identifying a major or program of study, whereas only 13 percent of their peers with college-going parents do so (Chen, 2005). For many, their dream consisted entirely of *getting into* college, but they were unable to see further. For those students, being *undecided* about a major has huge implications. In Tennessee's state colleges and universities before 2017 and the institutions of the University System of Georgia before 2019 (National Academies of Sciences, Engineering, and Medicine, 2019; Denley, 2022), most students who began college undecided dropped out before they ever choose a particular direction. This initial decision to begin undecided is a largely a result of the way that higher education structures that choice, and the way information about that choice is provided.

Schwartz (2005) has argued for a "paradox of choice"—that having too many options can lead to a decision paralysis. There has been much careful analysis of how decisions are made in the face of an abundance of choice (Tversky and Kahneman, 1974; Kahneman and Tversky, 1979; Kahneman, 2011). Researchers have found that when presented with too many choices, people fall back on a variety of rules of thumb or anecdotal evidence to make decisions. Or they may rely on biases such as cognitive ease or the halo effect, and when one of the choices is to choose later, decision paralysis takes hold. In choosing college majors, theory plays out in reality. When presented with a college's dizzying array of majors or programs, students are all too ready to believe that "later" they will be in a better position to choose a direction, and when the choice to choose later is available, undecided becomes the natural default.

Happily, the behavioral economics research on the effects of choice paralysis also provides a solution to this barrier. Rather than requiring them to choose from an endless alphabetical array of program names, institutions can help students benefit from a modified choice architecture in which they initially select from a smaller number of broader possibilities (Iyengar et al., 2004; Shah and Wolford, 2007).

So, by introducing a set of eight or so *academic focus areas* such as arts, humanities, STEM (courses in science, technology, engineering, and mathematics), health sciences, education, and business, more than 99 percent of incoming freshmen in both the Tennessee and Georgia state systems were able to successfully choose either a program or an academic focus area in which to begin their freshman year (Denley, 2016c).

Once a student identifies the direction of their programmatic focus, it is crucial that among their first-year courses are subjects that they could associate with that choice, and that provide them a taste of what is to come. University websites provide little information to their students about what is involved in successfully completing the program, and students often discover too late that the picture they had of that discipline differs from reality (Kirst and Venezia, 2004; Smith and Wertlieb, 2005). Although students may think that they have an interest in a particular area, they have often received little information about whether their academic abilities give them a realistic chance of successfully completing that program. What is more, they may associate each discipline with a limited number of careers and eliminate disciplines from their list of choices because those specific jobs are unappealing, without realizing the true variety of career opportunities that lie on the other side of graduation. Often, poorer choices are made in situations of an abundance of choice, using these fallback methods, than in situations with more limited choice. In fact, the literature on “choice overload” suggests that too many options can result in several adverse experiences, including a depletion of cognitive resources and postdecision feelings of regret (Schwartz, 2005; Guided Pathways, 2014).

Jenkins and Cho (2014) found a clear impact on the success rate of community college students when they earn at least nine credit hours in their program during their first academic year. This impact plays out no less strongly across both colleges and universities (Denley, 2016c, 2022). Indeed, in both Tennessee and Georgia, students who successfully completed at least nine credit hours in their academic area of focus in their first year were more than 40 percent more likely to complete their degree than their colleagues who did not. In fact, most of the increase in graduation rate was experienced by those students who merely attempt those courses.

Once again, it is the traditional structure of higher education, which leaves these touch-point experiences until the junior year, that creates the barrier to student success. The early introduction of academic focus areas allows campuses to design their curricular and co-curricular pathways with success in mind right from the start. Departments are able to redesign course sequences to ensure that students have those crucial academic touch points beginning in the first year. Institutions are also able to provide a wide variety of inside- and outside-the-classroom experiences that help students build an identity around their academic direction as they refine their broad choice to a particular program. What is more, this can all be knitted together with career exploration as students begin to make connections between what they are studying and future career possibilities.

As well as coursework that connects with their choices, it is crucial that students have success in foundational material. A structural analysis of the system-wide degree curricula in Tennessee and Georgia confirmed that the structure is highly connected, yet fragile, with mathematics and English at its very core. The small-world graph structure (Denley, 2016a) suggests that success and failure alike spread from these two learning areas across the curriculum. Consequently, success, or lack thereof, in this coursework is about much more than passing a math or English course. It is about graduating or not. Again, this theory is borne out in real data. In the University System of Georgia, before 2018, students who were successful in first-year math and writing courses were more than 10 times more likely to graduate (66 percent) than those who were not (6 percent). In Tennessee's Community Colleges, there was a factor of 3 difference in the graduation rates of students (Denley, 2016a). These differences in graduation rates remained true even when the data were further disaggregated by student demographic variables and by preparation. Suffice to say, improving student success in introductory mathematics and English courses plays an enormous role in improving not only mathematics and English outcomes, but also a student's likelihood to complete credentials of value.

Although there is a rich collection of strategies that can improve student learning in mathematics and English courses (e.g., Mathematics Association of America, 2017; National Council of Teachers of English, 2018), ironically the most fundamental barrier is the traditional approach to developmental education. Despite the intention of providing a supportive pathway for students who are not well prepared, the long sequence structure of traditional remediation composed of noncredit courses means that those students rarely complete the credit-bearing courses required for graduation (Complete College America, 2012). Again, it is the structure that has created a roadblock to student success.

Changes in remedial education that place students directly into gateway courses with intensive tutoring in conjunction with courses being taken for credit (a practice known as "corequisite remediation") have been shown to significantly improve these outcomes, in some cases doubling or even tripling student success rates in freshman math and English courses (Denley, 2016b, 2021b; Logue et al., 2019; National Academies of Sciences, Engineering, and Medicine, 2019; Complete College America, 2021). This was certainly the case at colleges and universities in the Tennessee and Georgia systems.

Studies of the corequisite outcomes (e.g., Denley, 2016b) show that while students across the full preparation spectrum are successful in the corequisite model, the most unsuccessful students often experience a lack of success in all of their classes. Furthermore, this lack of success is not linked with a lack of preparation but rather to noncognitive factors. What is more, these same noncognitive learning mindsets appear to have an important role in student success writ large (Lazowski and Hulleman, 2016; Broda et al., 2018; Yeager et al., 2019). Four specific learning mindsets have been shown to improve student grades and retention particularly among Black, Latino, Indigenous and first-generation student populations. Paying attention to strategies surrounding these mindsets has been shown to be particularly effective in the corequisite context (Tibbetts et al., 2022). These four mindsets are:

1. The belief that intelligence can be developed through hard work, the use of effective strategies, and help from others when needed (growth mindset).
2. Perceptions of the purpose and relevance of educational content. Specifically, the belief that one's schoolwork is valuable because it is connected to a larger purpose or is relevant to one's life (purpose and value).
3. Uncertainty about the quality of one's social and academic bonds (belonging uncertainty).
4. Perception that one's instructor has a growth mindset about their students' learning (faculty mindset).

Despite the strong evidence for these pedagogical classroom strategies, the structure of faculty professional development creates a barrier to their use. As faculty, we are all well trained in our own discipline, but few doctoral programs expose future faculty members to aspects of the pedagogies these mindsets require.

In 2018, the University System of Georgia implemented the Chancellors Learning Scholars Program. This system-wide professional development initiative involved more than 3,000 faculty across all 26 universities and colleges. Three hundred of the system's finest classroom professors facilitated learning communities of their peers in discussions about how to introduce evidence-based academic mindset practices into their classrooms. The faculty involved shared their insights and experiences in two wonderful book collections that tell the stories of their students' newfound success (Galle and Domizi, 2021a, 2021b).

Lastly, as students navigate their first year, the intensity of their course load plays a surprisingly important role. Recent research has looked more deeply into the Fifteen-to-Finish strategy, first introduced in Hawaii's universities and colleges. A propensity score analysis (Hagood, 2018) shows that while it is advantageous for students at every preparation level to attempt a 15-hour schedule, in fact every student improves their graduation rate compared with their statistical twin by increasing their course-taking intensity: increasing from 6 credits to 9, or 9 credits to 12, or 12 credits to 15 all have benefit. What is more, these advantages compound semester by semester. On average, a student in Georgia who attempted 30 credit hours in the first semester was 13 percentage points more likely to graduate than an identical colleague who took fewer hours.

Once again, this analysis asks pointed questions about the structure of higher education. The number of hours that a student enrolls in is heavily influenced by advising practices (having fewer advising hours actually harms student progress) and the way in which the course schedule is constructed. Have we ensured that the courses are scheduled at the right times, in the right modalities, and with the right capacities to allow as many students as possible to take as full a schedule as their lives allow? Furthermore, have we pressure-tested the curricular pathways that we create, to ensure that students really are able to enroll in those courses and are not blocked by required courses offered at times that conflict, or perhaps not offered at all?

The Momentum Year Framework

The evidence for system-scale structural barriers to student success is compelling, as is the promise of increases in student success by addressing these root issues. But to carry out this work across a whole system of institutions requires knitting these findings together into a coherent framework and a shared vision. The Momentum Year framework, as it has come to be known, applies this set of evidence to provide an integrated set of practices to remove these structural barriers and create conditions for improved student success.

The following three elements create a Momentum Year for students. Students should:

1. Start their college careers by making a purposeful choice in a focus area or program of study that they link to an eventual career direction.
2. Be provided experiences that help them develop a productive academic mindset.
3. Follow clearly sequenced program maps in their first year that include:
   - core English and math
   - 9 credits in the student's academic area of focus
   - as close as possible to 30 total credits.

Before we discuss how this framework was implemented in Georgia's universities and colleges, we should pause to make several observations. First, the phenomena behind these pieces of evidence appear to be ubiquitous. The University System of Georgia consists of 26 public universities and colleges. From big to small, rural to urban, historically Black colleges and Universities (HBCUs) to Hispanic-serving institutions (HSIs), open enrollment to selective research universities, the system spans the diversity of institutions found nationally in American higher education. Despite that variety, these student success phenomena were found at every institution. Indeed, the strategies grew out of earlier analytical and implemented work in the 19 Tennessee Board of Regents' state universities and colleges, where they too appeared at every community college and university in the system. While it was important that institutions implemented these strategies within their campus context, it was equally important that the strategies were coordinated with policy and programmatic support from the system.

Second, the effects are enormous. Most often, when we think about transformation in higher education, we talk about changes that move measures a percent here or percent there. Instead, these phenomena point to opportunities for doubling or even tripling graduation rates if we could create a different experience for particular student populations.

Our ability to create that different experience is not a distant mystery, but an evidence-based reality. There are proven strategies, based on research and large-scale data, that affect students in just these ways. We did not need to wonder how to begin. What is more, we are learning more each day about how to refine these strategies. For instance, recent work in curricular analytics (Heileman et al., 2018) provides a framework to analyze how the complexity of course sequencing or a curriculum can influence student success. At the same time, new research is shedding light on the most effective format for the corequisite model of developmental education, utilizing the same instructor with two hours of corequisite instruction whenever possible (Denley, 2021a).

Lastly, these strategies, while not focusing exclusively on historically minoritized or underserved groups of students, nonetheless have demonstrated that they dramatically close historical outcome disparities. All students are more successful; those who have been historically less well served have the largest gains in outcomes. Work remains to be done to understand how these strategies should be refined to meet challenges provided by a cultural context that is specifically informed by race or income.

Implementing Momentum Year Strategies

The Momentum Year framework provides coherence and structure to a suite of evidence-based student success strategies. But it also provides an approach to implementation that respects institutional context while ensuring all students experience a strong start for their academic careers. The Momentum Year is not a menu of strategies to be chosen from à la carte, but is instead an interwoven recipe of strategies, powerful individually but further amplified by their gestalt. From 2017 to 2021, the University System of Georgia (USG) undertook the first comprehensive student success strategy to address American college completion at a statewide scale.

At the first Momentum Year Summit in spring 2018, leadership teams from each institution created an implementation plan for their campus to fully implement the Momentum Year framework by fall 2019. Their plans included fully scaling corequisite learning support and the complete elimination of prerequisite developmental courses. By fall 2019, all 26 institutions in the USG had implemented reforms that ensure that all students began their academic careers with a Momentum Year.

At the system level, the University System of Georgia created the policy, incentive, and resource structures to fully implement the Momentum Year strategies at every one of our institutions. This work also required a change in the approach of the system itself, assembling an academic and student affairs team to act as a support for campus innovation while employing an approach that utilized the full scope and structure of the system.

Institutions developed a range of approaches that adapted the strategy framework to their own campus context. This campus work is far too voluminous to list here, whether default schedules built around learning communities focused on student's programs of study, enhanced academic and career services, engagement in transition to college programming (such as orientations and welcome weeks), better application of math pathways that shift students into a first math course aligned with their major, or the use of predictive analytics and chatbots in advising. Instead, I draw your attention to the yearly reports of the work by Complete College Georgia (2023). Suffice it to say, this work was not a series of initiatives but a fundamental rethinking of the way in which each campus engaged its students along the journey of their first year.

The Impact of the Momentum Year

This Momentum Year work in Georgia, which grew out of earlier work in Tennessee, involved thousands of faculty and staff across every campus and has already shown its success. Through the full implementation of the corequisite model in both states, success rates in freshman math and English courses have doubled. All groups—including Black and Latino students, students from low-income households, and first-generation college students—are passing these crucial gateway courses at similar rates.

Graduation and retention rates also grew to an all-time high. Tennessee saw a 42 percent increase in community college three-year graduation rates, with an 87 percent increase for minority students, and a 26 percent increase in university four-year graduation rates, with a 51 percent increase for minority students.

In Georgia, four-year graduation rates rose by 20 percent, and graduation rates for African American students and first-generation students increased by more than 30 percent. Graduation rates at Georgia's HBCUs increased by 50 percent over that same period. The increases in these and other key metrics were not limited to only some schools, but also were realized across the full spectrum of institutions in both states, from Tennessee's open-access community colleges to the University of Georgia and Georgia Tech.

The number of degrees conferred in Georgia set a new record (72,929) in 2021, an increase of 12 percent since 2017 when the Momentum Year work began and 33 percent over the previous decade. The gains were particularly marked for African American students seeking bachelor's degrees, with a 54 percent increase in the number of degrees conferred, and for Hispanic and Latino students seeking bachelor's degrees, who witnessed a 270 percent increase in their number over a 10-year period. These increases far outstripped the increase in enrollment over those same periods. Given the ubiquitous nature of the barriers that the Momentum Year framework has demonstrated it can overcome, one can hardly help but wonder how American higher education might be affected if the framework were replicated state by state.

Looking to the Future: Expanding the Momentum Year Framework to a Broader Momentum Approach

The work of the Momentum Year has thus far focused on eliminating institutional obstacles and the root causes of inequity in the freshman year—historic systemic barriers begin from the start. Yet this work cannot end with efforts focused on the first year alone. We must remove the barriers not only in the first year but also across the full span of the student experience.

To this end, I propose a new conceptual framework, the Momentum

Approach, that broadens the paradigm of each strand of the Momentum Year framework to a more general setting. I believe that this framework provides a tool to analyze how the barriers that we have unearthed, which so profoundly affect the first year, have parallels in every corner of higher education.

The Momentum Approach Framework

- Deepening purposeful choices
- Cultivating productive academic mindsets
- Maintaining full momentum along a clear pathway
- Heightening engagement
- Completing critical milestones

This expanded framework allows a new set of lenses through which to assess the full student journey from K–12 and navigating college, to graduation and the transition to one's career. It also sketches the outlines of a research agenda and a search for new evidence-based practices—for these new lenses bring into clear focus how much we do not yet know. In the coming paragraphs, I offer examples that illustrate how this expanded framework is already being used to inform and implement far-reaching initiatives at a system scale, and the potential amplified impact that those initiatives can bring about.

The Momentum Approach allows recognition that the initial program or focus area choice is but one of a sequence of crucial choices that need to be made—all of which need to be structured and informed in ways shaped by improving student success. Along that journey, feeling that you are studying what you thought you chose is important from the start, but so too are high-impact practices to heighten and deepen the learning experience and the student's commitment to their chosen path. English and math are critical, but they are only the first two of a sequence of critical milestone courses and experiences students must successfully navigate. While we are only now beginning to understand the noncognitive barriers that learners face in the first year, they are no less important all along the journey. As a result, we need to explore how institutional practices can derail students throughout the entire student experience and develop innovative strategies that result in equitable graduation and transitions to the workforce and vibrant careers.

The Momentum Approach provides a framework to understand the root causes for disparity along the length of higher education. It also provides a tool to do just that across the breadth of the student experience. For, just as it is important to recognize systematic barriers along the curricular journey, it is no less crucial to also do this work in understanding the links between student success and financial aid, student life, transfer, and other campus and system policies, practices, and processes. Each of these areas surfaces individual and complexly interwoven systematic barriers to student success both across the student body and within the context of a student's race or income level.

Implementing this phase of the work entails developing mechanisms to transform the culture of institutions. Efforts might focus on hiring faculty and staff who either bring experiences that reflect the experiences of students, faculty and staff development that builds their capacity to both hear and respond to student voices, or the reframing of workloads and intrinsic career development structures that recognize and reward faculty and staff involvement and their contribution to the work of student success.

One illustration is the University System of Georgia's application of the Momentum Approach framework to financial aid in the Know More Borrow Less Initiative. This work eventually employed dynamic digital communications, video resources, and chatbots, all aimed at ensuring that as students made decisions about their financial aid, they did so with the best personalized information possible. Yet the work grew out of the initial question posed by the Momentum Approach: How do students make purposeful choices about their financial aid? Surprisingly, the data suggested that students viewed their decision about financial aid not as a decision of how much to borrow, but instead as question of whether to opt-out of borrowing. By default, students either chose to borrow all they were offered or opted out, but only a vanishingly small percentage chose something in between, no matter their expected family contribution. Understanding that existing choice architecture enabled the creation of resources that truly informed student decisions. Much work yet needs to be done to think through the remainder of the framework: How might a financial aid pathway be structured, and what are the critical milestones and their connections to student success?

The Momentum Approach also provides a lens through which to analyze higher education throughout its depth at system, institution, and classroom levels. From the vantage point of a state system, the *purposeful choice* strand might consider what kinds of degree programs should be offered for students to choose from. Higher education today reaches well past graduation, extending into secondary education and throughout each person's life. As such, it is incumbent on colleges and universities to create the learning experiences and credentials that enable that lifetime of learning so critical for a lifetime of productivity.

Answering this call, we created the Nexus Degree, which was introduced in Georgia in 2018. It is the first new classification of degree in the United States since 1898, when the associate's degree was first introduced. The Nexus Degree curriculum combines an internship-style learning experience with a curriculum that is planned in conjunction with a major industry sector. The very structure of the Nexus Degree places purposeful choice as an intrinsic character of the degree itself.

As a new standalone, entry-level credential for a high-demand field, a Nexus Degree may be earned in combination with a traditional bachelor's degree to create a twenty-first-century liberal arts degree experience, but it may also be earned by a student who has already earned an undergraduate degree but who wishes to return to higher education to either redirect their career path or add to their existing credential portfolio in their field. Since its approval, more than a dozen Nexus Degrees have been created at seven USG universities in areas as diverse as block-chain machine learning, postproduction film, and financial technology cybersecurity. The first of many Nexus Degree graduates were awarded their degrees in December 2020. The Nexus Degree likely marks the beginning of a new wave of new degree credentials that provide the nimbleness that the modern learner really needs to be able to choose.

Lastly, at least within the confines of this chapter, we might view the classroom experience through Momentum Approach lenses. Deepening purposeful choice raises the classroom question of why this material is there to learn. What is its purpose? How does it connect with other material? Strategies such as transparency in learning and teaching have brought to the fore a focus on promoting student consciousness of how they learn, and how the structure of the learning experience might have been built to enhance their learning experience.

As we have already seen, the student perception of their faculty member's approach to learning is proving to have enormous influence on quality learning. What is far less clear today is how, at scale, we might implement strategies that change those student perceptions and the faculty attitudes that shape them. Nevertheless, raising faculty awareness of learning mindsets, and all of the ways their classroom dynamics might play a part in shaping the mindsets of their students, will be of tremendous coming import.

In the creation of the Momentum Year, we considered the design principles that shape curricular pathways for student success. That concept is no less important at the classroom scale. How should the learning experiences be sequenced and paced? Research (Yeager et al., 2014) demonstrates how changing the nature of providing feedback with a view to improvement across the scale of the course can engage students in new modes of learning. Of course, as we design those learning pathways, we need to identify the critical concepts on which all others rise and fall, and the best strategies to allow them to be mastered.

Finally, as we think about engaged learning, high-impact practices as described by the American Association of Colleges and Universities (AAC&U) come immediately to mind. But so too do modern approaches to learning science, such as *small teaching* techniques that can be employed to provide both instruction and deeply engaging learning experiences. Perhaps faculty learning communities such as those created by the Chancellor's Learning Scholars in Georgia provide a mechanism at scale to light a path to raising faculty awareness of these strategies and practices more broadly.

Conclusion

I was asked to look into the future to for what is possible in terms of system-wide curricular innovation, with an eye on increasing student success. As you read this chapter from the vantage point of your own institution or system, I hope that it prompts some probing questions about how your own structures materially contribute to your students' lack of success at scale, and what can be done about those failings. The Momentum Year strategies now have evidence from systems in two states and the promise of more from a third. That evidence convinces me that it is only with a comprehensive integrated approach that we will make any lasting progress on our quest for equitable outcomes.

The Momentum Approach framework in many ways demonstrates how much we yet do not know. But by working together to identify both the remaining barriers and strategies needed to remove them, I am confident that a decade from now we will see higher education with an unstoppable momentum of increasing student success.

References

Broda, Michael, John Yun, Barbara Schneider, David S. Yeager, Gregory M. Walton, and Matthew Diemer. "Reducing Inequality in Academic Success for Incoming College Students: A Randomized Trial of Growth Mindset and Belonging Interventions." *Journal of Research on Educational Effectiveness* 11, no. 3 (2018): 317–38.

Chen, X. *First Generation Students in Postsecondary Education: A Look at Their College Transcripts*. Washington, DC: National Center for Educational Statistics, 2005.

Complete College America. *Remediation Higher Education's Bridge to Nowhere*. Washington, DC: Complete College America, 2012.

Complete College America. *No Room for Doubt*. Washington, DC: Complete College America, 2021.

Complete College Georgia. "Campus Plan Updates." Accessed November 6, 2023, https://completega.org/content/campus-completion-plans.

Denley, Tristan. "Student Success, Curricular Structure and Course Revitalization." *TBR Technical Brief* No. 4 (Fall 2016a).

Denley, Tristan. "Co-requisite Remediation Full Implementation Analysis." *TBR Technical Brief* No. 3 (August 2016b).

Denley, Tristan. "Choice Architecture, Academic Foci and Guided Pathways." *TBR Technical Brief* No. 2 (August 2016c).

Denley, Tristan. "Comparing CoRequisite Strategy Combinations." *University System of Georgia Academic Affairs Technical Brief* No. 2 (January 2021a).

Denley, Tristan. "Scaling Developmental Education." *University System of Georgia Academic Affairs Technical Brief* No. 1 (January 2021b).

Denley, Tristan. "Predictive Analytics and Choice Architecture and Their Role in System-Scale Student Success. In *Higher Education Systems Redesigned*, 97–120. Albany: State University of New York Press, 2022.

Galle, Jeffrey W., and Denise Pinette Domizi, eds. *Faculty Learning Communities: Chancellor's Learning Scholars for Student Success*. Lanham, MD: Rowman and Littlefield, 2021a.

Galle, Jeffrey W., and Denise Pinette Domizi, eds. *Campus Conversations: Student Success Pedagogies in Practice*. Lanham, MD: Rowman and Littlefield 2021b.

Hagood, L. "Momentum Course Load Analysis." *University System of Georgia Research and Policy Brief* (2018).

Heileman, Gregory L., Chaouki T. Abdallah, Ahmad Slim, and Michael Hickman. "Curricular Analytics: A Framework for Quantifying the Impact of Curricular Reforms and Pedagogical Innovations." *arXiv*:1811.09676 (2018).

Iyengar, S., G. Huberman, and W. Jiang. "How Much Choice Is Too Much? Contributions to 401(k) Retirement Plans." In *Pension Design and Structure: New Lessons from Behavioral Finance*, edited by Olivia S. Mitchell, and Stephen P. Utkus. Oxford: Oxford University Press, 2004.

Jenkins, D., and S.-W. Cho. "Get with the Program . . . And Finish It: Building Guided Pathways to Accelerate Student Learning and Success." In "The College Completion Agenda: Practical Approaches for Reaching the Big Goal," edited by B. C. Phillips and J. E. Horowitz. Special issue, *New Directions for Community Colleges* 164 (2014): 27–35.

Kahneman, D. *Thinking Fast, Thinking Slow*. New York: Farrar, Straus and Giroux, 2011.

Kahneman, D., and A. Tversky. "Prospect Theory: An Analysis of Decision under Risk." *Econometrica* 47, no. 4 (1979): 263–92.

Kirst, M. W., and A. Venezia, eds. *From High School to College: Improving Opportunities for Success in Postsecondary Education*. San Francisco: Jossey-Bass, 2004.

Lazowski, R. A., and C. S. Hulleman. "Motivation Interventions in Education: A Meta-Analytic Review." *Review of Educational Research* 86, no. 2 (2016): 602–40.

Logue, A. W., D. Douglas, and M. Watanabe-Rose. "Corequisite Mathematics Remediation: Results over Time and in Different Contexts." *Educational Evaluation and Policy Analysis* 41, no. 3 (2019).

Mathematics Association of America. *Guide to Evidence-Based Instructional Practices in Undergraduate Mathematics*. Washington, DC: Mathematics Association of America, 2017.

National Academies of Sciences, Engineering, and Medicine. *Increasing Student Success in Developmental Mathematics Proceedings of a Workshop*. Washington, DC: National Academies of Sciences, Engineering, and Medicine, March 2019.

National Council of Teachers of English. "Understanding and Teaching Writing: Guiding Principles." November 14, 2018, https://ncte.org/statement/teaching composition/.

Schwartz, B. *The Paradox of Choice: Why More Is Less*. New York: Harper Perennial, 2005.
Shah, A. M., and G. Wolford. "Buying Behavior as a Function of Parametric Variation of Number of Choices." *Psychological Science* 18, no. 5 (2007): 369–70.
Smith, J., and E. Wertlieb. "Do First-Year College Students' Expectations Align with their First-Year Experiences?" NASPA *Journal* 42, no. 2 (Winter 2005).
Tibbetts, Y., J. DeCoster, M. K. Francis, C. L. Williams, D. A. Totonchi, G. A. Lee, and C. S. Hulleman. *Learning Mindsets Matter for Students in Corequisite Courses (Executive Summary)*. Denver, CO: Strong Start to Finish, Education Commission of the States, 2022.
Tversky, A., and D. Kahneman. "Judgement under Uncertainty: Heuristics and Biases." *Science*, n.s. 185, no. 4157 (1974): 1124–31.
Yeager, D. S., V. Purdie-Vaughns, J. Garcia, N. Apfel, P. Brzustoski, A. Master, W. T. Hessert, M. E. Williams, and G. L. Cohen. "Breaking the Cycle of Mistrust: Wise Interventions to Provide Critical Feedback across the Racial Divide." *Journal of Experimental Psychology: General* 143, no. 2 (2014): 804–24.
Yeager, D. S., P. Hanselman, G. M. Walton, J. S. Murray, R. Crosnoe, et al. "A National Experiment Reveals Where a Growth Mindset Improves Achievement." *Nature* 573 (2019): 364–69.

7

The Lean University System

Focusing on Value

STEVEN J. PATIN

"**LEAN MANAGEMENT**" offers a compelling mechanism for reimagining how university systems serve their constituencies. This chapter investigates how lean can improve university systems by helping them deliver greater value to those they serve. It begins with a description of lean's origins, defines lean, explains key lean concepts and approaches, identifies conditions for its success, and highlights lean's benefits. It then shifts to what is currently occurring in lean higher education, followed by what is possible for public university systems that adopt lean practices. It identifies the conditions for successful lean transformation and the barriers that systems must overcome. Finally, the chapter provides a vision of future possibilities for lean university systems as they serve their students, their institutions, and their states.

The Lean University System: Focusing on Value

Lean is a management philosophy and approach that was born in manufacturing but has also proven effective in other business sectors (Cavdur et al., 2019). In 2000, the academic literature began to reflect lean's beneficial extensions to financial institutions, health care, and government agencies and demonstrated that lean theory is applicable and transferable to service sectors. Despite its potential to improve outcomes, with a few exceptions, higher education has been slower to adopt lean than other sectors (Waterbury, 2008). This chapter explores lean's applicability in postsecondary education. Specifically, it investigates how lean can improve university systems by helping them deliver greater value to those they serve. Lean thinking can help university systems improve their administrative and academic processes in ways that provide stakeholders and customers with the value they expect, when they expect it, and to the level of quality they seek (Balzer, 2010).

Lean thinking is about imagining what is possible for the customer. In higher education, the prime customer is the student, but it could also include an agency or firm contracting with the university for research or training and development support. This chapter is not a cookbook for a lean transformation. Rather, it seeks to evoke our imagination by describing lean concepts and encouraging systems to develop actionable plans that fit their own unique cultures and circumstances. Nor does it suggest that lean is the panacea for all that is imperfect in public university systems. The chapter intends to stimulate an understanding of how the phenomenon of lean has powerfully transformed other complex and important enterprises. Further, it intends to encourage university system stakeholders to imagine what is possible for enhanced system performance in service to students if they adopt lean and pursue a lean transformation.

The Lean Story

An early step in the development of lean took place in 1784, when Eli Whitney patented the cotton gin and with it a standard process to separate sticky green seeds from within the white cotton bolls that grew prolifically in the southeastern United States (Schur, 2021). He later developed a process that used specialized machines to mass-produce muskets with interchangeable parts. Whitney thus changed the course of American agriculture and industry, and in doing so, he not only contributed to a revolution in agricultural productivity but also conceived some of the fundamental concepts of what would later be termed lean.

He established that replicable standard work could more cost-efficiently deliver large-scale, high-quality outputs, with benefits to an increasing population.

Lean further evolved on the assembly lines of the Ford Motor Company in 1913, when Henry Ford operationalized flow production, a process-driven system that combined standard work, interchangeable parts, and moving conveyance (Lean Enterprise Institute, 2023). He mass-produced the Model T with specialized machines, templates, and repeatable processes when other automakers continued to use general-purpose tools and nonstandard craft processes. Ford revolutionized production, albeit for a single chassis with nearly identical specifications (Parkes, 2015). As customers eventually sought options such as color, body type, and performance, Ford's competitors answered that demand. But when confronted with their heterogeneous components and assembly processes, they were unable to replicate the efficiencies and the overwhelming success of the original Model T line.

Through the 1930s and resuming after World War II, Kiichiro Toyoda and Taiichi Ohno from Japan's Toyota Corporation evaluated Ford's concepts and their application in the early years of the American automobile industry and created the Toyota Production System (TPS) (Lean Enterprise Institute, 2023). TPS adapted Ford's production flow to account for volume and demand, optimally configured machines, monitored quality, and sequenced process steps so that one step could inform the next step in the process. Taiichi (1988) later operationalized just-in-time logistics as a key component of TPS.

In the 1980s, researchers from the Massachusetts Institute of Technology's International Motor Vehicle Program (IMVP) evaluated TPS, drew upon its lessons, and coined the term "lean" to describe the paradigm-changing concept (Krafcik, 1988). James Womack, Daniel Jones, and Daniel Roos documented their research in *The Machine That Changed the World* (2007). This seminal volume initiated the contemporary lean movement and has inspired enterprises around the world in all industries to adopt lean and transform their production flow in service to their customers. Lean's evolution and history set the stage for defining its components and characteristics as a management philosophy, a mindset, and a set of broadly applicable business tools (Lean Enterprise Institute, 2023)

Lean Defined

Lean is first a management philosophy obsessively focused on customer-defined value (da Luz Peralta et al., 2020). It unifies an organization's employees working in diverse roles under a framework that is consistent and understandable to them. It clarifies the organization's overall operational strategy and helps employees understand their roles within it. Lean guides decision-making at all levels of an organization such that, without specific guidance from the top, employees in a lean enterprise know how to think and act, and they feel empowered to do so (Lean Enterprise Institute, 2023).

Lean is also a mindset that the success of an enterprise results directly from the value it delivers to its customers (Yamamoto and Bellgran, 2010). Any activity that diverts attention from value creation is considered wasteful and impedes a lean organization's success. Success might be the accumulation of wealth, advancement of an idea or cause, manufacture of a product, provision of a service, or other output of an organization. In a lean organization, all employees are equally accountable for continuous improvement toward the objective of value creation (Womack et al., 2007).

Finally, lean is a set of widely available tools and practices that support its philosophy and mindset (Sudip et al., 2010). Lean is not a mechanism for cost-cutting or eliminating positions, though it can result in lower operating costs. Its real purpose is to create the capacity for an organization to deliver greater value and top-line revenue growth rather than bottom-line cost reduction.

Lean Concepts

Lean is best described by explaining how lean systems operate and what to expect in a lean enterprise. Although these concepts help to define lean, a true change in an organization's management model is possible only if the new approach becomes a part of an organization's culture of everyday work as evidenced by employees' behaviors and attitudes (Maciąg, 2019).

Lean begins and ends with value (Rania, 2013). A lean enterprise maximizes its organizational energy to deliver value, defined as the results and outcomes an enterprise provides to its customers at their request and to the standard they require. A perhaps controversial idea when applied to higher education, in a lean organization, customers (not producers) determine what is valuable and measure it by what they are willing to pay for (Womack and Jones, 1996).

Gemba is a Japanese term for the "real place," where the truth is revealed, the time and place where the value sought by customers is created, where an organization's value-creating forces meet customer needs (Kampmeier, 1997; Liebengood et al., 2013). For example, in health care, it is where the healing process begins for a patient; in retail, it is where consumers first use the product they have purchased; and in service industries, it is where the service solves the customer's problem or satisfies their need. The activities closest to the site of value creation are those most important to customers and thus most important to a lean enterprise. Those activities furthest from the customer, while often necessary, are the least important (Gesinger, 2016).

Effort or energy expended by a firm that does not deliver value to customers is considered in a lean organization to be waste, or *muda* in Japanese (Suárez-Barraza et al., 2016). Since waste obstructs value creation, lean organizations obsessively drive it out of processes. Categories of waste include defects, overproduction, waiting, non-utilization of available talent, transportation, inventory, motion, and extra processing. While some waste is necessary and unavoidable—such as human resources, legal, finance, and procurement functions—and while the employees who perform these functions are important members of the overall effort, they do not deliver value directly to customers (Mor et al., 2019; Walters et al., 2020). As a result, an organization should expend the bare minimum of energy in pursuing such efficiency measures as process standardization, automation, consolidation, and outsourcing.

An example of unnecessary waste is approval requirements that an organization inserts into purchasing, hiring, contracting, and other processes. It can be difficult to determine when approvals are necessary and at what level in an organization they must occur. Are they required by law or regulation, or are they just mechanisms to enforce internal control? For higher education, this means resource reallocation from wasteful administrative and academic processes to value-added activities for students, research funders, employers, and the communities served by colleges and universities.

A lean enterprise seeks to develop and practice standard work, a predictable and replicable process that achieves valuable work outcomes while minimizing unnecessary variance and complexity, that is, waste (Labach, 2010). When a firm uses standard work consistently, wasteful deviations become obvious and avoidable and serve as a resource for reallocation to more customer-valued products and services. Although lean organizations seek to create value for customers through standard work, in some cases, customers find variance or uniqueness to be valuable, and they are willing to pay for these differentiating attributes. Customers might select a manufacturer that uniquely approaches environmental sustainability, for example. In higher education, a spiritual, residential life, national service component, or a unique pedagogy are deviations from standard approaches that some students value. In lean, it is not wasteful to accommodate customer-defined value first, and then strive for standardization of that process.

In lean, instead of producers pushing value, customers pull the value that in turn flows from the organization (Womack and Jones, 1996). A lean organization makes items or provides services when (and only when) a customer demands them, and does so quickly and without wasteful interruptions (Khorasani et al., 2017). One step triggers and flows seamlessly to the next without interruption or waiting, and adequate resources are provided for the immediate execution of each step in a process (Onofrei et al, 2021). Imagine the possibilities for higher education if it defined value in its customers' terms rather than its own. We will explore some of these possibilities below.

Lean enterprises seek continuous improvement of all standard work processes and procedures, at all levels of the organization, and all stakeholders, including customers, contribute to continuous improvement within an enterprise (Gonzalez-Aleu, 2018). They do so in the spirit of *kaizen*, which is Japanese for "good change." *Kaizen* are small, incremental changes that have a long-term effect; they can be structured, deliberate improvement team efforts or the simple, grassroots efforts of individuals (Imai, 1986; Galeazzo et al., 2021).

Hoshin kanri, a Japanese term for management pointing the way, is a strategic planning approach used by lean practitioners to identify strategic goals and guide the future needs of organizations (Testani and Ramakrishnan, 2013). This approach to planning orients entire organizations toward common visions or goals in alignment with implementation in daily management practices.

One example for how management points the way is by practicing and modeling mutual respect across a lean organization's workforce (Coetzee et al., 2019). An organization is only lean to the extent that its people respect each other's unique professional contributions toward providing value to customers. Lean managers respect the expertise of value-creating employees by observing their work, implementing their ideas for continuous improvement, redefining standard work based on their expertise, providing resources, and removing barriers to value delivery. Employees reciprocate respect by trusting that managers are working on their behalf, and the organization as a whole celebrates the employees who contribute to continuous improvement (Uusitalo et al., 2019).

Lean Benefits

Numerous organizations have found that adoption of lean improves productivity and eliminates waste, allowing them to create more value for customers with fewer resources (Dresch et al., 2019). For example, Nike, the athletic apparel giant, has reported that compared to factories that did not adopt lean, those that did experienced defect rates 50 percent lower, factory productivity 20 percent higher, integration time of new products 30 percent faster, and delivery lead times 40 percent shorter (Association for Manufacturing Excellence, 2012). Another example comes from the aircraft manufacturer Boeing, which introduced lean to its commercial aircraft division in 1996 and has since expanded lean company wide. Boeing has experienced 40 percent productivity improvements and 300 percent improvement in material defect rates in some of its business units (US Environmental Protection Agency, 2000).

Lean also has a profound effect on employee satisfaction and engagement because lean organizations recognize and encourage their employees to have a more active voice in decision-making regarding value-creating activities (Ross, 2002). The trusting relationships that develop in lean organizations enhance social exchanges between employees and employers, resulting in participative knowledge-sharing (Hamid et al., 2020; Wang et al., 2015).

Conditions for a Lean Transformation

The first condition for lean transformation is that the organization must understand what customers value (Womack et al., 2007). Other stakeholders may have an opinion about what is valuable, but only customer-defined value drives decision-making and resource allocation in a lean organization. Lean enterprises do not assume what customers find valuable. Rather, they ask customers directly and observe customer behavior at the point of customer interaction (Arumugam et al., 2012).

The second condition is a clear definition of the value stream—the sequential inputs, activities, and outputs that create value for customers—which helps the lean enterprise to identify standard work (Singh et al., 2020; Naga Vamsi and Sharma, 2014). Then the organization observes standard work, monitors the quality of outputs, and identifies defects that may be the result of deviations from standard work or imperfections in the value stream. In each case, the lean organization continuously re-channels an organization's defects or waste into value-creating capacity.

The third condition is lean leadership, which is the cooperation of employees and leaders in their mutual quest to deliver value, crossing divisional boundaries and supporting a thorough, long-term vision of the organization's value-producing processes, all the while holding everyone throughout the organization accountable for meeting lean commitments. The lean leader's role transforms from managing processes to developing and coaching people using lean principles to empowering them for ownership and responsibility for value creation. While implementing lean tools alone will account for 20 percent of the effort in successful lean transformations, the remaining 80 percent of the effort is expended on developing leaders' practices and behaviors, and their ability to build cultures of shared value, reflection, and continuous improvement.

Lean in Higher Education

Although not yet to the level of adoption as in the manufacturing, retail, service, health care, and K–12 education sectors, lean has also benefited higher education (Höfer and Naeve, 2017). Further expansion in the higher education sector will require a unique application and pace of change for effective adoption. In the K–12 space, it is important to recognize the pathbreaking work of the Carnegie Foundation and its model of "improvement science." That model is being adapted to university systems through a collaboration between Carnegie and the National Association of System Heads (NASH). And at the academic institution level, early adopters of lean within the United States include the Universities of Central Oklahoma, Iowa, New Orleans, and Scranton, along with Bowling Green State University and Rensselaer Polytechnic Institute (Balzer, 2010). Internationally, Cardiff University and the University of St. Andrews have been lean innovators (Hines and Lethbridge, 2008).

Campus-level improvements, which directly create value for students, have been most visible. For example, lean value stream mapping and continuous improvement allowed a large public university to reduce the lead time for its procurement process by 50 percent (Lean Advisors, 2023), allowing it to reallocate scarce resources into student-serving functions. Algonquin College drove a 25 percent improvement in the processing time for student timetable delivery and a 95 percent reduction in processing time for college information mailers. These noteworthy examples demonstrate how academic institutions have used lean to improve isolated processes. But the higher power of lean is in changing the paradigm—unifying the entirety of the organization toward value creation.

There are, unfortunately, few examples of broader applications at the university system level, where there is an opportunity to eliminate non-value-added waste in such areas as student transfer and financial aid processes, academic program collaboration, and administrative processes. What characteristics of university systems make them well suited as lean enterprises? What might be the barriers to the adoption of lean? How can system structures support campuses as value-creating entities? These are some of the questions I now explore.

The University System

At the most general level, a system is an organized collection of components (or subsystems) integrated to accomplish an overall purpose, common across its components. Similarly, university systems have been organized to serve a shared public purpose through their component campuses, based on the intended value of the whole being greater than the sum of their parts. In the United States, responsibility for public higher education is largely a state responsibility. And as an alternative to multiple separate institutions focused on their own interests, states have established systems to manage that public higher education mission effectively, efficiently, and apolitically.

NASH (2023) defines a public higher education system as "a group of two or more colleges or universities, each having substantial autonomy and headed by a chief executive or operating officer, all under a single governing board, which is served by a system chief executive officer." Some of these systems have a common mission across the system. An example would be the University of California, where all campuses are doctoral research universities. Other systems—such as those in Alaska, Georgia, Hawaii, Illinois, and Wisconsin—can be described as complex organizations that have numerous institutions with distinctly different missions and separate accreditation, all operating under a single governing board with a system chief executive. In the most effective systems, each constituent campus has its unique strategic plan, governance structure, and academic programs; however, the campuses function in the context of a system strategic plan, or framework, and systemwide academic, finance, and other policies. While all systems share some basic characteristics, they vary in organizational structure and governance roles, levels of autonomy, cross-institutional relationships, and authority within their sponsoring states as a result of historical, political, economic, geographic, and cultural factors.

While university systems can be seen as the aggregation of their institutions, offices, policies, processes, and personnel, they have the potential to serve as the leading organizational force for creating value greater than the sum of those aggregated parts (Berdahl, 2014). Their success in this regard varies by system and is the subject of spirited debate both within and outside those systems. Their components typically include appointed governing bodies and administration, system offices, the campuses or independently accredited institutions, and the customers of the system. The governing body is typically a board of regents or trustees appointed by the governor or elected by a defined constituency and charged with the establishment of policies and the quality of outcomes of the system. It may also hold fiduciary and legal responsibility for the system as a single "body corporate," such as is the case in Alaska (Ak. Const. Art. VII, § 2). The system office, under the direction of the system chief executive (president or chancellor), executes the direction of the governing board, advocates externally, and provides shared services in support of all campuses and institutions. Although the terms "system office" and "system" are often inappropriately conflated, a system office is only a component of the system.

Conditions for a Lean University System

A lean transformation is challenging for any organization to accomplish, and in a university system, it requires stakeholders at the board, system office, campus, and customer levels to understand lean principles and commit to practicing them. Results take time, and outcomes can be worse before they become better (Yamamoto and Bellgran, 2010). Lean is not an immediate fix to an organization's problems; it is a long-term endeavor designed to elicit deep and enduring operational and cultural change in service to the customer. Like any business strategy, an organization cannot abandon lean at the first sign of difficulty. Nor can it selectively choose where it is lean and where it is not (Testani and Ramakrishnan, 2011). Lean is not about the destination but about the journey—the pursuit of continuous improvement—because in the face of ever changing social conditions, demands, and expectations, there will always be something to improve, value to create, and waste to eliminate.

To be lean, stakeholders at all levels within a university system must appreciate that value creation for constituents is the singular goal and that lean is the paradigm that unifies the system toward it. The lean journey must be a shared interest, and participants must understand not only their roles as value creators or contributors, but also those of their colleagues. In short, stakeholders must view the system as a system—the synergy of necessary and unique parts working together toward the common goal of maximizing constituent-defined value.

Yes, lean is unapologetically a business approach. Some within the academy suggest universities cannot be run like businesses. They "condemn the efficiency mentality as an attribute for business, one not appropriate for higher learning" (Zimpher, 2013). They are correct to assert that public university systems do not exist to maximize profits, but a lean business is not about profits; rather, it is about delivering value to constituents. A lean university system must acknowledge its customers as its students, the citizens of its sponsoring community or state, and those people or organizations who benefit from its teaching, research, and service. While certainly critical to value creation, employees of the systems or their campuses are not customers. Neither are government or benefactors. Who are? Some debate whether students are customers of universities and suggest that such a distinction makes academic depth, breadth, and rigor beholden to student desires (Halbesleben et al., 2003; Finney and Finney, 2010). Others suggest that students are customers because they pay for a service and have the power to withhold payment if that service is not delivered (Watjatrakul, 2014). I would argue that students as customers can (and effectively do) define the value they seek and pull that value from systems without unduly compromising quality and academic rigor (Webster and Hammond, 2009). The most competitive higher educational institutions, both private and public, often have higher percentages of out-of-state students paying premium tuition rates, indicating students' willingness to pay more for what and where they find value (Waheeduzzaman, 2007). The rapid rise of private primarily online institutions (e.g., American Public University, Western Governor's University) and remote programs within traditional institutions (Arizona State University, Purdue University, University of Maryland) is a testament to the primacy of student choice.

To succeed in transforming university systems into more lean organizations, systems must recognize that the location of value creation occurs at the campus level, so value-creating forces and resources within systems must be concentrated at this location through processes such as teaching, research, service, and a welcoming environment (Petruzzellis and Romanazzi, 2010). Students have demanded that the academic environment serve their needs by providing more streamlined academic processes, more standardized administrative processes, and more individualized student support processes (Waterbury, 2008).

Students are willing to pay for value in accessible, high-quality academic programs; efficient systems for managing their academic experience; supportive services such as advising and career planning; high-quality facilities and infrastructure; enjoyable and engaging experiences such as athletics, social events, entertainment, culture; a welcoming and inclusive environment; and minimal overhead for administration and governance (Watjatrakul, 2014). Those who benefit from research are willing to pay for value in contributions to bodies of knowledge, economic development, and solutions to societal problems. Sponsoring communities are willing to pay for the economic benefits of a knowledge economy and community quality-of-life enhancements (Bracic,

2018). For example, students within a system may find finance to be a valuable undergraduate degree, thereby creating through their enrollment demand for finance programs, internships, certificates, and courses. A sponsoring community might look to the university system to increase cultural awareness and understanding to improve race relations and economic growth. Industries looking for environmentally sustainable practices may solicit research products from university systems.

Value-creating and non-value-creating are lean concepts that, if taken out of context, can understandably be misunderstood or even offensive to some. In lean, value-creating activities and actors provide direct constituent-facing outcomes. Faculty and select staff have a unique role as the prime value-creating forces in a lean university system (Cavallone et al., 2020). They connect with customers directly in their classrooms, research labs, and offices, and deliver the value that the system unifies to create (Schweikhart, 2012). Customers define the value that faculty deliver in their demand for scholarly disciplines, research, and service (Singh, 2021). While customers define the scope and quantity of value, faculty are the stewards of academic standards, quality, of rigor. It is the unique role of faculty to determine the breadth and depth of scholarly activity within courses and programs (Niehaus and Williams, 2016). The role of administration in scholarly and service activity is to respect the unique contributions of faculty, quietly observe value-creating activity, and eliminate distracting factors that cause deviations to faculty's standard work. Similarly, faculty should avoid non-value-creating management activities, as they distract from their unique role in value creation and are the sole expertise and purview of staff and administration (Perry, 2002).

A lean university system might seek to improve student value by including its member institutions in a Common Core curriculum where students access and receive credit for core courses through any system institution and different modalities. System institutions could create greater value by maintaining a standard academic calendar, financial aid program, learning management system, grading policy, and daily course schedule—all to create greater utility, flexibility, and access for students (Emiliani, 2004). For example, students at small campuses in rural locations can gain access to offerings from larger campuses in the system without leaving their hometowns. At the same time, system-level initiatives may also encroach, or appear to encroach, upon the autonomy and discretion of the system's institutions, thus creating tension within the ranks even when students may benefit from the initiative.

Necessary but non-value-creating roles of university systems include governance and oversight for constituent institutions, system-level marketing and branding, advocacy with federal and state legislators and agencies, and shared support for business operations (such as human resources and collective bargaining, enterprise-level information technology, procurement, finance, and legal services) (Emiliani, 2004). In a lean system, these functions would be performed by the administration at the campus level or centrally by the system office on behalf of the campuses where resources and energy are optimized through synergies, focus, and economies of scale (Brown, 2012). These functions are far from the point of value creation and therefore can be optimized by efficient shared processes and energies and the value of scale.

In a lean university system, the system office serves the needs of campuses, where value is created. For example, a system could consolidate many human resources functions and services for employees at the system level to create efficiencies and a more consistent service experience for employees at the campus. These services could even be outsourced to an external human resources provider, as is the trend in many large enterprises (Willcocks et al., 2013). Other human resources functions, such as the evaluation of faculty for tenure or selection of new faculty, may be more appropriately performed at the campus level. In contrast, consolidating information technology under unified, cloud-enabled platforms can improve its effectiveness, consume fewer resources, foster intercampus faculty collaboration, and support wider student access and choice (Mugridge and Sweeney, 2015).

The Lean Public University System

Like most organizations, university systems have legacy ideas, policies, and practices that can be difficult to change, even if they are barriers to value creation (Ford, 2011). Stakeholders within the system must set aside parochial motives, abandon their need for control, trust and respect their colleagues, and be willing to pivot from legacy conventions and ideas (Alarcón-del-amo et al., 2016). They must focus on their own roles within the system while honoring and not encroaching upon the unique expertise of colleagues. They must set aside what they feel is valuable and focus on what their customers find valuable. Faculty's primary allegiance must be to students and not their scholarly disciplines. In a lean university, disciplines are a means to an end, which is to maximize customer-defined value.

Lean may help systems realize two tiers of outcomes. First, process efficiency created through lean can create resource savings to be directed toward what students value in their academic programs, support facilities, and services. Second, lean can directly influence value-creating activities through standardized, streamlined, and consistently delivered curricula, standardized syllabi, and open-access educational resources.

In a lean university system, all employees understand lean and their unique roles in bringing it about (Flumerfelt et al., 2016). Even isolated individuals or small groups that do not comprehend lean principles can derail a lean transformation. Lean training must be universal, consistent, and thorough with cognitive and affective domain outcomes (Waterbury, 2015).

A university system cannot be lean without trust among stakeholders (Clément et al., 2020). Governing bodies and administration must respect the unique expertise of value-creating faculty and staff, supporting and trusting them to develop and maintain standard work to provide customer-defined value. Standardization of work imposed top-down by administration rather than from the point of value creation may be seen as yet another application of bureaucratic accountability and control rather than a new and innovative approach to value creation (Stecher and Kirby, 2004). Value-creating employees must trust that the administration is listening to their needs and removing obstacles, and those non-value-creating activities that are necessary are performed cost-effectively. All stakeholders must trust that their colleagues continue to strive for continuous improvement, and that they will be supported in that spirit and practice. Most importantly, a bond of trust between the system and its customers that value delivery must be the forefront priority of the university system.

The struggle for control to protect the status quo that sometimes occurs in a legacy university system will stall a lean transformation and, consequently, value creation for students. In a lean system, management should not control what happens at the point of value creation, and value-creating employees should not attempt to control management (Lawrence and Ott, 2013). Governance bodies should exist to develop and maintain curricula and scholarly standards and provide input to management, not to encroach upon management decisions for self-serving interests (Tanner and Fitzpatrick, 2006). Similarly, employees collectively bargain for wages, benefits, and working conditions, not to influence management decisions regarding the mission and purpose of the employer (Wickens, 2008). Institutions and departments in a lean system do not compete or harbor self-serving motives or interests. Instead, they see that the success of the entire system in creating customer-defined value is the barometer by which parts of the system—campuses, departments, and offices—must be measured.

A Vision for the Future

This chapter has defined lean and outlined how organizations in general and university systems in particular can experience and sustain a lean transformation. Given these conditions, a lean system can be realized if the higher education community is genuinely committed to maximizing value creation on behalf of its students. It has not been presented as a recipe for an actionable lean transformation because one size does not fit all, and a lean transformation plan is specific to an organization's ability and tolerance for change. For some, broad and far-reaching transformative change is appropriate. Others will be better suited for smaller and incremental changes. And for still others, the conditions may be such that the pursuit of lean likely will fail.

Future lean systems may embed lean teachers within all offices and departments to teach lean concepts to system employees and assist them as they implement lean (Sisson and Elshennawy, 2015). The University of St. Andrews in Scotland provides an example whereby lean consultants work with university stakeholders to share knowledge and experience and implement lean thinking within the university (University of St. Andrews, 2023).

The lean university of the future will then focus the preponderance of its energy on delivering customer-defined value. It will actively engage customers through surveys, needs assessments, focus groups, and direct observation of behaviors. It will base curricular offerings, research focus areas, service initiatives, and campus environmental enhancements on what customers indicate to be valuable (Kazancoglu and Ozkan-Ozen, 2019).

The point of value creation will be the center of gravity for future lean university systems, not the president's or chancellor's office. Stakeholders at all levels will routinely observe the value-creating activity firsthand to understand their unique contribution to it. Administrators will use their observations to obtain and allocate scarce resources in support of faculty and other value-creating employees. Academic programs will generate a greater level of student satisfaction, in part through precise expectations, clarity for lectures and assignments, standard formats for deliverables, coordinated curricular pace between classes, and better use of students' increasingly scarce time to put toward their goals (Emiliani, 2004).

The lean university system will map its value streams, create standard work definitions, and identify sources of waste within them. Employees will approach sources of waste with an active, continuous improvement program with measurable metrics for accountability, and to assess progress, and they will share success and celebrate progress within communities of lean practice and with senior administrators.

Customers will pull value from the lean system university using simple, practical, integrated automated systems that allow accessible value to flow without interruption or waste. Employees, management, and administration will gain and maintain mutual respect based on communication, trust, and acknowledgment of unique and interdependent roles and expertise.

Employees at all levels within university systems will understand lean and use it in their everyday work. Through lean, they feel empowered to share the truth and work in the spirit of continuous improvement, and they are engaged and committed to the mission and outcomes of the university system.

System offices and campuses understand and embrace their unique roles in the lean system and work together on behalf of customers. Campuses perform the value-creating activities of teaching, research, service, and providing a welcoming and enjoyable environment for faculty, staff, and students, all built on a strong commitment to freedom of scholarly and creative thought. System offices perform non-value-creating but necessary services in support of the campuses, taking full advantage of synergies and economies of scale to create efficiencies and eliminate waste. Systems measure their effectiveness based on the value they deliver and the waste they eliminate in satisfaction of their customers' needs.

Students benefit from a more affordable and streamlined experience as they develop intellectually and socially, feel welcome, and enjoy their experience. Students also learn the value of lean through their academic experience and carry that valuable knowledge into the many workplaces that are well on the lean path. Society receives the benefits of research, and sponsoring communities benefit economically or socially from the university system's product.

This chapter presents only a conceptual framework for lean in university systems, along with a projection of its advantages and an identification of some of its barriers. There remains a need for system-level practical examples and further research from which to draw lessons learned. When a system leads the way, commits to lean, and embarks on a lean transformation, more public university systems will be empowered and inspired to use lean to increase value for their customers.

Those systems will be rewarded with exciting futures with endless possibilities for sustainably creating ever more value for their students and other constituencies they serve.

References

Alarcón-del-amo, M., C. Casablancas-segura, and J. Llonch. (2016). "Responsive and Proactive Stakeholder Orientation in Public Universities: Antecedents and Consequences." *Higher Education* 72, no. 2 (2016): 131–51. http://dx.doi.org/10.1007/s10734-015-9942-2.

Association for Manufacturing Excellence. (2012). "Nike Reports Lean Production Success." May 18, 2012, https://www.ame.org/target/articles/2012/nike-reports-lean-production-success.

Arumugam, V., J. Antony, and A. Douglas. (2012). "Observation: A Lean Tool for Improving the Effectiveness of Lean Six Sigma." *TQM Journal* 24, no. 3 (2012): 275–87. http://dx.doi.org/10.1108/17542731211226781.

Balzer, W. (2010). *Lean Higher Education: Increasing the Value and Performance of University Processes*. Boca Raton, FL: CRC Press.

Berdahl, R. (2014). *Thoughts on the History of University Systems in the United States*. Berkeley, CA: Center for Studies in Higher Education. https://cshe.berkeley.edu/publications/thoughts-history-university-systems-us-robert-berdahl.

Bracic, A. (2018). "For Better Science: The Benefits of Community Engagement in Research." *PS, Political Science and Politics* 51, no. 3 (2018): 550–53. http://dx.doi.org/10.1017/S1049096518000446.

Brown, C. (2012). "Application of the Balanced Scorecard in Higher Education: Opportunities and Challenges." *Planning for Higher Education* 40, no. 4 (2012): 40–50. https://uiwtx.idm.oclc.org/login?url=https://www.proquest.com/scholarly-journals/application-balanced-scorecard-higher-education/docview/1272106398/se-2?accountid=7139.

da Luz Peralta, C. B., M. E. Echeveste, F. H. Lermen, A. Marcon, and G. Tortorella. "A Framework Proposition to Identify Customer Value through Lean Practices: IMS." *Journal of Manufacturing Technology Management* 31, no. 4 (2020): 725–47. http://dx.doi.org/10.1108/JMTM-06-2019-0209.

Cavallone, M., R. Manna, and R. Palumbo. (2020). "Filling in the Gaps in Higher Education Quality: An Analysis of Italian Students' Value Expectations and Perceptions." *International Journal of Educational Management* 34, no 1 (2020): 203–16. http://dx.doi.org/10.1108/IJEM-06-2019-0189.

Cavdur, F., B. Yagmahan, E. Oguzcan, N. Arslan, and N. Sahan. (2019). "Lean Service System Design: A Simulation-Based VSM Case Study." *Business Process Management Journal* 25, no. 7 (2019): 1802–21. http://dx.doi.org/10.1108/BPMJ-02-2018-0057.

Coetzee, R., L. van Dyk, and K. R. van der Merwe. (2019). "Towards Addressing Respect for People During Lean Implementation." *International Journal of Lean Six Sigma* 10, no. 3 (2019): 830–54. http://dx.doi.org/10.1108/IJLSS-07-2017-0081.

Clément, L., C. Fernet, A. J., S. Morin, and S. Austin. (2020). "In Whom College Teachers Trust? On the Role of Specific Trust Referents and Basic Psychological Needs in Optimal Functioning at Work." *Higher Education* 80, no. 3 (2020): 511–30. http://dx.doi.org/10.1007/s10734-019-00496-z.

Dresch, A., D. R. Veit, P. Nascimento de Lima, P. L. Daniel, and C. C. Dalila (2019). "Inducing Brazilian Manufacturing SMEs Productivity with Lean Tools." *International Journal of Productivity and Performance Management* 68, no. 1 (2019): 69–87. http://dx.doi.org.uiwtx.idm.oclc.org/10.1108/IJPPM-10-2017-0248.

Emiliani, M. L. (2004). "Improving Business School Courses by Applying Lean Principles and Practices. *Quality Assurance in Education* 12, no. 4 (2004): 175–87. http://dx.doi.org/10.1108/09684880410561596.

Finney, T., and R. Finney. (2010). "Are Students Their Universities' Customers? An Exploratory Study." *Education and Training* 52, no. 4 (2010): 276–91. http://dx.doi.org/10.1108/00400911011050954.

Flumerfelt, S., A. C. Alves, C. P. Leão, and D. L. Wade. (2016). "What Do Organizational Leaders Need from Lean Graduate Programming." *European Journal of Training and Development* 40, no. 5 (2016): 302–20. http://dx.doi.org/10.1108/EJTD-01-2015-0005.

Ford, M. C. (2011). "The Roles of the President, Faculty, and Staff in Cultivating the Commitment and Engagement Necessary to Produce Revitalization at Faith-Based Colleges." Doctoral diss., University of Pennsylvania. Order No. 3455407. https://uiwtx.idm.oclc.org/login?url=https://www.proquest.com/dissertations-theses/roles-president-faculty-staff-cultivating/docview/868666670/se-2?accountid=7139.

Galeazzo, A., A. Furlan, and A. Vinelli. (2021). "The Role of Employees' Participation and Managers' Authority on Continuous Improvement and Performance." *International Journal of Operations and Production Management* 41, no. 13 (2021): 34–64. http://dx.doi.org.uiwtx.idm.oclc.org/10.1108/IJOPM-07-2020-0482.

Gesinger, S. (2016). "Experiential Learning: Using Gemba Walks to Connect with Employees." *Professional Safety* 61, no. 2 (2016): 33–36. https://uiwtx.idm.oclc.org/login?url=https://www.proquest.com/scholarly-journals/experiential-learning-using-gemba-walks-connect/docview/1765137209/se-2?accountid=7139.

Gonzalez-Aleu, F., E. M. Van Aken, J. Cross, and W. J. Glover. (2018). "Continuous Improvement Project within Kaizen: Critical Success Factors in Hospitals." *TQM Journal* 30, no. 4 (2018): 335–55. http://dx.doi.org.uiwtx.idm.oclc.org/10.1108/TQM-12-2017-0175.

Halbesleben, J. R. B., J. A. H. Becker, and M. R. Buckley. (2003). "Considering the Labor Contributions of Students: An Alternative to the Student-as-Customer Metaphor." *Journal of Education for Business* 78, no. 5 (2003): 255–57. https://uiwtx.idm.oclc.org/login?url=https://www.proquest.com/scholarly-journals/considering-labor-contributions-students/docview/202819526/se-2?accountid=7139.

Hamid, R. B. A., M. D. B. Ismail, and I. R. B. Ismail. (2020). "Importance of Employee Participation in Lean Thinking and Their Competency towards Employee Innovative Behaviour." *South East Asian Journal of Management* 14, no. 1 (2020): 23–43. https://uiwtx.idm.oclc.org/login?url=https://www.proquest.com/scholarly-journals/importance-employee-participation-lean-thinking/docview/2522189630/se-2?accountid=7139.

Hines, P., and S. Lethbridge. (2008). "New Development: Creating a Lean University." *Public Money and Management* 28, no. 1 (2008): 53–56. https://uiwtx.idm.oclc.org/login?url=https://www.proquest.com/scholarly-journals/new-development-creating-lean-university/docview/36946569/se-2?accountid=7139.

Höfer, S., and J. Naeve. (2017). "The Application of Lean Management in Higher Education." *International Journal of Contemporary Management* 16 (2017): 63–80. http://dx.doi.org.uiwtx.idm.oclc.org/10.4467/24498939IJCM.17.038.8261.

Imai, M. (1986). *Kaizen: The Key to Japan's Competitive Success*. New York: McGraw-Hill.

Kampmeier, C. (1997). "Gemba Kaizen: A Commonsense, Low-Cost Approach to Management." *Journal of Management Consulting* 9, no. 4 (1997): 68. https://uiwtx.idm.oclc.org/login?url=https://www.proquest.com/scholarly-journals/gemba-kaizen-commonsense-low-cost-approach/docview/215895075/se-2?accountid=7139.

Kazancoglu, Y., and Y. Ozkan-Ozen. (2019). "Lean in Higher Education: A Proposed Model for Lean Transformation in a Business School with MCDM Application." *Quality Assurance in Education* 27, no. 1 (2019): 82–102. http://dx.doi.org.uiwtx.idm.oclc.org/10.1108/QAE-12-2016-0089.

Khorasani, S. T., J. Cross, R. Feizi, and M. S. Islam. (2017). "Application of Lean Tools in Medication Ordering Systems for Hospital." *IIE Annual Conference Proceedings* 67: 1145–50. https://uiwtx.idm.oclc.org/login?url=https://www.proquest.com/scholarly-journals/application-lean-tools-medication-ordering/docview/1951123137/se-2?accountid=7139.

Krafcik, J. F. (1988). "Triumph of the Lean Production System." *Sloan Management Review* 30, no. 1 (1988): 41. https://uiwtx.idm.oclc.org/login?url=https://www-proquest-com.uiwtx.idm.oclc.org/scholarly-journals/triumph-lean-production-system/docview/224963951/se-2?accountid=7139.

Lawrence, J., and M. Ott. (2013). "Faculty Perceptions of Organizational Politics." *Review of Higher Education* 36, no. 2 (2013): 145–78. https://uiwtx.idm.oclc.org/login?url=https://www.proquest.com/scholarly-journals/faculty-perceptions-organizational-politics/docview/1265601250/se-2?accountid=7139.

Lean Advisors. (2023) "Improving the Procurement Process at UTPA." Accessed December 28, 2023, https://www.leanadvisors.com/lean-success-stories/education/improving-the-procurement-process-at-utpafigure-3-detailed-process-map-of-procurement-process-at-utpa-current-state-the-more-detailed-map-also-allowed-the-team-to-measure-the-individual-process-steps-from-a-time-standpoint.-as-part-of-the-vsm-process.

Lean Enterprise Institute. (2023). "A Brief History of Lean." Accessed December 28, 2023, https://www.lean.org/explore-lean/a-brief-history-of-lean/.

Labach, E. J. (2010). "Using Standard Work Tools for Process Improvement." *Journal of Business Case Studies* 6, no. 1 (2010): 39–47. https://uiwtx.idm.oclc.org/login?url=https://www.proquest.com/scholarly-journals/using-standard-work-tools-process-improvement/docview/214859523/se-2?accountid=7139.

Liebengood, S. M., M. Cooper, and P. Nagy. (2013). "Going to the Gemba: Identifying Opportunities for Improvement in Radiology." *Journal of the American College of Radiology* 10, no. 12 (2013): 977–79. https://www.jacr.org/article/S1546-1440(13)00519-X/fulltext.

Maciąg, J. (2019). *Lean Culture in Higher Education: Towards Continuous Improvement*. London: Palgrave Macmillan. https://books.google.com/books?hl=en&lr=&id=CtaMDwAAQBAJ&oi=fnd&pg=PR9&dq=APA+citation+Lean+Culture+in+Higher+Education:+Towards+Continuous+Improvement&ots=vVkUaJyo-J&sig=r1sbeXNaPTWOo6jlfnEQWw9YI-g#v=onepage&q&f=false.

Madhani, P. M. (2020). "Lean Six Sigma Deployment in Finance and Financial Services: Enhancing Competitive Advantages." *IUP Journal of Operations Management* 19, no. 3, 25–49. https://uiwtx.idm.oclc.org/login?url=https://www-proquest-com.uiwtx.idm.oclc.org/scholarly-journals/lean-six-sigma-deployment-finance-financial/docview/2460797829/se-2?accountid=7139.

Mor, R. S., A. Bhardwaj, S. Singh, and A. Sachdeva. (2019). "Productivity Gains through Standardization-of-Work in a Manufacturing Company: IMS." *Journal of Manufacturing Technology Management* 30, no. 6 (2019): 899–919. http://dx.doi.org/10.1108/JMTM-07-2017-0151.

Mugridge, R. L., and M. Sweeney. (2015). "Data Center Consolidation at the University at Albany." *Information Technology and Libraries (Online)* 34, no. 4 (2015): 18–29. https://uiwtx.idm.oclc.org/login?url=https://www.proquest.com/scholarly-journals/data-center-consolidation-at-university-albany/docview/1761153664/se-2.

Naga Vamsi, K. J., and A. Sharma. (2014). "Lean Manufacturing Implementation Using Value Stream Mapping as a Tool: A Case Study from Auto Components Industry." *International Journal of Lean Six Sigma* 5, no. 1 (2014): 89–116. http://dx.doi.org.uiwtx.idm.oclc.org/10.1108/IJLSS-04-2012-0002.

National Association of System Heads. (2023). "About NASH." Accessed December 28, 2023, http://nashonline.org/about/.

Niehaus, E., and L. Williams. (2016). "Faculty Transformation in Curriculum Transformation: The Role of Faculty Development in Campus Internationalization." *Innovative Higher Education* 41, no. 1 (2016): 59–74. http://dx.doi.org/10.1007/s10755-015-9334-7.

Onofrei, G., B. Fynes, H. Nguyen, and H. A. Amir. (2021). "Quality and Lean Practices Synergies: A Swift Even Flow Perspective." *International Journal of Quality and Reliability Management* 38, no. 1 (2021): 98–115. http://dx.doi.org/10.1108/IJQRM-11-2019-0360.

Parkes, A. (2015). "Lean Management Genesis." *Management* 19, no. 2 (2015): 106–21. http://dx.doi.org.uiwtx.idm.oclc.org/10.1515/manment-2015-0017.

Perry, W. L. (2002). "Roles and Responsibilities of Program Administrators as Perceived by Physical Therapist Program Administrators and Faculty." *Journal of Physical Therapy Education* 16, no. 2 (2002): 9–15. http://dx.doi.org/10.1097/00001416-200207000-00003.

Petruzzellis, L., and S. Romanazzi. (2010). "Educational Value: How Students Choose University: Evidence from an Italian University." *International Journal of Educational Management* 24, no. 2 (2010): 139–58. http://dx.doi.org/10.1108/09513541011020954.

Rania, A. M. (2013). "A Model for Applying Lean Thinking to Value Creation." *International Journal of Lean Six Sigma* 4, no. 2 (2013): 204–24. http://dx.doi.org/10.1108/20401461311319365.

Ross, J. R. (2002). "Evaluating Lean Manufacturing Benefits (Presentation Supporting Paper)." *IIE Annual Conference Proceedings*, 1–6.

Schur, J. (2021). "Eli Whitney's Patent for the Cotton Gin." National Archives. Last reviewed December 16, 2021, https://www.archives.gov/education/lessons/cotton-gin-patent.

Schweikhart, S. S. (2012). "An Interview with John Toussaint." *Journal of Health Administration Education* 29, no. 4 (2012): https://uiwtx.idm.oclc.org/login?url=https://www.proquest.com/scholarly-journals/interview-with-john-toussaint/docview/1271954911/se-2?accountid=7139.

Singh, J., H. Singh, A. Singh, and J. Singh. (2020). "Managing Industrial Operations by Lean Thinking Using Value Stream Mapping and Six Sigma in Manufacturing Unit: Case Studies." *Management Decision* 58, no. 6 (2020): 111. http://dx.doi.org.uiwtx.idm.oclc.org/10.1108/MD-04-2017-0332.

Singh, J. (2021). "Applying Lean Methodology to Curriculum Revision and Internship Placement Process—A Case Study." *Journal of Research in Innovative Teaching and Learning* 14, no. 2 (2021): 288–305. http://dx.doi.org/10.1108/JRIT-05-2019-0055.

Sisson, J., and A. Elshennawy. (2015). "Achieving Success with Lean." *International Journal of Lean Six Sigma* 6, no. 3 (2015): 263–80. http://dx.doi.org.uiwtx.idm.oclc.org/10.1108/IJLSS-07-2014-0024.

Stecher, B., and S. Kirby, eds. (2004). *Organizational Improvement and Accountability: Lessons for Education from Other Sectors*. Santa Monica, CA: RAND.

Suárez-Barraza, M. F., S. Dahlgaard-Park, F. G. Rodríguez-González, and C. Durán-Arechiga. (2016). "In Search of 'Muda' through the TKJ Diagram." *International Journal of Quality and Service Sciences* 8, no. 3 (2016): 377–94. http://dx.doi.org/10.1108/IJQSS-04-2016-0028.

Sudip, K., A. Chakraborty, and R. Bhattacharya. (2010). "Effects of Lean Tools in Small Scale Enterprises." *Drishtikon: A Management Journal* 2, no. 1 (2010): https://uiwtx.idm.oclc.org/login?url=https://www.proquest.com/scholarly-journals/effects-lean-tools-small-scale-enterprises/docview/1477996646/se-2?accountid=7139.

Taiichi, O. (1988). *Toyota Production System: Beyond Large-Scale Production*. Milton Park, UK: Taylor and Francis.

Tanner, C., and J. Fitzpatrick. (2006). "What Ever Happened to Faculty Governance?" *Journal of Nursing Education* 45, no. 9 (2006): 339–40. https://uiwtx.idm.oclc.org/login?url=https://www.proquest.com/scholarly-journals/what-ever-happened-faculty-governance/docview/203970107/se-2?accountid=7139.

Testani, M. V., and S. Ramakrishnan. (2011). "Lean Transformation Leadership Model: Leadership's Role in Creating Lean Culture." *IIE Annual Conference Proceedings* (2011): 1–8. https://uiwtx.idm.oclc.org/login?url=https://www.proquest.com/scholarly-journals/lean-transformation-leadership-model-leaderships/docview/1190410600/se-2?accountid=7139.

Testani, M., and S. Ramakrishnan. (2013). "Leader-Centric Hoshin Planning: A Systemic Approach for Sustaining an Enterprise-Wide Lean Transformation." *IIE Annual Conference Proceedings* (2013): 1006–13. https://uiwtx.idm.oclc.org/login?url=https://www.proquest.com/scholarly-journals/leader-centric-hoshin-planning-systemic-approach/docview/1471959868/se-2?accountid=7139.

US Environmental Protection Agency. (2000). *Pursuing Perfection: Case Studies Examining Lean Manufacturing Strategies, Pollution Prevention, and Environmental Regulatory Management Implications*. Washington, DC: US Environmental Protection Agency. https://www.epa.gov/sites/default/files/2013-11/documents/perfection.pdf.

University of St. Andrews. (2023). "St. Andrews Lean Consulting." Accessed December 28, 2023, https://www.st-andrews.ac.uk/business-services/lean/.

Uusitalo, P., O. Seppänen, A. Peltokorpi, and H. Olivieri. (2019). "Solving Design Management Problems Using Lean Design Management: The Role of Trust." *Engineering, Construction and Architectural Management* 26, no. 7 (2019): 1387–405. http://dx.doi.org.uiwtx.idm.oclc.org/10.1108/ECAM-03-2018-0135.

Wang, H., Y. Yen, and J. Tseng. (2015). "Knowledge Sharing in Knowledge Workers: The Roles of Social Exchange Theory and the Theory of Planned Behavior." *Innovation: Management, Policy and Practice* 17, no. 4 (2015): 450–65. http://dx.doi.org/10.1080/14479338.2015.1129283.

Walters, L. M., M. A. Nickerson, and L. A. Hall. (2020). "Improving the 1040 Process by Applying Lean Principles: A Case Study." *TQM Journal* 32, no. 2 (2020): 249–67. http://dx.doi.org/10.1108/TQM-02-2019-0048.

Waterbury, T. (2008). "Lean in Higher Education: A Delphi Study to Develop Performance Metrics and an Educational Lean Improvement Model for Academic Environments." Doctoral dissertation, Capella University.

Waterbury, T. (2015). "Learning from the Pioneers: A Multiple-Case Analysis of Implementing Lean in Higher Education." *International Journal of Quality and Reliability Management* 32, no. 9 (2015): 934. http://dx.doi.org/10.1108/IJQRM-08-2014-0125.

Waheeduzzaman, A. N. M. (2007). "States, Demographics and Competitiveness of America's Best Universities." *Competitiveness Review* 17, no. 1 (2007): 77–93. http://dx.doi.org/10.1108/10595420710816632.

Watjatrakul, B. (2014). "Factors Affecting Students' Intentions to Study at Universities Adopting the 'Student-as-Customer' Concept." *International Journal of Educational Management* 28, no. 6 (2014): 676–93. http://dx.doi.org/10.1108/IJEM-09-2013-0135.

Webster, R. L., and K. L. Hammond. (2009). "Are Students and Their Parents Viewed as Customers by AACSB-International Member Schools? Survey Results and Implications for University Business School Leaders." *Allied Academies International Conference Academy of Educational Leadership Proceedings* 14, no. 2 (2009): 51. https://uiwtx.idm.oclc.org/login?url=https://www.proquest.com/scholarly-journals/are-students-their-parents-viewed-as-customers/docview/192405837/se-2?accountid=713.

Wickens, C. M. (2008). "The Organizational Impact of University Labor Unions." *Higher Education* 56, no. 5 (2008): 545–64. http://dx.doi.org/10.1007/s10734-008-9110-z.

Willcocks, L., D. Feeny, and M. Lacity. (2013). "Transforming a Human Resource Function through Shared Services and Joint-Venture Outsourcing: The BAE Systems-Xchanging Enterprise Partnership 2001–2012." *Journal of Information Technology Teaching Cases* 3, no. 1 (2013): 29–42. http://dx.doi.org/10.1057/jittc.2012.15.

Womack, J. P., and D. T. Jones. (1996). *Lean Thinking: Banish Waste and Create Wealth in Your Corporation*. New York: Simon & Schuster.

Womack, J. P., D. T. Jones, and D. Roos. (2007). *The Machine That Changed the World*. New York: Simon & Schuster.

Yamamoto, Y., and M. Bellgran. (2010). "Fundamental Mindset That Drives Improvements towards Lean Production." *Assembly Automation* 30, no. 2 (2010): 124–30. http://dx.doi.org/10.1108/01445151011029754.

Zimpher, N. (2013). "Systemness: Unpacking the Value of Higher Education Systems." In *Higher Education Systems 3.0: Harnessing Systemness, Delivering Performance*, edited by J. Lane and B. Johnstone, 27–44. Albany: State University of New York Press.

8 | Online Systems

WALLACE E. BOSTON

The Future of Online Systems

THE 65 PUBLIC UNIVERSITY and systems in the United States have evolved from the ground up. Campus centered, with satellites in strategic locations, they receive the majority of their state's postsecondary education funding. Faculty members at public universities were among the first to explore the innovative possibilities of electronic classroom instruction at a distance before and after the rise of the Internet.

The Alfred P. Sloan Foundation's Anytime, Anyplace Learning Program funded the establishment of the Sloan Consortium of Colleges and Universities in 1999. Early recipients of grants included distance-learning providers such as the University of Maryland University College and Penn State's World Campus. Among the grantees benefitting from $72 million of the program's largesse were the State University of New York (SUNY), University of Central Florida, and University of Illinois. All three institutions developed substantial online learning programs (Online Learning Consortium, 2022).

While universities within public systems may have substantial online enrollments, there are few centralized system initiatives. Until recently, UMass Online served only as a website catalog for a listing of the courses offered by the University of Massachusetts campuses at Amherst, Boston, Dartmouth, and Lowell, as well as at UMass Medical School. With the UMass purchase and rebranding of Brandman University as UMass Global, an online nonprofit university previously owned by California's Chapman University, it will be interesting to see if it and UMass Online centralize their operations.

Purdue University's purchase of Kaplan University set the stage for bringing a separate online operating division under the branding and operating control of a nonprofit, state-supported university. The University of Arizona purchased Ashford University, an online former for-profit university, and renamed it the University of Arizona Global Campus. Purdue set the bar with its Purdue Global brand, followed by Arizona, and now UMass. In the first two cases, OPM (online program management) services were provided by the former for-profit corporate owners of the online universities. The University of Arizona (UofA) Global Campus recently cancelled its OPM agreement with Zovio, its former for-profit owner. Less than a year after the cancellation of the OPM contract, the UofA announced that the UofA Global Campus would operate under the University of Arizona and not as a separate entity.

This was followed by one of the earliest online pioneers, the University of Phoenix, announcing that it had signed a contract to be sold to the University of Idaho. Unlike the Kaplan University sale to Purdue and the Ashford University sale to the University of Arizona, there is no OPM contract involved in this deal post-transaction. While the first two transactions were initially controversial, the integration and operations of the large online universities appear to be stable. The notoriety of the University of Phoenix, whose enrollment approached 500,000 at its peak, may make it difficult for the University of Idaho transaction to close. Current online enrollments are estimated to be approximately 85,000, and the University of Phoenix states that they have substantially improved the recruitment and persistence of students. Assuming the Idaho/Phoenix transaction closes, there are just four regionally accredited for-profit universities with substantial enrollment that could be attractive acquisition candidates.

To date, nearly all of the online initiatives at public institutions have occurred through individual universities and not through state systems. The primary explanation as to why system initiation has not occurred stems from the fact that few state systems offer a centralized or collective curriculum, instead choosing to delegate the academic responsibilities of member institutions to the individual universities. But wholly online degree programs do not require a physical presence on campus and are "game changers." Recommendations for how systems can benefit through centralized, online programs and courses will be included at this chapter's conclusion.

Fixed versus Variable-Cost Models: Do They Conflict with Online Offerings?

Adding online courses at a university that operates in-person courses on a campus should be relatively easy in an environment where learning management systems, Internet access, and access to mobile devices are all incorporated into daily campus operations. The sudden onset of the COVID-19 pandemic forced most colleges and universities to operate remotely in the spring of 2020. In most cases, the transition in higher education happened quicker and smoother than it did in K–12 public schools, primarily because of two decades of experience delivering online instruction and thanks to its older, more independent, and more technologically savvy students.

Despite substantial progress, online courses and programs are a recent innovation in higher education. Campuses have been the platform for systems' program delivery for half a century or more. As commitments in public funding for higher education increased commensurate with increases in student enrollments, the number of physical campuses expanded. As state funding priorities shifted and higher education funding per student decreased, some costs were cut and others shifted onto students, but the number of campuses in most cases was not cut, largely for political reasons beyond the ability of the system to control. The cost of operating a physical campus at a minimally targeted number of students and academic programs is largely fixed. When the number of programs are fixed and enrollments increase, the increase in expenses is marginal. When enrollments decrease, it is difficult to decrease expenses so long as the same number of programs are maintained.

By contrast, the most successful online operations of nonprofit and for-profit universities use a variable-cost model. Most faculty teaching in online programs are part-time. Full-time faculty are instructors who are not on a tenure track and are not expected to conduct research. Part-time faculty are hired based on the scheduled online course starts. The largest online programs offer many more course and program starts in a year than the traditional campus operating model. Rio Salado College, a two-year public college in Arizona, offers 50 starts per year, as does Ashford University, now operated as the University of Arizona Global Campus.

While none of these online institutions began their operations in this variable-cost manner, they evolved into it in response largely to student demand. As the number of their courses and student enrollments increased, the online course operating schedules increased as well, based on growing and changing student demand. With no need to find a physical classroom available in a campus building, the online dean can add another section of a course or additional courses to the online operating schedule almost any time, contracting with part-time faculty to teach those classes.

The for-profit online American Public University System (APUS) originally offered three semester starts a year through its two institutions, American Military University and American Public University. As the number of students increased, APUS doubled its annual starts to six by starting new online courses every other month. By 2002, APUS leadership realized that working adult students demanded flexible course availability, so they doubled the six starts per year to twelve. While some months continue to exhibit stronger enrollments (notably September and January), enrollments are reasonably distributed among the other ten months, including November and December, because APUS has operated this way for the past two decades and students know that they can start a class on the first day of any month. APUS was able to grow its enrollments to approximately 90,000 students by capitalizing on the variable-cost nature of its operations and the fact that there was no need to expand its physical plant to accommodate additional programs, courses, and sections. One example of this flexibility is that on the first Monday of each month, APUS offers more than 100 sections of its English 101 course. If each section has 25 students enrolled and the courses are eight weeks in length, the overlapping instruction would require physical classrooms for 5,000 students each month at a traditional university. By contrast, APUS's online operating costs are primarily limited to the costs for instructing each section as well as any course materials cost.

Operating online courses and certificates can be done cost-effectively using a variable-cost, incremental cost model. But planning for a large-scale online operation requires close coordination of operating costs. Many institutions have valid concerns about campus-based students choosing online courses so they can attend class from their homes or dorm rooms. As the campuses responded to the pandemic, conducting online classes for everyone was necessary.

Institutions have found it difficult to manage returning to in-person classes versus continuing to operate online classes during the multiple waves of COVID-19 (five and counting in the United States as of February 2022). Most institutions returned to campus operations, but with tacit acknowledgment that instructors could teach online and students could attend class online until the risk of infection was substantially reduced.

The distraction of the pandemic did not solve the dilemma of operating online and on-campus courses simultaneously. To date, no systems have operated both under traditional campus leadership hierarchies. Large online operations usually operate under a dean unless a separate institution and brand has been established, such as Purdue Global, University of Arizona Global, and UMass Global. Those institutions are separately accredited and have presidents who report to the chief executive of the main campus.

The pandemic may have turned the tide of resistance to teaching and taking courses online. College and university students in the class of 2022 have spent more than half of their undergraduate years taking online classes because of the multiple waves of the pandemic. Athletes, commuting students, and working students have enjoyed the flexibility of not having to find parking spots on campus and walk to a distant building to attend class.

There is no better time than the present for state systems to consider the cost benefit of centralizing online operations, particularly from a back-office and administrative perspective. Successful online programs offer academic advising, tutoring, and other services online. Student services and academic departments are more coordinated online than on campus.

In the summer of 2020, the leadership team at Educause called for "digital transformation" as a grand strategy for the major challenges of higher education (Grajek and Brooks, 2020). Initially, Educause's researchers identified student success, institutions' financial health, institutions' reputation and relevance, and institutions' external competition as the top four challenges of higher education. University and college information technology (IT) executives were surveyed in August 2019 to assess their institutions' readiness and ability to utilize digital technologies to solve these grand challenges.

Only 13 percent of the IT executives surveyed indicated that their institutions were engaged in a digital transformation. Approximately two-thirds believed that a digital transformation was more important than ever. All were asked to rate 17 specific benefits associated with digital transformation and whether those benefits were minor, moderate, or major. Over 75 percent of respondents indicated that each of the 17 benefits would be at least moderate.

As Educause's researchers were analyzing the survey data and writing the report, COVID-19 struck. As a result, a fifth grand challenge was added: the pandemic. The researchers called attention to its influence on crisis mitigation; the health and safety of faculty, staff, and students; and digital transformation.

Campus operations will likely never return to "normal." The pandemic has accelerated attention to numerous issues, including digital learning. System leaders could use the digital transformation framework proposed by Educause as a guide to collect data and craft a strategic solution.

Standardization: Pros and Cons

Early installations of information systems on college and university campuses were cumbersome. Payroll and benefits functions were automated first, with bursars and accounts payable following. Customized or homegrown student information systems (SISs) evolved to handle registration, transcripts, and more. Later, many colleges followed their peers, replacing their homegrown systems with those offered by specialized, larger software companies.

While many colleges and universities have transitioned from highly customized systems to the more widely accepted SISs and learning management systems, standardization of policies, procedures, and processes is rare and expensive, even though it is a key condition for system initiatives that expand student access and success though intercampus collaboration.

State systems from Maryland to California have evaluated and established transfer equivalencies over the years for graduates of their two-year colleges to transfer to their four-year institutions. Despite these established guide paths and others, students continue to lose credits in the transfer process, delaying their completion and adding to the financial burden on students and institutions.

More recently, several systems have established standards for general education credits that apply to all colleges and universities in the system and/or state. The Texas Higher Education Coordinating Board (THECB) established the Texas General Education Core Curriculum, effective in the fall of 2014. The 42 semester-credit-hour curriculum consists of eight component areas (communication; mathematics; life and physical science; language, philosophy, and culture; creative arts; American history; government/political science; and social and behavioral sciences) and a component area option (THECB, 2022). All public institutions are required by statute to organize their general education courses in these areas in order to facilitate transfer of lower-level courses among Texas public institutions and systems.

While implementing this law required coordination among its public institutions, the Texas model does not mandate standardized courses; rather, it is a framework through which each institution's courses are identified and categorized. There are benefits of designing and building system-specific online general education courses ranging from an easier transfer of semester credit hours to lower course instructional costs to classroom and utility costs for offering these courses online instead of in person. Based on the design of the Texas framework, it appears that public higher education in the United States is not yet ready politically to require faculty to teach courses centrally designed and prescribed, even though that could facilitate development and delivery of best-in-class courses and more accurate analysis of assessment and learning outcomes, in addition to reducing barriers to student access and lowering costs across the system.

General education courses are the most frequently taught courses (because they're required) in higher education and are cited among other explanations reasons for the first-year student dropout rate. Several explanations of this include the length of time elapsed since the working adult student attended formal education classes, the need for remedial or refresher courses in reading, writing, and math, as well as the students' desire to take courses in their program of interest and not the mandated general education courses. Given the sophisticated adaptive learning tools widely available today, there is no logical reason why a system could not invest time and money in the faculty and technology to build the best general education courses available. These sophisticated and high-quality courses could increase student success rates as well as decrease instructor preparation time and operating costs for classes conducted online.

Constraints

Governance may be the biggest impediment for systems going online in a smart way. Most systems have delegated academic operations to individually accredited institutions. The few examples of a separate online operation outside of individual institutions have met with limited success. For example, though not a university system, California's Calbright College, an online two-year start-up with substantial state funding, has failed to gain any traction in enrollment thus far. A simple Internet search delivers far more results for online courses at the existing California two-year colleges.

UMass Online is an example of a brand representing a university system. In reality, UMass Online simply operates a website that promotes the online offerings of five member institutions: UMass Amherst, Boston, Dartmouth, Lowell, and Medical School. According to a former system head, UMass Online did not capture Massachusetts residents who enrolled at Southern New Hampshire University and other online programs, so UMass purchased Brandman University from Chapman University and rebranded it as the University of Massachusetts Global. There are only so many large online universities operating successfully, and integrating them within an existing system and its incumbent institutions will not be easy, but it is arguably easier to do that than it is to build a 40,000-plus student online university.

Choosing Campus Offerings: Who, What, Where, and When?

Several states have developed platforms that host online courses offered by public institutions in that state. UMass Online has operated that way for years. A recent addition is Online Idaho, which was funded through federal coronavirus relief funds distributed to the state of Idaho. It is an online technology platform represented as a collaboration between the state's eight public colleges and universities and several Idaho state agencies, including the Idaho State Board of Education.

The platform currently operates as an online course catalog passing through a link for course registrations and payments to the college offering the course(s) selected by a student. After the site is fully implemented, students will be able to register and pay for a course at the Online Idaho site (Critchfield, 2020).

Early reports from Idaho publications indicate an enthusiasm for the sharing platform. Provided enrollments are modest, the system may work as designed. If online enrollments increase and cannibalize campus-based enrollments, institutions will complain. Achieving a proper balance of course offerings is never easy in a system. Some faculty and their institutions may view this as an opportunity and contribute more online courses to the platform than their "share" of state higher education funds. Will that enthusiastic response be offset by an institution or institutions that resist and don't contribute? Not many provosts want to report to the president that funding from the state was reduced because their faculty resisted providing online courses to the state's platform. How online tuition revenues and expenses are allocated among the eight public universities will undoubtedly be important to Online Idaho's long-term success. It's too soon to know whether the proposed purchase of the University of Phoenix by the University of Idaho will close. But its integration could substantially impact the operation of Online Idaho.

Operating Online at Scale

Leaving aside some of the traditional concerns about revenue and cost allocations between academic and administrative departments, one of the key questions for systems leaders is, At what point will the online operation operate at scale?

To answer this question, operating goals need to be determined. Is the purpose of operating online to meet the needs of the campus-based students, or to reach students who are unable or unwilling to attend classes on campus? If the purpose is to serve only the existing students on campus, online courses will never operate at scale without deeply affecting campus-based operations, with a net negative effect. If, however, the goal is to serve students who are unable or unwilling to attend campus-based classes, a deeper analysis is required. The recent announcement of an online initiative by the University of North Carolina System provided a targeted incremental online student enrollment of 24,000. Tuition revenues from 24,000 incremental students should more than cover the operating costs, unless the system finds it difficult to attract that number of students without spending a disproportionate amount of money on advertising and admissions.

Most online only students are nontraditional, older than 25, and generally work full-time while attending college part-time. Work deadlines, family obligations, and/or financial issues will cause them to stop out. In order to prevent the stop-out from becoming a drop-out, flexible semester starts need to be offered. An online operation can initially mimic the campus start schedule (trimester, quarterly starts, etc.), but a competitive option is to offer monthly starts, noting that there are some online offerings with nearly weekly starts.

Not all programs need to be offered online. It's better to work with enrollment management to determine which programs are best offered online based on the needs of students and of the community. It's also a good idea to consider the potential cannibalization impact of online programs on campus enrollments.

To accommodate the nontraditional start schedule, the system should organize and operate the online "institution" separately. Until enrollments increase and a regular cadence of frequent (monthly) starts occurs, the most effective way to schedule faculty is to hire part-time instructors.

An effective online operation should enable the student to apply online, be accepted online, apply for financial aid online, and enroll for classes online. Those are the easier components to establish. In order to enroll for classes, an online course schedule should be posted that enables the student to plan for their courses within the academic year selected. That requires a four- to five-month schedule of classes if course starts are offered monthly.

Providing academic advising to online students remotely is vital as well. Given many reasons for stop-outs, regular contacts from program advisors can encourage a student to reenroll before dropping out.

A rule of thumb established by many institutions is a minimum level of enrollment for each online class. Some institutions choose to base the course enrollment minimum on the number of students needed to cover the adjunct instructor's compensation per course. For each student enrolled in a course beyond the minimum, the direct cost contribution margin is positive. If course minimum enrollment levels are established and part-time instructors are hired for each course, a break-even point can be calculated based on the enrollment needed to cover the fixed or semi-fixed costs for operating costs dedicated to the online programs.

At the highest levels of online student enrollments, the opportunity to operate at scale is high if the institution(s) is willing to spend the marketing dollars necessary to recruit students. A recent example is the announcement by the University of Maryland Global Campus (UMGC) to spend $500 million over six years to increase its enrollment (McKenzie, 2019). At the time of the announcement, UMGC's 90,000 part-time students were reported as 48,432 full-time-equivalent students, an important fact to consider in planning. Nonetheless, UMGC believed it was important to increase its student enrollments in order to maintain competitiveness with other institutions offering online courses and programs.

It's notable that there are approximately just 30 institutions with online enrollments in excess of 20,000 students (Lederman, 2019). Two of these institutions—Western Governors University and Southern New Hampshire University—have more than 100,000 students each. To achieve its enrollment growth, Southern New Hampshire University (SNHU) spent $137 million on marketing costs in 2017 (McKenzie, 2019). Note that these two institutions are not members of university systems.

While the potential for online enrollments may seem unlimited, know that it is not. Regardless of the idealism espoused by policymakers, not everyone is interested in earning a degree, much less earning it online. Another caution is how important it is to establish a solid online curriculum, instruction, and academic support platform before investing in marketing to expand enrollments. And even if it is determined that there is market demand, enrollments will not meet expectations if—as is often the case—there is insufficient investment in marketing.

Did COVID-19 Accelerate the Transition to Offering Online Programs?

The onset of the COVID-19 pandemic caused many universities to shutter their campus classes and convert all courses to online in the spring 2020 semester. While campus-based classes have resumed in person since then, the continuing waves of COVID-19 infections have triggered periodic returns to online instruction for campus-based students.

While campuses rightly were lauded for their quick conversion of courses from face-to-face to online, seasoned online course instructional designers were quick to point out that designing a course to be taught most effectively online is not the same as loading a syllabus into a learning management system and expecting students to upload assignments while watching live Zoom calls or prerecorded videos.

Despite its many human and other costs, the notable benefit of the pandemic is that the "cat is out of the bag" as far as online education goes. Those who may have been detractors of online education are more likely to have seen the potential for students to learn as well online as well as in person. Students who were hesitant to register for online courses have seen the advantages of reducing commuting time to campus or dealing with the difficulties of working through a campus-based schedule while working off campus or participating in an athletic team or club. In a few cases, faculty have gained access to students from distant locations, generating tuition revenue for their institutions.

Systems leaders should take advantage of their recent experiences with online instruction and expand online curriculum system wide over the next few years. Properly designed and implemented online programs can increase enrollments and expand geographical outreach for most institutions. Costs of design and implementation can be shared across the system.

University and Employer Partnerships: Will Online Facilitate More of Them?

Workforce development funding comes from both federal sources (such as the Workforce Innovation and Opportunity Act, or WIOA) and state sources. The Education Commission of the States (ECS) tracks the states that go beyond WIOA requirements and specifically link education with workforce development boards. As of this writing, 31 states provide workforce development funding through the state education agency, 29 states provide workforce development funding through the state higher education office, and 32 states provide workforce development funding through the community and or technical college system (ECS, 2021).

State systems, as they are currently organized, are ideally positioned to provide workforce development programs distributed across their state's population centers. Thanks to automation, the percentage of human jobs (jobs that can only be performed by humans) continues to increase in the United States. Employers will expect human workers to be creative, solve complex problems, and think critically. Those traits are enhanced by a college education. State systems can partner with employers to provide them the educated and trained employee that they are seeking.

The University System of Maryland has led a five-campus initiative working with Maryland's Department of Development to increase the number of students graduating with cybersecurity credentials. Increasing the numbers of graduates with cyber-credentials aligns with Maryland's tax incentives designed to attract cybersecurity businesses to relocate to the state. The system's community college partners have also participated in this initiative. The scale and resources of the system allowed it to make this partnership successful.

Offering online courses and programs can only increase the opportunities for systems to partner with employers. Location no longer matters when courses and curriculum operate online. Universities don't have to worry about arranging for instructors to teach workers on-site, and companies don't have to worry about arranging space for classes, nor do they have to worry about interrupting their operations with classes held for selected employees in rooms not normally reserved for such training.

Evidence abounds that several major information technology companies like Amazon, Google, and Intel are developing online curricula for workers in existing locations as well as future locations. Local universities with a strong background in offering and teaching online courses should be able to implement more partnerships through online offerings than are currently offered face-to-face. An important role for systems is to form, manage, and support those partnerships.

Will Partnerships between Private and Public Systems Grow?

The acquisitions of Purdue University Global, University of Arizona Global, and UMass Global are notable for the number of online students each institution brought to its new brand affiliate. In two of those cases, Purdue Global and Arizona Global, a contractual arrangement with the seller provides OPM services to the online entity (note that the University of Arizona Global cancelled its OPM contract with Zovio). Most of those services are directed to marketing and admissions, whose outcomes are critical for providing a return to the system and to the seller.

The University of North Carolina (UNC) System announcement that it plans to launch an internal unit to build and host online courses and programs for all 17 of its members was not a surprise (Smalley, 2021). The surprise was the scope and ambition of a plan that intends to enroll more than 24,000 "incremental" enrollments system wide while establishing 120 new online degree programs by the 2026–27 academic year.

The $97 million set aside by UNC from federal pandemic relief funds will not begin to cover the costs of an initiative of this size and scope. Outside experts interviewed at the time of the UNC's announcement noted that $1 million to develop each online program was a conservative estimate given that some OPMs have spent $3 to $4 million per degree in program development costs. That would indicate $120 million in program development costs before spending additional sums on infrastructure, administration, and marketing.

Conservative estimates place the higher education marketing costs per new online student at $5,000. That will require an estimated $120 million in marketing expenses for the 24,000 incremental students the UNC System plans to enroll, assuming 100 percent student retention and no new recruits to replace graduating students. Obviously, both of those assumptions are unrealistic. The system cited the 60,000 North Carolina residents who are currently enrolled in online programs at other "outside" institutions such as Strayer University and Liberty University as a group that they would like to capture. They also noted that there are approximately one million working adults living in North Carolina who have earned some college credits without earning a degree. The initiative's planners believe that capturing potential students from this group will enhance its enrollment potential.

It will take a lot of cooperation for UNC's member institutions to support this initiative. There are already online students enrolled at most of the 17 UNC institutions, and the details for sharing revenues and expenses have not been outlined as of this date. If there is an entity that can support an initiative of this size and ambition from a monetary perspective, UNC can afford it. The likely outcome, however, is that the proposal will not meet its targets for online degrees or enrollment by the end of 2026–27. If UNC can solve the political issues and unite its member institutions in embracing this new entity, it will likely achieve this level of enrollment at some later date and after spending a much larger sum than originally funded.

One question that every system leader should ask when contemplating an idea like this is, Could or would any of the existing OPMs be willing or able to complete the plan's objectives? It is almost impossible to believe that Coursera or 2U could build out the hundreds of courses and 120 programs in five years. Enrolling 24,000 incremental students is achievable, but at substantial cost for advertising and admissions coordinators responsible for discussing enrollment options with prospective students.

Will a Private System "White Label" Its Courses and Programs for Public Systems?

Another option, admittedly unprecedented, is contracting with other universities, private and public, to use their online courses and programs as an intermediate "white label" solution until the system can build out their own courses and programs. While it is a possibility that this could occur, it is less likely given the approval process required by faculty and departments for new courses and programs. There may be issues with accrediting bodies for such arrangements.

In addition to the challenges just noted, white labeling with a university that may not be in the regular business of licensing its online courses may also lead to potential exposure for an institution from an Americans with Disabilities Act (ADA) compliance perspective if the course is designed to utilize components from the originating university's systems and websites that are not accessible to the licensing institution. This challenge is mitigated by the approach taken by states such as Texas, where a core curriculum exists for general education courses, and a simple memorandum of understanding or transfer agreement makes it easier to utilize online courses from other institutions rather than licensing the course shell and loading it on another learning management system.

Technology Infrastructure: Is Standardization Possible on Campus and Online?

Standardization in technology infrastructure has been elusive in higher education. While there are system-wide contracts for vendors offering learning management systems (LMSs) and other products utilized for online courses, there is little standardization in course curriculum, content, evaluation, registration, scheduling, or design. Given the issues of shared governance with faculty, LMS standardization is not a sure thing, but it is more likely to happen before course curriculum and content standardization.

Another key consideration is security. While operating in the cloud is cheaper than operating a physical computer facility on or off campus, it does not mitigate the need for information security. Colleges and universities have legal obligations to protect student data as well as research results from government contracts. Operating an LMS that is accessible 24 hours a day, 7 days a week from any device with access to the Internet requires a heightened awareness of data security and cybersecurity requirements. An unscreened link posted in an online course could provide criminals with access to the institution's data and systems. Electronic vigilance and training are critical to evading the constant probes from cybercriminals. As the online course and program offerings of their member institutions increase, systems should take the lead in investigating the security readiness of their institutions in order to reduce their exposure to hackers and cybercriminals.

Technology in the Online Class: Content Development and Sharing

At the beginning of the COVID-19 pandemic, the two- to three-week conversion of thousands of traditional college courses to online courses accentuated and broadened the awareness that well-designed online courses are different than an online syllabus, online quizzes, email, and videotaped lectures.

Preparing for the chance that courses offered in the fall of 2020 could be online, over the summer of 2020, many institutions hired instructional designers to work with professors to develop and build better online courses. Professors with course lecture notes and PowerPoint slide decks crafted over years were asked to share that content with designers in order to build more effective asynchronous online courses.

Even when an institution previously required all scheduled courses and their related materials to be hosted in an LMS, it is not likely that it mandated the standardization of syllabi across the institution, school, or department. Well-crafted syllabi include institution and department learning objectives, institution and department policies, assignments, and the rubrics used for grading. When standardized, an LMS can become a searchable database for content that needs to be updated or utilized for the development of a similar course.

All major LMS vendors offer access to a learning content management system (LCMS) that is compatible with their software. For example, D2L offers a built-in LCMS as a feature of their LMS. An LCMS is more than a repository for course content. When the classification and categorization for course content are designed effectively, the LCMS becomes a valuable resource for instructional designers and instructors tasked with building new courses or updating current courses.

Whether the digitized course content consists of books, chapters, documents, videos, audio recordings, and the like, an LCMS provides a central repository shared by everyone (with proper permissions) responsible for designing online courses. Courses can be designed to automatically access the most recent version of a specific content item or be locked into an older version until the person responsible for the course content approves the update.

At a large institution or across a university system, a well-developed LCMS is a valuable resource. But it takes time to develop, maintain, and update an LCMS, so many institutions choose not to utilize one. Developing a system-wide LCMS would be difficult without substantial standardization of courses and content across the system's campuses.

Unique to some online courses, generally those in the STEM or math areas, are adaptive learning tools, which are typically licensed by vendors other than the LMS vendor. Some adaptive learning tools operate with algorithms that choose learning pathways based on the answer selected by the student(s). More sophisticated adaptive learning tools may utilize artificial intelligence tools such as neural network analysis. Whenever these tools are utilized, administrators should determine whether additional compliance steps are necessary to conform to applicable artificial intelligence ethics policies.

Building an Online Student Support Infrastructure

Whenever an institution enrolls online students, its student support infrastructure may not be ready for a student who works full-time, accesses the course and course materials asynchronously, and lives quite a distance away from the campus. If the institution has scheduled online courses more frequently than campus-based courses, student advising may need to develop a different pace and mode of interaction with the online student.

When students spend most of their time in the electronic classroom during evenings and weekends, tutoring services, the technology help desk, and library access may need to increase to a 24-hours-a-day, 7-days-a-week schedule in order to meet the needs of these students. The online American Public University System, for example, enrolls more than 50,000 students who are active-duty military servicemembers stationed across the world. Not only do the student support functions need to operate during most hours of the day every day of the year, but the scheduling tool used to arrange an online appointment needs to accommodate time zone differences of more than 12 hours.

If a separate student support department is not going to be established, each manager of the existing student support departments needs to address how their department will meet the needs of students enrolled at a distance. Importantly, many departments should not budget their services based on FTEs. Part-time students are individuals who need student support services regardless of how many courses they enroll in each semester. Providing adequate budgetary support may minimize some of the reluctance of departments to make changes in order to accommodate online students.

Systems can leverage their scale and resources to build centralized student support services operating extended hours to meet the needs of working adult, online students attending member institutions. Centralizing these operations reduces system-wide costs per student and provides more expanded services that can be increased on a marginal cost basis as enrollments increase.

Hybrid Models: A Panacea or Another Operating Problem?

With the multiple waves of the pandemic having different effects on cities, states, and colleges and universities, hybrid learning has become a more prevalent option on many campuses. In some cases where governors have mandated the offering of in-person classes at state institutions, faculty and administrators sidestepped those orders by offering hybrid classes that were more online than they were face-to-face.

Hybrid classes may be the future of higher education. The Lumina Foundation argued in a 2021 editorial that hybrid learning provides a better and more flexible education for students than the traditional in-person experience (Howard, 2021). Today's college students are older, and nearly half of them work full-time. The flexibility of online courses meets their needs better than attending a traditional class on a campus that may be difficult to attend when scheduled. Lumina also argues that a majority of Black and Hispanic families believe that online classes meet their needs better than traditional classes (Howard, 2021).

I am a parent of two college athletes. Many of their classes moved to online or hybrid after the beginning of the pandemic. The hybrid classes have allowed them and their teammates to make up for classes missed because of conflicts with competition and practice schedules as well as to submit assignments and take proctored tests and exams without sitting in a traditional classroom. It's likely that their classmates who have part-time or full-time jobs have benefitted as well.

Who wins? Will there be a few large online course and program providers, or will there be many? Can systems collaborate with their institutions to take advantage of their collective resources and scale to match their online enrollments with their campus-based enrollments?

Lumina and others argue that it's time to revamp the format of college education and make classes accessible to anyone at any time and from any place. We have the technology and the knowledge to accommodate a transformation like this. Systems have the leadership and resources necessary to make these changes permanent, though they often face serious pushback from on-campus stakeholders and even accreditors.

There is a strong argument that public institutions will increase their enrollment of adult students once they offer competitive online courses and programs like the leaders in the online community. With strong partnerships with state workforce development initiatives and private sector employers, systems should be able to leverage their expertise, size, and resources. An added plus is that in-state tuition is a major differential when comparing similar programs and services offered by private nonprofit and for-profit institutions.

But systems cannot naively assume that additional students will enroll in a traditional format that has merely been enhanced with the availability of online classes. Student support services meeting the needs of working adults are arguably as important as lower-cost tuition. Centralized student support services for online students can arguably be offered at a higher level of service and a lower cost per student if the system coordinates their development with its member institutions.

Over time, with support and leadership from their systems, member institutions should collaborate with curriculum and online course design. There is no longer a need to offer duplicative courses when all courses are available online. Tactics for sharing tuition revenues and online expenses need to be developed, but a system enhanced by a substantial breadth of relevant online courses and programs ultimately will benefit students as well as their member institutions and the taxpayers who support them.

Course-sharing platforms are another potential option for systems and their member institutions to leverage existing online courses while expanding member institutions' course catalogs, maximize the frequency of course offerings, improve student retention, increase revenues, and decrease operating and course development expenses.

The largest course-sharing platform in terms of participating institutions is operated by Acadeum (www.acadeum.com), based in Austin, Texas. With more than 450 member institutions, the Acadeum platform allows institutions the opportunity to participate in multiple consortial agreements, enabling them to share their courses with other members as a teaching institution or have their students take courses offered by other members as a home institution.

The consortial agreements are superior to standard transfer credit agreements for students in that they offer financial aid eligibility, transparent payment processes, the ability to transfer grades as well as credits, and assurance that completed courses will be accepted and transcribed. The hassles of transfer course approval and processing transcripts are eliminated. For the institution, course-sharing through consortial agreements assures the course equivalency/transfer eligibility and provides quality control over the courses students can access. The Acadeum platform provides a student portal and an advisor portal for approval of the course(s) selected by the students. The platform also provides electronic billing between institutions. In addition to expanding the number of online courses available to a member institution, the varied start dates for courses provides flexibility for home institution students who have dropped or withdrawn from a course and need to enroll in another course starting during the existing term to maintain academic standing or eligibility for continued financial aid.

The Texas A&M University System (TAMUS) uses Acadeum's course-sharing platform to power their intra-system course-sharing initiative. TAMUS identified that a lack of course availability at students' home institutions in scheduling was a contributing factor to 180,000 stop-out students across 12 campuses over the past decade. TAMUS worked to identify key data points to inform their system-wide course-sharing efforts and found that approximately 103 courses were needed by students, but half were not scheduled at their home institution for the next two terms. The system-based consortial agreement allowed students to seamlessly and timely attend these courses at member institutions (Gibson, 2022).

While a handful of institutions currently enroll more than a fifth of online students, systems have the best chance at catching up. To do this, system leaders need to understand the costs involved as well as the need for collaboration across institutions to share costs and revenues. Developing the infrastructure and support necessary for online students will not be easy. It will, however, be necessary to meet the needs of online students if a system's goal is to be the dominant online provider in their area. Large employers and localized industries prefer to have a single point of contact to help them build partnerships with multiple institutions distributed across a state's geography. Systems have been that point of contact for on-the-ground programs, and they should recognize the advantages that expanded online offerings provide to these partnerships.

References

Critchfield, D. (2020). "Idaho Online Will Improve Distance Learning in Higher Education." *Idaho State Journal*. July 17, 2020, https://www.idahostatejournal.com/opinion/columns/idaho-online-will-improve-distance-learning-in-higher-education/article_555f88f8-b514-5bb2-b828-c84e69bc7540.html.

ECS. Education Commission of the States. (2021). *Education and Workforce Development Connections 2021: Workforce Funding*. 50 *State Comparison*. Denver: ECS. https://reports.ecs.org/comparisons/education-and-workforce-development-connections-2021-03.

Gibson, Shonda. (2022). "The Texas A&M University System: Identifying Opportunities for Impact and Progress." Acadeum. Accessed December 22, 2022, https://academ1.wistia.com/medias/7v3ekof2ll?utm_campaign=Wally%20Boston%20Book&utm_source=Inv&utm_medium=TAMU%20Video.

Grajek, Susan, and Christopher Brooks. (2020). "A Grand Strategy for Grand Challenges." *Educause Review* 3, 10–22.

Howard, Danette. (2021). "Today's Students Need Hybrid Learning Models." Higher Ed Dive. November 1, 2021, https://www.highereddive.com/news/todays-students-need-hybrid-learning-models/609242/.

Lederman, Doug. (2019). "The Biggest Movers Online." *Inside Higher Ed*. December 17, 2019, https://www.insidehighered.com/digital-learning/article/2019/12/17/colleges-and-universities-most-online-students-2018.

McKenzie, Lindsay. (2019). "UMUC 2.0." *Inside Higher Ed*. March 13, 2019, https://www.insidehighered.com/digital-learning/article/2019/03/13/university-maryland-university-college-will-change-name-and.

Online Learning Consortium. "Our History." Accessed January 28, 2022, https://onlinelearningconsortium.org/about/history/.

Smalley, S. (2021). "UNC's $97 Million Plan to Reach Adult Online Learners." *Inside Higher Ed*. December 9, 2021, https://www.insidehighered.com/news/2021/12/09/unc-system-launch-ambitious-97-million-ed-tech-start.

THECB. Texas Higher Education Coordinating Board. (2022). "Texas General Education Core Curriculum WebCenter." Accessed January 22, 2022, http://board.thecb.state.tx.us/apps/TCC/.

9 | Partnering with Purpose

Collaborations for the Future

DEMARÉE K. MICHELAU

Introduction

THE YEARS SPENT NAVIGATING the COVID-19 pandemic were challenging, stressful, and taxing. In the early days, it was apparent that the risks and impacts were serious, but how the virus was transmitted, how long it would last, who was most vulnerable, and whether we would find a way to prevent or treat it were unclear. As we look back, it is difficult to imagine that we believed it was possible in just a couple of weeks to "flatten the curve" or reduce the number of people sick with COVID-19 so it did not overwhelm our health care system. Our nation's postsecondary leaders were soon disabused of that idea because many quickly realized that they needed to change what they were doing and how they were doing it if they were to continue serving students, conducting research, and providing public services. They transitioned to remote instruction within just a couple of weeks, and many campuses effectively stayed closed for face-to-face instruction for the next year. And while states had different approaches to the pandemic—some implementing strict lockdown measures and others allowing individual choice with respect to preventative measures—it was apparent that the world was facing a prolonged period of dislocation and uncertainty.

Nearly three years later, one of the indisputable lessons of the pandemic is its variable impacts on different populations. The pandemic surfaced societal inequities that we knew existed but were magnified and worsened under the sharp spotlight of the COVID-19 crisis (Harper, 2020). The inequities experienced by poverty-affected individuals and those from minoritized populations—in health, housing, employment, and education—were especially distressing. Our nation's students also suffered, especially those from racial and ethnic minority populations and those who were already experiencing housing and food insecurity (Cornett and Fletcher, 2022). It adversely affected their financial situations, mental health, and academic performance (Webster et al., 2021). It was also challenging for our postsecondary systems and institutions, many of which faced declining enrollments and financial uncertainty despite an influx of one-time federal dollars designed to support students and institutions during the crisis. According to the National Student Clearinghouse Research Center, as of spring 2022, there were 1.4 million fewer undergraduate students than before the pandemic, with losses concentrated in the community colleges (National Student Clearinghouse Research Center, 2022). There were more than 827,000 fewer students in community colleges since spring 2020 (National Student Clearinghouse Research Center, 2022). And, in a post-COVID-19 world, the economic recovery has been uncertain and fragile, including higher housing inflation, raising fears of a recession (FRED Blog, 2023).

But challenging times present opportunities. This is a unique moment in history for higher education, especially for postsecondary education systems that educate approximately 75 percent of the country's public four-year college students. As the country emerges from the COVID-19 pandemic, system leaders, led by the National Association of System Heads (NASH), have been energized in new ways and have coalesced around the "Power of Systems,":, a bold initiative that is intended to "deliver real progress for student success while tackling systemic inequities that too often stand in the way" (NASH, 2023). This vision for tomorrow cannot be realized with scattershot solutions and one-off fixes. Postsecondary education systems, and specifically public postsecondary education systems, are in a position to lead—and part of that leadership will center on meaningful, deliberate collaboration. As leaders committed to this initiative reimagine how they do business and serve the students of tomorrow, a key factor of their success will center on meaningful collaboration. This chapter focuses on the pressures on higher education that will drive postsecondary system leaders toward collaboration and how leaders can maximize their system's full potential by rethinking how and with whom they collaborate—how they partner with purpose.

What Is Collaboration?

Merriam-Webster (2023) provides two definitions of collaboration. The first is "the action of working with someone to produce or create something," and the second is to "to cooperate with or willingly assist an enemy of one's country and especially an occupying force." That sums up the two different ways that collaboration is often viewed in postsecondary education—working with someone with a mutual goal in mind or cooperating with an enemy. Higher education in the United States is inherently competitive along multiple dimensions. Institutions compete for students, funding, leaders, faculty, bragging rights, and in any arena where money or prestige can be found. Dennis Jones, president emeritus of the National Center for Higher Education Management Systems (NCHEMS)—a private nonprofit 501(c)(3) organization whose mission is to improve strategic decision-making in higher education for states and institutions in the United States and abroad—is quoted as saying that "institutional collaboration is an unnatural act." It is unnatural because of the inherent competition that exists among and even within institutions, whether they are in a system or in different systems; collaboration is not intuitive, nor is it frequently seen as an obvious solution to pressing problems. Yet collaboration does exist and thrive in postsecondary education, and many of the most prominent examples are found in public higher education systems. The challenge is to make collaboration natural, worthwhile, and effective at scale. Postsecondary education systems are in the ideal position to lead this change in institutional cultures. Nancy Zimpher (2013), chancellor emeritus of the State University of New York (SUNY), notes that "higher education systems have an advantage over individual institutions in that they can harness the collective efforts of multiple institutions and channel those efforts to specific communities through a broad array of institutions and other outlets."

Pressures on Higher Education

If the forces of nature are generally working against collaboration in higher education, then what makes us think that effective and meaningful collaboration is desirable, let alone possible? In short, other, stronger forces will make collaboration a necessary tool, rather than an option, for system leaders to keep in their toolbox. Three pressures on US postsecondary education will drive leaders toward effective collaboration—demographic change, constrained and uncertain resources for postsecondary education funding, and an urgency to convey the value of postsecondary education.

Demographic Change

For the past 40 years, the Western Interstate Commission for Higher Education (WICHE) has produced Knocking at the College Door: Projections of High School Graduates, which provides data and projections on high school graduate populations for all 50 states, the District of Columbia, and selected US territories and outlying areas, including information about the race/ethnicity of public school graduates and the number of private school graduates. The latest data, which project the number of high school graduates out to 2037, show a clear shift in the demographic makeup of our student populations. This shift is marked by fewer high school graduates overall and a diversification of the student pipeline along racial and socioeconomic dimensions (Bransberger et al., 2020). Specifically, US high school graduates are projected to peak in number at about 3.9 million with the class of 2025, after having steadily increased since the mid-1990s (Bransberger et al., 2020). Further, the US population is growing older, and by 2035, older adults defined as age 65 and up are projected to outnumber children under the age of 18 for the first time in the nation's history (US Census Bureau, 2019).

The implications of these demographic changes are multifaceted and uncertain. But one thing is clear: fewer students in the pipeline and a changing racial and ethnic composition of the student population will challenge postsecondary systems and assumptions about how they serve adult learners, as well as those students who have not historically been served well by the higher education enterprise. Successfully reaching these new populations of students will require innovative partnerships that may have been previously overlooked.

Postsecondary Education Funding

In March 2020, many state legislators, governors, and postsecondary education leaders were predicting dire outlooks for their state, system, and institutional budgets. That same month, Moody's Investors Service, a global risk assessment firm, issued a report shifting its outlook for the higher education sector from stable to negative. Citing "the potential for disruption in enrollment patterns, state support, endowment income and philanthropy, and research grants and contracts," the report noted reduced revenue, higher expenses, and continued unknown risks (Moody's Investor Service, 2020).

Fortunately, help was on the way, at least for some of higher education. As a result of three stimulus bills passed by Congress in 2020 and 2021, states and institutions received an unprecedented amount of federal relief funding. In March 2020, Congress passed the Coronavirus Aid, Relief, and Economic Security (CARES) Act, which allotted approximately $14 billion to the Office of Postsecondary Education as the Higher Education Emergency Relief Fund (HEERF) (US Department of Education, 2021). Of those funds, more than $6 billion were required to go directly to students in the form of emergency financial aid grants for expenses related to the disruption of campus operations due to COVID-19. Institutions received the balance. In addition, through the CARES Act legislation, Congress set aside approximately $3 billion for the Governor's Emergency Education Relief (GEER) Fund. The US Department of Education awarded these grants to state governor's offices based on a formula stipulated in the legislation that considered the state's relative population of individuals age 5 through 24 and the state's relative number of children counted under section 1124(c) of the Elementary and Secondary Education Act of 1965 (ESEA) (Office of Elementary and Secondary Education, 2023). The Coronavirus Response and Relief Supplemental Appropriations (CRRSA) Act of 2021 was then signed into law on December 27, 2020, and provided an additional $1.3 billion as a supplement to the GEER II Fund (Office of Elementary and Secondary Education, 2023). In addition, in March 2021, Congress passed the American Rescue Plan, which established the HEERF III Fund and provided $39.6 billion to support higher education institutions serving students and ensure continued learning during the COVID-19 pandemic (US Department of Education, 2023). There are a variety of stipulations attached to the use of these funds along with a deadline to spend all COVID-19 relief dollars by September 2024. While enrollments and tuition revenue declined since the pandemic began, and declined significantly in the two-year sector, states increased funding to postsecondary education by 4.5 percent in fiscal year 2021. Notably, postsecondary systems, despite their important role, were not eligible for these funds, which certainly constrained the ability of systems to fulfill their governing and coordinating role.

While this influx of dollars was critical to prevent fiscal disaster and essential for COVID response, this support was a one-time, nonrecurring event. These funds cannot address the recurring structural challenges facing our universities. So, states, systems, and institutions, ideally working together, must begin planning for what will happen when the federal dollars are no longer available. Higher education systems could lead the way in making lasting strategic investments that support the students of tomorrow and institutional viability. The restrictions placed on the federal dollars requiring one-time investments are a powerful incentive for systems to identify viable partners so they can sustain the critical investments begun during the pandemic.

The financial future for postsecondary education is uncertain, and declining enrollments in large portions of the country, especially within the two-year sector, are likely to continue. Expanding and scaling collaborations with proven success records in mitigating these negative impacts are worth considering as systems look to lead into the future.

The Perceived Value of Postsecondary Education

Postsecondary education is vital for economic mobility and for supporting an engaged citizenry. Importantly, data show that education and training beyond high school pay off for the individual and society (Carnevale et al., 2011). Increasingly, however, postsecondary education is fighting narratives that there is little to no value in obtaining a postsecondary degree because of cost or that the higher education enterprise is inappropriately bringing politics and ideology (generally viewed by critics as "liberal") into a student's pursuit of credential. In 2019, the Pew Research Center released research showing that while most people in the United States see value in higher education, an undercurrent of dissatisfaction is growing, often linked to partisanship (Pew Research Center, 2019). Recent research from Public Agenda shows that only 49 percent of Americans think the economic benefits of a college education outweigh the costs, and young people without degrees are the most skeptical. But Public Agenda's research also suggests strong cross-partisan support for the idea that a college education has positive impacts on "people's ability to earn a good living and on their state's capacity to attract employers." They also found that most Republicans (about 71 percent) think liberal, politically correct institutions in which conservatives cannot speak freely are at least somewhat of a problem, with about 44 percent of Democrats and 51 percent of Independents believing that as well (Schleifer et al., 2022).

Citing issues such as limits on free speech on campus and suspicion about admissions decisions, the vocal dissatisfaction of some (particularly of conservatives) is that campus faculty are overwhelmingly liberal and their political views affect students' educational experience.

As is typically the case, the reality is more nuanced than the narrative, with differences among sectors, career stages, and geographical regions (Jaschik, 2017). And research from the Higher Education Research Institute shows that while for decades there had been an increasing proportion of faculty who leaned toward the left end of the political continuum, it leveled out around 2010–11 and has held steady at roughly 50 percent since then (Stolzenberg et al., 2019).

Since 2020, while the political divide in American society continues to deepen, there does seem to be increasing optimism for postsecondary education (Lederman, 2022). But while polls suggest that higher education is faring better in the public eye than before, it is difficult and likely unwise to be content with the current state of affairs. Looking ahead to the next 5, 10, 20 years, for students and society as whole to reap the benefits of higher education, it is imperative to reclaim the narrative around the value of postsecondary education by continuing to demonstrate both private and public benefits. Postsecondary education systems must be viewed as trustworthy, valuable partners of government, employers, and families. The most effective way to do this is through collectively serving students, families, and communities so that they experience the benefits of the value provided.

Potential Collaborative Solutions

The world has changed since COVID-19 began its rapid and deadly spread across the globe. Business as usual will not be effective nor sustainable given the pressures facing higher education today, but collaborative solutions, led by postsecondary education systems at scale, can be an effective strategy for better serving students and sustaining the enterprise in the future. A wide array of potential collaborative solutions achieves different goals and methods. For instance, some collaborations save money, some provide better service, and some do both; but being strategic and disciplined about partnership will lay the groundwork for success. Below are three examples of potential collaborations for consideration.

Scaling Partnerships with Employers

Most geographic areas of the country and many career fields, including higher education, are feeling intense workforce pressures. Part of this dynamic is due to a shifting work context. More people prefer to work remotely, help wanted signs are ubiquitous, teachers and health care workers are warning of the long-term effects of COVID-19 on recruitment and retention in their professions, and it seems that every employer is short-staffed. It is likely that more retirees leaving the workforce, significant demographic shifts in the emerging workforce, and the impact of declining birth rates on the future workforce will put further stress on a fragile employment market. Given these realities, higher education is in position to lead in the recovery, but not in the same ways as before the pandemic, when we could expect a constantly increasing supply of high school graduates entering postsecondary education.

Higher education will need to reach out to untapped populations such as adult learners (e.g., those with some college and no degree) and other potential students much more effectively, but where can we find them? And how can we serve them? Many are already in the workforce, so we must rethink how higher education, business, and industry collaborate for the benefit of all students, employers, and society. But this begs the question: Why is successful collaboration with business and industry at significant scale not already happening?

First, collaborations are time and staff intensive. Especially during and after the pandemic, higher education leaders, faculty, and staff are feeling intense demands on their time, making any additional claims on that time an unattractive option. Considering this, if there are not clear benefits to all sides of the partnership, then collaboration often does not happen. Second, competition is inherent in higher education, and in that context, working together is not part of the culture and is often viewed with suspicion. Third, partnerships often depend on champions, those who lead or work hard toward a particular goal and secure the support of others in achieving that goal. Those collaborations tend to be impactful and valued, but not conducted at scale, and they often fade when the champions move on. Finally, higher education is predominantly internally focused, with rewards and incentives that do not support partnerships with entities outside the higher education ecosystem. For example, faculty promotion and the awarding of tenure is seldom dependent on involvement in collaborative activities, especially outside the academy. Clearly these are generalizations, and there are examples of partnerships worthy of emulation, but those done at scale tend to be the exception and not the rule, and in a changing landscape, we must rethink how we partner with purpose and with whom. This is where postsecondary education systems are poised to lead.

One possibility is for systems to partner with state and local government and/or school districts. In all states, state and local governments are major employers, and in many communities, the local school district is the largest employer. Many people employed in these sectors have not obtained a postsecondary credential or are interested in pursuing additional education, but these are employers who likely value and support postsecondary education. Systems could intentionally partner with these entities at scale to bring back adults who have some college but no credential to complete and support any desired additional education. By offering tuition discounts, targeted programs, convenient scheduling, online courses and programs, competency-based credit, or streamlined educational opportunities such as high-value certificates, they would reach adult students where they are in their trajectory, and support their success while promoting retention and advancement in key positions in the community.

Establishing the partnership is only the first step in a longer process, however. The institutions within the systems need to be prepared to serve the students they are attracting. Many colleges and universities across the country already serve diverse student populations, including adults, and some do it very well. They have designed their instructional modalities and schedules, student services, campus facilities, and supports to promote academic success. But many more have not yet figured out the magic formula or even recognized that making changes to business-as-usual is necessary for their future sustainability and success as an institution. They are successful at supporting a traditional college student who is 18 to 24 years old and lives in the residence halls, but that supply of high school students is dwindling. This will drive institutions to reconsider how they serve students who come to their institutions with new and different needs because the students they have historically relied on will no longer sustain them. Postsecondary systems can and should support their campuses in serving the changing needs of diverse student populations.

WICHE has conducted higher education needs assessments and strategic planning efforts in partnership with compact members. This work typically includes focus groups, key informant interviews, and surveys with various constituent groups, including employers. Regardless of how the data are collected, when employers are asked about what they need for their workforce, they inevitably cite "people skills." Employers need people who know how to answer a phone, show up to work on time, collaborate with others, and act appropriately in a professional setting. One of the most effective ways to acquire such skills is through work-based learning, or programs that combine an educational pathway toward a credential with meaningful work experience. These programs require strong partnership between the institution and the employer, and they benefit both. There are countless work-based learning programs embedded in our institutions, and a few institutions in which work-based learning is the foundation of their model. But to meet future workforce demands, respond to the needs of employers, and demonstrate the value of postsecondary education, students will be served best if these work-based learning initiatives are conducted at scale. Postsecondary education systems are in a unique position to engage in such large-scale collaborations with employers that implement work-based learning opportunities. And for those systems that serve rural areas where there may be fewer employers with whom to connect, online work-based learning opportunities are also worth exploring.

Scaling partnerships with business and industry that result in meaningful work-based learning opportunities and clear pathways to employment with living wages will demonstrate value to students, families, and policymakers. Especially during times of economic uncertainty and concerns about a looming recession, system leaders have an opportunity to lead in the recovery, but they will be more effective if they strategically partner with others who can support the recovery. If higher education can be seen as the pathway toward a more stable economic recovery, everyone benefits.

Another area of partnership with industry that is especially promising and equally challenging is cross-sector research collaboration. A recent report from the Association of Public and Land-Grant Universities (APLU) notes that while collaborative university-industry research and development has benefits for universities, industry, and the US economy, it is costly and other barriers—such as differing goals and incentives and lack of capacity for pursuing these relationships—get in the way (APLU, 2022). Their research shows, however, that there are institutional strategies that can bridge the chasm. These include but are not limited to goal alignment, developing mutual trust, leadership that clearly articulates support for industry partnerships, and effective structures for relationship management. Taking these lessons a step further, depending on their structure, postsecondary education systems may be even better positioned than individual institutions to lead in this area if they can implement strategies consistent with these important lessons.

Leveraging and Redesigning System Resources

Demographic pressures, particularly in the Northeast and Midwest, where populations are declining, are driving new ways of leveraging partnerships for systems to survive and thrive despite a tendency for collaborations to disintegrate when resources are scarce. For instance, the Pennsylvania State System of Higher Education (2023) is implementing a system redesign that involves university integrations with the goals of increasing student opportunities and ensuring institutional viability. Connecticut, Maine, and Vermont are also going through major structural transformations. Enrollment declines and mounting financial pressures have driven these major changes, and they will have impacts for years to come.

In the West, where the demographic projections are not as dire, pressure is still mounting, particularly on rural institutions. Like other regions, some postsecondary education systems in the West are organized so that they centralize key functions, such as budget and finance, legal affairs, government relations, advancement, information security, payroll, and so on. Other systems are less centralized with considerable institutional autonomy. Recently, some less centralized systems have engaged in efforts to identify ways to leverage economies of scale, sometimes spurred by their state legislatures or governors. Whatever the impetus, context must be considered in devising a response if initiatives are to be successful. Systems that are composed of similar institutions in terms of mission and status, as opposed to a mix of institutions with differing missions and different sectors, may find achieving these efficiencies easier, but that is not always the case. Demographic shifts and enrollment pressures are likely to drive systems into partnerships that consolidate these types of services, which perhaps were not on the horizon just a few years ago. For instance, in 2020, the South Dakota State Legislature passed Senate Bill 55, which required the South Dakota Board of Regents to "assemble a task force to study the operations and functions of the institutions of higher education under the board's authority" (SD SB55 (2020)). The task force was composed of 20 individuals who represented various geographic areas of the state, included four representatives from the Joint Committee on Appropriations, and was chaired by Brian Maher, the now former executive director and chief executive officer of the South Dakota Board of Regents (2021). Over six months, the task force worked collaboratively to develop 35 recommendations designed to improve the quality and effectiveness of the regental operations (South Dakota Board of Regents, 2021).

Mergers and acquisitions are not yet a key feature of the public higher education landscape in the West, but some institutions are exploring unique partnerships in which they can rely on back-office operations, such as procurement and information technology, at other more resourced institutions that are either nearby, part of a different system within the same state, or within their own system. It is reasonable to expect that these types of collaborations will expand and should be explored strategically and deliberately over time. For those systems in which collaboration in these areas are foreign or uncomfortable, this requires a complete rethinking of business operations and takes time to be done well. It needs to be done deliberately, carefully, and with patience or it is doomed to fail.

Course-Sharing Partnerships between Postsecondary Institutions

Another collaborative solution that has promise at scale is course-sharing. Two higher education systems in the West—Montana and Idaho—have recently launched statewide course-sharing initiatives. In 2021, the Montana University System created the Montana Virtual Campus, which provides access to courses and programs across the university system. By leveraging what each institution offers, the course-sharing initiative collectively expands access to academic programs for Montana students wherever they are in the state (Montana University System, 2023). Similarly, with support from the Office of the Idaho State Board of Education, through Online Idaho, the state's public colleges and universities offer an array of online courses and programs supported by experienced faculty. Initially spurred by the COVID-19 pandemic, the board launched this course-sharing initiative aimed at consolidating online courses, streamlining pathways to degrees and certificates, and improving digital learning infrastructure for all of Idaho's public eight higher education institutions (University of Idaho, 2023).

Other course-sharing initiatives are program or field specific and can be a model for system leaders. For instance, NEXus—the Nursing Education Xchange—is a consortium of institutions that offer online doctoral programs in nursing through course-sharing (https://winnexus.org). This initiative expands capacity in a desperately needed profession. Strategically implementing course-sharing initiatives in high-needs fields and in a way that supports adult students who may be place committed is one way that system leaders can expand access for students in times of fiscal volatility while being more responsive to evolving labor needs.

Any collaborative partnership should be closely examined to ensure compliance with state laws and regulations as well as accreditation requirements. A mechanism for evaluating effectiveness and program fidelity should be established in the early stages so that prudent decisions can be made along the way.

Regional Compacts as Devices for Next-Level Collaboration

Almost all US postsecondary systems are in states that are members of one of the four regional higher education compacts: Midwestern Higher Education Compact (MHEC), New England Board of Higher Education (NEBHE), Southern Regional Education Board (SREB), and WICHE. Working together with the compacts to leverage opportunities for next-level collaboration is an area ripe for further exploration.

WICHE—an interstate compact of western states, territories, and freely associated states committed to increasing access to high-quality higher education for all residents of the West—was founded almost 70 years ago based on the idea that collaboration and resource-sharing in higher education would strengthen western states both individually and collectively as a region (Abbot, 2004). Today, in an increasingly divided political and socioeconomic environment, collaboration in postsecondary education is even more important.

Since 1988, WICHE has coordinated the Western Undergraduate Exchange (WUE), an agreement among WICHE's 16 member states that provides nonresident tuition savings for western students at more than 160 participating public colleges and universities. WICHE also coordinates a similar program at the graduate level, the Western Regional Graduate Program (WRGP). Both programs allow institutions to charge up to 150 percent of resident tuition, and institutions are afforded a great deal of flexibility in which programs they offer. Most WUE institutions make all or most majors available at the WUE rate, and while institutions may set more stringent admissions standards for WUE students, many do not. In academic year 2022–23, 46,1110 WUE students and their families saved more than $520 million in tuition, and 3,269 students saved nearly $58 million in tuition through WRGP.

Demographics and changing patterns in nonresident tuition rates are having an effect on these types of programs and partnerships in some regions and states. Competition for enrollment has become fierce, with some systems and institutions eliminating nonresident tuition altogether. Those who choose this path may experience considerable financial impact, but the rationale is that the fallout would be worse had they not.

Is it possible that regions could leverage these long-standing partnerships that have been built through their exchanges to take course-sharing to the next level with a focus on sharing programs? Course-sharing is already gaining steam as a viable strategy for supporting student success and institutional sustainability, and in areas that are especially hard hit by demographic change and face a dismal financial future, a new way of collaboration could be a path forward.

For many years, WICHE and SREB have supported course-sharing partnerships that benefit students and institutions. Recently, SREB announced a course-sharing consortium among historically Black colleges and universities (HBCUs) and minority-serving institutions (MSIs) aimed at helping students stay on the path to on-time graduation by expanding access to courses (SREB, 2022). This initiative crosses state lines and supports institutions with similar missions.

While higher educational systems are an obvious locus for creating opportunities for shared services, the regional compacts can take the scale of collaboration to the next level. MHEC has long been a leader in providing joint purchasing opportunities for their compact states, covering areas like property insurance, student health insurance, academic-related areas of interest, and technology (MHEC, 2023). The compact also collaborates with the other regional higher education compacts, including WICHE, SREB, and NEBHE, to provide these savings opportunities to states, institutions, and other entities to extend that reach and benefit across the country. As enrollment challenges and financial uncertainties loom, system leaders could consider working with their regional compacts to explore current and new areas in which to leverage their purchasing power. By working with compact partners that have experience in implementing joint purchasing agreements, systems can operate more efficiently, and system leaders, especially those from smaller systems that do not have the same purchasing power as the larger ones, can help identify new areas of beneficial cost-savings programs.

System leaders must also demonstrate how the value of postsecondary education extends beyond the financial benefit to an individual and positively impacts society. WICHE works collaboratively with its compact members to strengthen higher education, workforce development, and behavioral health throughout the region and works to address some of society's most pressing needs. With a similar sentiment, Zimpher (2013, 33) asks, "How can US higher education put its imprint on the most challenging problems of our day?" One could argue that one of the most pressing problems facing the United States today is misinformation and the eroding confidence in our democracy. Imagine for a moment if every credential—whether two- or four-year degrees or even certificates—required some service learning or civic engagement component. Systems could drive such a change that would not only support students becoming more informed and participatory citizens, but also would provide them with useful skills akin to work-based learning. System leaders would do well to work with NASH and other partners to identify tangible ways to shift the narrative and be perceived as valuable partners in supporting the health of the nation's democracy.

Tips for Partnering with Purpose

Like interstate compacts, which are the hubs of collaboration for and among states, postsecondary education systems are the hubs of collaboration for institutions, and successful leaders will strategically develop and maintain effective collaborations at all levels. Whether as a way to lead during significant demographic shifts, to manage systems and institutions during volatile financial times, or to thrive in an increasingly politically charged environment, leaders who forge and maintain meaningful partnerships will stand apart from the rest. With common goals, coordination on key strategies, and centralized governance and authority, postsecondary systems already have a head start, but it takes continuous effort to reap the benefits of the system over time.

Have you ever been on a team that worked in perfect harmony? Each member of the team likely understood their role, even if they came to the project with a different perspective. Team members trusted each other, and even when there were bumps in the road, the group achieved the intended goal. Now think for a moment of a time when you were on a team full of acrimony. The project or task probably lacked direction, or worse, people could not work together because they lacked trust. We have all been in these situations at one time or another, and they are not pleasant; worse yet, they are doomed to fail. Reaching the finish line takes a long time, and often the finished product is not what you hoped it would be.

What sets these two scenarios apart? Many factors support successful collaboration, and a strong body of literature from other fields can teach us important lessons. In sum, successful collaborations are:

1. *Strategic and purposeful*. Zimpher (2013, 31) asserts that for any system or institution to be competitive in the twenty-first century, it must be mission driven; it should also have a "well-articulated identity, a vision for the future, and a plan for moving forward." The identity, vision, and plan will be best served with disciplined collaboration as a key component. The most successful collaborations are well thought out, planned, and directed to a larger goal. Working with leadership to identify areas that are ripe for collaboration, and that benefit the system as a whole as well as the individual institutions within it, can surface opportunities and solve problems that previously seemed unsolvable. Clear direction that collaboration in key areas is expected and valued is an important signal to the institutions and their leaders that partnering with purpose will be rewarded.

2. *Mutually beneficial*. Successful collaborations involve partners who see the collaboration as beneficial to them, their organization, or their interest. The foundation of any successful collaboration is mutual agreement and an investment in the goal, and the value-add of the partnership must be evident. Often, partners in a collaboration have different agendas, perspectives, and styles, which can make

a partnership stronger if managed appropriately. Ensuring that the work is mutually beneficial in some way will foster a successful collaboration.

3. *Clear expectations*. People have different understandings of what collaboration means and how it happens. For some, collaboration comes naturally, and it is in their DNA. For others, it is difficult. Setting clear expectations at the outset may lead to a greater likelihood of success. This might involve setting regular check-in meetings, relying on a mutually agreed-upon project management software, or differentiating roles and responsibilities, but most important is being clear with expectations.

4. *Owned and not bought-in*. Higher education leaders working toward some sort of change often refer to the act of securing "buy-in." Buy-in is when people agree with something that you have presented or suggested. Buy-in is a shaky proposition because it relies on convincing people of the value of an idea. It is also hard when tough decisions, such as the loss of programs or faculty and staff, are required. Instead, successful collaborations rely on ownership of an idea, or a vested interest. People who own a proposition will work hard to ensure its success and sustainability.

5. *Able to leverage partner strengths*. Collaboration is second nature and intuitive to some people, and it requires more effort from others. Whether accepting of or resistant to collaboration, successful leaders recognize their own strengths as they relate to collaboration. Likewise, partners need to assess the skills, attributes, and abilities they bring to the partnership. Ensuring everyone's strengths are maximized and that everyone fulfills the expectations supports effective collaboration.

6. *Sustainable*. Often a successful collaboration is dependent on personalities. Good things happened because two (or maybe more) individuals came together around a common interest, worked well together, and were eager to succeed. But if one of the partners retires, moves on from their position, or focuses on different priorities, the

partnership can fall apart. Partnering for long-term success involves developing structures that support sustained partnership. This might include developing multiple points of contact between the partnering organizations, writing clear statements of work or expectations, formally adding the responsibility to a person's position description, or incentivizing the partnership through financial or other rewards. In other words, bake collaboration into the system and make an unnatural act, natural. When the goal is something that others depend on, it is prudent to prepare for the possibility that one of the partners fails to live up to their end of the bargain.

Conclusion

As the world emerged from the pandemic, and postsecondary education system leaders contemplate how they will lead into the future, effective collaboration will be an important consideration. Demographic pressures, constrained and uncertain resources (or lack thereof), and how the public perceives the value of postsecondary education will push us toward scalable collaborations that better serve diverse student populations and keep our institutions viable. The Power of Systems initiative is strategic collaboration at its best, and postsecondary systems can engage with this example for success. In the context of this bold initiative, postsecondary education system leaders have an opportunity to be disciplined and strategic about the types of partnerships that will be beneficial for their students, institutions, and their communities. And while higher education cannot alone solve the problems facing society today, we can meaningfully contribute and earn the public trust that will sustain us for years to come.

References

Abbot, Frank C. *A History of the Western Interstate Commission for Higher Education: The First 40 Years*. Boulder, CO: Western Interstate Commission for Higher Education, 2004. https://www.wiche.edu/wp-content/uploads/2018/resources/First40Years.pdf.

APLU. American Association of Public and Land-Grant Universities. *Driving U.S.*

Competitiveness through Improved University-Industry Partnerships. Washington, DC: APLU, January 2022. https://www.aplu.org/library/driving-us-competitiveness-through-improved-university-industry-partnerships/file.

Bransberger, Peace, Colleen Falkenstern, and Patrick Lane. *Knocking at the College Door: Projections of High School Graduates*. Boulder, CO: Western Interstate Commission for Higher Education, 2020. https://knocking.wiche.edu/.

Carnevale, Anthony P., Stephen J. Rose, and Ban Cheah. *The College Pay Off: Education, Occupations, Lifetime Earnings*." Washington, DC: Georgetown University Center on Education and the Workforce, 2011. https://cew.georgetown.edu/cew-reports/the-college-payoff/.

Cornett, Allyson, and Carla Fletcher. "The Impacts of COVID-19 on the Experiences of Students with Basic Needs Insecurity: Evidence from a National Survey." *Journal of Student Financial Aid* 51, no. 1 (2022): Article 1, https://ir.library.louisville.edu/jsfa/vol51/iss1/1/.

Harper, Shaun R. "COVID-19 and the Racial Equity Implications of Reopening College and University Campuses." *American Journal of Education* 127 (November 2020): https://www.journals.uchicago.edu/doi/epdf/10.1086/711095.

FRED Blog. "Complementing Public Data with Private Data." November 6, 2023, https://fredblog.stlouisfed.org/2023/11/complementing-public-data-with-orivate-data/.

Jaschik, Scott. "Professors and Politics: What the Research Says." *Inside Higher Ed*. February 27, 2017, https://www.insidehighered.com/news/2017/02/27/research-confirms-professors-lean-left-questions-assumptions-about-what-means.

Lederman, Doug. "Public's Impression of Higher Education Improves (Somewhat)." *Inside Higher Ed*. March 14, 2022, https://www.insidehighered.com/news/2022/03/14/public-opinion-higher-education-takes-turn-better.

Merriam-Webster. S.v. "collaborate." Accessed November 7, 2023, https://www.merriam-webster.com/dictionary/collaborate.

MHEC. Midwestern Higher Education Compact. "Contracts." Accessed November 8, 2023, https://www.mhec.org/contracts.

Montana University System. "Montana Virtual Campus." Accessed November 7, 2023, https://courseshare.mus.edu/.

Moody's Investors Service. "Outlook Shifts to Negative as coronavirus Outbreak Increases Downside Risks." March 18, 2020, https://seic.com/sites/default/files/Moodys%20Research%20HigherEd%20Outlook.pdf.

NASH. National Association of System Heads. "About the Power of Systems." Accessed December 28, 2023, https://nash.edu/about-power-of-systems/#:~:text=The%20Power%20of%20Systems%20takes,often%20stand%20in%20the%20way.

National Student Clearinghouse Research Center. "Overview: Spring 2022 Enrollment Estimates." May 26, 2022, https://nscresearchcenter.org/wp-content/uploads/CTEE_Report_Spring_2022.pdf.

Office of Elementary and Secondary Education. "Governor's Emergency Education Relief Fund." Last modified October 19, 2023, https://oese.ed.gov/offices/education-stabilization-fund/governors-emergency-education-relief-fund/.

Pennsylvania State System of Higher Education. "System Redesign: The Road

Forward." Accessed December 28, 2023, https://www.passhe.edu/system-redesign/index.html.
Pew Research Center. "The Growing Partisan Divide in Views of Higher Education." August 19, 2019, https://www.pewresearch.org/social-trends/2019/08/19/the-growing-partisan-divide-in-views-of-higher-education-2/.
Schleifer, David, Will Friedman, and Erin McNally. *America's Hidden Common Ground on Public Higher Education: What's Wrong and How to Fix It*. Brooklyn, NY: Public Agenda, July 2022. https://www.publicagenda.org/wp-content/uploads/2022/07/Public-Agenda-HCG-Higher-Ed-Report-FINAL.pdf.
South Dakota Board of Regents. *Report of the Senate Bill 55 Task Force*. Pierre: South Dakota Board of Regents, October 2021. https://www.sdbor.edu/administrative-offices/infogovtrelations/Documents/SB%2055%20Full%20Report.October%202021.pdf.
SREB. Southern Regional Education Board. May 2022. "SREB HBCU-MSI Course-Sharing Consortium to Expand Range of Options for Students." https://www.sreb.org/news/sreb-hbcu-msi-course-sharing-consortium-expand-range-options-students.
State Higher Education Executive Officers. *SHEF State Higher Education Finance: FY 2021*. Boulder, CO: State Higher Education Executive Officers, 2022. https://shef.sheeo.org/.
Stolzenberg, E. B., M. K. Eagan, H. B. Zimmerman, J. Berdan Lozano, N. M. Cesar-Davis, M. C. Aragon, and C. Rios-Aguilar. *Undergraduate Teaching Faculty: The HERI Faculty Survey 2016–2017*. Los Angeles: Cooperative Institutional Research Program, 2019.
University of Idaho. "Online Idaho." Accessed November 7, 2023, https://online.idaho.edu/.
US Census Bureau. *The Graying of America: More Older Adults Than Kids by 2035*. Washington, DC: US Census Bureau, 2019. https://www.census.gov/library/stories/2018/03/graying-america.html.
US Department of Education. "CARES Act: Higher Education Emergency Relief Fund." Last updated January 29, 2021, https://www2.ed.gov/about/offices/list/ope/caresact.html.
US Department of Education. "ARP: American Rescue Plan (HEERF III)." Last updated August 30, 2023, https://www2.ed.gov/about/offices/list/ope/arp.html.
Webster, J., C. Fletcher, A. Cornett, and C. Knaff. *Student Financial Wellness Survey Report: Fall 2020*. San Antonio, TX: Trellis, 2021. https://www.trelliscompany.org/student-financial-wellness-survey-2021/.
Zimpher, Nancy. "Systemness: Unpacking the Value of Higher Education Systems." In *Higher Education Systems 3.0: Harnessing Systemness, Delivering Performance*, edited by Jason E. Lane and D. Bruce Johnstone. Albany: State University of New York Press, 2013.

10 | Lessons from Multi-Stakeholder Consortia for Public Higher Education Systems

STAKEHOLDER ALIGNMENT COLLABORATIVE

Joel Cutcher-Gershenfeld, Karen S. Baker, Nicholas Berente, Helen M. Berman, Alan Blatecky, Anita Say Chan, Alysia Garmulewicz, Ron Hutchins, Alyssa Mikytuck, Barbara B. Mittleman, Alyson Gounden Rock, Rajesh Sampath, Namchul Shin, Pips Veazey, Susan Winter, Kimberly E. Zarecor

OVER THE CENTURIES, higher education has evolved in ways that closely track the dominant technologies and the associated social systems in society. This pattern can be seen in higher education overall and, more specifically, with public higher education systems in the United States. As technical and social systems evolved, so did the structure of higher education. With each successive era, new combinations of social and technical systems defined the era, but prior sets of social and technical systems did not disappear. Prior sets of technical and social systems were still present in important ways but no longer played a dominant role for the era (Piore and Sable, 1984).

We are now in a postindustrial, digital era. The challenge for public higher education systems is to lead, adapt, or fall behind as new institutional arrangements move to the foreground. Will public higher education systems help to define the current era, or will other organizational forms become definitional for education and research? In other words, how will US public higher education systems evolve in this digital age?

Many argue that a key institutional feature of the digital age involves different forms of multi-stakeholder collaboration, alliances, and consortia (Dougherty and Dunne, 2011; Heidl et al., 2014; Olsen et al., 2016; Giudici et al., 2018; Stakeholder Alignment Collaborative, forthcoming).

These institutional arrangements operate laterally across organizational lines and are enabled by digital infrastructures and platforms. Multi-stakeholder consortia are not new, but they take on a different complexion and greater importance in the current era. Individual universities and public higher education systems are deeply involved in the formation of consortia, which are smaller and more agile and adaptive than the universities and public higher education systems themselves.

Our goal in this chapter is to present lessons from the multi-stakeholder consortia for public higher education systems, with the aim of informing the adaptation needed to re-create these systems of higher education. The Stakeholder Alignment Collaborative has decades of collective experience—through research and practice—with dozens of multi-stakeholder consortia. From our work with these consortia, we identify four critical lessons for higher education systems around: (1) forging a shared vision, (2) fostering internal alignment to enable lateral alignment, (3) staying agile with minimal structures, and (4) establishing rules to change rules. In order to motivate these four lessons, we present first the evolution of higher education in relation to four broad eras in society, ultimately arguing that the current post-industrial digital era requires higher education systems to lead, adapt, or be superseded by innovations that are a better fit with the current and emerging era.

Higher Education Evolving with the Institutions of Society

A brief review of selected highlights from key eras in higher education suggests that the overall social systems have coevolved with the dominant technologies and logics of successive eras. In the first era, described below, US higher education was influenced heavily by the guild structure of work as well as by religious institutions. This evolved during two waves of industrialization. After briefly describing these three eras, we provide a sketch of the challenges associated with the contemporary, postindustrial, digital era, which is in the spirit of many studies that document eras in higher education (McGuinness, 2016).

This view of successive eras builds on the Piore and Sabel (1984) thesis that the social and technical arrangements from prior eras do not disappear but are no longer dominant in the subsequent era. There has been some debate among us, however, over the exact metaphor to use in this context. In some respects, the successive eras can be thought of as layers of sediment in public higher education systems, with the newest layers sitting on top and events occasionally revealing underlying layers. For example, the campuses in the current California State System rest on a layer of having been "normal" schools educating teachers, overlayed with a layer of becoming full liberal arts colleges, and further overlayed with a layer, in several cases, of becoming research universities. Alternatively, the layers can be thought of as a software stack, where higher layers in public higher education systems draw on and depend on lower layers from earlier eras. This metaphor is evident, for example, in how public university systems invest in promising new technologies that have commercial potential and then provide incentives for fields and disciplines to work together in new ways. Some members of our research team even suggested a more playful metaphor, but one that has some validity—that of decorator crabs that gather whatever flora, fauna, and other items that happen to be nearby and take on those additional features as part of their outer shell. In this context, virtually all public higher education systems claim to reflect the unique cultures, histories, geographies, economies of their states. This can be seen in a small way, for example, in the justification sometimes given for Texas having seven separate public higher education systems, which is that "everything is bigger in Texas." In a larger sense, the economic priorities signaled by public higher education systems take on the look and feel of the associated regional economies and societies. As the following brief review suggests, there are elements of all three of these metaphors in play.

Era 1: Guilds and Religious Institutions

Modern Western universities were founded about 1,000 years ago and taught mainly theology, but also secular subjects such as logic and rhetoric. They developed from the Latin Church *studia generalia*, which were spurred by papal bulls, and taught mainly by educated monks and clerks. *Universitas* originally meant the grouping of "a number of persons into one body, a society, company, community, guild, corporation, etc." (Charlton and Short, 1966). These early universities had a guild structure and comprised students and teachers. They were self-regulating and determined the qualifications of their members, building on the concepts of guilds as repositories for craft expertise.

The self-regulation continued into the modern era, with the first universities founded in the United States in the mid to late 1600s, modeled on English and Scottish universities. Although the separation of church and state was an important institutional arrangement in the United States, this was not extended to higher education since these were private organizations, mostly tied to Protestant belief systems and focused entirely on the education of white men (women were not admitted and anti-literacy laws prohibited Blacks from attending until 1833, when Oberlin College was the first coeducational university and the first university to admit Black students).

Era 2: Industrial Revolution

The Morrill Land-Grant Colleges Acts of 1862 and 1890 accelerated the founding of public institutions of higher education with a mission to support the "agricultural and mechanistic arts." As society—farms as well as factories—became mechanized, land-grant universities were intended to prepare citizens to support this industrialized society (Geiger, 2015). The second Morrill Act increased funding for historically Black colleges and universities (HBCUs), further opening higher education up by race. Networks of public "normal" schools were established so that women could be trained to become teachers. The rise of mass production coincided with, and in many ways drove, this growth in public higher education. The universities were asked to feed society's need for research and graduates educated in practical fields such as engineering, agriculture, mining, and education. As this happened, the guild-based model merged with a more factory-like logic for education and research.

In examining the succession of eras in society, Piore and Sabel (1984) document how the rise of mass production did not replace craft production. Craft workers were still needed to make and repair the machines for mass production, but the logic of mass production came to the fore. With the change, some organizations adapted, and some new forms emerged. For example, some craft unions, such as the International Association of Machinists, evolved to become industrial unions. At the same time, a new breed of industrial unions in the auto, steel, and other industries emerged, with their own association (the Congress of Industrial Organizations) that competed with the traditional craft association (the American Federation of Labor). Eventually, of course, the two associations merged, and new generations of service unions emerged. In a similar way, most religious-based private universities evolved to be more secular in approach and more inclusive in admissions, but public and private universities still retained some guild-like features centered on fields and disciplines.

Era 3: Multinational, Multidivisional Corporations

The rise of the multinational corporation, which emphasized the logics of consolidation, efficiency, and multidivisional structures still operated under the broad umbrella of mass production, but with institutional arrangements that could support a vastly larger scale and scope. The same shift can be found in higher education. Many of the state systems were formed just after World War II at a time when the resources provided by the GI Bill resulted in a major expansion in the numbers of people being educated, and the rise of the military-industrial complex required inputs from large-scale research universities. Corporate logic came to higher education in part through state university systems. For example, the State University of New York (SUNY) system was formed in 1948, consolidating 29 institutions at the time (it now spans 64 colleges and universities). This reflected a view that coordination was needed to provide, as the SUNY mission states, "educational services of the highest quality, with the broadest possible access, fully representative of all segments of the population in a complete range of academic, professional and vocational postsecondary programs" (New York State Senate, 2014).

While the logic of consolidation was strong at this historical juncture, it was not absolute. For example, California also has a separate state college system with roots in the 1921 consolidation of "normal" schools that were rebranded as teacher colleges. A 1933 report commissioned by the university system and conducted by the Carnegie Foundation criticized the encroachment by the teacher colleges on the liberal arts missions of the universities. Although the recommendation was for the teacher colleges to pull back from the turf of the universities, the change that took place was just the opposite. The report was galvanizing for teachers' colleges, resulting in an even stronger assertion of their independent ability to operate as more than just trade schools (Gerth, 2010). So, the case still involves movement away from the craft logic of a trade school, yet not a full embrace of consolidation. A more inclusive framework was embodied in the 1960 Master Plan for California Higher Education, led by Clark Kerr with the goal of balancing "competing demands of fostering excellence and guaranteeing educational access for all" (Warren, 2011). This codified the three-tier structure of the system, with interconnections among elite research universities, comprehensive four-year universities, and two-year community colleges.

Further, the twentieth century saw the rise of industrial collaborations with higher education throughout the Cold War—typically described in terms of "R&D consortia"—which were deemed a critical organizational form for realizing national priorities (Kash, 1968; Patterson, 1970). R&D consortia are intended to build national capabilities in fields with rapid technological advancement to support industrial competitiveness (Evan and Olk, 1990; Aldrich and Sasaki, 1995). R&D consortia typically involve private corporations, universities, and other institutional stakeholders, yet they operate outside the bounds of any of the member organizational hierarchies. They are voluntary and produce public and private goods. These consortia are characteristic of this third era, but they are also a precursor for the consortia that are expanding in importance in a fourth postindustrial era.

Era 4: Postindustrial Digital Revolution

We are now in a postindustrial digital era with broad implications for higher education. Piore and Sabel earned a MacArthur "genius grant" for anticipating this second industrial divide superseding both craft and mass production. In this era, Piore and Sabel (1984) highlight institutional arrangements that support "flexible specialization." Instead of single, multinational and multidivisional organizations, regional agglomerations of small, flexible firms are key to this flexibility. Piore and Sabel cite the textile and garment firms in northern Italy as an example. This distributed form is able to respond to fashion trends more quickly and serve niche markets more effectively than the established parts of the industry.

Today, there is a growing movement building out the dimensions of this postindustrial age, seeing it as a fourth industrial era (Schwab, 2016), a fifth technological revolution (Perez, 2002), a second machine age (Brynjolfsson and McAfee, 2014), and a third digital revolution (Gershenfeld et al., 2017). What is consistent across these conceptions is the view that the current era is experiencing an epochal shift with digital technologies as enabler, and often even a key driver.

At the core of the digital logic are accelerating rates of change, combined with modular components (bits or bytes) that can be assembled and disassembled, continually opening up new forms of innovation (Yoo et al., 2010; Gershenfeld et al., 2017). Organizations need to be agile and respond rapidly to changes and opportunities (Child and McGrath, 2001; Sambamurthy et al., 2003). Commonly accepted industrial dynamics no longer hold (McGrath, 2013). The effects of digital logics are both flexibility and fragmentation, with an expanded role for platforms and underlying architectures to provide ongoing coherence. Digitally enabled platforms have become a dominant institutional form for production in the digital age (Parker et al., 2016). A host of new digital platforms and infrastructure enabled a variety of novel open, multiparty arrangements (Dougherty and Dunne, 2011; Lavie and Drori, 2012; Heidl et al., 2014; Olsen et al., 2016; Giudici et al., 2018).

Universities and public higher education systems, at best, achieve linear rates of change, posing the challenge of coevolving with fast-changing technologies. The global COVID-19 pandemic accelerated the use of digital learning platforms by universities as vast numbers of courses were adapted for virtual delivery. Concurrently, there has been an accelerated role of digital technologies in research (spanning the sciences, social sciences, humanities, and other domains), particularly around the sharing and reuse of digital data, the expanding role of cloud computing, the use of digital notebooks in labs, the use of artificial intelligence (AI) and machine learning (ML) in research, and many other developments. Further, the digital modularity is reflected in the concurrent rise of credentialing systems, niche degree programs, and diverse stakeholder groups, each with distinctive expectations of higher education. But it is not clear how universities and public higher education systems will evolve to address these fast-emerging bundles of social and technical advances. Too often, key policies and procedures are unchanged or only modified with small, incremental adjustments. In our research, we have found multi-stakeholder consortia to serve as a model for how systems can evolve in this emerging digital era.

Enter Multi-Stakeholder Consortia

Consortia are collaborative arrangements among individuals, organizations, and institutions in which the members are both independent and interdependent, working to accomplish together what they can't accomplish separately. Multi-stakeholder consortia are not, in themselves, a digital institutional form. These lateral collaborative arrangements emerged in the second half of the twentieth century (Kash, 1968; Evan and Olk, 1990; Aldrich and Sasaki, 1995); today, certain types of multi-stakeholder consortia are relevant to higher education systems. These include consortia centered on teaching, energy, investments, religion, and countless other topics. There are also long-standing consortia associated with sports, some of which dwarf the university systems.

Further, university systems can be thought of as multi-stakeholder consortia, even though they are not voluntary per se, as they are established by law with authority vested in a board, which is delegated to an executive who in turn delegates authority to campuses in the system. In this sense, they have both a legal hierarchical structure as well as a less formal, but no less relevant, lateral structure across the system.

Our focus here is on a new array of consortia that are connected to digital platforms and directly involved in work with data, computing, digital fabrication, and other postindustrial undertakings (Stakeholder Alignment Collaborative, 2022). Universities play key roles in these consortia, even though the consortia operate in agile and adaptive ways that contrast with the supporting universities. These consortia are vastly smaller in scale and scope compared to university systems. University systems operate with multibillion-dollar annual budgets, while even the largest consortia that we have studied have annual budgets of a few million dollars. Still, these smaller and newer lateral arrangements do have lessons to offer to university systems.

For more than a decade, the members of the Stakeholder Alignment Collaborative have been studying the formation and operation of multi-stakeholder consortia focused on the open sharing of research data and cyberinfrastructure capabilities. As reported in an article in the *Stanford Social Innovation Review*, we have been able to identify 24 consortia formed between 1950 and 1999, with the aim of advancing the open sharing of data in science, cyberinfrastructure, and related matters. In contrast, we have been able to identify 97 consortia with comparable missions that were created between 2000 and 2020. Considering that the first period is 50 years and the second period is 20 years, this represents a tenfold increase in the formation of this type of consortia (Stakeholder Alignment Collaborative, 2022).

Examples of consortia from the first period in which one or more of the coauthors of this chapter have a direct connection (with the year of formation) include the Protein Data Bank (PDB; https://www.rcsb.org/) (1971); the Long-Term Ecological Research Network (LTER; https://lternet.edu) (1980); and Internet2 (1997). Examples of consortia from the second period in which we have direct experience include the Quilt

(2000; https://www.thequilt.net/), the BioMarkers Consortium (2006), the Interdisciplinary Earth Data Alliance (IEDA; https://www.iedadata.org) (2010), the Research Data Alliance (RDA; https://www.rd-alliance.org/) (2012), the Campus Research Computing Consortium (CaRCC; https://carcc.org/) (2017), and the Minority Serving Cyberinfrastructure Consortium (MS-CC; https://www.ms-cc.org/) (2018).

Computing and data infrastructure is also provided by the commercial sector through cloud storage and countless software applications. In addition, there are large numbers of open-source platforms with both nonprofit and commercial support systems within the larger research data and computing ecosystem. Universities have both administrative (email, networking, student, finance, etc.) and research computing domains. Research computing might be further divided into library and information services, including repositories and advanced computing capabilities for academic research that ultimately feed into cyberinfrastructure.

The increase in lateral connections among stakeholders involved with research data and computing is a product of the current postindustrial, digital era in at least two ways. First, the amount of data itself has increased exponentially with digitization, making curation and sharing a vastly larger enterprise that is not easily managed by any one institution. Second, the tools of digital communication make lateral coordination easier for parties interested in working together, which in turn makes the boundaries associated with traditional institutional arrangements more permeable. So, what can we learn from these research data and computing consortia?

Lesson 1: Forge and Sustain a Shared Vision

In a commentary in *Nature* on "Five Ways Consortia Can Catalyze Open Science," we highlight the importance of a shared vision (with an emphasis on "shared") (Stakeholder Alignment Collaborative, 2017). In helping to facilitate the formation of new consortia, a first challenge is to identify the different types of stakeholders, which, for the consortia we have been studying, includes diverse fields and disciplines, funding agencies, publishers, commercial organizations, citizen scientists, and others. Getting a sufficient number of these stakeholders to share a vision for what is possible with more open data and more available cyberinfrastructure invariably surfaces a complex mix of common and competing interests.

At first, the elements of a visioning process tend to be general aspirational statements, and some coaching is needed to get to a more substantive vision that takes into account the full landscape of stakeholders and interests. For example, consider this vision statement for the Minority Serving Cyberinfrastructure Consortium, which includes HBCUs, tribal colleges and universities (TCUs), Hispanic-serving institutions (HSIs), and other MSIs:

> We envision a transformational partnership to promote advanced cyberinfrastructure (CI) capabilities on HBCU, TCU, HSI, and MSI campuses. We are advancing connections across campuses around data, research computing, teaching, curriculum development, professional development, and capacity-building. We will learn and grow as a consortium, lifting up all participating institutions by advancing cyberinfrastructure for research and education across diverse fields, disciplines, and communities in ways that reflect the unique voices and interests of our communities. We will engage as full contributors to the global research and education community.

This defines the classic elements of who, what, where, why, and how. It does not include "when" since it is designed to be enduring.

As challenging as it is to construct a shared vision when launching a new consortium, it is even more challenging to maintain that shared vision as the mix of stakeholders changes and the underlying interests that are "at stake" also evolve. For example, when it comes to cyberinfrastructure, MS-CC has to take into account the growth of cloud and edge computing, the ever increasing importance of cybersecurity, and the universities' expanding relationships with local communities around bridging digital divides.

For many state university systems, it will be challenging to revisit their founding vision and ensure sufficient alignment such that the vision is fully shared today. This involves going beyond a surface-level alignment. Recall the SUNY mission, which was for "educational services of the highest quality, with the broadest possible access, fully representative of all segments of the population in a complete range of academic, professional and vocational postsecondary programs." It does not take much scratching of the surface to find considerable debate about how the diverse campuses in the SUNY systems should be aligned around what it takes to have the highest quality, the broadest access, and the most complete representation of academic, professional, and vocational programs. Even in a less complex public system, such as the University of Illinois System, the forging of a shared vision is complicated by the different composition of the three campuses in that system—an original flagship land-grant campus, a former urban extension campus that has evolved into a full-featured research university with a medical school, and a former community college pioneering distance learning technologies as a four-year college. This challenge reflects both the variation in types of campuses in most systems as well as the many incentives in higher education for each campus to advance its own interest as its top priority, rather than those of the system as a whole.

Our first recommendation is for shared visioning processes to happen on a periodic basis, as well as when needed in the face of disruptive events, such as the current pandemic. Some of us were involved in an effort to build a shared vision with the University of Alaska in the midst of a major funding crisis. Our lesson from that initiative was that the competing interests and underlying fears surfaced much faster than the common interests. In addition, the interests of the status quo (e.g., institutional autonomy from the system and job security for faculty and staff) overwhelmed the interests for increased intercampus collaboration, more responsiveness to state needs, and greater operational cost-effectiveness. In order to take these dynamics into account, we further recommend that such visioning processes be multiyear and multistage undertakings.

What is key is to see the development of a shared vision as a negotiated process. All negotiations involved a mix of forcing and fostering

(Walton et al., 1994), which is to be expected with higher education systems. In the SUNY case, for example, some forcing was required for this to become a shared vision. This happened with the requirement that all new academic program proposals stipulate how they were aligned with the strategic plan. At the same time, this forced compliance needed to be accompanied by fostering dialogue and shared appreciation for how the vision is evolving in practice.

Lesson 2: Foster Internal Alignment for Lateral Alignment

In an article in the *MIT Sloan Management Review* on "The Art of Managing Complex Collaborations," a few of us highlighted the importance of alignment within stakeholders as well as alignment across stakeholders (Knight et al., 2015). This element builds on a classic lesson from negotiation theory (Walton and McKersie, 1965; Walton et al., 1994). In labor negotiations, for example, it is common to say that a labor agreement actually requires three agreements—one within labor, one within management, and one between the two. Most labor negotiators will report that the agreements within are often much harder to achieve than the agreements between the two parties. In the context of multi-stakeholder consortia, it is not three agreements to get one, but with n stakeholders it is at least $n + 1$ agreements (and more if we consider coalitions).

This dynamic surfaces quickly during the formation of a consortium. A group of formal and informal leaders will see the need for a consortium, come together to forge a draft vision statement and spell out terms of engagement (often documented in a charter), and then indicate that they need to go back to their home organizations to ensure support. This sets in motion an iterative process between lessons 1 and 2—iterating between an increasingly shared vision and the internal alignment dynamics within the member organizations. This puts these representatives in what are termed "boundary-spanning" roles where they bridge the boundary of their existing organization and the new venture being launched (Tushman, 1977). Boundary spanners always face the dilemma of not "forgetting where they came from," while also embracing and advancing something new.

For university systems contemplating agile and adaptive responses that bridge organizational boundaries in a postindustrial digital era, there will need to be regular processes for internal alignment. In the section below on "Looking Ahead," we note the forums for shared governance mentioned in the SUNY system, which are a partial step in this direction. This includes many "role-alike groups" (e.g., academic officers, business officers, deans, and others who meet regularly across the institutions). We learned from another contributor to this volume that there are approximately 85 such groups in the SUNY system.

Without these types of established forums, distinct stakeholder groups need to be assembled and will have to go through trust-building and other dynamics on an ad hoc basis. Looking ahead, there will be a need for even more forums so that stakeholder groups can achieve sufficient alignment for action in ways that save on wasted or misdirected efforts and accelerated progress where there is alignment.

It is ironic that stable, well-structured forums are needed for flexible adaptation, particularly when the adaptation can be disruptive to these forums. Here we run up against a long-standing institutional challenge, which Robert Michels termed "the iron law of oligarchy" (2001). When studying political parties and labor unions, Michels observed that new democratic arrangements will invariably concentrate power in a small group of leaders in order to ensure their continued existence. This helps to explain why internal alignment is challenging—these institutional forces lead to an embrace of the status quo. It suggests that public higher education systems will be slow to change and avoid changes that disrupt the dominant role of those in positions of power and authority or that are secured by tenure or the terms of a collective bargaining agreement, which ironically may be the faculty, staff, and administrators of the institutions within the system rather than the "system office."

Just as negotiation theory helps us to see the importance of internal alignment for lateral alignment, the role of lateral alignment is important in advancing internal alignment. Too often, negotiations are undercut as one or more parties gets locked into a specific position. The antidote is to appreciate the underlying interests of the party—for any one position, there are any number of interests that are "at stake" (Fisher et al., 2011). This leads to a further recommendation, which is that internal stakeholder forums need training in interest-based approaches to negotiation. When discussing potential new initiatives and other changes, they need to be able to appreciate what is important to others and why it is important. Even if they disagree on the positions, an appreciation of the underlying interests helps to foster exploration of additional options that better take into account all of the relevant interests. For example, MS-CC has identified six major stakeholder groups and specified the value proposition for each, as follows:

> *Researchers and Educators*: Harnessing the power of data and computing resources to advance the frontiers of knowledge in ways that are aligned with the mission of HBCUs, TCUs, HSIs, and other minority serving colleges and universities—spanning science, engineering, social science, humanities, arts, and other domains.
>
> *Students*: Students at HBCUs, TCUs, HSIs, and other minority serving colleges and universities addressing issues of importance to them with data and computing capabilities, as well as preparing to be the next generation workforce—including future cyberinfrastructure professionals.
>
> *Cyberinfrastructure Professionals*: Connecting cyberinfrastructure professionals across HBCUs, TCUs, HSIs, and other minority serving colleges and universities so we can accomplish together what we can't do separately—including building capability, bringing in funding, establishing career paths, advancing knowledge, and pioneering new technologies.
>
> *Campus Leaders*: Making wise investments in the capabilities needed for a post-industrial, digital world—advancing the mission and impact of HBCUs, TCUs, HSIs, and other minority serving colleges and universities.
>
> *Industry Partners*: Enabling industry leaders to coordinate engagement with HBCUs, TCUs, HSIs, and other minority serving colleges and univer-

sities around new technologies, services, resources, and next-generation talent relevant to research and educational cyberinfrastructure.

Foundations and Funding Agencies: Enabling foundations and funding agencies to coordinate engagement with HBCUs, TCUs, HSIs, and other minority serving colleges and universities around research priorities and community development relevant to research and educational cyberinfrastructure.

Beginning with an appreciation for these interests is more constructive than having each group react in an ad hoc way to any given position. Ideally, stakeholder groups can then help one another with their respective internal alignment challenges, which then makes possible lateral alignment across stakeholders.

Lesson 3: Stay Agile with Minimum Viable Structures

In our article in the *Stanford Social Innovation Review* titled "When Launching a Collaboration, Keep It Agile," we suggest that broad societal challenges cannot be addressed by any one organization and need to be addressed in agile and adaptive ways (Stakeholder Alignment Collaborative, 2022). To do so, we introduce the idea of a minimum viable consortium (MVC) as a point of departure, which would then allow for adjustments at liminal thresholds. This formulation draws on the concept from entrepreneurial organizations of a "minimum viable product." Rather than beginning with a full-featured offering, starting with the minimum viable option allows for learning and adjustment from early customer interactions.

In documenting a set of illustrative minimum viable consortia, we found that there was great variance in just what the minimum was. For the MS-CC noted above, the MVC for the first two years was a small volunteer steering committee. In time, MS-CC partnered with Internet2 (https://internet2.edu/) to form a temporary fiscal arrangement that allowed for the receipt of a National Science Foundation (NSF) enabling grant and the hiring of initial staff. By contrast, the BioMarkers Consortium (https://fnih.org/our-programs/biomarkers-consortium/)

encompassed from the beginning a complex and highly regulated domain involving large pharmaceutical companies, small- and medium-sized biotech companies, the National Institutes of Health (NIH), the Food and Drug Administration (FDA), universities, and patient advocacy organizations. In this case, the MVC at launch depended on a pre-committee that defined policy, drafted the charter, gained alignment, enabled future change, and more for nearly two years prior to launch, followed by a highly structured organization with an executive committee, four steering committees (Cancer, Inflammation and Immunity, Metabolic Disorders, and Neuroscience), and a professional staff. In another case, the National Data Service began with less than the MVC and was not able to achieve the critical mass needed for ongoing, full-scale operations consistent with their initial vision.

We also introduce the term "liminal" as a way of describing how these consortia adjust over time. Though there are multiple meanings of liminality, we focus on the idea of reaching certain thresholds and then pivoting, adjusting, expanding, or shrinking. The liminal adjustment is analogous to how an adolescent becomes an adult. In a somewhat similar way, multi-stakeholder consortia are liminal as the mix of stakeholders and interests change, along with broader contextual changes. But the liminality is not always in the direction of greater maturity and increased stability (as suggested by the adjustment to adulthood by an adolescent).

For university systems, there are two implications. First, as they launch new initiatives of one kind or another, they can employ the MVC approach. Such initiative may focus on leading-edge research issues, such as aspects of AI, social determinants of health, climate change, micro-credential initiatives, and countless other topics. The implication is that these initiatives should begin with the minimum viable structure so that they can be agile and adaptive. When they were founded, most public university systems had an expectation of stable public support, which has eroded over the decades. Now the expectation is for innovation and entrepreneurship efforts to generate the revenue to provide sustaining support.

Second, and more challenging, university systems need to increase their capacity to change and adapt in liminal ways. This may include radical restructuring. As we noted with the previous reference to Michels's "iron law of oligarchy," this may drive public higher education systems toward increasing central concentration of decision-making. Resource constraints may also drive moves toward centralization even though what may be needed is a more agile, decentralized model.

Even more problematic is when both of these conflicting logics—increasing and decreasing structure—simultaneously make sense. At the core, institutions need to do two things for society: create value and mitigate harm (Cutcher-Gershenfeld and Isaac, 2018). This can happen in many ways—some with more central structure and some with less. There are inherent tensions. For example, a more decentralized structure enables individual campuses to be more agile but may make the system as a whole less agile. For public higher education systems, we argue that this moment represents a key liminal threshold, and it is important to foster a dialogue with both internal and external stakeholders that begins with all options on the table, as well as an emergent experimental approach.

Lesson 4: Establish Rules to Change the Rules

Knight et al. (2015) also highlighted the importance of routines to change the routines, that is, the importance of consortia and partnerships having rules to change the rules, thereby instantiating the notion of change. When multi-stakeholder consortia are launched, the chartering process may contain a clause indicating that the charter is a living document. While all university systems have founding documents that are far more complex than these charters and that include mechanisms for making adjustments, these systems rarely make major changes in how they are governed.

University systems can learn from multi-stakeholder consortia by adopting a more agile and adaptable approach to governance. This can take the form of experiments in structure and process that begin with more clearly stated rules for changing the rules. A good example can be found at the University of Illinois Urbana-Champaign, which has one of the world's premier engineering programs. Over the years, the requirements for the various engineering degrees have become more and more rigorous, and many students in the four-year engineering programs need five years to graduate. Of equally great concern, the barrier to adding anything new to the curricula was high. The university responded by empowering all engineering professors to offer any new course once and have it count toward any degree without needing any prior approval other than the standard process for any new course. This way, when making the case for a change in engineering degree requirements, a faculty member had results of their experimental course to present. This same thinking could be applied at a systems level, where policies have built-in flexibility for experimentation for time-bound periods. Before launching a system-wide initiative on micro credentials, for example, campuses could be invited to self-nominate degree programs that might better reach target audiences by being converted into stackable micro-credentials. Similarly, given the US Supreme Court's decision prohibiting the consideration of race in higher education admissions, a system may want to experiment with policies based on socioeconomic status, first-generation status, and other criteria. Rules that allow for experimentation on different campuses and tracking impacts (with overall coordination on legal compliance) can provide a way for institutions to advance their missions of reaching diverse populations.

Arizona State University is well known for an institutional arrangement that simultaneously supports faculty who want to operate in traditional disciplines and departments, as well as those who want to form new cross-disciplinary collaborations. On the positive side, this arrangement has led to a wide range of innovative groupings of faculty, staff, and students. On the negative side, this arrangement has given rise to clusters of like-minded groups, some highly integrative and some traditional, with the risk of reduced cross-fertilization. These are complex dynamics, and managing a system that operates this way is challenging when it comes to allocating resources, even as it fosters experimentation and innovation.

Our recommendation is for state systems to experiment with a range of new models on various campuses—where there is a foundation of stakeholder support and clear learning objectives. The results will not always meet the initial learning objectives, and positive unanticipated learning benefits may also be one result, but it is good discipline—and conforms with the scientific method—to generate the objectives and make them public at the start of each experiment.

Looking Forward

Public higher education systems have always had to be responsive to diverse stakeholders. This is reflected in the forums that these systems establish. For example, the SUNY system created a Faculty Council of Community Colleges in 1967, an Association of Council Members and College Trustees in 1970, and a SUNY Student Assembly in 1973 (SUNY, 2022). Today, the array of relevant stakeholder groups is vast; as noted previously, there are approximately 85 role-alike groups in the SUNY system today.

A positive aspect of the increasingly broad mix of stakeholders with expectations for higher education has been the broader access and increasing diversity. In 1940, 5.5 percent of men and 3.8 percent of women had completed four years or more of college education. By 1950, it was 7.3 percent of men and 5.2 percent of women, still a small proportion of the population. There has been steady growth over the decades, with a reversal in the genders in 2015. By 2020, 38.3 percent of women and 36.7 percent of men had completed four years or more of college education (Statista, 2023). At the same time, there are gendered power relations at play in universities that maintain long-entrenched inequalities (Burkinshaw and White, 2017). Nontransparent criteria hamper women's progress, such as a gendered workload imbalance and organizational citizenship behavior being unequally distributed by gender. Similarly, on most campuses, faculty of color are faced with disproportionate workloads when it comes to service, mentoring, and other roles intended to address racial equity in higher education (Matthew, 2016). The restrictions on the use of race in university admissions may further chill efforts to increase racial diversity in faculty and staff. These identity issues can't be effectively resolved by individual campuses or even individual university systems. It will take broader coalitions to find paths forward that comply with the law, while still enabling progress in advancing diverse and inclusive communities on campuses.

Concurrently, there is growing attention on many campuses and in the media on the value of non-Western perspectives, the interests of communities in what is termed the Global South, and the institutional legacies of white privilege, gender status advantage, and class privilege. There is growing resistance to the unequal structures at play in higher education, particularly on the part of younger generations (Burkinshaw and White, 2017). Leading professions, such as those computer and information science, are now reaching out today to the "missing millions" (Blatecky et al., 2021). The challenges are not limited to defined categories of race, gender, disability, or others because the lived experience of most individuals is intersectional (Crenshaw, 1991). Further, issues of identity are associated with increasingly deep divides along ideological lines and other dimensions (accelerated by digital technologies) and visible in a distrust of science by some, cancel culture by others, and gaps in access for too many. Again, these matters will require consortia of various types so that institutions can accomplish together what they can't do separately.

The overall challenge for universities and public higher education systems in this postindustrial digital era is to be agile and adaptive, while simultaneously being broader and more inclusive. The good news is that lateral connections by communities of practice, with digital enablers, are advancing these diverse interests in ways that are not limited by institutional boundaries. These identity-based consortia represent defined voices that can contribute to institutional innovation as well as provide opportunities for continuing education. More challenging is that there are not clear standards and protocols guiding the engagement of these consortia. An important first principle going forward is an appreciation of the essential dignity of all individuals and groups (Hicks, 2011), with the corollary that there is room in higher education for all groups, provided that they respect the essential dignity of others.

Conclusion

The multi-stakeholder university-affiliated consortia associated with research data and computing are evidence that universities are adapting to the digital age, but these consortia are too often hidden, marginal institutional arrangements. For the most part, universities and public higher education systems are not internalizing the lessons from these consortia to inform institutional innovation and change. There is much to learn from these institutional experiments happening within and around higher education itself (if they were more visible). Public higher education systems risk missing an opportunity for healthy evolution if the lessons are not learned and cultivated.

Formal university procedures for documenting and controlling interinstitutional partnership agreements, memoranda of understanding, charters, and other formal membership arrangements only capture a small subset of the lateral collaborative arrangements in place. These procedures miss the many individuals who are attracted to consortia for learning, problem-solving, and knowledge-building. For those who are bureaucratically minded, these more informal lateral arrangements are risky and need to be monitored and controlled. We argue here that the risk in the twenty-first century is not about being entangled in hard-to-control consortia; instead, the risk is to miss out on being part of many such arrangements.

Multi-stakeholder consortia that use the "minimum viable" approach have the potential to achieve short-term gains, being disbanded when goals are met, or evolving into long-term, high-impact initiatives. Important as this potential is, we have argued that multi-stakeholder consortia are important for another reason—as agile and adaptive institutional arrangements, they can be instructive to the much larger and more complex university systems themselves. After all, at their core, university systems *are* multi-stakeholder consortia. By learning from these smaller and more recently formed consortia, the university systems can be better at being what they are.

References

Aldrich, H. E., and T. Sasaki. 1995. "R&D Consortia in the United States and Japan." *Research Policy* 24(2), 301–16.

Blatecky, A., D. Clarke, J. Cutcher-Gershenfeld, D. Dent, R. Hipp, A. Hunsinger, A. Kuslikas, and L. Michael. 2021. *The Missing Millions: Democratizing Computation and Data to Bridge Digital Divides and Increase Access to Science for Underrepresented Communities*. Washington, DC: National Science Foundation. https://www.rti.org/publication/missing-millions/fulltext.pdf.

Brynjolfsson, E., and A. McAfee. 2014. *The Second Machine Age: Work, Progress, and Prosperity in a Time of Brilliant Technologies*. New York: W. W. Norton.

Burkinshaw, P., and K. White. 2017. "Fixing the Women or Fixing Universities: Women in HE Leadership." *Administrative Sciences* 7(3), 30.

Charlton, L. T., and C. Short. 1966. *A Latin Dictionary*. Oxford: Clarendon Press.

Child, J., and R. G. McGrath. 2001. "Organizations Unfettered: Organizational Form in an Information-Intensive Economy." *Academy of Management Journal* 44(6), 1135–48.

Crenshaw, K. 1991. "Mapping the Margins: Intersectionality, Identity Politics, and Violence against Women of Color." *Stanford Law Review* 43(6), 1241–99, https://doi.org/10.2307/1229039.

Cutcher-Gershenfeld, J., and J. Isaac. 2018. "Creating Value and Mitigating Harm: Assessing Institutional Objectives in Australian Industrial Relations." *Economic and Labour Relations Review* (April), 1–26, doi:10.1177/1035304618767263.

Dougherty, D., and D. Dunne. 2011. "Organizing Ecologies of Complex Innovation." *Organization Science* 22, 1214–23, http://doi.org/10.1287/orsc.1100.0605.

Evan, W. M., and P. Olk. 1990. "R&D Consortia: A New US Organizational Form." *MIT Sloan Management Review* 31(3), 37.

Fisher, R., W. Ury, and B. Patton. 2011. *Getting to Yes: Negotiating Agreement without Giving In*. 3rd ed. New York: Penguin.

Geiger, R. 2015. *The History of American Higher Education: Learning and Culture from the Founding to World War II*. Princeton, NJ: Princeton University Press.

Gershenfeld, N., A. Gershenfeld, and J. Cutcher-Gershenfeld. 2017. *Designing Reality: How to Survive and Thrive in the Third Digital Revolution*. New York: Basic Books.

Gerth, D. R. 2010. *The People's University: A History of the California State University*. Berkeley, CA: Berkeley Public Policy Press.

Giudici, A., P. Reinmoeller, and D. Ravasi. 2018. "Open-System Orchestration as a Relational Source of Sensing Capabilities: Evidence from a Venture Association." *Academy of Management Journal* 61(4), 1369–402.

Heidl, R. A., H. K. Steensma, and C. Phelps. 2014. "Divisive Faultlines and the Unplanned Dissolutions of Multipartner Alliances." *Organization Science* 25(5), 1351–71.

Hicks, D. 2011. *Dignity: Its Essential Role in Resolving Conflict*. New Haven, CT: Yale University Press.

Kash, D. E. 1968. "Research and Development at the University: The Direction of Federal Support and Opportunities for Response by Consortia Are Changing." *Science* 160(3834), 1313–18.

Knight, E., J. Cutcher-Gershenfeld, and B. Mittleman. 2015. "The Art of Managing Complex Collaborations." *MIT Sloan Management Review* 57(1), 16–19.

Lavie, D., and I. Drori. 2012. "Collaborating for Knowledge Creation and Application: The Case of Nanotechnology Research Programs. *Organization Science* 23(3), 704–24.

Matthew, P. A. 2016. "What Is Faculty Diversity Worth to a University?" *The Atlantic*, November 23, 2016.

McGrath, R. G. 2013. *The End of Competitive Advantage: How to Keep Your Strategy Moving as Fast as Your Business*. Cambridge, MA: Harvard Business Review Press.

McGuinness, A. C. 2016. "State Policy Leadership for the Future: History of State Coordination and Governance and Alternatives for the Future." Education Commission of the States. May 16, 2016, https://www.ecs.org/state-policy-leadership-for-the-future-history-of-state-coordination-and-governance-and-alternatives-for-the-future/.

Michels, R. 2001. *Political Parties: A Sociological Study of the Oligarchical Tendencies of Modern Democracy*. Translated by Eden and Cedar Paul. Kitchener, ON: Batoche Books.

New York State Senate. 2014. "Consolidated Laws of New York: Chapter 16, Article 8, Section 351, State University Mission." September 22, 2014, https://www.nysenate.gov/legislation/laws/EDN/351.

Olsen, A. Ø., W. Sofka, and C. Grimpe. 2016. "Coordinated Exploration for Grand Challenges: The Role of Advocacy Groups in Search Consortia." *Academy of Management Journal* 59(6), 2232–55.

Parker, G. G., M. W. Van Alstyne, and S. P. Choudary. 2016. *Platform Revolution: How Networked Markets Are Transforming the Economy and How to Make Them Work for You*. New York: W. W. Norton.

Patterson, L. D. 1970. *Consortia in American Higher Education*. Report 7. Washington, DC: George Washington University. https://eric.ed.gov/?id=ED043800.

Perez, C. 2002. *Technological Revolutions and Financial Capital: The Dynamics of Bubbles and Golden Ages*. Cheltenham, UK: Edward Elgar.

Piore, M., and C. Sabel. 1984. *The Second Industrial Divide: Possibilities for Prosperity*. New York: Basic Books.

Sambamurthy, V., A. Bharadwaj, and V. Grover. 2003. "Shaping Agility through Digital Options: Reconceptualizing the Role of Information Technology in Contemporary Firms." *MIS Quarterly* 27(2), 237–63.

Schwab, K. 2016. *The Fourth Industrial Revolution*. New York: Crown Business.

Stakeholder Alignment Collaborative. 2017. "Five Ways Consortia Can Catalyze Open Science." *Nature* 543, 615–18.

Stakeholder Alignment Collaborative. 2022. "When Launching a Collaboration, Keep It Agile." *Stanford Social Innovation Review* (Spring 2022).

Stakeholder Alignment Collaborative. Forthcoming. *The Consortia Century: Aligning for Impact*. New York: Oxford University Press.

Statista. 2023. "Percentage of the U.S. Population Who Have Completed Four Years of College or More from 1940 to 2022, by Gender." July 21, 2023, https://www.statista.com/statistics/184272/educational-attainment-of-college

-diploma-or-higher-by-gender/#:~:text=In%20an%20impressive%20increase%20from,percent%20of%20women%20in%201940.

SUNY. State University of New York. 2022. "Shared Governance." Accessed November 9, 2023, https://www.suny.edu/about/shared-governance/.

Tushman, M. L. 1977. "Special Boundary Roles in the Innovation Process." *Administrative Science Quarterly* 22(4), 587–605, doi:10.2307/2392402.

Walton, R., J. Cutcher-Gershenfeld, and R. McKersie. 1994. *Strategic Negotiations: A Theory of Change in Labor-Management Relations*. Boston: Harvard Business School Press.

Walton, R., and R. McKersie. 1965. *A Behavioral Theory of Labor Negotiations*. New York: McGraw-Hill.

Warren, Jeffrey E. 2011. "UC, Where Are Your Native Sons and Daughters?" *SFGate*, July 14, 2011.

Yoo, Y., O. Henfridsson, and K. Lyytinen. 2010. "Research Commentary—The New Organizing Logic of Digital Innovation: An Agenda for Information Systems Research." *Information Systems Research* 21(4), 724–35.

11 |

The International Engagements of Higher Education Systems in the United States

What's the Current State, and What Does the Future Hold?

JASON E. LANE AND JESSICA SCHUELLER

WHEN ONE THINKS of the purposes of multicampus university systems, international activities would likely not make the top of the list. Systems are typically viewed as a variation of a "state agency," with more bureaucratic roles like allocating funding, regulating activities, and coordinating academic offerings across campuses. Yet systems are not state agencies, at least not in the traditional sense. While composed of multiple campuses, often with separate missions and institutional accreditations, systems have a single governing board responsible for all campuses and a shared system administration that operates on behalf of the governing board. In fact, a number of system administrations do engage in international activities, ranging from coordinating study abroad opportunities to operating overseas offices.

While these activities often get little attention in the mainstream press or in broader higher education conversation, system administrations do serve important roles in supporting various internationalization activities and managing the risks that are inevitably associated with such activities. And this work may be increasingly important in the future. The COVID-19 pandemic illustrated how vulnerable institutions are to shocks to the international education ecosystem. For example, with planes grounded, embassies closed, and quarantines implemented, international mobility came to a screeching halt—significantly reducing the number of students studying abroad, limiting the ability for international students to study in their location of choice, and shifting international research collaborations online.

Many systems are involved in facilitating internationalization policies, activities, and procedures from a central office or coordination point. Systems, because of their large scope and scale, may have better opportunities for stabilizing international engagements than individual campuses. For example, about 20 years ago, the State University of New York (SUNY) established a bilateral, dual-degree relationship with Turkey. Rather than have individual campuses in New York work with individual campuses in Turkey, the SUNY system entered an agreement with Turkey's higher education agency (YÖK/CoHE). According to Lane et al. (2015):

> The overarching strategic goal for the partnership itself was to leverage SUNY's scale as a system to create a meaningful, multifaceted, long-term partnership that could grow to include more campuses and possibly be replicated in other countries. The idea was to go beyond the traditional student and faculty exchange relationships and develop a framework for a broad, yet intimate partnership, that included many aspects. The decision to make the joint/double degree the heart of the relationship allowed for the creation of a tangible and formal foundation, on which other activities could be built and sustained (e.g., institutional information and data-sharing, student and faculty exchange, study abroad, faculty research collaboration, etc.). (7–8)

Their chapter goes on to illustrate that the system-to-system relationship not only allowed for a broader framework, but also created a critical mass of champions across multiple campuses to collaborate and creatively solve problems. In addition, when one institution within the system became less engaged, the system would identify a different campus partner to pick up the relationship. Thus, because the principal actors were SUNY administration and YÖK/CoHE, the overall relationship was much more stable and secure than what would typically be the case in an institution-to-institution relationship.

The stability that could be provided via system engagements in international activities may become even more important as traditional geopolitical relationships destabilize, ranging from economic discord between the United States and China to Russia's invasion of Ukraine. This falls in line with the predictions of famed organizational theorist Henry Mintzberg (1989), who observed that organizations create structures to buffer their operational core from environmental instability. In today's environment, enrollment management and governmental affairs offices gain importance given the increasing instability of enrollments and government relations. Now, everything from research to recruitment has an international dimension, and those dimensions are increasingly tied to the institution's reputation, revenue, and rankings (Lane and Kinser, 2016). As such, it only makes sense that we would see some systems, with a larger economy of scale and the ability to pool financial, human, and programmatic resources across campuses, play a stronger role in supporting and facilitating the international activities within and among their constituent campuses.

In this chapter, we revisit the topic of the internationalization of higher education systems, first explored by Lane (2013) in the book *Higher Education Systems 3.0*, which outlined the primary international functions of system offices in the United States. In addition, we explore the increasingly international approach of US systems in collaborating with systems abroad. This cross-system collaboration sets the background for a brief ex-course into two areas in which systemness is being applied to internationalization activities in other countries: the European Universities Initiative and Cross-National Regional Universities. With US systems increasingly facilitating system-wide internationalization initiatives and the trend of system-to-system international partnerships, this chapter sets the stage for understanding how systemness can be complementary to internationalization aims and conducive to system-to-system international initiatives that bring public higher education in two or more countries together for the betterment of the student experience and broader societal aims.

International Functions of System Offices

The results and findings presented in this chapter are grounded in data collected for the original study and supplemented with a new analysis of the websites of 51 public higher education systems in the United States (conducted in July 2022). The approach for the web analysis was threefold. First, systems' website navigation was reviewed for references to international or study abroad initiatives. Second, the search functionality was used with the keywords *global*, *international*, and *study abroad* to explore content on the site further. Third, system strategic plans, when available, were reviewed using the same keywords to triangulate the website findings. In total, 29 of the 51 systems (57 percent) had some mention of internationalization initiatives on either their website or in their strategic plan. These materials were then reviewed thematically according to the framework for systemness set forth in Lane (2013), which includes functions and themes related to the internationalization activity of systems. Table 11.1 gives the results of this analysis.

In 2013, eight systems were identified as having an active central engagement in internationalization. In 2022, we located thirteen such systems, which included six of the eight originally identified offices, as two that existed in 2013 no longer existed at the time of this writ-

Table 11.1 Functions and themes of system internationalization activity

Area of Activity	Number of Systems	Percentage
Functions		
Campus coordination	12	41
Outreach and promotion	17	59
Study abroad	15	51
Recruitment	4	13
Collaboration	12	41
Themes		
Planning, steering, and coordination	13	45
Programs: student exchanges and study abroad	13	45
Promotion, research, and recruitment	9	31
Policies and policing	11	38

Note: These data only include systems with internationalization initiatives (n = 29).

Table 11.2 Systems identified with international offices in 2013 and 2022

System	2013	2022	Number of Campuses	Number of Students
California State University	X	X	23	485,550
Oregon University System	X		—	—
State University of New York	X	X	64	370,114
University of California	X	X	10	280,000
University of Massachusetts	X		5	72,796
University of North Carolina System	X	X	17	244,507
University of Wisconsin System	X	X	15	165,000
University System of Georgia	X	X	28	340,638
Arkansas State University System		X	7	37,000
University of Hawai'i System		X	10	57,052
University System of Maryland		X	12	168,126
Nevada System of Higher Education		X	8	108,047
Pennsylvania State System of Higher Education		X	14	93,000
Washington State University		X	7	31,478
Total	8	13		

Source: Adapted from Lane (2013) with data from system websites in 2022.

ing.[1] (See table 11.2 for a comparison.) Just because an office was not identified in 2013 does not necessarily mean it did not exist. We do believe the data indicate both the potential instability of such offices at the system level as well a likely overall growth in them over the past decade. This count does not include several other systems that were engaged in coordinating or convening campus international officers but did not have an identifiable official office explicitly dedicated to international programs.

Further, as can be seen in table 11.3, there is no consistency in how these offices are named. Some take a more functional description in the label, such as *international programs*. Others capture the tie to the academic program, identifying it as *international education and engagement*. A set also uses more modern terms such as *global affairs* and *inter-*

1. The Oregon University System was disbanded by the state government, along with its system international office (Paulsen, 2015). The University of Nebraska System made the operational decision to close the office and devolve the functions entirely to the campuses.

Table 11.3 Sample of system-level international offices and selected functions

System	International Office	Primary Area	Selection of Functions
California State University	International Programs (CSU IP)	• Programs • Promotion	• Campus coordination • Outreach and promotion • Study abroad • Collaboration
University System of Georgia	International Education	• Planning • Promotion • Programs • Policies and policing	• Campus coordination • Outreach and promotion • Study abroad
University of Hawaii	International Initiatives	• Planning • Promotion • Programs • Policies and policing	• Campus coordination • Outreach and promotion • Study abroad • Collaboration
State University of New York	Office of Global Affairs	• Planning • Promotion • Programs • Policies and policing	• Campus coordination • Outreach and promotion • Study abroad • Recruitment • Collaboration
Washington State University	Office of International Programs	• Planning • Promotion • Programs • Policies and policing	• Campus coordination • Outreach and promotion • Study abroad • Recruitment • Collaboration
University of Wisconsin	International Education and Engagement	• Planning • Promotion • Programs • Policies and policing	• Campus coordination • Outreach and promotion • Study abroad • Collaboration

national relations, which seem to reflect a broader mission of strategic engagement, reaching beyond academic and regulatory matters.

There is also little consistency in the exact tasks system administration international education offices carry out. While the areas of responsibility vary considerably among offices, many system-level international offices with central coordination tend to be relatively comprehensive in the primary areas of engagement and functions. Some offices have a fairly narrow mission, focusing mostly or only on study abroad and international student exchanges. In other cases, systems such as the University of Maine have taken on leadership roles in advancing system-wide international recruitment initiatives (Office of Strategic Procurement, 2015). Responsibilities also include facilitating campus coordination in areas of the international research and overseeing academic offerings, promoting the internationalization of the curriculum within constituent campuses, supporting international collaborations by campus faculty, and managing legal requirements associated with sponsoring student and scholar visas.

System Internationalization Activity Themes: The 4 P's

The activity of system international offices can be summarized in four primary areas: (1) planning, steering, and coordination; (2) programs: student exchanges and study abroad; (3) promotion, research, and recruitment; and (4) policies and policing. (See also tables 11.2 and 11.3.) Next, each of these areas will be defined, and recent activities within each will be highlighted.

Planning, Steering, and Coordination

Planning encompasses "multi-campus coordination that aims to steer institutions in a similar direction," whether that be through coordinating offices, committees, or advisory boards (Lane, 2013, 269). With planning, systems may develop strategy documents to guide their work. The University of Nebraska System's (2016) "A Strategy for Global Engagement" is a standalone document intended to guide efforts across the system. This can be contrasted with the Minnesota State University System's strategic plan, which embedded "global impact" as part of its overall strategic priorities (Minnesota State University, 2017).

One manifestation of coordination is the development of offices with this specific mission, and we identified 13 systems with such an office. The University System of Georgia (USG) has one of the most robust system-wide coordination efforts for international education, coordinating such activities as education abroad, international student and scholar services, the English as a Second Language (ESL) program, advocacy, policymaking reporting, and administration (USG, 2023a). In addition to administering several programs centrally, this office also convenes the System Council on International Education, which provides for campus representatives to coordinate and collaborate, as well informs system decision-making (USG, 2023b).

One of the more intriguing planning functions of the University of Georgia System is the Consortium for Analysis of Student Success through International Education (CASSIE), which conducts research on the relationship between student success and international education. CASSIE is a joint effort between USG's Office of International Education, Office of Research and Policy Analysis, and the Institute of International Education and is funded by the US Department of Education's International and Foreign Language Education Office (Institute of International Education, 2020; USG, 2019, 2023c). Their findings inform decision-making at both the campus and system levels.

Systems can also coordinate specific projects across campuses and across countries. The Colorado State University System leads the North American Agricultural Advisory Network, which brings together myriad stakeholders across Canada, Mexico, and the United States on issues related to agricultural and rural development. The network is headquartered within the CSU's Spur campus in Denver, and its steering committee, coordinated by CSU System staff, includes the three highest-ranking agricultural officials for Canada, Mexico, and the United States (Colorado State University System, 2023; North American Agricultural Advisory Network, 2023). This partnership seeks to better the food, water, agriculture, and rural needs of all three countries while simultaneously serving the state's interests and aims for its higher education system. This project is indicative that planning and coordination for international programs is encompassing study abroad and increasingly enhancing system-wide and system-to-system (or system-to-government) international programs.

Programs: Student Exchanges and Study Abroad

Programs involve system-wide support for a range of international education activities, which could include student and faculty mobility, as well as virtual mobility, and other programs specifically designed to support global engagements. Study abroad is one area where some systems have been particularly active. For SUNY, state statute dictates the system is responsible for oversight of all study abroad programs, which now entails approving all study abroad programs and facilitating what is essentially a multicampus consortium that enables any student within SUNY to participate in programs offered by other SUNY campuses (SUNY, 2023a). In fact, many systems allow students to choose from programs at any institution in the system. The Louisiana State University System, Nebraska State College System, City University of New York (CUNY), and Pennsylvania State System of Higher Education (PASSHE) have similar programs (CUNY, 2023a; Nebraska State College System, 2023; PASSHE, 2023; University of Louisiana System, 2023).

Programmatic offerings extend beyond education abroad. As mentioned above, Colorado State University System facilitates research programming. SUNY has the Collaborative Online International Learning (COIL) Center, which supports SUNY campuses as well as institutions outside of SUNY in implementing virtual mobility activities. The University System of Georgia facilitates a system-wide ESL program. Each of these represent any number of programs system administrations can and do administer across the system.

Promotion, Research, and Recruitment

The areas of promotion, research, and recruitment are characterized by systems "helping to promote and market the system and constituent campuses in overseas markets as well as provide infrastructure to support campuses' international recruitment efforts" (Lane, 2013, 273). Such collaborative recruitment efforts are not new or unique to systems. The "Study State" initiatives (e.g., Study New York, Study Illinois), are state-level efforts to promote all the colleges and universities in the state to international students.

Systems have engaged in similar efforts for their constituent campuses. One example is the University of Maine System, which uses a joint call for proposals to manage and coordinate the system-wide promotion and recruitment of international students to both degree and English-language programs (Office of Strategic Procurement, 2015). The Washington State University System's International Programs Office on the Pullman campus provides the backbone support for all of the system's five campuses, including in the area of student recruitment. Previously, SUNY's Office of Global Affairs managed several system-level contracts with recruiting agents, which campuses could opt in to using rather than negotiating their own contracts (Lane, 2013).

We also observe system-level activities to standardize communication with prospective international students. For example, some systems provide a central website targeting the international student audience (CUNY, 2023b; University of Massachusetts System, 2023; Minnesota State University System, 2023a; North Dakota University System, 2023; University of Maine System, 2023). These webpages vary markedly, with the North Dakota University System providing a simple welcome, to CUNY offering a more comprehensive set of system-level resources. These websites effectively serve as a front door to each system, quickly redirecting the viewer to each campus website to information on admissions and related matters. The webpages exemplify the tension that exists in this space in that systems are often able to provide supports and encouragements, but it is the campuses that ultimately are responsible for admissions and other activities.

Websites are not the only shared informational resources. Some systems have jointly developed international student handbooks with information on the state, its institutions, programming, and policies, as well as arrival to-dos (USG, 2023d, 2023e). Both the CUNY and Minnesota State systems have developed a joint guide for international student career development (CUNY, 2023c; Minnesota State University System, 2023b). These efforts evidence a "value add" of the system that facilitates the creation of resources that can be used across campuses, rather than each campus having to create similar materials. On this note, promotion does not necessarily indicate an outward facing activity. The Minnesota State System regularly awards an Innovation in Global Education Award to faculty and staff who advance global understanding through courses, projects, research, faculty and student exchanges, study abroad, internships, foreign language, service learning, and other services (Minnesota State University System, 2023c).

Policies and Policing

A fourth activity area for systems is the development and enforcement of policies as well as the ongoing policing of related campus activities. Many systems regulate campus activities through policies. Systems such as the University of California and the University of Texas have international travel and activities policies that all campuses must adhere to (University of California System, 2017; University of Texas System, 2023). Although joint policies and policing of internationalization were the least frequent themes found in the analysis, these activities tend not be formally recognized on mission statements and strategy documents. Several systems, including the Southern Illinois University System, University of Illinois System, University of Massachusetts System, and University of Nebraska system, and Nevada System of Higher Education (NSHE) put out joint messages of support against the COVID-19 online education decision for international students (Southern Illinois University System, 2020; University of Illinois System, 2020; University of Massachusetts System, 2020; University of Nebraska System, 2023). Involvement in policies and policing may continue to increase owing to new federal policies seeking to restrict and monitor research collaborations with Chinese students and scholars (see Bauer-Wolf, 2021; Fischer, 2022).

Policing may be one of the most important activities, though it is also one of the most difficult to identify. To some extent, all system offices engage in oversight of campus activities, and these efforts typically relate to protecting various constituencies (e.g., students, faculty, staff) or working to minimize risk and limit system liabilities. Yet such efforts are rarely documented as a "function" of an office.

One example of how policing can work comes from when one of the coauthors (Lane) oversaw SUNY's Office of Global Affairs. Staff at the system administration learned that one of the community colleges within the system was making plans to enroll approximately 200 new Chinese students as part of a strategy to address declining enrollments. But prior enrollment data showed the campus had no more than a dozen international students in any one year. Two staff from the system administration (including Lane) visited the campus president to discuss the situation. They learned the institution was working with a recruiter to bring in the students and that there were barely any support structures at the institution or in the surrounding community for those students. Alarm bells immediately went off that such a situation was likely not to be successful for either the students or the institution, and the resulting negative publicity could have ripple effects for recruiting from China across the system. In this case, system administrators worked with the campus to reduce the planned number of new students and brokered relationships with other system campuses to provide some of the needed supports, such as ESL courses. The initiative ended up collapsing before it began, but it would have likely been much worse had the system not intervened. Such oversight is an important function of systems, but one that is rarely publicly documented.

There are also more formal aspects of policing in which systems may play an increasingly important role. For example, the federal government has recently become more concerned about the foreign influence on research and educational activities, resulting in prosecution of some foreign-born faculty members and new legislation that increases accountability (Mervis, 2020). As a result, in 2022, the University of Texas System initiated audits of two campuses focused on issues of foreign influence (see Stephens, 2022; Wertz, 2022). While the results are limited and confidential, they illustrate another type of system-level policing of institutional international activities. It is likely that as governmental scrutiny of a range of issues from foreign entanglements of faculty to concerns over exporting of intellectual property increases, system-level oversight and policing of such activities will also increase.

Revisiting Systems: Still a Domestic Orientation?

Much of the intersection between systems and internationalization has been focused on intrasystem collaboration and partnerships. Some systems have moved their inward looking orientation on internationalization matters (e.g., policy development and policing of domestic campuses) to be pursue more external, foreign engagements, however.

For example, SUNY Korea is a branch campus that offers degrees from two SUNY campuses (i.e., Fashion Institute of Technology and Stony Brook) and for which the system provides partial oversight. The Center for Leadership and Sustainable Development, a joint effort between SUNY and the University of the West Indies (UWI) system, builds collaborations between the partners and collectively addresses issues of inequity tied to the Caribbean diaspora (SUNY, 2023b).

Another type of activity entails US systems entering into partnership with systems overseas, such as the relationship between SUNY and Turkey's YÖK/CoHE highlighted at the beginning of the chapter. Some international cross-system partnerships and activities were developed on the basis of sister state agreements such as Wisconsin, whereas more recent activity in this area has been initiated through open calls for international system-wide partners, such as with the Nevada system (NSHE, 2018; Wisconsin Department of Public Instruction, 2023).

One form of an international cross-system partnership involves the state systems in two countries collaborating on joint international programs. For example, in Germany, the State of Hessen's government has international partnerships with three state university systems from abroad: Massachusetts, Wisconsin, and Queensland (Australia). Through a joint international education program, students can study abroad at any institution within the respective system (TU Darmstadt, 2023a, 2023b). Whereas the Hessen-Wisconsin system partnership dates to 1998, more recent activity in this area was initiated through open calls for international system-to-system partnerships. An example is the Nevada System of Higher Education, which used an open call to actively seek out system-to-system international partnerships. As a result of the call, the system signed a memorandum of understanding (MOU) with the higher education system in the state of Tamaulipas, Mexico, in 2019 (NSHE, 2018, 2019). The goal of the MOU is to foster the exchange of students and staff, as well as to forge new research collaborations that address the needs of both the US and Mexican states. Dual-degree programs, language training, and joint conferences round out the integrated collaboration agenda (NSHE, 2019).

These examples may portend a future state where systems become more actively involved in the brokering and facilitating of international relationships and outposts. Operating a campus or office overseas can be more economical if it serves the needs of multiple campuses, rather than each campus having its own location. One interesting area will be to see if international branch campuses that are part of a system, such as Texas A&M Qatar or Texas Tech Costa Rica, begin to work with more than one campus in the system. Both of those branches are affiliated with a campus in their systems, College Station and Lubbock, respectively, but it would be possible for each International Branch Campus (IBC) to become an extension of the system as a whole, rather than one individual campus within.

Similarly, it is likely that we will also see systems brokering relationships with other systems or government agencies similar to the relationships outlined above. Partnering at the system/government level has several opportunities from being able to navigate/change policy barriers to attracting funding to support the efforts. Yet at the end of the day, the work of educating students or conducting research will likely occur at the campus level. As Lane et al. (2015) noted:

> The system could leverage its size, scope, and scalability to attract partners with similar characteristics and create partnership opportunities that might not otherwise be possible for campuses. Yet, the students, faculty, programs, and degrees exist at campuses; and thus, the success of any system-to-system partnership would depend on the interest and willingness of campuses to engage. (7–8)

Thus any new system-level engagements will still entail the collaboration between and among campuses and the system administration.

The Future of Systemness and Internationalization: Supranational Systems

The examples of international system-wide, system-to-system collaboration are illustrative of the potential for addressing internationalization activities more effectively through systemness. An extended view from abroad reveals even more efforts to enhance system-wide cohesion of internationalization activities for the benefit of students, staff, and society. The new European Universities Initiative (EUI) and the growth of Cross-National Regional Universities emphasize the importance of and interest in combining resources to increase the efficiency and effectiveness of educational institutions and internationalization initiatives.

European Universities Initiative

Members states of the European Union (EU) have been systematically integrating their educational systems since the onset of the Bologna process in 1999 (Zahavi and Friedman, 2019). This involved the establishment of a common framework for degree programs and a joint credit point system, among other initiatives such as the Erasmus Program, which made student, staff, and scholar mobility seamless across institutions in different EU countries. This undertaking is illustrative of systemness on its own, in that the convergence of educational systems across a continent worked to leverage the power and strengths of each member state and its institutions to better serve students and society (Zahavi and Friedman, 2019).

The most recent, large-scale integration attempt of the European Union within the higher education arena maximizes the previous work done with Erasmus (Cino Pagliarello, 2022). Through the new European Universities Initiative (EUI), sets of universities across Europe form alliances that become joint institutions (Gunn, 2020). Each alliance has a theme related to service to society—students, researchers, and staff then collaborate across all institutions within an alliance to work on activities related to the theme and its aim (Cino Pagliarello, 2022). This represents a "systemic goal-oriented mode" of governance, in which nation-states play a smaller role compared to the European Union, the EUI alliances, and individual institutions (Capano and Pritoni, 2019). Together, the alliances create a network of systems that works collectively to enhance collaboration and impact across the member states and higher education institutions' communities.

Cross-National Regional Universities

A cross-national regional university (RU) is defined as "an institution of higher education which involves a group of countries in a designated region that collaborate to establish a university offering degree and pre-degree courses, conducting research and serving the needs of the region" (Knight and Zhang, 2022, 115). These entities are distinct from the regional universities commonly found in the United States to serve specific domestic regions. Examples include the University of the South Pacific, the University of Central Asia, South Asian University, and the Pan African University. They "involve multiple governments cooperating to establish a new institution serving students in a particular region and responding to regional needs and priorities" (Knight and Zhang, 2022, 115). Typically, a group of countries in the same region (culturally, politically, and/or geographically) convene to establish a university that aims to serve the teaching and research needs of the cross-national region. RUs are governed by multiple universities and therefore do not have one "parent institution" but rather a joint governing board—similar to systems in the United States. Although RUs are under-researched, most RUs were established before 2000, with only three created in the past two decades (Knight and Zhang, 2022, 125).

The Pan African University (PAU) illustrates how systemness is being applied at a RU. The PAU was developed in cooperation with African and international organizations as well as the African Union and select African universities. It comprises five regional research institutions docked on to local universities. The institutes aim to provide continent-wide educational opportunities in disciplines relevant to African development and prosperity. Not only does the PAU increase continent-wide student and researcher mobility, but it also acts as a hub for networking within each discipline. National governments also benefit from involvement in the PAU through increased research output and by being situated as regional leaders. At the core of the PAU is the aim of addressing societal issues facing the continent (Knight, 2019). By leveraging multiple public higher education institutions across several countries, the

PAU benefits from systemness as it serves African students and societies across the continent (Martin et al., 2022).

Toward the Future

Our review indicates that not every system administration is actively engaged in international engagements, but it does appear that more systems have become engaged in these efforts over the past decade. And our prediction is that we will continue to see system engagement continue to increase given the intensifying destabilization of the geopolitical order, enhanced state and federal scrutiny of campus international activities, and the COVID-19 pandemic's illustration of impact of large-scale disruption to the international education sector. As we look toward the future, we see the potential for systems to play a major role in a number of international activities.

- *Research partnerships*. Many of the greatest challenges facing humankind (e.g., pandemics, climate change, food scarcity, security, populism, and the distrust of science) require cross-national and cross-disciplinary collaborations to develop effective rsponses. While the work of research happens at the campus level and between faculty, we see growing interest among international funders, foundations, and governments to establish shared frameworks to support this work, and those actors would prefer to work with entities that represent multiple institutions. In the United States, we are likely to see systems, particularly those that represent one or more research universities, become more engaged in brokering these large-scale partnerships.
- *International student recruitment*. The international student market is becoming more fraught and competitive. As campuses look to have their international student enrollments rebound from their collapse during the pandemic, systems can play a role in enhancing recruitment efforts from marketing the system (and constituent campuses) overseas to developing shared contracting with recruitment

agents. These efforts could also include partnerships with other systems or governments to recruit students to the system's campuses.

- *Overseas presence*. As noted above, some institutions have begun to develop an international presence, from branch campuses to outreach offices. Physical presence can be useful beachheads for developing local partnerships, recruiting students, and raising both reputation and revenue. But managing these presences can be complicated and involve dealing with a range of issues from international tax regulations to foreign accreditation requirements. Managing these presences at the system level may make more sense than having them undertaken by individual campuses. For example, SUNY Korea offers degrees of two campuses within SUNY, capitalizing on both the system's name as well as the fixed costs already invested in the campus. This same campus also has the potential to operate as an Asian hub for all SUNY campuses. It may also be possible that systems collaborate with other state agencies so that these presences both serve the system's campuses and work to advance other state priorities, particularly in the area of economic development. It will be important as these efforts evolve not to re-create variations of colonization. Consideration should be given to working through constructive relationships with foreign governments, institutions, and peoples to advance mutually beneficial efforts.

Systems are already engaged in international efforts, though most of these efforts are currently focused on domestic aspects of this work. In the future, we are likely to see systems engage in more offshore activities, such as those described above. The reemergence of nationalism seeks to re-create and restrengthen political and cultural borders that have been dismantled over the last several decades. Yet pandemics and climate change do not see such borders and will wash over them as easily as a wave upon a beach. Research and education have been the fundamental form of international cooperation for centuries. To effectively address the many challenges facing humankind, let alone the need to improve international relations and intercultural understanding, it is imperative that we continue to grow international engagements, not pull back from them. To do so, in light of the increasing pressures against such work, systems can, and must, play an increasing role in facilitating, supporting, and leading the global engagements of the higher education sector.

References

Bauer-Wolf, J. (2021). "Bill Would Give Federal Agencies New Oversight of Colleges' Foreign Dealings." Higher Ed Dive. April 23, 2021, https://www.highereddive.com/news/bill-would-give-federal-agencies-new-oversight-of-colleges-foreign-dealing/598892/.

Capano, G., and Pritoni, A. (2019). "Varieties of Hybrid Systemic Governance in European Higher Education." *Higher Education Quarterly* 73(1), 10–28.

Cino Pagliarello, M. (2022). "Higher Education in the single Market Between (Trans)National Integration and Supranationalisation: Exploring the European Universities Initiative." *Journal of European Integration* 44(1), 149–64.

Colorado State University System. (2023). "Top North American Agriculture Leaders Will Help Guide New International Advisory Network on Extension." Accessed November 10, 2023, https://csusystem.edu/top-north-american-agriculture-leaders-will-help-guide-new-international-advisory-network-on-extension/.

CUNY. City University of New York. (2023a). "Programs." Accessed November 10, 2023, https://www1.cuny.edu/sites/global/students/programs/.

CUNY. City University of New York. (2023b). "International Education." Accessed November 10, 2023, https://www.cuny.edu/academics/academic-programs/international-education/.

CUNY. City University of New York. (2023c). "International Student Guide." Accessed November 10, 2023, https://www1.cuny.edu/international/sec4-1.html.

Fischer, K. (2022). "Is Geopolitics Closing the Door on Open Research?" *Chronicle of Higher Education*. April 19, 2022, https://www.chronicle.com/article/is-geopolitics-closing-the-door-on-open-research?cid2=gen_login_refresh&cid=gen_sign_in.

Gunn, A. (2020). "The European Universities Initiative: A Study of Alliance Formation in Higher Education." In *European Higher Education Area: Challenges for a New Decade*, edited by Adrian Curaj, Ligia Deca, and Remus Pricopie, 13–30. New York: Springer.

Institute for International Education (IIE). (2020). *Research Brief: University System of Georgia's CASSIE Project Shows Positive Impact of International Education on Student Success*. New York: IIE. https://www.iie.org/publications/cassie-research-brief/.

Knight, J. (2019). *Knowledge Diplomacy in Action*. London: British Council.

Knight, J., and Zhang, Y. (2022). "Regional Universities around the World: An Analysis of Single Campus, Multi-campus and Virtual Models." In *Reconfiguring National, Institutional and Human Strategies for the 21st Century: Converging*

Internationalizations, edited by L. Cremonini, J. Taylor, and K. M. Joshi, 113–31. New York: Springer International.

Lane, J. (2013). "The Systemness of Internationalization Strategies: How Higher Education Systems Are Aiding Institutions with Globalization." In *Higher Education Systems 3.0: Harnessing Systemness, Delivering Performance*, edited by J. Lane, 251–82. Albany: State University of New York Press.

Lane, J., and Kinser, K. (2016). "Rankings, Higher Education Internationalisation and National Strategies: TradeOffs, Policy Levers and (Un)intended Outcomes." In *Global Rankings and the Geopolitics of Higher Education*, edited by E. Hazelkorn. Milton Park, UK: Routledge.

Lane, J. E., K. Krebs, and L. Thompson. (2015). *Leveraging System Assets to Strengthen Campus Internationalization: Strategic Planning and the Role of Leadership*. International Briefs for Higher Education Leaders, No. 5. Washington, DC: American Council on Education.

Martin, R., N. Zimpher, J. Lane, and J. Johnsen. (2022). "Leveraging the Power of Systemness to Improve the Success of Students and Society." *Change: The Magazine of Higher Learning* 54(4), 38–44.

Mervis, J. (2020). "Report Finds Holes in U.S. Policies on Foreign Influence in Research." *Science*, December 28, 2020. https://www.science.org/content/article/report-finds-holes-us-policies-foreign-influence-research.

Minnesota State University. (2017). "University Strategic Directions 2016–2021." September 6, 2017, https://www.mnsu.edu/globalassets/student-success-analytics-and-integrated-planning/integrated-planning/strategic_direction_goals_and_objectives_9_6_17.pdf.

Minnesota State University System. (2023a). "International Students." Accessed November 10, 2023, https://www.minnstate.edu/admissions/international.html.

Minnesota State University System. (2023b). "International Students Career Planning Resources." Accessed November 10, 2023, https://www.minnstate.edu/careerexploration/interactive/workbook_international_students.html.

Minnesota State University System. (2023c). "Innovation in Global Education Award." Accessed November 10, 2023, https://minnstate.edu/system/asa/awards/asa-awards/documents/global-education-award.pdf.

Mintzberg, H. (1989). "The Structuring of Organizations." In *Readings in Strategic Management*, edited by D. Asch and C. Bowman, 322–52. London: Macmillan Education UK.

Nebraska State College System. (2023). "Study Abroad Opportunities." Accessed November 10, 2023, https://www.nscs.edu/information-for/students/study-abroad.

North American Agricultural Advisory Network. (2023). "Homepage." Accessed November 10, 2023, https://naaan.csusystem.edu/.

North Dakota University System. (2023). "International Students." Accessed November 10, 2023, https://ndus.edu/international-students/.

NSHE. Nevada System of Higher Education. (2018). "NSHE Seeks International System-Wide Partnerships." October 19, 2018, https://nshe.nevada.edu/2018/10/nshe-seeks-international-system-wide-partnerships/.

NSHE. Nevada System of Higher Education. (2019). "Regents Approve International

Partnership with Higher Education System in Tamaulipas Mexico." March 1, 2019, https://nshe.nevada.edu/system-administration/news/2019/03/regents-approve-international-partnership-with-higher-education-system-in-tamaulipas-mexico/.

Office of Strategic Procurement. (2015). *Request for Qualification: Promotion and Recruitment of International Students*. RFQ 37-16. Orono: University of Maine System. https://www.maine.edu/strategic-procurement/wp-content/uploads/sites/5/2017/06/37-16_Promotion_and_Recruitment_International_Students.pdf.

PASSHE. Pennsylvania State System of Higher Education. (2023). "International Studies." Accessed November 10, 2023, https://www.passhe.edu/offices/asa/international/index.html.

Paulsen, D. (2015). "The End of the Oregon University System." *Eugene Weekly*, July 9, 2015. https://eugeneweekly.com/2015/07/09/the-end-of-the-oregon-university-system/.

Southern Illinois University System. (2020). "Supporting Our International Students." July 12, 2020, https://siusystem.edu/president/presidential-messages/supporting-our-international-students.shtml.

Stephens, T. (2022). *Confidential Audit Report: Foreign Influence on Research*. Audit Report No. R2204 [Memorandum]. Dallas: University of Texas. https://www.utsystem.edu/sites/default/files/documents/ut-system-reports/2022/utd-foreign-influence-research-summary-memo-confidential-report/utd-foreign-influence-research-summary-memo-confidential-report.pdf.

SUNY. State University of New York. (2023a). "Study the World." Accessed November 10, 2023, https://www.suny.edu/studyabroad/.

SUNY. State University of New York. (2023b). "SUNY UWI Leadership Team." Accessed November 10, 2023, https://www.uwi.edu/sunyuwicenter/about/suny-uwi-leadership-team.

TU Darmstadt. (2023a). "Hessen-Massachusetts Program." Accessed November 10, 2023, https://www.tu-darmstadt.de/studieren/studierende_tu/auslandsaufenthalte/austauschprogramme_outbound/austausch_in_die_welt/austauschprogramme_hessen/hessen_massachusetts/hessen_massachusetts_landesprogramm.en.jsp#:~:text=The%20Hessen%2DMassachusetts%20Program%2C%20an,Massachusetts%20System%20free%20of%20charge.

TU Darmstadt. (2023b). "Hessen-Wisconsin Program." Accessed November 10, 2023, https://www.tu-darmstadt.de/studieren/studierende_tu/auslandsaufenthalte/austauschprogramme_outbound/austausch_in_die_welt/austauschprogramme_hessen/hessen_wisconsin/hessen_wisconsin_landesprogramm.en.jsp.

University of California System. (2017). "International Activities." June 23, 2017, https://policy.ucop.edu/doc/2300651/InternationalActivities.

University of Illinois System. (2020). "Importance of Our International Students." July 8, 2020, https://news.uillinois.edu/view/7815/312469872.

University of Louisiana System. (2023). "Study Abroad." Accessed November 10, 2023, https://www.ulsystem.edu/students/study-abroad/.

University of Maine System. (2023). "International Students." Accessed November 10, 2023, https://www.maine.edu/students/international/.

University of Massachusetts System. (2020). "Statement by UMass President Marty Meehan Regarding the Rescinding of ICE Guidance on International Students." July 14, 2020, https://www.massachusetts.edu/news/statement-umass-president-marty-meehan-regarding-rescinding-ice-guidance-international.

University of Massachusetts System. (2023). "International Students." Accessed November 10, 2023, https://www.massachusetts.edu/education/international-student-applicants.

University of Nebraska System. (2016). "A Strategy for Global Engagement at the University of Nebraska." June 29, 2016, https://nebraska.edu/docs/global/Global_Engage_Broch_Pages.pdf.

University of Nebraska System. (2023). "International Student Access." Accessed November 10, 2023, https://its.nebraska.edu/covid-19/international-student-access.

University of Texas System. (2023). "Systemwide International Policies and Programs." Accessed November 10, 2023, https://utsystem.edu/offices/risk-management/systemwide-international-policies-and-programs.

USG. University System of Georgia. (2019). "Students Benefit from International Education Opportunities." November 22, 2019, https://www.usg.edu/news/release/students_benefit_from_international_education_opportunities.

USG. University System of Georgia. (2023a). "System Council on International Education (SCIE)." Last modified October 26, 2023, https://www.usg.edu/international_education/usg_resources/scie_information.

USG. University System of Georgia. (2023b). "International Education, Academic Affairs Division." Accessed November 10, 2023, https://www.usg.edu/international_education/.

USG. University System of Georgia. (2023c). "The Consortium for Analysis of Student Success through International Education." Accessed November 10, 2023, https://www.usg.edu/cassie.

USG. University System of Georgia. (2023d). "International Students: Informational Resources." Accessed November 10, 2023, https://www.usg.edu/information/international_students/.

USG. University System of Georgia. (2023e). "International Student Manual." Accessed November 10, 2023, https://www.usg.edu/international_education/assets/international_education/documents/USG_International_Student_Manual.pdf.

Wertz, L. (2022). *Reporting of Foreign Gifts and Contracts*. Audit Report No. 22-106 [Memorandum]. Dallas: University of Texas. https://www.utsystem.edu/sites/default/files/documents/ut-system-reports/2022/utep-reporting-of-foreign-gifts-and-contracts-report/utep-reporting-of-foreign-gifts-and-contracts-report.pdf.

Wisconsin Department of Public Instruction. (2023). "Germany." Accessed November 10, 2023, https://dpi.wi.gov/international-education/german.

Zahavi, H., and Y. Friedman. (2019). "The Bologna Process: An International Higher Education Regime. *European Journal of Higher Education* 9(1), 23–39.

12 |

Leveraging Systems to Increase Diversity, Equity, and Inclusion at Institutions of Higher Education

KHALEEL SEECHARAN AND DARREN GREENO

Summary

THE CURRENT STATE of higher education reflects larger social stratification in the United States. This stratification is the result of a long history. Higher education in America was originally created to train the elite, wealthy, and predetermined leaders of society. As higher education opened to people beyond the highest economic and social strata, its archaic foundations have resulted in education disparities for the many disenfranchised and vulnerable members of society. Now, with more than 75 percent of students enrolled in public colleges and universities that are part of multicampus systems, systems have opportunities to address these education disparities at scale. We can utilize the current infrastructure and ecosystem of higher education—multicampus systems in the pursuit of diversity, equity, and inclusion (DEI) efforts—and utilize "systemness" to address the needs of students from communities historically underserved and marginalized by postsecondary education. DEI initiatives are vital to address both historical and current racial and ethnic disparities in admissions, achievement, retention, degree conferral, and more. Many terms are used in the field of inclusive excellence; for simplicity, we use DEI while acknowledging other terms such as belonging and justice. DEI, as noted by the American Psychological Association (2021), is a framework that promotes fair treatment and participation of all people, especially populations that have been historically underrepresented because of their background, identity, disability, or other characteristic. Diversity refers to the representation or composition of various social identity groups in a work group, organization, or community. Equity involves providing resources according to the contextual help needed for diverse populations to achieve success. Inclusion strives for an environment that offers affirmation, celebration, and appreciation for different approaches, perspectives, and experiences. This chapter is a reflection on the opportunity to use the unique power of systems to operationalize more inclusive and equitable practices in higher education.

Introduction

American higher education began in the colonial era with the founding of Harvard College in 1636 to train men for ministry. Other denominations across the colonies followed suit, adapting programs to meet leadership needs. As Harvard was considered too liberal, Yale was created to train orthodox ministers; Brown deviated from the norm by admitting white Christian men of many denominations. The College of William and Mary expanded beyond the ministry and was created to train lawyers, politicians, and plantation owners in the South. The University of Pennsylvania, reflecting the character of its founder Benjamin Franklin, further expanded the vision in 1765 to include practical fields such as medicine.

The first institutions accessible to the broader public came in 1785 and 1789 with the establishment of the University of Georgia and North Carolina's state university system, respectively (Carlton, 2022). Public institutions were rare and politically divisive; the Morrill Land-Grant Act of 1862 was passed only after Southern Democrats, who had previously opposed the bill, seceded from the Union. This act reimagined federal support for public higher education by granting federal land to states, which would in turn monetize the land to support the founding and funding of state-led public institutions and university systems, leading to the founding of 69 universities (National Archives, 2022). While the Morrill Act ensured availability of higher education to the public for the first time, the land granted was seized under threat and duress from Native American tribes; if treaties were agreed upon, the federal government rarely followed through with the agreement (Williams et al., 2022).

Reflecting the deep racism in the country in the years before and after the Civil War, Black students were discouraged or explicitly prohibited from white institutions of higher education, leading to the establishment of historically Black colleges and universities (HBCUs). The first HBCU was Cheyney University (1837) in Pennsylvania; others included the University of the District of Columbia (1851), Lincoln University (1854), and Wilberforce University (1856). The second Morrill Act of 1890 was created to develop separate land-grant HBCUs, resulting in the majority of present-day HBCU institutions (National Archives, 2022). Prior to desegregation in the 1950s and 1960s, nearly all Black students enrolled in postsecondary institutions were at HBCUs (HBCU First, 2022).

Women's education was also largely disregarded, with postsecondary education primarily consisting of finishing schools prior to the development of Georgia Female College—now known as Georgia's Wesleyan College—the first four-year institution to grant degrees to women. In 1840, Catherine Brewer would be the first woman in the United States to graduate with a bachelor's degree. In 1862 at Oberlin College, Mary Jane Patterson was the first Black woman to graduate with a bachelor's degree (Fourtané, 2021), more than 200 years after the establishment of Harvard College and 25 years after establishment of Cheyney College.

With nearly 400 years of history, reverberations of discrimination, exclusion, and atrocities continue to be felt in US higher education. Widespread public postsecondary education was only possible with the forced seizure and expulsion of Native people from their land; Black students only gained access to segregated education a little over 100 years ago, and desegregated education just over 50 years ago; and women across racial and ethnic groups were last to access higher education, with Black women being the latest to access higher education in the United States. But we can reframe this history to understand that access to higher education across socioeconomic status, race/ethnicity, and gender is the foundation of diversity, equity, and inclusion initiatives at institutions today.

DEI initiatives are vital to address both historical and current racial and ethnic disparities that exist in admissions, achievement, retention, degree conferral, and more. Data on degrees conferred by aggregated racial and ethnic groups for 2018–19 illustrate significantly lower percentages of attainment for associate's, bachelor's, master's, and doctoral degrees among Black, Latino, Asian/Pacific Islander, American Indian/Alaska Native, and multiracial students (National Center for Education Statistics, 2020). The pre-pandemic data suggest that students from marginalized populations are at higher risk of nondegree conferral status. Contrasted with the US census data for population ages 18–24, the aggregated data by ethnicity and race indicates, in most instances, greater disparity in Black, Hispanic, and American Indian/Alaska Native populations in degrees conferred past the associate's degree level (fig. 12.1).

The COVID-19 pandemic exacerbated challenges—for instance, marginalized students who felt isolated prior to the pandemic experienced

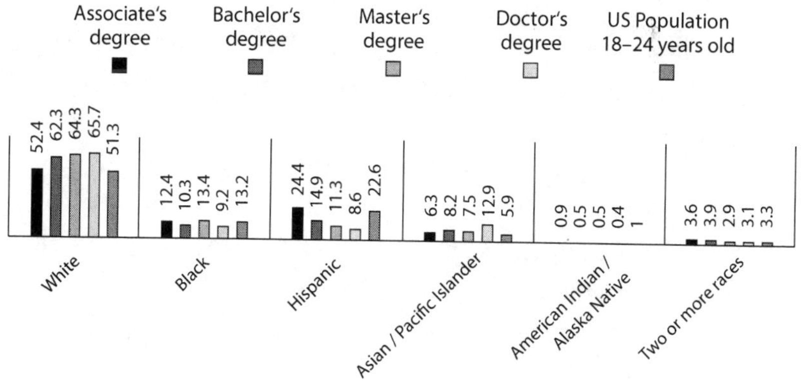

Figure 12.1 Degrees conferred by postsecondary institutions to 18- to 24-year-olds* by race/ethnicity, 2018–19.

* Each demographic's respective percentage of US population. 18–24 years old is indicated in the rightmost column.

challenges with online learning, connecting with faculty, and feeling a sense of involvement with the institution (Vetro, 2021). Increased remote learning during the pandemic also highlighted disparities in access to broadband and related technologies necessary for student learning done at home.

Systems in Higher Education

The public higher education ecosystem is composed of public colleges and university systems that are responsible for employment, legal governing, policy making, and fiduciary activities. Systems are used by 44 of 50 states to manage higher education within the state, and 75 percent of four-year college and university students are enrolled in a system institution (Martin et al., 2022). Understanding DEI within a system context is critical to build a sustainable, scalable DEI implementation plan.

The Power of Systems, outlined by the National Association of System Heads (NASH), is based on the concept of "systemness" where, in aggregate, the system holds more power than a collection of single institutions, and thereby has the opportunity to generate normative change. The Power of Systems agenda includes five "Imperatives" that utilize systemness to achieve targeted transformative outcomes.

1. The Learning Imperative details a flexible, responsive, precision-education strategy to meet the needs of each student.
2. The Talent Imperative details civic engagement and global awareness to allow for flexibility in the changing workforce landscape.
3. The Equity Imperative impresses upon the need for dismantlement of structural and systemic barriers.
4. The Investment Imperative outlines resource-sharing and re-investment in students and facilities.
5. The Systemness Imperative surveys political, strategic, and normative solutions that can be scaled across higher education systems.

This agenda is geared toward system leaders to serve as a guide when undergoing transformational efforts. We keep the Power of Systems agenda in mind when reviewing brief case studies of two systems. First is a public university, the University of Missouri (UM) System, whose DEI efforts grew out of immediate crises. The second is the California System of Community Colleges, the largest system of community colleges in the United States.

Case 1: The University of Missouri System

The UM system includes four campuses that serve more than 70,000 students; its size and breadth of services establish it as an economic generator for the state of Missouri, as well as a microcosm of social and political issues in the state. After a series of racist incidents at the University of Missouri-Columbia (UM Columbia) and the fatal shooting of Michael Brown by a white police officer in Ferguson, Missouri, in 2015, students led peaceful, highly publicized protests. The high prominence of the university in Missouri ensured that any protest would be widely disruptive. These protests were meant to bring attention to the UM system's inadequate response to campus crises, a systemic breakdown in communication, and the absence of any infrastructure to bring in the voices and experiences of diverse and historically marginalized perspectives into decision-making on campus. The lack of meaningful action from the UM system, combined with the escalation of the protests—which included a boycott by the UM football team and a hunger strike by a student leader—ultimately led to the resignation of the university president and wider system instability. At its core, this instability arose from a lack of infrastructure to support DEI initiatives and subsequent lack of infrastructure to respond to crises.

In response, the UM system hired its first vice chancellor for diversity, equity, and inclusion, Kevin G. McDonald. His role focused on addressing the immediate racial crises, establishing infrastructure for rebuilding the campus community, and developing interventions for the UM system to reimagine their DEI-related efforts. Using the American Association of Colleges and Universities (AAC&U) Inclusive Excellence Framework as a tool to include the voice of community-based constituents, McDonald and other leaders within the UM system sought to harness the energy and expertise of the broader community. Briefly, the Inclusive Excellence Framework has four primary elements: (1) a focus on student intellectual and social development; (2) a purposeful development and utilization of organizational resources to enhance student learning; (3) attention to the cultural differences learners bring to the educational experience and that enhance the enterprise; and (4) a welcoming community that engages all of its diversity in the service of student and organizational learning.

The shift to engaging with the UM Columbia community allowed historically marginalized voices to help shape new policies and practices at UM Columbia and across the UM system. The community-building process involved convenings to discuss and provide guidance on the impact of reporting DEI policies, practices, and developmental goals, and developing strategies to leverage institutional political savvy and support during turbulent times. The emphasis on co-creation opened the door for protestors to support development of new DEI practices, as well as leaders on every campus involved in decision-making and availability of funds centrally located to support ongoing DEI initiatives.

Other work included improved transparency and accessibility of information to provide open-source materials related to DEI work, equity audits across the UM system to identify broken or outdated practices, and financial incentives for schools and units to construct and implement adaptable and appropriate DEI plans that closed equity gaps. McDonald's office was able to build infrastructure, community, and transparency within the UM system capable of DEI restructuring and crisis response.

Currently, the UM system is headed by Mun Y. Choi, who collaboratively leads the system and the flagship campus in Columbia, with chancellors leading the other three institutions. The UM system now includes DEI as a key department with four focus areas: Inclusive Excellence, Information Gathering, Title IX, and Programs. The UM system adopted the Inclusive Excellence Framework and used it to guide the development of DEI policies and practices for each of the four campuses. Inclusive Excellence plans are the result of a system-wide strategic initiative adopted in 2015 to serve the UM system, most recently updated during the 2017–18 academic year. The five- to seven-year plans address issues of access and success, institutional climate and intergroup relations, education and scholarship, institutional infrastructure, and community involvement. With $3.4 million in funding to develop new programs, enhance existing programs, provide salary support for new positions, and award scholarships, there is a commitment to address inequities and to fund DEI initiatives.

The American Council on Education has reported on the success of the University of Missouri System's initiatives: *Speaking Truth and Acting with Integrity: Confronting Challenges of Campus Racial Climate* (2018) and *Leading after a Racial Crisis: Weaving a Campus Tapestry of Diversity and Inclusion* (2020) address issues related to critical decision-making during a crisis.

Case 2: The California System of Community Colleges

The California System of Community Colleges (CCC) is the largest public institution of higher education in the United States, with 116 colleges and 1.8 million students. The racial/ethnic makeup of this student body is as follows: 46 percent Hispanic, 24 percent white, 11 percent Asian, 6 percent African American, 4 percent multiethnic, 3 percent Filipino, less than 1 percent American Indian/Alaskan Native, less than 1 percent Pacific Islander, and 6 percent unknown (California Community Colleges Chancellor's Office, 2022). The CCC's governing board was awarded the 2022 Equity Award from the National Association of Community College Trustees for its work to promote institutional diversity in its system. This award was granted in honor of the board's "Vision for Success" operating philosophy, which involves system goals and commitments that make DEI and accessibility within and across institutions transparent and accessible. Their Vision of Success goals identify core commitments to preparing students for workforce demands. Other foci include reducing equity gaps for students who transfer to the University of California and California State University systems; a goal to close equity gaps within 10 years; and the implementation of DEI criteria in performance evaluations for all employees in the CCC to ensure DEI is a priority in the interactions with faculty, staff, and students.

The CCC system utilizes collaboration among leadership within and among institutions. The work of the Academic Senate is actively involved in DEI initiatives and includes representation of faculty from marginalized communities (California Community Colleges Chancellor's Office, 2020). The Academic Senate developed a project on anti-racism education and acknowledged the need to assess and advance effective anti-racism practices for the purpose of professional development. The project centers national conversations on the racial violence and pain constituents feel as members of marginalized communities. The project offers a space where students, faculty, and administrators can address their work on social justice to further support their experiences with injustice, oppression, and inequity. Through the development of this project, faculty members can contribute to the system-level decision-making processes. System leadership acknowledges the importance of every person who is asked to share perspectives on the journey to facilitate diversity, equity, inclusion, and accessibility (DEIA) at each institution within the system.

The measurement of progress is a focal point in the communication of actions related to DEIA efforts. Three core outcomes of these efforts are critical to the DEIA journey: celebrating cultural diversity; promoting equity through equity-minded policies and practices; and fostering inclusion through employee recruitment, hiring, and retention. A "Call to Action" in 2020 served to unite the system head, college leadership, and other key stakeholders in focusing on DEIA efforts. This included the creation of anti-racist policies and practices that include embedding DEIA competencies and criteria into employee evaluations and tenure review processes; updating the student grievance process to provide clear steps for students to raise concerns and resolve acts of racism, microaggressions, and discomfort; reevaluating and including DEIA in district equal employment opportunity plans (EEO) to demonstrate an ongoing action-oriented commitment; encouraging mentorship opportunities between students and faculty; and providing professional learning resources focused on institutional bias, structural racism, and their impact on campus culture and student success.

At the system leadership level, Interim Chancellor Daisy Gonzalez has made several actionable steps to facilitate DEIA efforts within the CCC system. She has advocated for state legislation to end the controversial practice of high-stakes student placement tests, instead facilitating direct access to transfer-level English and math courses with appropriate academic support. This legislation, over four years, resulted in an increase in the completion of transfer-level courses—49 to 67 percent in English and 26 to 50 percent in math—shortening the time to degree completion. Chancellor Gonzalez was instrumental in the system's integration of a funding strategy to allocate funds to districts serving low-income students. Her approaches have prioritized students and focused on closing student opportunity gaps, promoting student success, and supporting degree completion. She is also transparent with her intersectional background as a Latina, former foster youth, and first-generation college student; she understands the power in identity and leadership and understands the role representation plays in the empowerment of students, faculty, and administrators from marginalized communities—who comprise a significant population of the CCC community.

The CCC system has integrated DEIA initiatives into multiple broad and targeted levels of their system, a strategy that supports scalability and sustainability of initiatives. Transparent communication, community engagement, and a student-first perspective have supported an environment for transformative change to take place and grow. Given the size and scale of the CCC system, these successes indicate potential for replicability across institutions of higher education.

Future Directions: A Systemness Approach to DEI

Although the power of systems to improve DEI efforts is significant, we recognize the current and future challenges to DEI improvement—especially within an anti-DEI political landscape—may be equally significant. Several states have enacted legislation that limits or bans DEI work, oftentimes without concrete instruction for implementation or enforcement. And yet our systems of higher education continue to become more diverse—US census data shows us that colleges and universities will be serving a majority-minority student body in the coming decades. Higher education practitioners must adapt to better serve this increasingly diverse student body, while navigating political impediments explicitly designed to challenge progress. Working within antagonistic political environments places additional burdens on equity practitioners (often faculty and staff of color). System-level actors need to understand the day-to-day strain that faculty and staff experience while engaging and furthering DEI initiatives and construct policies to support these efforts.

At the institution level, challenges to DEI improvement may be caused by internal politics, funding, or both. Supporting DEI efforts—or even locating a DEI office—is an inherently political act. For example, DEI efforts are typically siloed within departments, divisions, and schools. Oftentimes, a single chief diversity officer (CDO) is charged with responding to a crisis or fixing equity gaps on a small scale and is then expected to replicate success across a system. These structures are unsustainable, ineffective, and inequitable in their distribution of labor. A systems approach to DEI improvement shifts responsibility from the unit, school, or CDO to the institutional community and creates a model for system-level actors to be facilitators of DEI improvement as opposed to bystanders. Using a systems approach, we can build inclusive and supportive structures through a community of practice aimed at supporting inclusive excellence regardless of changing political trends.

Multicampus systems can and have been leveraged to foster meaningful change that positively affects students and the communities surrounding college and university campuses, as exemplified in our case studies. Facilitation by system actors and institutional commitment to DEI can become tangible through historical context, an understanding of current challenges, and strategies implemented in our case studies, outlined below.

Utilizing Frameworks

The NASH Framework, AAC&U Inclusive Equity model, and Inclusive Excellence models can be blueprints for multistep strategies to develop scalable and sustainable DEI strategies. These frameworks and models can be tailored to individual institutions or systems as a whole and can lay out clear guideposts for college and university leaders to follow throughout the implementation of DEI initiatives. If utilized transparently, these frameworks serve as communicative tools, as well as means to measure and document institutional change.

For example, the NASH Framework provides systems and their campuses eleven categories for self-assessment and action: public commitment, leadership, data, policy, curriculum and co-curriculum, student success interventions and treatment, faculty and staff hiring, retention, promotion and rewards, professional development, and community engagement. The framework allows systems to assess which of their categories have strong practice and which have less activity. Learning from the self-assessment, utilizing cross-campus or cross-sector teams, leads to specific actions and improvements to advance systemness-inclusive excellence.

Resource Allocation

The allocation of monetary, physical, and staffing resources purposely targeted to achieve DEI goals articulated by and for the system community is necessary for sustained DEI success. These resources should be presented concurrently with structure and strategies for follow-up to ensure accountability and proper resource allocation as determined by needs of each system, department, or community.

Mandates and Incentives

System-wide and statewide mandates or incentives can be utilized to close equity gaps when coupled with resources, goals, and opportunities for customization and adaptability to circumstance. To make meaningful progress, institutions may need to focus their resources on DEI improvement with the same rigor they would seek to increase their research activity, for example. A classification or ranking structure where campus and systems seek the prestige of DEI distinction may incentivize such concerted efforts. At minimum, mandatory or incentivized DEI efforts can lead to innovative and successful initiatives that can be adapted for scale across the system.

Leadership

Effective, flexible, and knowledgeable leadership is essential for DEI initiatives to succeed within a community and at scale. Without tokenizing individuals, bringing on talent and teams with lived and professional experience who can inform the restructuring of a system with nuance and perspective provides a sustainable model for success that promotes longevity beyond the tenure of a single individual. Fostering and supporting leaders who treat higher education as a system within a society is a perspective necessary for normative change at scale.

Community Engagement

Systems must reenvision the campus community to include external stakeholders in the communities where the campuses exist. Community engagement can take many forms: listening sessions, town halls, events, open door policies, and more. These changes in engagement for both students and the larger community grants opportunity for historically overlooked and excluded perspectives to provide innovative ideas to individual and systems problems.

Communication and Transparency

Honest and transparent communication increases accessibility and humility. Communication and transparency regarding challenges and failures, coupled with purposeful community engagement, can lead to effective cross-system communication via data-sharing agreements and facilitate solution-building from the individual to system level.

Strategic Planning and Reconceptualization

Instead of retrofitting surface level initiatives, often arising from crisis situations rooted in historic problems within higher education systems, utilize strategic planning to reconceptualize a system that promotes efficacy, sustainability, and scalability. For DEI initiatives to thrive, they should develop a supportive ecosystem around the most marginalized student, the most marginalized community, and continue to build each level. Developing a system that advocates and addresses the concerns of the most disenfranchised ultimately creates a fluid and adaptable system that addresses the needs of all, throughout potential changes or crises.

Dismantling Systems of Injustice

Active dismantling of archaic, marginalizing systems of injustice can seem too monumental. But systems are powerful in aggregate and have far more reach and influence than their current perceived capacity. Mandates, trainings, policies, incentives, and utilizing the transformative and liberatory power of education itself can all work toward reducing equity gaps. Everyday changes, implemented at a wide scale, can amount to long-term change.

Student Focus

All initiatives should, at their core, remain student focused. Polling and working with the student community on current challenges fosters community and trust, building a strong student and alumni network that the larger system can continue to utilize post-matriculation. In addition, rooting change in the overarching interests of students can serve as a common goal across disparate parts of an organization or system.

Advocacy and State Legislation

The power of a system in aggregate can influence and advocate for state policy changes and legislation to support the student community at large. Systems can and should work toward protecting the rights and advancing the interests of students, especially in a climate of social regression.

Adapting for Sustainability

Systems of higher education are faced with a dichotomous tension in which they must serve a majority "minority" student population with diverse needs and objectives at the same time they are restricted or banned via state legislation from utilizing funds to directly and transparently address the needs of the evolving student body. How, then, do systems adapt? Restructuring DEI plans and initiatives for sustainability and longevity are key. Building a community of inclusive practitioners shares the weight of the workload across the system. Adapting DEI efforts to withstand legal challenges may contribute to the construction of new methods to support marginalized students. Systems should support these innovative practices and seek to replicate those that are successful. Leveraging systems to disseminate best practices—especially those that provide a road map for DEI improvement within antagonistic political climates—will reinforce the necessity of continued DEI efforts and create a systems-facilitated environment of mutual aid.

Conclusions

Systems cannot change using surface-level initiatives that lack adequate support or resources; systems also cannot be torn down and rebuilt hastily without intention, care, and understanding of how systemic problems were established and cemented. Normative change is a transformative goal that can be achieved through smaller actions implemented at large scale. Utilizing the power of systems, we can look to examples of successful change and change agents beyond the ivory tower, among practitioners doing work in real time to implement smaller, transformative changes. The DEI work leading us into the future will be scaled, sustainable adaptations of current interventions that actively dismantle inequities and contribute to a reconceptualization of the power of systems to develop a fundamentally more equitable society.

References

American Council on Education. (2018). *Speaking Truth and Acting with Integrity: Confronting Challenges of Campus Racial Climate*. Washington, DC: American Council on Education.

American Council on Education. (2020). *Leading after a Racial Crisis: Weaving a Campus Tapestry of Diversity and Inclusion*. Washington, DC: American Council on Education.

American Psychological Association. (2021). *Equity, Diversity and Inclusion Framework*. Washington, DC: American Psychological Association. https://www.apa.org/about/apa/equity-diversity-inclusion/framework.pdf.

California Community Colleges Chancellor's Office. (2020). *Vision for Success, Diversity, Equity and Inclusion Taskforce*. Sacramento: California Community Colleges Chancellor's Office. https://www.cccco.edu/-/media/CCCCO-Website/Reports/CCCCO_DEI_Report.pdf.

California Community Colleges Chancellor's Office. (2022). "Student Enrollment and Demographics." Accessed November 10, 2022, https://www.cccco.edu/About-Us/Chancellors-Office/Divisions/Digital-Innovation-and-Infrastructure/research-data-analytics/data-snapshot/student-demographics.

Carlton, G. (2022). "The History of Public Universities in the U.S." BestColleges. November 10, 2022, https://www.bestcolleges.com/blog/public-universities-history/.

Fourtané, S. (2021). "Black Women in Higher Education: Navigating Cultural Adversity throughout the Centuries." Fierce Education. April 23, 2021, https://www.fierceeducation.com/administration/black-women-higher-education-navigating-cultural-adversity-throughout-centuries.

HBCU First. (2022). "A History of Historically Black Colleges and Universities." Accessed November 10, 2022, https://hbcufirst.com/resources/hbcu-history-timeline.

Martin, R., N. Zimpher, J. Lane, and J. Johnsen. (2022). "Leveraging the Power of Systemness to Improve the Success of Students and Society." *Change: The Magazine of Higher Learning* 54(4), 38–44, doi:10.1080/00091383.2022.2078154.

National Archives. (2022). "Morrill Act (1862)." Accessed November 10, 2022, https://www.archives.gov/milestone-documents/morrill-act.

Vetro, V. (2021). "College during a Pandemic: A Qualitative Exploration of Community College First-Generation Students' Mattering and Persistence Experiences." In *Journal of Higher Education Management* 36(1), 93–103.

Williams, R., S. M. Gavazzi, M. E. Roberts, B. W. Snyder, J. N. Low, C. Hoy, M. L. Chaatsmith, and M. Charles. (2022). "'Let Us Tell the Story of Our Land and

Place': Tribal Leaders on the Seizure and Sale of Territories Benefiting Land-Grant Universities." *Tribal College Journal of American Indian* 33(4), https://tribalcollegejournal.org/let-us-tell-the-story-of-our-land-and-place-tribal-leaders-on-the-seizure-and-sale-of-territories-benefiting-land-grant-universities/.

13 | The Emergence of Intelligence Machines and Cyberspace

Framing the Challenge to University Systems and Suggesting a Three-Level Strategy of Resilience

MARK HAGEROTT

Introduction

IT IS IMPOSSIBLE to predict the future with any certainty, but evidence is accumulating that our economy, society, and higher education are moving from a period of relative equilibrium into a period of disequilibria. In response, there is a growing literature on reforming the university.[1] But there seems to be a relative lack of work on the future of state university systems, and therefore this volume fills an important need for policymakers, governing boards, scholars, and systems heads like myself. So, how to approach the problem of thinking about and then planning and preparing for this future of disruption? This paper builds on the supposition that the emergence of artificial intelligence (AI) affecting human, machine, and data systems is the underlying driver of disruption.[2] As disruptive forces gather momentum, the effects will be felt on a grand scale, at the macrolevel, with serious implications for the microlevel. Current and future waves of technological disruption will shake and then reshape education, our society, economy, and government. State university systems will be challenged to thrive, or in some cases even to survive, the disruption. But state systems have yet another calling: across history, the academy has been a tool for society to navigate and even thrive through disruptive change, and we are being called upon to do so again, this time during the transition to a digitized, artificially intelligent world.

This chapter will approach the future with humility. It does not attempt to make detailed predictions and recommendations, but it does suggest that system leaders adopt organizational resilience as one strategy to navigate change. And exactly *because we cannot predict* future disruptions with certainty, institutions will fare better if they create and preserve resilience at three levels: (1) day-to-day *reliability*, (2) periodic *adaptability*, and (3) less frequent but essential capacity for *transformability*. Resilience efforts will be better aligned to the future by understanding that digitization is creating a world of intersecting intelligent actors, represented as realms of *human*, *robotic*, and *cyberspace of software and data*. Leaders must build resilience in the human, machine, and the cyberspace of software data while reliably meeting the day-to-day needs of students. No small challenge.

But there is a complicating factor on the road to a digitizing future: cyber-insecurity. As we discuss later in this chapter, the problems posed by cyber may now be exceeding the capabilities of individual campuses. State university systems will play a key role helping those campuses as well as our states and larger society navigate this digital security challenge. But for some systems and states, the scale of the problem, and the needed speed of response to digitization in general and cybersecurity in particular, may overwhelm state budgets and human capital resources, requiring a larger effort from state systems. This chapter will conclude with a sketch of a possible new such program.

As system leaders prepare to face and hopefully thrive through the digital challenges ahead, how might we frame changes to our environment, the new realms of activity? Historical perspective helps inform this framework.

A Framework for Action: Three Intersecting Realms of Action and Being

The most powerful force of change, and a threat to the well-being of much of human-centric society if left unmanaged, is the uncontrolled, accelerating invention, adoption, and concentration of power associated with digital technology. A multitude of increasingly intelligent digital inventions, robotic and in cyberspace, relentlessly pile one upon another, exerting social-economic change on a grand scale, at the *macrolevel* of how work and social interaction are carried out. Digital technology is changing the very structure of life and society and economy.

To be sure, changing technologies have affected society and economy in the past. At the small scale, or *microlevel*, a person is compelled many times in their lifetime to adapt to one technology or another. But something began to change at the socio-economy's *macrolevel* as technology began to digitize. Our socio-economy has been inundated with waves of digital innovation. Typed letters were replaced by faxes and then email, and now intelligent email assistants draft letters. Factories and warehouses with intelligent robots hold few if any human workers and therefore remain dark while the machines work. Offices were once full of humans thinking and working with desktop computers and spreadsheets, but now these data are analyzed and stored in "the cloud" by increasingly intelligent "self-learning" algorithms and massive data centers. And the humans who are left increasingly work from home. Friends used to be people in our physical neighborhoods and schools, but now they can be anywhere. They may not even be human at all, as in the case of Amazon's Alexa.

With the explosion of advanced digital technology, trillions of chips, sensors, computers, autonomous machines, and what may be a Turing-like breakthrough in AI, we are witnessing *macro* change, the emergence of new artificial worlds. Reduced to its simplest, a planet that was dominated by a realm of human-centric activity is now being joined by other realms of digital activity and being. The socio-economic-military activity emerging between artificial actors in these two realms *can now occur with little or no direct human control*. The emergences of the Robotic and Cyberspace Realms are moreover nearly simultaneous and will challenge the privileged place of human-centric systems that has defined history to this point.[3] Figure 13.1 shows a depiction of the three realms. The three realms overlap to compose a Venn diagram of the robotic, the cyber, and the human.

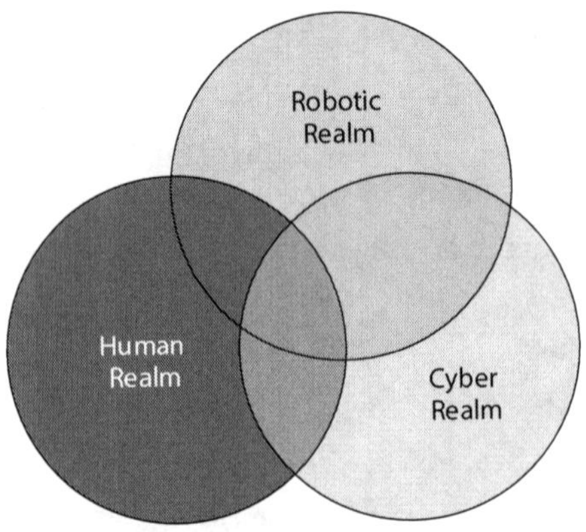

Figure 13.1 Framing the impact of AI-powered robotic and cyber technologies: a world of three realms emerges to challenge higher education. The emergence of the robotic and cyber-realms, powered by AI, will require increased investments in state educational systems to achieve speed and scale of response.

The Emergence of Advanced Robotics and Cyberspace: Early Evidence of Risk to Human Well-Being

Society is now experiencing the emerging nexus of artificial intelligence, in digital machines, and the cloud of data (or cyberspace). But all is not well where cyberspace and digital machines intersect at the level of regions, cities, and household economies. As the digital world grows, financial benefits accrue to only a small portion of the population, with large swaths of the country left behind or left insecure.

Where cyberspace and digital machines intersect with regions, cities, and households outside the tech hubs, signs of distress are mounting. Darkening clouds of hacking and privacy abuses, misinformation and disinformation, and lack of equal access cast a shadow of social, employment, and political insecurity. The workers and wages outside of the tech hubs and digital professions are coming under increased pressure, and there is no certainty that an advanced digital economy can absorb the human workforce, a possibility considered by Brynjolfsson and McAfee in The *Race against the Machine*.[4]

Also alarming is a rapid increase in child depression and suicide, a major shift that scientists associate with the widespread penetration of society by highly advanced communication and computational devices—

smartphones—and the growth of social media sites.[5] A multitude of digital creators and the insiders of the companies creating these products have argued that users are not actually customers, but themselves are the product.[6]

Growing concern about accelerating artificial intelligence and implications for higher education systems is highlighted by the emergence of ChatGPT, produced by the OpenAI consortium, late in 2022. Within a few short weeks, this highly capable chatbot accumulated over 100 million users and passed various standards of human expertise, to include standardized test sections for college applications and sections of MBA exams. Multiple companies and organizations began to adopt the technology to increase productivity. The speed at which this form of AI experienced a growing user base—and a similar concomitant explosion in related questions, from the potential for plagiaristic abuses to effects on student mental health—prompted President Biden to convene consultative bodies and entire nations in the European Union to institute a pause of AI research. More than 1,000 scientists, engineers, and business leaders—including a cofounder of OpenAI, Elon Musk, and a leading AI researcher, Stuart Russel—signed an open letter supporting a six-month pause.

Lastly, human-centric cultural values are being affected by the emergence of these two realms of intelligent machines. And if we doubt the significance of the social issues surrounding the emergence of advanced technological systems guided by ever more capable artificially intelligent software, consider that the Biden administration recently called for a new Digital Bill of Rights for AI.[7] All of these disruptive developments are further support of the recommendations in this chapter, that system leaders must meet the AI-digital challenge by maintaining campus day-to-day reliability, periodic adaptability, and occasional transformability.

Who Can Help Society Transition? State University Systems Will Be Leaders

The likelihood that the technical elites in Silicon Valley can tackle a challenge of such a magnitude is doubtful, in part owing to a lack of trust from the public. Amazon was driven out of New York City; Facebook paid a $5 billion fine for privacy violations, and many argue that it and other social media companies should be more strictly regulated. All this news springs from an eroding fabric of public trust and vanishing opportunity in the fast-emerging digital system enveloping the nation's social, technical, and economic sectors.

But the punitive and reactive policies increasingly coming out of political circles (e.g., to break up Facebook) are also evidence of a shortage of well-aimed, future-oriented ideas to help people build a better future for themselves. Who can help navigate the road ahead? Educational institutions will be at the center of such efforts. State systems appear especially well positioned to play a central role.

State systems are poised to act, but how? The exact contours of the emergence of cyberspace and intelligent robotics will remain unknown for decades. Yet university systems and the states will have to successfully navigate their emergence and flourish in them when they mature. An approach that includes a strategy of creating and maintaining organization resilience across the realms of the human, machine, and cyberspace software systems is essential. But first, what do we mean by resilience?

What Is Resilience?

There are multiple definitions of resilience and a growing body of literature about it.[8] But for purposes of this chapter, we focus on the organizational level of the campus and system and break resilience into three levels: day-to-day *reliability*, periodic *adaptability*, and less frequent but no less important, the ability of an organization to achieve bursts of *transformability*.

Level 1: Day-to-day *reliability* to care for and preserve the human, machine, and data systems against the effects of thermodynamic and social entropy. It means reliably passing knowledge to and preparing the next generation of students, machine systems, and algorithms with the data and knowledge created by previous generations. Examples include data servers that are reliable, distributed, and possibly colocated with power generation; bandwidth that is adequate and broadly distributed; educational software that reliably interacts with myriad student devices anywhere on campus; power supplies that are stable and have built in redundancy; students, staff, and faculty that are protected from infection and disease; and machines that remain "healthy" in the face of computer viruses.

Level 2: Periodic *adaptability* in face of external change. This component of resilience involves adapting human, machine, and data systems to include their organization, processes, and composition to changes in the external environment. Examples include campus or system budgets that are able to fund the construction of new buildings to adapt to increased student enrollment; systems that demonstrate adaptation to a shock to the system such as COVID, which required large increased bandwidth and computing capacity for distance learning and adaptive human systems such as housing density and hygiene requirements where in-person presence was essential.

Level 3: *Transformability* when confronted by the emergence of new environments or paradigmatic change in other exogenous factors. Transformability could involve the human, machine, or data elements of a university system, or any combination of the three. Transformability also includes the ability to overcome organizational barriers to create new processes, organization types, new fields of knowledge, or expand experimental programs to a qualitatively different scale. Examples are creation of new fields of knowledge, new professions, and new types of institutions. We can see these changes across history in the case of emergent organizations of state systems, land-grant universities, community colleges, and entirely online universities. These innovations were transformative in that no amount of day-to-day work or incremental adaptation at America's venerable Ivy League colleges would have met the needs now met by these new entities.

How might the framework we derive help locate areas of effort and intervention to ensure day-to-day reliability, adaptability within the capacity of existing systems, and major transformability? Some suggestions follow.

Resilience as a Strategy to Navigate Emerging Intelligent Machines and Cyberspace

Many leaders no doubt consider the resilience of their enterprise, but they may circumscribe the concept too narrowly. As the head of a state higher education system of 11 campuses, I frequently see the concept confined to the sustainment and restoration of day-to-day operations. But resilience extends well beyond these narrow constructs. Campus leaders must value and support all three levels of resilience: daily reliability, focused adaptability, and smaller teams working on transformability. But campuses must also align much of their efforts on the new realms emerging around advanced digital technology.

Using the framework represented in figure 13.1, we can situate numerous tasks: Is the challenge we face human centric, or is it the result of an overlap of human and cyberspace issues, such as distance learning or social media bullying? Issues of this type must be approached carefully, as they are fraught with sensitive privacy and health policies, laws, and ethics. In contrast, if we identify the issue to be deeply embedded in the realm of cyberspace, situated perhaps among software programs in the cloud, far removed from issues of student welfare, then such decision-making may be less complex and relatively free of ethical concerns, and addressed more quickly.

Approaching resilience from the perspective of this framework might also help illuminate issues related to adaptability and longer-term transformability. There is consensus that AI is rapidly advancing, perhaps soon to break barriers once considered the purview of science fiction.[9] Higher education leaders may soon confront profound questions of where to apply AI at speed, and where to go slowly. In general, if AI will affect human populations, we should proceed more slowly. If the application of AI is relatively remote from human interaction, then we should continue to adopt AI at speed. Recent mishaps illustrate this point. During COVID, some applicants were denied admissions based on AI algorithms that resulted in socioeconomic and ethnic profiling.[10]

Another area with transformational implications is the nature of cyberspace, or the "metaverse." If Mark Zuckerberg is correct, as other tech leaders seem to agree, that the metaverse (or cyberspace in figure 13.1) will become a place for living, learning, and working, then what steps must we take to transform the academic experience to make such possibilities accessible to your students and faculty, including disadvantaged groups? Achieving the needed speed and scale of effective action in the lagging states, regions, and struggling groups is problematic and will require state- and system-wide coordinated action.

As robotics and AI advance, leaders will be confronted with the question of if and then how to augment or replace selective human labor forces on campus and in the university system. Leaders now confront the possibility that American workforce participation rates may not recover from the shock of COVID. If so, how might leaders transform more of their campus operations by moving them deeper into the robotic realm, resulting in more robots and fewer if any human workers in some university functions.[11]

What is becoming clear is that intelligent machines and clouds of data become more affordable if brought to scale. Therefore, as the costs associated with these two realms increase— more high-performance computing (HPC), AI, machine learning, big data storage capacities, cybersecurity—smaller campuses will be severely challenged to keep pace for the sake of their students and the campus enterprise. It may be time to pool more of these resources centrally rather than distributed at various campuses, and to place them at the university system offices to ensure equitable and cost-effective sharing and access.

Questions of cost, scale, and governance will challenge systems as they digitize, but so will another factor that is simply existential: cybersecurity. A failure to provide for adequate cybersecurity will impede resilience at all three levels of our model: day-to-day reliability, adaptability, and transformability.

Cybersecurity for the University System: Human, Machine, and Cyberspace

The quest for digital security and resilience takes on yet more urgency in the wake of the COVID pandemic, as students, faculty, and staff study and work anywhere, anytime, via digital technology. Moreover, workers and consumers both in state government and the economy in general expect to do more via digital technology.

Words struggle to convey the threats posed by cybercriminals and rogue nation-states in the recesses of the Dark Web, as they increasingly focus their efforts to threaten campuses and state systems. The problem has been with us for decades, since early digital systems emerged on a handful of university campuses in 1969, and then these systems proliferated and grew exponentially but without parallel adaptation or transformation of security architectures. The reality is simple: our data systems will never be entirely secure, but they must be resilient in the face of eventual compromise.

Worrisome trends are developing in universities and colleges, as higher education is seeing a rapid increase in the number of campuses falling victim to hacking, in the form of both criminal ransomware and purposeful exploitation by state actors. And the attacks can be devasting and disruptive. Some states saw major campuses and even medical schools and affiliated hospitals return to "paper and pencil" while experts unlocked systems that had been hacked.[12]

The threat to campuses is growing at an accelerating rate. By some measures, ransomware attacks on colleges and universities rose almost 50 percent in 2021 alone.[13] In one case, a college was forced to close in part due to a persistent and especially damaging cyberattack and ransomware lockup of key admissions databases.[14]

While nonstate, criminal organizations focus more on ransomware attacks, a second threat emanates from what are called advanced persistent threats (APTs) from nation-state actors. It is now well established that certain powerful nations are methodically targeting higher education for intellectual property for economic advantage. The losses have been extraordinary, and in some cases brought a standstill to major university research operations.[15]

So, how to approach this problem? The framework proposed in this chapter helps to organize thinking about the scope of the cyberthreat to our faculty, staff, and students; to our machines that keep the campus enterprise running; and to our essential data, from research IP to student records. Thus a strategy going forward is to be able to provide day-to-day reliability to our students and faculty while fending off and mitigating the effects of a breach, becoming more adaptive and, if need be, transformative in our approaches to digital security by scaling up and teaming with other campuses, state governments, businesses, and the federal government (more on this possible initiative below).

What can our campuses do to improve resilience in the face of inevitable cyberthreats? First is training or awareness of our students, faculty, and staff. Many breaches involve human error. Phishing, when a hacker sends out fake emails to encourage a human to click on or open the portal to the cyberattack, is the most common threat. Training will help reduce the incidence of this type of breach, yet in many university systems, such training is optional. In my view, such training should be made mandatory as a condition to access any university system or network.

A second approach is to adopt a "zero trust" mentality between humans and machines and the data cloud. This approach is becoming increasingly standard in most companies, and if our campuses are not adopting these practices, we should, at speed. To achieve this and other cybersecurity improvements will require a whole-of-system, whole-of-campus effort, including governance changes at multiple levels. While it is beyond the scope of this chapter to go into the details of many other highly recommended measures—especially two-factor authentication and end-point security—several resources are available for system leaders to consider.[16]

One important consideration is the longer-term trajectory of cyberattacks. Evidence shows that attackers are changing their focus and shifting toward relatively more vulnerable targets, diverting from strongly defended, larger enterprises and instead targeting smaller enterprises that may have weaker countermeasures and fewer resources to spend on security.[17] While it is early in this trend, smaller higher education campuses and those without the financial and technical benefits of scale provided by a system may fall into this growing vulnerability category.

Looking to the medium and long term, it is possible the cyberthreat will exceed more campuses' resources and technical staff capability and leave them unable to effectively protect their human, machine, and data realms on their own. Improving cybersecurity needs to become a "whole-of-community" endeavor, where faculty, staff, administrators, boards, legislatures, and governors support this priority. The trajectory of rising costs, complexity, and insurability appear to argue for a greater role of state university systems leading the collaborative effort among campuses.

But the challenge of cybersecurity does not end at the college quad or system office. Rather, campuses and state systems will be expected to provide more assistance to state governments, their citizenry, and businesses as they struggle to access more cyber-knowledge and upskilled cybersecurity work force. The issue has grown to such proportions that the Biden administration in July 2022 proposed a national initiative focused on cybersecurity education, training, and workforce development.[18] The cyber-workforce now numbers in the multiple millions, but the gaps are extraordinary, estimated most recently at almost 750,000 unfilled cybersecurity-related positions.

As discussed in the preceding sections, state university systems face a daunting set of challenges presented by the emergence of intelligent machine robotics and cyberspace. In addition, because these two drivers of change are digital in nature, higher education leaders will also confront an epic security challenge. While transforming and securing their campus systems will consume enormous time and resources, these state systems must also assist their respective state residents, businesses, and governments during this time of transition, just as we did in previous macro-transitions, such as from an economy based on agriculture to one based on manufacturing. It may be that this combination of challenges is too much for system leaders to navigate without both major resource investment and reallocation and a level of collaboration with the federal government that is transformative: a system of systems approach.

A Proposal to Meet the Challenge of Intelligent Machines, Cyberspace, and Security: A New Digital-Cyber Land-Grant Program

In the 1860s, President Abraham Lincoln created the land-grant university system to support the nation's agriculture and industry to develop and adapt to new science and technology. Today, the nation needs a transformed university system on a similar scale to catalyze the transition to a world of intelligent machines and software.

The timing is right, as we see a massive shift in federal government priorities, such as of the behemoth CHIPS and Science Act. This act, which may exceed $200 billion, stands as a testament of the scale of the transformation and adaptation that is required to respond to accelerating digitization. But this new program is directed and ultimately controlled by the federal government. The states and state university systems should also transform, with control remaining with the states. How? State systems require a similar resource infusion and new structure, a Digital-Cyber Land-Grant Act, where resources are controlled by each state, funded and structured to respond to digitization. Unfortunately, the federal higher education law does not even recognize systems, much less provide resources to them.

Five Key Features

This nationwide Digital-Cyber Land-Grant Act[19] would form a network of state systems using advanced technology to deliver both technical and more general education on campuses located across the country. It would move beyond the limits of existing physical plants and the existing structures of faculty hierarchy and tenure to provide a wide range of skills and competencies to students and people in the workforce nationwide.

This proposed system has the following key features.

- States that join this transformative effort would commit to supporting the best of both online and brick-and-mortar education that offered expanded technical and nontechnical curricula that help campuses, systems, and states respond to the emerging realms of intelligent machines and cyberspace.
- University systems in the new initiative should offer an accelerated approach to tenure and promotion for faculty working on cyber-issues, including those in the ethics, law, and humanities who focus on the digital transformation of our society.
- The network should offer innovative funding mechanisms that do not place further burden on hard-pressed states and students, but rather draw from the coffers of the social media giants.
- The federal government should create tax incentives for contributions to university endowments (such as tax credits vs. tax deductions) so that the coming wave of wealthy Internet philanthropists will have reason to provide support to systems covered by the Digital-Cyber Land-Grant Act.
- Incentives should be created for technology companies and leading high-tech universities to help staff and partner with the new universities' faculties and programs. Joint appointments could be offered to digital-skilled faculty from leading public universities, perhaps in partnership with leading private institutions, who would teach or conduct research at one of the systems covered by the act, which would also benefit industry.

How to Pay for a Digital-Cyber Land-Grant System?

In the 1860s, the Morrill Act, so critical to national adaptation and transformation, was funded by land grants. The new colleges used the proceeds from sales of large tracts of land to establish and build their institutions.

Today, most all the three-dimensional space of new land is accounted for, but the fourth-dimensional "land" of cyberspace is almost untapped and might grow for decades (if not perpetually). The foundation of cyberspace—the Internet, upon which the social media giants derive their wealth—was built by a US government program funded by taxpayers.

The allocation of this new cyber-land could help pay for the new system of state systems. Given the substantial negative consequences of social media on the nation's citizens, children, and democracy, levying an educational tax on social media corporations makes sense morally, not unlike the taxes levied on gambling, cigarettes, and alcohol.

In the end, the rationale of this initiative is not punitive but rather centered around a social obligation of companies to reinvest in the future of the nation. By leading this charge and helping to fund the Digital-Cyber Land-Grant Act, social media companies will also expand their workforce, increase their access to researchers and inventors, and gain more of society's—and, not to be overlooked, Congress's—goodwill.

Conclusion

The future is at the intersections of three realms: the human and the emerging realms of artificially intelligent robotics and cyberspace. All Americans should reap the benefits of these new realms, but to do so will require a reformed educational system, and state systems will be on the leading edge. Yet the contours of the future are unknown; thus system leaders should adopt as part of their strategy an emphasis on resilience. Resilience is not just day-to-day reliability, but also adaptability and periodic transformability of the system of campuses. Strategy will be threatened by rising costs associated with digitization and cyber-insecurity. State systems must also serve their respective stakeholders, the residents of their state, the business community, and government. Taken together, this is a tall order that may be beyond the resources and span of control of system leaders. It is time for a transformation of independent state systems into a "system of state systems" as part of a new Digital-Cyber Land-Grant Act that remains under the leadership of each state. With such a nationwide effort, focused on the challenges of digitization, more regions, states, and cities can access the knowledge and resources to weave a better future in the emerging digital socioeconomic system. Having such a system of state systems will allow the nation to achieve a scale of response that is more cost-effective; to expand the scope to more underserved populations and regions; and to achieve both these transformative goals at greater speed. The urgency of the challenge is hard to exaggerate. The Biden administration, Congress, state governments, Silicon Valley elites, and higher education should come together to create the digital-cyber land-grant university and college system. Just as the land-grant system transformed higher education to catalyze agricultural and industrial capacity across a growing nation in the nineteenth century, so can a digital-cyber land-grant system provide the educational foundation needed to ensure economic and democratic vitality and security for the entire nation in the twenty-first century.

Notes

1. Michael Crow and William Debars, *The Fifth Wave: The Evolution of American Higher Education* (Baltimore: Johns Hopkins University Press, 2020). See also Brian Alexander, *Academic Next: The Futures of Higher Education* (Baltimore: Johns Hopkins University Press, 2020).

2. Stuart Russel, *Machine Compatible: Artificial Intelligence and the Problem of Control* (New York: Viking, 2019); Eric Schmidt, Henry Kissinger, and Daniel Huttenlocher, *The Age of AI and Our Human Future* (New York: Little, Brown, 2021).

3. Mark Hagerott, "Covid Is Accelerating Digital Transformation: What Could Be the Downside for Humanity, and What to Do about It," *Northern Plains Ethics Journal* 8, no. 1 (Fall 2020). This framework has also been presented in multiple venues the past 15 years, to include award-winning articles on defense strategy (2006); Naval War College (2007); CNA Corporation (2007); presentations at universities in France (2011), at Yale (2013), and in Annapolis (2014); University of South Dakota (2019); the Geneva Convention CCW (2014); Pentagon (2012), navy senior leaders (2015), army senior engineers (2014), National Security Agency/US Cyber Command (2014); Naval Postgraduate School (2016); US TRANSCOM (2017); US Chambers of Commerce annual meeting (2015); TEDx (2016); and a variation of this framework published in American and European edited volumes. This framework was presented most recently at Northern Plains Ethics Institute in November 2019, on the eve of COVID pandemic, and an extended essay on this topic was published by NPEJ in late 2020. COVID adds new urgency to explain what is happening, and how to frame the emergence of intelligent machines and software.

4. Eric Brynjolfsson and Andrew McAfee, *The Race against the Machine: How the Digital Revolution Is Accelerating Innovation, Driving Productivity, and Irreversibly Transforming Employment and the Economy* (Lexington, KY: Digital Free Press, 2011).

5. Jean M. Twenge, *iGEN: Why Today's Super-Connected Kids Are Growing Up Less Rebellious, More Tolerant, Less Happy—And Completely Unprepared for Adulthood and (What This Means for the Rest of Us)* (New York: Atria Books, 2017).

6. Links to this report can be found in the show notes to *The Social Dilemma*, directed by Jeff Orlowski (Los Gatos, CA: Netflix, 2020), https://www.netflix.com/title/81254224.

7. "Join the Effort to Create a Bill of Rights for an Automated Society," White House press release, November 10, 2021, https://www.whitehouse.gov/ostp/news-updates/2021/11/10/join-the-effort-to-create-a-bill-of-rights-for-an-automated-society/.

8. Resilience theory has typically been confined engineering studies, and as a nuclear engineer, I was trained to consider resilience in most all our systems. For the larger engineering field, see David D. Woods, "Four Concepts for Resilience and the Implications for the Future of Resilience Engineering," *Reliability and Engineering and System Safety* 141 (2015). In academia, however, resilience has more commonly been associated with the learner/student level, as in what makes a resilient student. For a recent discussion of this type of resilience, see "What Are We Learning about Academic Resilience?," Liberal Education, July 2, 2020, https://www.aacu.org/liberaleducation/articles/what-are-we-learning-about-academic-resilience. In the past couple years, questions of resilience have begun to be applied to studies of the university. See Romulo Pinheiro and Mitchell Young, "The University as an Adaptive Resilient Organization: A Complex Systems Perspective," in *Theory and Method in Higher Education Research*, vol. 3, edited by Jeroen Huisman and Malcolm Tight (Bingley, UK: Emerald Publishing Group, 2017). Also of value are discussions of systems control and societal evolution, such as in James Beniger, *The Control Revolution: Technological and Economic Origins of the Information Society* (Cambridge, MA: Harvard University Press, 1986), chap. 3.

9. Russel, *Machine Compatible*; Schmidt et al., *The Age of AI*.

10. Tom Simonite, "Meet the Secret Algorithm That's Keeping Students Out of College," *Wired*, July 10, 2020, https://www.wired.com/story/algorithm-set-students-grades-altered-futures/.

11. Michael Joseph, "Rise of the (Fast Food) Robots: How labor Shortages Are Accelerating Automation," *Fortune*, November 29, 2021, https://fortune.com/2021/11/29/fast-food-robots-labor-shortage-automation-pandemic/.

12. Sarah Coble, "Nebraska Medicine Data Breach Settlement Approved," *Info Security Magazine*, June 9, 2021, https://www.infosecurity-magazine.com/news/nebraska-medicine-data-breach/#:~:text=Omaha%2Dbased%20Nebraska%20Medicine%20suffered,the%20postponement%20of%20patient%20appointments.

13. "The State of Ransomware in Education" (white paper, Sophos, Ottawa, July 2022), https://assets.sophos.com/X24WTUEQ/at/pgvqxjrfq4kf7njrncc7b9jp/sophos-state-of-ransomware-education-2022-wp.pdf.

14. Dan Lohrman, "College Closing Another Sad Milestone for Ransomware Impact," Government Technology, May 15, 2022, https://www.govtech.com/blogs/lohrmann-on-cybersecurity/college-closing-another-sad-milestone-for-ransomware-impact.

15. Felicia Schwartz, "Penn State's Engineering School Computers Hacked: One Group of Hackers Apparently Based in China," *Wall Street Journal*, May 16, 2015, https://www.wsj.com/articles/penn-states-engineering-school-computers-hacked-1431804110.

16. *Cyber Risk Oversight for Governing Boards* (Washington DC: Association of Governing Boards and Internet Security Agency, 2021); see also online resources at CISA, the Cybersecurity and Infrastructure Security Agency, accessed November 13, 2023, https://www.cisa.gov/cyber-incident-response.

17. Howard Kass, "Why Ransomware Hacks Prefer Small Businesses Rather Than Rich Enterprises," MSSP Alert, April 22, 2022, https://www.msspalert.com/cybersecurity-research/why-ransomware-attacks-prefer-small-business-targets-rather-than-rich-enterprises/.

18. "Fact Sheet: National Cyber Workforce and Education Summit," The White House, July 21, 2022, https://www.whitehouse.gov/briefing-room/statements-releases/2022/07/21/fact-sheet-national-cyber-workforce-and-education-summit/.

19. Mark Hagerott, "Time for a Digital-Cyber Land Grant System," *Issues in Science and Technology* (Winter 2020): https://issues.org/time-for-a-digital-cyber-land-grant-system/; idem, "Silicon Valley Must Help Rural America: Here's How," *Chronicle of Higher Education*, September 23, 2018, https://www.chronicle.com/article/silicon-valley-must-help-rural-america-heres-how/.

Part III

LEADING THE FUTURE

14 |

Shared Governance in University Systems

GEORGE BLUMENTHAL

Introduction

IN THE UNITED STATES, almost all colleges and universities have some form of academic senate or council to provide a meaningful role for faculty participation in the governance of the institution. Indeed, based on a recent survey by the American Association of University Professors, faculty governance has gained in importance over the past half century.[1]

The situation is quite different at the university system level, however. Today, the vast majority of university systems—present in 44 of the nation's 50 states—do not have a faculty-driven governance component at the system-wide level. This chapter will make the case that a system-wide faculty senate provides significant benefits through its input to both academic leaders and boards of trustees or regents. Some might argue that the last thing a system needs is another major outlet for faculty voices, but in most cases, the potential benefits of such a system far outweigh the risks. This is especially true for university systems, which are expected to lead their institutions in new ways and to create value that is greater than the sum of their parts.

Both the role and the benefits associated with a system-wide academic senate may depend strongly on the type of university system in which it resides. Homogeneous university systems are those in which the individual campuses have similar missions and serve similar student bodies. An example might be the 23 campuses of the California State University system. Some homogeneous systems consist of research universities only, some are made up of community colleges, and some may be teaching colleges. A heterogeneous system is one in which its component campuses serve different roles. For example, the University of Wisconsin system and the State University of New York include research universities, state colleges, and community colleges. Some systems could be a hybrid of the two types. For example, the University of California consists of nine full-service research universities, a free-standing law school, and one health sciences campus with a strong research portfolio. For the discussion here, such hybrid systems can be thought of as homogeneous.

Board governance can also be a distinguishing feature of university systems. Some systems are overseen by a single governing board. In other systems, each campus may have its own governing board, although there may also be a global governing board as well, with certain responsibilities resting at the system board level and others at the campus boards. An example of this would be the California Community College (CCC) system , where each campus (or district) has an elected board of trustees, but there is also a system-wide California Board of Governors.[2] Another would be the State University System of Florida, with its boards of trustees for each institution and a board of governors over the entire system.

In the next section, I review the role of academic senates on individual university campuses. Following that, I provide a brief snapshot of currently existing system-wide academic senates and then discuss the roles, advantages, and challenges for system-wide shared governance for university systems of the future.

Role of the Academic Senate at Colleges and Universities

At individual college and university campuses, the existence and authority of the academic senate can derive from a number of sources. In some cases, the president establishes the academic senate and delegates authority to it. On other campuses, the board of trustees, or even the legislature, in the case of public universities, establishes the academic senate.

On most campuses, shared governance can manifest in a variety of structural forms. At the campus level, some academic senates operate through an elected representative assembly, some do their work through an executive committee, and some legislate in a town hall format with all faculty invited to participate. But whichever structure an academic senate adopts, the bulk of the work of the senate usually takes place within the senate's committee structure. The senate's legislative body usually appoints or elects senate committees, and each senate committee normally deals with a certain class of issues under the senate's purview.[3]

The delegated authority of a campus academic senate typically divides into two broad categories. One such category is the set of *academic* issues over which the senate has decision-making authority. The second category concerns university issues that lie within the purview of the campus administration (or trustees/regents), but the senate has the authority to provide consultation and input on these issues before a decision is made. Among US universities, there is considerable variation in what issues the senate may even consider as well as how those issues divide between these two categories. The discussion below considers an inclusive but not necessarily exhaustive list of such topics.

When a campus academic senate has primary authority over a set of issues, those issues are invariably and obviously academic in nature. The faculty represent the collective wisdom on academic issues and on the quality of academic programs, so the academic senate, as an expression of the faculty voice, should have authority over the quality of those programs.

An example of such delegated authority involves the courses and curricula offered by a university. Typically, the faculty in a department or school will determine the courses and curriculum to be offered by that unit based on the norms of their discipline. But the campus academic senate would normally review and approve such courses as a way of maintaining standards of quality and pedagogy across the campus. But the campus administration also has a key role here. It is the administration that funds the courses and curriculum by providing the faculty and space in which to offer the courses. This is an excellent example of shared governance—where the faculty senate determines the courses and course content, and the administration determines whether there are resources available to offer those courses and curricula. In this example, both the administration and the senate have a responsibility to assess whether there will be demand for new courses and curricula.

A campus academic senate may also have authority over grading policy and degree requirements. For grades, it is natural that there should be one single standard used throughout the campus. Because grading is fundamentally an academic activity, the campus senate often is the group that determines grading policy. Similarly, graduation degree requirements, though suggested by departments, often lie within the purview of the senate. This can be the case at the baccalaureate or the graduate level. Such senate oversight again ensures there is uniformity across the campus.

On some campuses, the academic senate also has the authority to set the academic criteria for the admission of new students. Even in such cases, the process of admitting and enrolling new students remains a purely administrative function.

There are several areas where the campus academic senate plays an important *advisory* function but has no direct authority. These areas include campus policies, academic personnel issues, and the campus budget. This right of the senate to be consulted may derive from the policy of the board of trustees/regents, or it may come from an administrative policy.

Faculty hiring and promotion is a clear example of where informed faculty input on the quality of a candidate must be a crucial aspect of the decision-making process, even though there is no question that the final decision rests somewhere within the administration or in the governing board. Many academic senates also have academic personnel committees that provide direct advice to the decision-maker on the quality of an academic personnel case. Such campus committees provide a check against unfairness at the departmental level, and they also work to apply campus standards uniformly across the campus. It is a measure of the academic health of a campus when the academic personnel decisions are rarely in conflict with the recommendations of the senate committee on academic personnel.

On questions of faculty discipline and termination, the academic senate has a key advisory role to play both in setting the campus policies and in the adjudication of individual cases. When there is a question of whether a faculty member should be disciplined or terminated, the normative standard, as defined by the American Association of University Professors, calls for that faculty member being afforded a hearing before a committee of their peers. Providing such a committee is usually within the purview of the academic senate, and there is a presumption that their recommendation plays a key role in the final decision of the administration.[4]

Another area where the academic senate may have a right to be consulted concerns the university's budget plan. There is no question that all budgetary authority rests with the administration, but the faculty on a campus have a legitimate interest in how budgetary allocations will affect the academic activities on campus. Meaningful consultation with the senate means that budgetary information and proposed plans be floated with the senate before decisions are made, thereby affording the appropriate senate body enough time to provide thoughtful feedback and input. This may delay final decisions, but the value added and buy-in among faculty from the consultation should make the process worthwhile. This is especially true during times of significant budget augmentations or reductions.

Academic freedom is central to the operation of the academic senate. Participants in senate debate must be guaranteed that the expression of their views will not undercut their own academic positions.

Consequently, the senate must play a key role in determining the academic freedom policies within a campus. Note that there is surprising variation in academic freedom policies within US universities at the present time. Moreover, the academic senate can play an essential role in investigating allegations that academic freedom has been violated. It is also the case that faculty grievants who allege violation of their academic freedom often have a right to an evidentiary hearing before a panel convened by the senate. The American Association of University Professors regards the right to such a hearing as essential to any meaningful academic freedom policy.

Finally, any discussion of campus academic senates should include a discussion of how the academic senate coexists with faculty collective bargaining on a campus. First of all, on some campuses, the faculty are not unionized. The academic senate on such campuses may include a committee dealing with faculty welfare issues, such as salary and benefits, but such a senate committee would serve only to inform the faculty and to provide advice and feedback to the administration. When there is collective bargaining of faculty, there can be two groups representing the faculty on the campus: the academic senate and the faculty union. In that case, it is crucial to clearly delineate the authority of the senate and the union. Typically, the union will bargain over salary, benefits, and other terms and conditions of employment, while the senate will deal with academic issues and provide consultation on budget and personnel issues. But the boundary between the two can become murky, and it is essential to identify which issues are senate issues and which lie within the purview of collective bargaining. Otherwise, the effectiveness and credibility of the senate as a key factor in academic quality will be undermined.

Current Snapshot of University System-Wide Academic Senates

The previous section included a discussion of the role of the academic senate within an individual campus. In the United States, most states have one or more university systems, which are collections of campuses acting under a single authority. Such systems may be homogeneous, where all campuses share a similar mission, or they may be heterogeneous, where, for example, some campuses may be research universities and others might be community colleges. Since all these systems have some form of administrative or board governance at the system level, it is worthwhile to examine the role of faculty governance at the system-wide level.

In a forthcoming research study, I examined 94 public higher education systems around the United States, looking for evidence of a system-wide academic senate. This list includes both university systems and community college systems. Of those 94 systems, only 13 (or 14 percent) demonstrated clear evidence of system-wide faculty governance. So, the immediate conclusion is that system-wide senates are by far the exception rather than the rule among university systems. Interestingly, of the 13 examples that exist, there are several that operate within heterogeneous university systems even though most are homogeneous systems. Seven of the system-wide senates are located in three states having more than one such system with a senate (California, Colorado, and New York). In most cases, the system-wide body is designated as an academic senate, though in a couple of cases, it is referred to as an academic council. In some cases, the system-wide senate operates through a representative assembly, although there are also some who are governed by a council of the chairs of the campus senates.

While there are some interesting and significant differences among these various academic senates, these differences will not be explored here. The key issue in this chapter is understanding the benefits and disadvantages of a system-wide senate. Therefore the remainder of this section will describe key attributes of the University of California (UC) system academic senate.[5] It turns out that the UC senate, with its long history, has a well-developed structure and a purview that is perhaps the strongest among all system-wide senates. Consequently, understanding the structure and purview of the UC system senate establishes a possible ceiling of what is possible within any university system.

The University of California academic senate is established by the Standing Orders of the UC Board of Regents. Those orders delegate to the senate certain decisions involving the academic activities of the university, and they assert the right of the senate to be consulted on budgetary and personnel decisions. This codification of the role of the academic senate occurred during a tumultuous period in the university's history in the aftermath of the First World War.[6]

The legislative body of the senate is the Academic Assembly, which consists of 60 members allocated roughly in proportion to the size of the faculty on each campus. The committees of the system-wide senate are all committees of the assembly. One such group is the Academic Council, which serves as the executive committee of the assembly and consists of the 10 chairs of the campus divisions as well as the chairs of several key senate committees. Importantly, the University of California has only one academic senate. The senate bodies that operate on each of the campuses, called divisions of the academic senate, all derive their authority from the system-wide senate. They deal with issues that the campus divisions have the authority to decide, subject to the authority of the system-wide senate bylaws and regulations. For example, campus divisions approve grading policy and major requirements for the campus.

One of the most important responsibilities of the UC system senate is to review and approve proposals from the campuses that establish new graduate and professional programs and schools. When a campus submits a proposal to establish a new graduate program, that proposal is vetted by a committee of the academic senate. That review is quite rigorous and includes sending the proposal to reviewers from the same discipline outside of UC to assess the quality of the proposed program. The senate must also assess the demand for such a program, whether there is an inappropriate duplication of effort with programs on other campuses, and whether there are adequate resources being allocated to ensure success of the program. No program can be established without the approval of the UC senate.

At UC, undergraduate degrees and programs are not reviewed for approval by the system-wide senate, but rather they are reviewed and approved by the campus divisions of the senate. Nonetheless, the system-wide senate does establish certain regulations and norms for undergraduate programs with which the individual campuses must conform. For example, some aspects of the UC grading policy are established at the system-wide level by the senate. Similarly, each campus senate has established its own unique general education requirements for undergraduate degrees, but the system-wide senate has set certain system-wide general education requirements for transfer students from community colleges. When they first enroll, community college students rarely know which UC campus they will be transferring to, so it makes sense to have one set of requirements for the whole system.

Another major academic area where the system-wide senate has significant authority concerns admissions policy and requirements for applicants to the University of California. Subject to regental approval, the senate establishes the criteria for admissions or transfer to any campus within UC. This is one of the most visible functions of the academic senate from the public's perspective. For example, it was the academic senate that established the set of high school courses that must be passed to qualify for admission to a UC campus[7] (and to any California State University campus as well).

Even the editorial board of UC Press is in fact a UC system-wide senate committee. This board determines which books may be published by the press and which academic areas are appropriate for the press to specialize in.

At the University of California, the president consults with the system-wide senate on the budget as well as on a wide range of system-wide policies. There is no collective bargaining on salary or benefits for UC professors because these issues are handled at the system-wide level, where there is no union certified to represent the faculty. Consequently, the senate's Faculty Welfare Committee, which is advisory in nature, plays an important role in determining UC faculty compensation. This group assesses salary and benefits proposals with the goal of maintaining competitiveness for the university. Several years ago, when UC was preparing to adopt a different pension benefit plan, the system-wide senate proposed an alternative plan, one that the president and the system ultimately adopted. The Faculty Welfare Committee, through a subcommittee composed of experts on health care, works closely with the university administration to develop and negotiate with insurers the modified health insurance plans that are offered each year to all employees. This partnership has long been recognized as highly beneficial throughout the university.

With a goal of maintaining a uniformly high-quality faculty, the UC system has an extensive list of academic personnel policies that are owned by the administration. Campuses do have the right to establish their own academic personnel policies, but only to the extent that they are consistent with system-wide policies. All changes to the system-wide personnel policy are carefully vetted with the system-wide senate, and the senate often proposes changes to those policies. For example, one of the most important system-wide policies at UC is the Faculty Code of Conduct, coupled with the procedures to be used in possible discipline or termination of faculty members. The system-wide senate's agreement to any changes in these policies is crucial both because the senate itself controls the process for senate committee hearings regarding discipline and because faculty buy-in to changes in the Code of Conduct would be essential for its success. Another example of a key academic policy is the university's academic freedom policy. UC has made several changes to that policy over the past 20 years, sometimes at the behest of the senate, but all changes have been strongly supported by the system-wide senate.

The influence of the UC academic senate extends as well to the Board of Regents of the university, where both the chair and vice chair of the senate sit ex officio as (nonvoting) representatives to the regents. This gives them the right to attend and speak at all sessions of the regents, including regents-only sessions. It also ensures that the voice of the academic senate is a part of all discussions at the regents' meetings. Unlike boards that include one or more faculty regents, who represent their own views, the UC faculty representatives to the regents are explicitly tasked with representing the views expressed by the senate.

Finally, California is unique among the states in having three postsecondary systems with distinctly different missions—UC, California State University, and California Community Colleges—all of which have system-wide academic senates. As a result, these three senates have formed a council called the Intersegmental Council of the Academic Senates (ICAS), which deals with issues such as student transfer from community colleges to four-year institutions. This group also collaboratively lobbies the state legislature on a range of issues, including higher education funding.

Why Establish a System-Wide Academic Senate?

This section explores some of the advantages, disadvantages, and challenges of establishing and maintaining a system-wide academic senate within university systems. For a system without a system-wide senate, starting one from scratch is not necessarily simple. To the extent that a system-wide senate represents an umbrella organization with authority over the campus senates, this requires the ceding of some authority from the individual campus senates, or it requires the withdrawal of the original delegation to the campus senates by the Board of Regents with subsequent redelegation to the system-wide senate, which is politically difficult to achieve. A simple first step could entail forming an academic council consisting of the chairs of the individual campus senates. Such a council could share best practices and coordinate the policies on the various campuses. Eventually, such a council could evolve into a more formal structure as it addresses system-wide issues such as transfer, coming closer to resembling the University of California senate described above. However it may occur, it is demonstrably possible to establish a system-wide senate where there was none before.

One of the major advantages of a system-wide senate is its ability to ensure quality and coordination of the academic programs across the system. This is an appropriate role for faculty. Such academic oversight can take many forms. For example, the senate may set up a system-wide grading policy or a policy on courses so that courses and the grading system on all campuses conform to a single standard. This might be especially useful in heterogeneous systems when considering transfer students and whether their courses should transfer with full credit and meet prerequisite requirements. Another academic issue revolves around the admissions policies within the university system. Some admissions issues may be best resolved for all campuses rather than campus by campus. For example, it might be wise for all campuses in a system to have a single policy on whether to require the SAT/ACT exam for admission to the university. These are areas where the faculty, collectively, should have a voice.

Another academic area where a system-wide senate can play an essential role is in the approval or review of degree programs. This would be especially true of degree programs that span multiple campuses within the system. The University of California system approval process for all new graduate and professional degrees was mentioned above. It is certainly true that individual campuses have the ability to review their own degree programs and proposals for new degrees. But despite the extra step that it inserts into the approval process, there are several advantages to system-wide senate review of degree proposals. The system-wide senate develops a higher level of expertise in evaluating such proposals than would be found on a campus, including successfully soliciting outside reviewers. It can also assess the demand for such degrees and do this in a way that is not subject to the pressures of their peers on the campus. The expectation is that system-wide review makes these degree programs better and provides credibility regarding their academic quality.

In addition to degree programs, there may be multicampus research centers within a system. For such centers, it seems highly appropriate that a system-wide senate have a role in evaluating and reviewing such centers. The same is true for research grant proposals offered by the system as a whole.

Another area where a system-wide senate can be of immense value is in facilitating intercampus faculty collaboration as a way of maximizing academic innovation. Such collaboration can be in research or teaching. In either case, the senate can help create programs with a critical mass of faculty and create economies of scale from smaller programs located on individual campuses. Some research and graduate programs might especially benefit from this arrangement, and it would allow virtual programs to draw upon faculty across the system. This would clearly benefit online program development and delivery.

There is a wide range of issues on which the university administration may want to consult with the system-wide senate before making a final decision. When a request for consultation is made, the system-wide senate should solicit views from their own system-wide committees and from the senates on each of the system's campuses. Then the appropriate senate body should consider all the feedback received and write a letter clearly expressing the views of the senate. It is a major advantage for the administration to receive a single response from the senate rather than getting responses from the individual campus senates. Presumably, if the administration makes a decision contrary to the recommendation of the senate, best practices dictate that there is feedback in which the administration explains why they made the decision they did.

There are any number of academic and nonacademic areas that clearly lie within administrative purview but where it might be appropriate and wise to consult with the system-wide senate. One such area would be the university's budget, where clear consultation allows there to be a united front between the faculty and the administration in supporting university priorities. This is especially important when the university's budget is being cut. Another topic for universities without faculty collective bargaining would be consultation on faculty wages and benefits. Any university administration would be better off having those discussions at the system level rather than at each individual campus.

One of the most fertile areas for system-wide senate consultation concerns academic personnel policy. Most systems have some academic personnel policies on the system-wide level. These might include policies concerning academic freedom and a faculty code of conduct with its corresponding procedures. It does make sense for some of these policies to reside at the system level—after all, it would be hard to justify having different codes of conduct or different academic freedom rights on the various campuses within a system. So, the system-wide senate should be the faculty body that weighs in on such issues of central importance to faculty. In addition, a system, whether homogeneous or heterogeneous, may have policies on faculty hiring and promotion that would apply to all campuses. Such policies would supersede any campus policies in order to attain some uniformity of standards across the system, reflecting the fact that in some systems the employer is the system, not the campus.

Similarly, having a system-wide academic senate can provide oversight and coordination among the individual campus senates. By establishing rules or bylaws governing how campus senates may operate, the system-wide senate can prevent disparities within the system. For example, specifying the membership in the senate through system-wide rules prevents having certain classes of faculty be senate members on one campus but not on another. Part-time faculty might be one of many examples where that might occur. Furthermore, a system-wide senate provides the opportunity for representatives from the corresponding campus senate committees to meet and coordinate the way that they operate. This ability to socialize the activities of the campus committees can contribute greatly to the efficiency of the campus senates.

The system-wide senate can also serve as a means of fostering faculty development and leadership. For example, in the UC system, four former system-wide senate chairs have become chancellors, and a much larger number have become provosts. The system-wide senate can also play an active role in leadership training aimed at faculty members.

Since a system-wide senate speaks for the faculty of the entire system, such a senate can significantly help in working with governing boards and even state legislatures. This allows the university to present a clear picture of faculty views to the governing board and the state. Because the senate structure is there and ready to respond quickly, it can increase the nimbleness and responsiveness to system-level pressures from the board or the state. It can also increase the credibility of the university to external agencies, for example, by having senate leadership testify at legislative hearings. As discussed above, a system-wide senate can also interface with the senates of other systems in the same state or region on issues of mutual concern, such as transfer requirements and course equivalencies.

Despite the advantages of establishing a system-wide senate, there are some challenges and potential disadvantages as well. The most obvious of these is administrative resistance. An administration may wonder why it should start an organization that may disagree with the administration on some system-wide issues. The answer here is obvious. Without giving up administrative decision-making power, the university is stronger if all perspectives are heard and considered. The senate's views will often add value. A related legitimate concern is that adding consultation also adds time to the process. Indeed, a standing joke at the University of California is that UC stands for "unending consultation." While it is true that consultation does add time to a decision-making process, it is also the case that trying to consult with individual campus senates would take much longer. For a system-wide senate to operate well, there must be clearly defined agreed-upon time frames by which the senate must respond to requests for consultation.

For systems with faculty collective bargaining at the system level, another challenge is maintaining a clear distinction between a faculty union and an academic senate. First, there is the question of membership. In some cases, the union and the senate will have the same membership, but that may not be the case for all systems. Temporary faculty, contingent faculty, and clinical faculty[8] are just three examples of faculty that might be in one group but not the other. Even more difficult is the challenge of maintaining clarity about the differing purviews of the union and the senate. This is particularly challenging for faculty who may hold leadership roles in one or both organizations. Generally speaking, the union should be dealing with faculty compensation and terms and conditions of employment, while the senate deals with academic and institutional issues. But there are issues that might be claimed by both groups, such as the faculty code of conduct and procedures for dismissal of faculty. The best practice is to have clarity about such issues from the very beginning.

Heterogeneous university systems, those whose colleges and universities have a broad range of missions, pose a different set of challenges for a system-wide senate. As already discussed, many issues faced by such systems can benefit from a system-wide senate, including the faculty code of conduct, academic freedom policy, course articulation policies, and transfer policies. With different missions on each campus, however, there may be much less room for uniformity on academic personnel policies or curricular policies, and it might not make sense to have degree approvals, such as graduate degrees, occur at the system level. In addition, if a system develops one or more virtual campuses, there may be a challenge regarding participation by those faculty in the senate, but in my view, there is no reason why the faculty of those virtual campuses cannot participate fully in both a campus senate and a system-wide senate.

Another awkward issue is the extent to which the campus senates are willing to cede some authority to a system-wide senate. Starting a system-wide senate by, for example, regularly convening a council of campus chairs does not require that authority flow from the campus to the system. As a system-wide senate develops, it may evolve into an umbrella organization of the senate, in which case it is important that the campuses see the system-wide senate as adding value and influence to the voice of faculty.

Concluding Remarks on University Systems of the Future

As we envision university systems of the future, we can imagine them evolving in ways that better meet the needs of the state that funds them and of the students they serve. That future also envisions that university systems enhance the quality of the teaching, research, and public service done on the individual campuses. One important ingredient of that successful future should involve meaningful shared governance at the system-wide level. In the years to come, university systems will face a broad range of external challenges, including demographics, technology, funding, and employment of their graduates, and these universities will need to be more responsive and more resilient. A strong system-wide senate will enable university systems to respond more effectively to these challenges.

This chapter has discussed some of the advantages and challenges associated with having a system-wide academic senate. Because those university systems having a system-wide senate are among the largest and highest-quality systems in the United States, it seems likely that additional systems will emulate these successful systems. The key point is that a system-wide senate can add real value to the discourse that occurs within a university system. The value of scale that applies to so many other aspects of university system operations can also apply to faculty governance.

One final point is that faculty have a major professional investment in the success of a campus and the system in which it resides. After all, students stay at a university for four years, leaders of universities have an average tenure of about five years, and even trustees or regents typically have terms of less than twelve years. Faculty who spend their careers at a university may stay for two to four *decades*. Since their personal and professional lives are so tied to the university, it makes sense that they should have a voice in university decision-making at all levels. This can only improve the loyalty and commitment of the faculty to their campus and the university system as a whole. That is what makes a university system strong.

Notes

1. American Association of University Professors, *The 2021 AAUP Shared Governance Survey: Findings on Faculty Roles by Decision-Making Areas* (Washington, DC: American Association of University Professors, 2021), https://www.aaup.org/sites/default/files/2021-AAUP-Shared-Governance-Survey-Findings-on-Faculty-Roles.pdf.
2. See "Board of Governors," California Community Colleges, accessed November 13, 2023, https://www.cccco.edu/About-Us/Board-of-Governors.
3. Note that on some campuses, even academic departments can serve as a senate committee for some purposes, such as determining the curriculum.
4. In some cases, where there is a collective bargaining agreement with a faculty union, the terms of the collective bargaining agreement might govern the process of discipline or termination.
5. "Welcome to the Academic Senate," University of California, accessed November 13, 2023, https://senate.universityofcalifornia.edu/.
6. See, e.g., John Aubrey Douglass, *Shared Governance at the University of California: An Historical Review*, CSHE.1.98 (Berkeley, CA: Center for Studies in Higher Education, 1998), https://cshe.berkeley.edu/sites/default/files/publications/1998_shared_governance_at_the_university_of_california_an_historical_review.pdf.
7. The so-called A-G requirement.

8. Temporary faculty are typically hired for a limited duration to teach one or more specific courses. Contingent faculty may be full-time, but they are not eligible for tenure, they usually have less job security, and they are often held to a different performance standard (such as in research) compared to regular faculty. Clinical faculty are physicians and other health care providers who participate in health education but whose primary role is provision of health care.

15

Governing Large

How Public University System Boards Can Help Shape the Future of American Higher Education

KEVIN P. REILLY

Introduction

IN RECENT YEARS, critical writing on the structure, membership, function, and authority of public university system boards has been expanding. Scholars and practitioners have addressed such questions as:

- Should university systems have a single, system-wide governing board, or a system board that devolves some of its authority to campus governing boards, or a system governing board in combination with campus advisory councils?
- At a time when state funding to all public higher education, including that to university systems, is shrinking in proportion to other funding sources, should state governors retain the authority to appoint most members, or should more seats be allotted to those representing organizations supplying more dollars, such as alumni associations, business leaders, foundation executives?
- Are public flagships in need of their own board separate from the system board overseeing other campuses, by virtue of their unparalleled size, large research portfolios, commercialization ventures, and national and international reach?
- Should public regional institutions, and community and tech-

nical colleges, be governed by one board to facilitate smoother pathways to student success?[1]

These are certainly reasonable questions. Those debating them have come up with different answers for different times and different places. The fact is that almost any of these arrangements, or combinations of them, can work in a particular state culture in a particular era, depending on what state and university leaders expect of their higher education institutions. As Tip O'Neill liked to proclaim, "All politics is local." Moreover, such questions are largely internally directed to the form of public higher education, instead of to the function it needs to perform for the external common good.

I will not rehash here the relative merits of various university system board constellations for the future, or the existential question of whether they are needed at all. Rather, I focus on three big, accelerating trends affecting the future of American higher education in the first part of this chapter. Then in the second part, I address what university system governing bodies might uniquely—or most effectively in comparison with single-institution boards—do to help shape those trends for the public good going forward.

This chapter assumes that system boards in some form will be around for a good long time. That assumption is based on the value their systems have demonstrated to date, as well as the nature of the challenging trends faced by society and the requirement for a coordinated, directed response from higher education to meet them in a global knowledge economy. To borrow an analogy from American constitutional history, the argument that will play out here is essentially that the country needs system boards now and in the future to see their charters as more akin to the US Constitution than to the Articles of Confederation.

Significant Trends for System Boards to Address

Student Demographics, and Student and Employer Behavior

We now have more than 17 million American undergraduates, and they are more diverse—in age, race, ethnicity, wealth, acknowledged gender identity, and family background—than ever before.[2] What once was a *selective* American higher education industry has become a *mass* industry, with aspirations toward *universal* availability. Today's students have differing expectations of what college can and should do for them, and they need to reach their goals using a wider variety of means than colleges have generally offered in the past. With the disruptions of the COVID era, the racial reckoning the country is facing after the murder of George Floyd, and the rise of student activism fueled in part by exploding social media, these expectations and needs will not be easy for colleges and universities to meet.

How can we best simultaneously serve the 18-year-old residential first-year student who wants to study international relations and become immersed in the full undergraduate experience of four-year campus life; the out-of-work 26-year-old with a high school diploma looking to earn an associate's degree related to a desired job in the electronic gaming industry; and the 38-year-old single working parent with two kids, a dog, and a mortgage who needs 20 more credits to complete a baccalaureate degree in business administration required to move up into the supervisory ranks? Even the answer to the question about the 18-year-old will be different now and in the future based upon massive innovation the COVID pandemic has forced on all our campuses.

The means at our disposal to answer these questions include online delivery, flipped classrooms, blended learning, accelerated semesters, collaborative learning, competency-based education, prior learning assessment, and joint degree and certificate programs with businesses and nonprofits. Some of these approaches can hold down the cost of delivering education and the price of earning it.

If, for instance, we don't force students to take courses that teach competencies they demonstrably already have, we can save money for both them and our institutions. We need to use such techniques to hold down expenditures more tightly. Many Americans, including influential elected officials, see higher education as just too expensive, and some believe the price puts it out of reach for them and their families.[3]

Among the students who do enroll and earn credentials, more and more of them zig-zag through multiple institutions along the way, in a behavior dubbed "student swirl." According to a 2016 report from the

National Student Clearinghouse Research Center, 64.5 percent of bachelor's degree recipients in 2014–15 had attended more than one institution, and 25 percent had attended more than two. There has been no update of these numbers because of the pandemic, but they are likely higher now.[4] Moreover, there has been a proliferation of new credentials short of a degree. Sean Gallagher, executive director of Northeastern University's Center for the Future of Higher Education and Talent Strategy, offers some eye-catching numbers related to this phenomenon:

- Strada Education Network's consumer polling has shown that 40 percent of working-age adults have earned some type of non-degree credential.
- The number of alternative credential "badges" awarded nearly doubled, from 24 million in 2018 to 43 million in 2020.
- Employer acceptance of a variety of credentials earned online has grown steadily, reaching more than 70 percent in 2021, up from 61 percent in 2018 and 40 percent in 2013.
- In a 2021 employer survey, 34 percent of HR leaders say their organizations have "skills-based hiring" strategies that de-emphasize degrees.

Gallagher puts it this way: "badging, embedding certificates into degrees and the idea of offering small credentials on the way to larger ones are emerging as key trends, and are ways that new types of credentials are augmenting and supplementing (rather than supplanting) degrees."[5]

Many students and employers are moving toward an anytime, anywhere learning approach to higher education. The advent of the do-it-yourself degree is increasingly upon us, with a range of credits, credentials, badges, certificates, and certifications offered in a variety of formats by academic institutions but also other entities and partners—businesses, industrial associations, the military, nonprofits, and government.

A university system that contains a wide variety of degree and certificate programs spanning multiple, affiliated campuses across the state, each with its own regional networks and partners, is ideally structured to respond to these trends. But the system governing board will typically have to step up to help the system realize its potential to accommodate the new student and employer proclivities. Stepping up will require strong board leadership and support for the system head in making difficult choices among competing options and in the face of well-entrenched interests.

Uncertain Enrollments, Volatile Funding, and Efficiency Pressures to Consolidate, Merge, or Close Campuses

Between 2010 and 2018, college enrollment nationally dropped 7 percent. Then, with the pandemic, further declines occurred without any indication that they would soon turn around.[6] Even without lingering effects of COVID dropouts or stop-outs, in a number of states, the shrinking pool of secondary school graduates will mean fewer potential postsecondary students in the years to come.

Both in these states and in those that find themselves in the contrasting situation of booming population growth and high school expansion, state funding for higher education is often unsteady.[7] These hard facts and the simultaneous pressure to freeze or lower tuition have strained resources on many campuses. All of this provokes heated discussions about ways to lower institutional expenses through such major moves as consolidation, merger, or even closure.

Take, for example, a recent editorial about the Pennsylvania State System of Higher Education in the *Pittsburgh Post-Gazette*. It argues, "For too long, the state system has tried to be all things to all people: 14 independent universities that . . . tried to be full-scale liberal arts and workforce training institutions." The editorial board recognizes the difficult work the system has done under Chancellor Daniel Greenstein's leadership in merging six of its campuses into two new regional institutions. But it goes on to raise a more fundamental issue:

> But still the state system seems to be oriented toward competing with larger, more prestigious, better funded institutions rather than crafting its own educational identity. We'd suggest that the system's students have already shown the path forward by their own educational choices: More

> than 40 percent study one of three professional disciplines—business, health and education. A considerable proportion of the remainder also pursue professional programs while, for instance, only 4 percent study all the "social sciences" combined.

The *Post-Gazette* editors do not leap to the position that given this student behavior only one campus in the system should offer philosophy or physics, but they do promote the notion that courses can and should be taught in these and other low-enrollment disciplines without having a department for them or major in them on every campus.[8]

Admittedly, Pennsylvania is a state with declining population, and the Pennsylvania State System of Higher Education is attempting to redefine itself, sitting astride the powerhouse Pennsylvania State University with 24 campuses of its own around the state and an online "World Campus." Nevertheless, I believe the kind of thinking and action going on there now will help set a pattern for other public university systems and their trustees as they struggle to remodel their systems—especially their comprehensive master's-level institutions in relation to flagships and urban research campuses—to meet the evolving realities of student demand and state financial support. System boards will have an essential leadership role in this remodeling.[9]

Criticism over the Role the University Plays (or Not) in Workforce Development and Big Social and Political Issues

While few Americans understand what governing boards of colleges and universities actually do, public university systems and their boards tend to be prominent features of state budget and political landscapes, given the systems' significant size and extensive reach. Board members and system heads are charged with navigating their organizations across these rocky landscapes in a climate of criticism, skepticism, and even hostility about the value of higher education. There is doubt that higher education can handle its own burning issues correctly—from affordability to campus safety to diversity of thought and free speech to student activism to racial reckoning on campuses.

In recent years, a spate of opinion polls has broadcast unsettling news about public attitudes toward the academic enterprise. A *Wall Street Journal*/NBC News survey found that just 49 percent of Americans believe a four-year degree will lead to a good job and higher lifetime earnings (despite incontrovertible evidence that it does for most degree holders). Only 25 percent of respondents in a New America poll say that higher education is fine the way it is, and only 3 percent of millennials share that sentiment.

Most disturbing, a Pew Research poll found that 58 percent of Republicans and Republican-leaning Independents believe that colleges and universities have a negative effect on the country. Even among trustees, more than half agree or strongly agree that the public's perception of higher education has declined over the past decade or more. Nearly three of every four believe that the price of a college degree is too expensive.[10]

A *New York Times* survey in 2016 asked what people thought the unemployment rate was for 25- to 34-year-olds who graduated from a four-year college. The responses were as follows.

- *Times* readers' average: 9.2 percent
- Google survey average answer: 6.5 percent
- Correct answer: 2.4 percent
- For those with only a high school degree, it's 7.4 percent[11]

This sort of basic misunderstanding—in some cases driven by purposeful disinformation—is rampant across many sectors of our society, not just higher education. It undermines faith in the country's largest, most important institutions, and provides fodder for dysfunctional, distracting political donnybrooks.

At a time of rapidly changing workforce needs, ever more rabid partisan politics, and supercharged culture wars, large collections of institutions such as university systems that are supposed to help produce the next generation of job-ready employees and simultaneously pursue a disinterested search for truth loom as tempting symbolic targets. Trustees of university systems will need to become more informed, forceful, persuasive advocates of their systems' roles in developing the talent and discoveries that will undergird the future of American democracy to turn this vulnerability on its head.

System Board Opportunities to Shape These Trends for the Better

The work of the Task Force on System Board Governance of the Association of Governing Boards of Universities and Colleges, which I chaired, might be summarized in three broad, forward looking recommendations to boards and their systems:

1. Develop a system-wide strategic plan for the social, educational, and economic future of your state and its communities.
2. Ensure that the vision, strategic plan, and competitive energy of the system and each campus are purposefully connected to the larger directions in which the state wants to move.
3. Engage in independent-minded governance of, and informed advocacy for, your system and its institutions.[12]

The sections of this chapter below present proven and promising approaches to using these key recommendations to address the trends I have outlined above.

Having the Right Tools

In a 2018 report on The *Future Roles and Responsibilities within the University of Colorado System*, the National Center for Higher Education Management Systems (NCHEMS) urges the system board to "focus system leadership primarily on issues that affect all campuses or relationships between and among campuses." It also offers an observation about the institutions in the Colorado system that would apply to most institutions in most systems. It says that they operate "under a single brandname, a single corporate structure, and a service organization that performs some centralized functions."[13] These remarks from NCHEMS raise the question of whether system boards generally have the tools and the discipline in using them to realize the promise of system structures and opportunities to engage with powerful trends such as those summarized above.

In that regard, what I call a "tools inventory" can be helpful:

- Does the board have a clear approach to setting goals and methods to achieve them as part of a strategic planning process based on: (1) the collective strengths of the campuses, (2) the opportunity to scale innovation at the system level, and (3) and state needs?
- Are there realistic stretch metrics to monitor the performance of each institution and the system as a whole? Do these metrics feature a set of specific deliverables for the social, educational, and economic future of the state and its communities?
- Are there common budget methodologies and a system-wide database that allow the board to judge fairly the progress all the players are making toward their goals?
- Does the board have accountability tools, short of "you're fired," to reward strong performance and get the attention of individuals who are not moving the enterprise forward at an acceptable pace?
- Does the board require balanced budgets at the campuses to help guide degree program development, elimination, and program array?
- Is there a culture of and rules for shared governance by the board with the institutional presidents and the faculty? If system goals are to have any chance of being achieved, both the presidents and the faculty need to be involved in setting them, and then take the lead in implementation.
- Do the board and the system head have system administration senior executives prepared to support the change necessary to help steer these trends?
- Are there policies, practices, or other deeply embedded behaviors that constrain the board's ability to govern effectively?

Only if a board accumulates these enterprise management tools and works up skill in using them across the system with its chief executive can it hope to meet the challenges of today and those on the horizon.[14] In my experience, most system boards have adequate authority to do that. Not all have the big vision, and the moxie, to do it.

Student Pathways through Multiple Educational Options: Policies, Initiatives, and Incentives

Many university systems contain a variety of institutions within them. Institutions may have different admissions standards; degree offerings; financial aid availability; cooperative learning, service learning, and internship opportunities; peer tutoring arrangements; career placement operations; study abroad programs; graduation requirements; and on and on. The advantages this variety holds for students is the individual's ability to find the most appropriate "fit."

The characteristics of student demographics and student and employer behavior I described above, which are taking hold ever more firmly, may produce a large wrinkle here. They may well mean that the fit in the future will be less with an institution than with a variety of courses, services, and credentials the student sees leading toward a particular job, career, professional or graduate school program, or even an informed, well-lived life.

William Sederburg, a former state commissioner of higher education, state legislator, and college president, anticipated this new definition of fit in provocative language back in 2016:

> The historical model of universities as stand-alone enterprises, with their own mission, admission standards, and academic programming, is not as applicable as it once was. Public universities, private colleges, community colleges, technical schools, and online institutions will increasingly be seen as nodes on multiple networks, and not as institutions with unique, well-defined roles.[15]

More and more students will want to access courses, services, and credentials from a number of institutions within a system. The potential for students to do that is one of the attractive strengths systems can offer, a leading value proposition for them. But for that value to be delivered, access will have to be seamless. For that to happen, system board-sanctioned and president-driven policies, initiatives, and incentives will have to be put in place to create clearer, cleaner—though no less academically rigorous—pathways for students through the networks Sederburg refers to. Following are examples that boards can adopt to ready their systems for optimal forward-looking service to students and the society.

Enacting Policies

- Enacting credit transfer policies that limit loss of credits and encourage application of them to majors and degree requirements, not just general education and electives.
- Enacting system-wide financial aid policies that allow students to take courses from multiple campuses while keeping their full-time status, and then receive a degree offered jointly by the system and campuses from which the student has completed coursework.
- Assigning primary or lead responsibility for online delivery to a single unit within the system.
- Making explicit policies that embody board expectations for closing equity gaps in student outcomes.
- Providing support for dual enrollment and early college high schools, where students can earn initial college credits as part of their secondary education. Studies have shown that particularly low-income students in early-college high schools are as much as three times more likely to complete a postsecondary degree than students assigned to control groups in those studies.[16]
- Requiring remedial education that includes credit-bearing content, recognized as such by all campuses in the system. Much research has demonstrated that this "corequisite" approach is more effective in enabling students to move toward degree completion than is offering noncredit remedial courses.[17]
- Developing a system-wide general education core and ensuring its portability across campuses.
- Enacting system-wide standards for awarding credit based on

prior learning assessment and through competency-based education.
- Creating system-wide academic calendars, grading policies, learning management systems, and application processes.

Initiatives and Incentives

- Ensuring a well-informed cadre of academic advisors focused on establishing clear (both easily understood and unobstructed) pathways for students to the degree, using all the resources of the entire system.
- Encouraging targeted use of need-based financial aid directed at opportune times to students throughout the system who are in most jeopardy of dropping out.
- Providing system-coordinated assistance to high school seniors and their families in applying for federal and state financial aid. It should include help in understanding the full cost of attendance and in decision-making around loan and debt levels. This initiative and the one immediately above are particularly important for system outreach to underserved and disadvantaged students at a time when the National Student Clearinghouse reports a 32 percent decline for Black students and a 20 percent decline for Hispanic students in public two-year colleges since 2019. The number of high school seniors applying for financial aid is down by 270,000 since 2019, with the largest drop among students from high-poverty high schools.[18] Not getting on the pathway in the first place is the surest way not to get to the end of it.
- Communicating expectations for early, transparent course scheduling at all institutions in the system.
- Offering board recognition of faculty on all the campuses who promote student success through effective teaching and interaction with students outside the classroom. The board can also encourage and reward faculty who participate in programs to develop their teaching skills for an increasingly diverse student body.
- Making explicit in the hiring and evaluation process a prefer-

ence for campus leaders who, while being strong advocates for their own institutions, will also be committed to collaborating with other campus leaders and the system head to broaden pathways to student success.[19]

To make these kinds of changes, the system president, board chair, and institutional leaders will need to have regular, genuine, respectful shared governance dialogue with the faculty about the compelling reasons for them, and how they are intended to be implemented with faculty input on how best their students can be served. Student voices must be brought into this mix as well, ideally via face-to-face meetings and periodic surveys of student interests and satisfaction. Especially in environments where faculty are unionized, these discussions will require patience and persistence. Part of the message from the board in the conversations should be a clear one that they expect the system and campus heads, working with the faculty, to deliver on these steps, and that they will be fully supported by the board in doing so.

An innovative recent instance of new system pathways for students is Google's partnership with the Connecticut State Colleges and Universities System. In October 2021, Google announced it was making its suite of career certificates available free to every community college and to every career and technical high school in the United States. The certificates are offered in four fields: information technology, data analytics, project management, and user experience design. The Connecticut System soon after became the first to offer all four across its campuses. Moreover, the certificates have been recommended for up to 12 college credits by the American Council on Education. The in-demand careers the certificates address have starting annual salaries in the $60,000 range, and Google has organized a consortium of 150 companies that have agreed to hire students who complete them.[20]

A different kind of system partnership pathway is a relatively new set of applied baccalaureate degrees. Institutions are now offering such degrees as bachelor of applied studies, bachelor of applied arts and sciences, and bachelor of science in applied computing. Designed primarily for working adults in cooperation with two-year institutions, they are typically baccalaureate-completion curricula built on associate degrees or two years' worth of credits earned at a community or technical college. They can therefore usually be completed in two more years via courses available online. These programs are partly a response to employers telling the university they want to develop their management cadre from employees who may start with them as technical personnel but show potential as supervisors—if they can earn a broadening bachelor's degree along the way.

Taking on Big Societal Challenges

University systems are uniquely positioned to take on the big challenges facing society because of their ability to pool capacity and expertise, leverage change across multiple institutions and locations, and direct resources to where they will have the most positive effect for their students and the state. A number of years ago, the American Association of State Colleges and Universities (AASCU) characterized its members as "Stewards of Place." State systems indeed play that role in every town or city where a campus is located, and for the state as a whole. Figuring out how to embed the institutions and the system more fully in a state needs agenda is a project where system board members, given their networks around the state and their connections to business and state and local government leaders, can make a major contribution.

Because of these connections, system board members can assist the university in striking partnerships with health care organizations, businesses and industry trade groups, school districts, and government to help strengthen their competitiveness and service to their clients. Many of these arrangements, if they are truly aimed at the most complex issues pressing on society, will be the kind of outside partnerships that need to involve more than one institution inside the system and cross-campus curricular content reinvigoration. Board members have the clout to encourage and incentivize that sort of powerful joint response from campuses across the state. Two examples from my own experience at the University of Wisconsin System illustrate the possibilities.

The first was a response to a health industry crisis faced by more than a few states—a shortage of well-educated nurses and an aging population requiring more, and more sophisticated, nursing care. Stimulated in part by members of the Board of Regents asking what the university system could do to tackle the problem, five of the Wisconsin system campuses offering bachelor of science in nursing (BSN) programs joined forces to develop our first-ever Collaborative Nursing Program.

Students, mostly employed as non-baccalaureate-prepared registered nurses at hospitals, assisted living and rehabilitation facilities, and nursing homes in far-flung communities large and small, could take courses from any of the five institutions and decide which one they wanted to award their BSN degree. Coursework was initially offered using what now seems like the ancient technology of closed-circuit television at regional sites. Currently known as the BSN@HOME with six institutions participating, the program is available entirely online, with nearly 3,000 graduates. The board publicly applauded this amalgam of curricular revision and integration, institutional cooperation, and instructional technology innovation as the system stretching itself, as only a statewide system could, to enhance the quality of life in Wisconsin.

The second program I will mention is the University of Wisconsin System reconfiguring an element of its research prowess to accelerate progress in a field with significant implications for energy use, sustainability, and Wisconsin's economy. Johnson Controls is an international electronics and heating, ventilation, and air conditioning (HVAC) equipment company with its American headquarters in the Milwaukee area. When it wanted to create a world-class center to advance research, development, and commercialization of energy storage technologies, it reached out to the university to establish three joint laboratories in engineering and applied science at the UW-Milwaukee and UW-Madison engineering schools.

The campuses appointed the company's scientists as adjunct professors who could sit on the doctoral committees for PhD students in engineering. Students were offered internships at the company, supervised by some of these same adjunct faculty. Johnson Controls funded graduate fellowships to support advanced student research projects at both institutions. It also endowed a professorship in energy storage research, with the person holding the position responsible for maintaining the research labs and overseeing graduate students at both campuses. When I visited the labs on the Milwaukee campus, company research scientists working there told me they had received multiple job offers and decided to accept the one from Johnson Controls because it allowed them to continue their research in a respected university environment in partnership with a range of university faculty.

At the public announcement of the initiative, the system board chair, company leaders, campus leaders, the governor, and I celebrated the coming together of the system's two research campuses with one of the state's premier corporations to position Wisconsin as a leader in a vital industry of the future. The future of successful system board governance will entail working closely with system leadership to discern such opportunities and seize them. I want to emphasize that in both these examples, faculty stepped up to make change because they saw an opportunity to use their expertise in new ways to assist their students in improving the lives of their fellow citizens.

After several years of service on a system board, diligent members will know more about the campuses in the system than anybody else not employed by one of them. Board members are what I will call "border runners" between the system and the public. They can uniquely bring state residents' questions, needs, and concerns into the university, while at the same time explaining the university's mission and work to their fellow citizens.

As stewards of the system's financial health, educational and research quality, and equity-mindedness, they should be informed, "loving critics"—neither blind defenders nor unhappy underminers. As advocates both for the taxpayers and the university system, they should help tell the system's story, indicating where it needs to do better but promulgating its value to the commonwealth, present and future.

This public advocacy function of board members of all political stripes is ever more important to keep public universities from being diverted and damaged as pawns in increasingly virulent partisan warfare.[21] To advocate adequately, system board members cannot be enamored of just one campus, program, or constituency. They might call on a particular example or two, but they have to educate themselves so they are able to tell the story of the system as a whole.

Conclusion

We now live in an open architecture/multiple modality/polyinstructional knowledge environment. The structures for delivery of education, the forms in which it can be delivered, and the instructional techniques available have all exploded. The traditional mode of offering information and perspective to students in classrooms in set time slots over a fixed number of weeks continues, of course. But around it has grown up a variety of anytime, anyplace, any-pace learning opportunities that burgeoning technologies make possible, and attractive, for today's student audiences. One of the effects of the COVID pandemic has been to drive more of these new approaches into the traditional one, making for transformational hybrid teaching experimentation that I believe will continue into the future.

The adjectives I used in the first sentence of the paragraph immediately above—"open," "multiple," and "polyinstructional"—capture the core direction of the work of university system boards as we move into the second quarter of the twenty-first century. A system board that finds ways with its chief executive officer to generate and support more learning and research opportunities of this kind, efficiently using the talent and resources on all its campuses, will model good system governance in the years ahead.

There is an irony in this. Student tendencies are a growing *centrifugal* force that requires a *centripetal* movement from university systems. To respond to student demands enabled and emboldened by technology to use more than one institution in the system as sources of learning, system heads and boards will have to govern more like the system is a unified institution, all parts of which students should be able to access with ease.

The irony will present new challenges to boards to grapple with cross-campus faculty governance, business operations, and technology platforms. It will reward boards that manage to concentrate intensely on student success while exercising the system-wide peripheral vision necessary to achieve it. How to do this without dampening the energy, entrepreneurialism, and identity of the individual institutions, how to move them to a relationship of more fruitful "coopetition" with each other, will take much careful listening, serious thinking, and courage. Thus successful system boards of the future will help move their systems from the more starkly "sovereign states" model of the Articles of Confederation to the more fully interconnected, power-sharing model of the US Constitution, one that respects local integrity while maximizing the advantages of the unity of the whole.

In *Characteristics of Effective Statewide Higher Education Leadership Organizations*, the National Center for Higher Education Management Systems recommends:

> Decentralize governing and operational responsibilities to the maximum degree possible, within a statewide framework of accountability. Institutions should be held accountable and rewarded for performance in relation to statewide goals as well as goals relevant to institutional missions.[22]

Holding institutions, and the system administration, accountable in this way will necessitate boards having and exercising the authority described in the "Having the Right Tools" section of this chapter. It should also precipitate vigorous debate about just what the new "maximum degree possible" is.

System boards might think of their systems in terms of a tile mosaic, with each tile (campus) polished to a high gloss in its own color, no two identical in shape and size, coming together as part of an integrated whole that amplifies the value of each part. The American public clearly has concerns about whether the nation possesses the ingenuity, entrepreneurship, and innovative skills to propel a twenty-first-century economy or solve critical social and environmental problems. With system boards, presidents, and campus leaders attentive to designing their mosaics as I have suggested, public university systems will play no small part in alleviating those concerns.

Notes

1. Questions of this type and related ones are taken up throughout in Jason E. Lane and D. Bruce Johnstone, eds., *Higher Education Systems 3.0: Harnessing Systemness, Delivering Performance* (Albany: State University of New York Press, 2013). For informative charts on system structures around the country, see National Center for Higher Education Management Systems, *Characteristics of Effective Statewide Higher Education Leadership Organizations* (Boulder, CO: National Center for Higher Education Management Systems, 2017), 24–30.

2. "Current Term Enrollment Estimates," National Student Clearinghouse Research Center, May 24, 2023, nscresearchcenter.org/current-term-enrollment-estimates/.

3. Anna Brown, "Most Americans Say Higher Ed Is Heading in Wrong Direction, but Partisans Disagree on Why," Pew Research Center, July 26, 2018, https://www.pewresearch.org/short-reads/2018/07/26/most-americans-say-higher-ed-is-heading-in-wrong-direction-but-partisans-disagree-on-why/.

4. National Student Clearinghouse Research Center, "Time to Degree—2016," September 18, 2016, nscresearchcenter.org/signaturereport11. See in particular Appendix C, Results Tables, Table 12 under the tab "Table 0—Descriptives." Furthermore, Doug Shapiro, executive director of the Clearinghouse Research Center, pointed out in a January 18, 2022, email to me that 54 percent had prior enrollments in two-year colleges, and 20 percent had earned associate degrees.

5. Sean Gallagher, "The Still-Evolving Future of University Credentials," *EdSurge*, December 21, 2021.

6. Gallagher, "The Still-Evolving Future of University Credentials."

7. William R. Doyle, Amberly B. Dziesinski, and Jennifer Delaney, "Modeling Volatility in Public Funding for Higher Education," *Journal of Education Finance* 46 (Spring 2021): 563–91.

8. "The State System Must Clarify a Muddled Mission," editorial in the *Pittsburgh Post-Gazette*, December 6, 2021.

9. For other cases of public university systems consolidation, see National Center for Higher Education Management Systems, *A Review of Consolidations of Postsecondary Systems: The Alaska, Minnesota, and Connecticut Cases* (Boulder, CO: National Center for Higher Education Management Systems, 2021). The Georgia System has also completed campus mergers in recent years. Interestingly, in a different kind of merger, the system boards in Nevada and Tennessee each voted in 2021 to merge a private college into their systems. See "A Look at Trends in College Consolidation since 2016," *Higher Ed Dive*, December 7, 2021. The University of Maine System has moved to unified accreditation for the entire system. In yet another sort of restructuring, as of this writing, Washington State University (WSU) is about 90 percent through a transition from a single institution with a president as CEO and five branch campuses to what it calls "an integrated university system." This system will have six campuses across the state—each with its own chancellor—a system president, and a single system-wide board. President Kirk Schulz is becoming the system president, with a new chancellor as CEO of the flagship campus in Pullman. As President Schulz explained in a January 6, 2022, conversation with me, he intends to focus on setting statewide strategic vision and direction, developing higher educa-

tion policy, setting philanthropic priorities, and representing WSU at the state and federal levels. This revamped structure is also meant to encourage individual campuses to align more fully with local community needs in an evolution of WSU's land-grant mission in a large state with a growing population. See more about the strategic plan at https://stage.web.wsu.edu/strategic-plan-transfer/the-wsu-system-today-4/.

10. Kevin P. Reilly and Richard Novak, "A Winter of Discontent: Tax Policy, Trust, and the Future of Higher Education," *Trusteeship* (January/February 2018): 11.

11. Kevin P. Reilly, "Common Sense on Colleges and Workforce Development," Inside Higher Ed, July 8, 2019, https://www.insidehighered.com/views/2019/07/08/some-recommended-approaches-higher-education-and-workplace-development-opinion.

12. Association of Governing Boards of Universities and Colleges, *Consequential Board Governance in Public Higher Education Systems* (Washington, DC: Association of Governing Boards of Universities and Colleges, 2016). See also Kevin P. Reilly, "Too Big to Fail," *Trusteeship* (January/February 2017).

13. National Higher Education Management Systems, *The Future Roles and Responsibilities within the University of Colorado System* (Boulder, CO: National Higher Education Management Systems, 2018), 13.

14. This section on system board tools is widely informed by a conversation I had with Daniel Greenstein, chancellor of the Pennsylvania State System of Higher Education, on December 20, 2021.

15. William Sederburg, "Commentary: The Uncertain Future of University Governance," *Chronicle of Higher Education*, February 29, 2016.

16. Deborah Delisle and Chris Gabrieli, "Opinion: We Face Another Lost Generation if We Don't Do Something about College Enrollment," *Hechinger Report*, December 27, 2021, 3.

17. Complete College America, *No Room for Doubt: Moving Corequisite Support from Idea to Imperative* (Indianapolis: Complete College America, 2021).

18. Delisle and Gabrieli, "We Face Another Lost Generation," 2.

19. These suggested policies, initiatives, and incentives are broadly informed by the National Association of System Heads (NASH) Imperatives for Higher Education Systems Success. See the NASH website at www.nashonline.org in the Big ReThink section.

20. Abigail Johnson Hess, "Google Is Giving All U.S. Community Colleges Free Access to Their 4 Career Certificates," CNBC Make It, October 29, 2021, https://www.cnbc.com/2021/10/29/google-gives-community-colleges-free-access-to-their-4-certificates.html.

21. The Association of Governing Boards of Universities and Colleges Guardians Project has developed materials to prepare trustees to speak and write persuasively about the "return on investment" of their university systems. See the website at www.agb.org/Guardians.

22. National Center for Higher Education Management Systems, *Characteristics of Effective Statewide Higher Education Leadership Organizations*, 9.

16 | Making Change Happen

ALLISON M. VAILLANCOURT

A GOVERNOR-BACKED PLAN to create a single and more coordinated higher education system in New Hampshire failed to gain traction.[1]

A widely announced merger between Marlboro College in Vermont and the University of Bridgeport in Connecticut fell apart.[2]

An initial effort to slash costs by consolidating administrative staff into a shared services model at the University of Michigan was blocked by faculty opposition.[3]

These are just a few of examples of highly visible higher education change initiatives that encountered insurmountable headwinds. At first glance, each of these change efforts made logical sense. A single higher education system could reduce administrative overhead and make it easier for students to move from earning associate's degrees to bachelor's degrees. The planned merger of two institutions in New England could have increased financial solvency for a struggling institution, while addressing land needs for the other. And moving administrative staff from multiple departments into a single shared services center promised to reduce costs, encourage consistency, and improve quality.

So, why did these seemingly good ideas fail to advance? Importantly, why have so many similar higher education reform efforts, including more than 100 institutional merger attempts in the past decade, faced opposition when moving from idea to execution? That is the question we will answer in this chapter. And once we have answered it, we will provide a practical framework designed to bring about the university system of the future through both incremental and transformational change.

What Needs to Change

Before we address strategies for making change in higher education happen, let's consider what higher education is facing in terms of pressure to adapt to the forces challenging its current operating model. Some of the forces are obvious, including declining state funding for higher education and demographic shifts that are reducing the number of traditional-age college students.[4] Perhaps less obvious are the "five new realities" that Arthur Levine and Scott Van Pelt outlined in their book *The Great Upheaval: Higher Education's Past, Present, and Uncertain Future*. That list includes competition from other content providers, increased power on the part of higher education consumers, demands for more accessible and digitally based learning, greater interest in outcomes-based learning, as well as more practical certifications and "just-in-time" education.[5]

These new realities can be added to an ongoing to-do list that includes responding to a litany of complaints about higher education that will sound familiar. Tuition is increasingly unaffordable. Student loan debt levels are too high. Completion rates are too low. The curriculum is not responsive to emerging labor market needs. Scheduling options are too rigid. Tenure can protect underperforming faculty.

Whether addressing new realities or reconsidering structural, financial, and accountability practices, higher education must be more flexible. And that leads us to an important question. Why does change inside higher education seem to be harder to achieve than change within other sectors? If we can answer this question, we might be better positioned to make progress.

Why Can't Higher Education Change?

In her *Inside Higher Ed* article "Why Can't Higher Education Change?" Kathy Johnson Bowles cites a handful of factors that are perceived to impede change within higher education. That list includes tenure, shared governance, multiple stakeholders, and accreditation processes. Johnson Bowles somewhat boldly asserts that none of these factors is a true barrier to progress; it is the way they are operationalized that is the problem. For example, she argues tenure tends to be awarded to homogenous thinkers who have a vested interest in maintaining the status quo. Unmanaged shared governance can lead to endless and unproductive debates. Higher education fears its stakeholders rather than engaging them. And accreditation processes designed to ensure quality can limit the ability to revise programs or introduce new courses in a timely way in response to emerging demands.[6]

It is easy and common to blame higher education structures and traditions for blocking change. While these features may complicate change efforts, this chapter argues that the real barrier to transformational change comes from something that is rarely recognized or acknowledged: underdeveloped change management expertise among would-be change agents.

Common Change Management Errors

When seeking to understand why apparently reasonable higher education change initiatives fail to succeed, we often find that the efforts lacked strategic change management plans. Too often, those who seek to transform higher education, or even modify pieces and parts of it, begin with a clever idea and see their role as selling it, rather than creating demand for it. They try to wear down those who oppose their ideas rather than seeking to learn from them. Notably, they see change as a logical exercise rather than an emotional experience.

Much has been written about common obstacles to change, and there is no shortage of failed higher education change experiments to illustrate these obstacles. Despite this, many of those committed to change efforts seem unaware of common change pitfalls and are therefore unprepared to avoid them. So, before offering guidance about how to make change happen, let's consider 10 common change tactics that tend to yield poor results.

1. *Providing a solution to an invisible problem.* Organizational and political leaders often see the need for change before others do. That is because they typically have more information than others and are often trained to notice and look for trends. Upon recognizing a need or challenge, leaders to propose a solution. The problem with this approach is that it assumes that others agree there is a problem to be solved, and that may not be the case. As a result, change initiatives can be viewed as disruptive and unnecessary. If there is no perceived need to change, most people will see no reason to be inconvenienced by doing things differently.

2. *Announcing rather than asking.* Even when there is general agreement about the need for change, the path to a better future may not be obvious. Change initiatives often fail when there is disagreement about the specific tactics for change. Rather than announcing big plans, effective change agents are more likely to surface a concern and work to build consensus about the best way to address it. There is a caveat to this advice, however.

When it comes to securing support for institutional consolidations, there is some evidence to suggest that announcing appears to work better than asking. Why? Because this leaves stakeholders to argue about how to implement the consolidation rather than debate whether it should occur. Researchers have cited the success of consolidations in university systems in both Georgia and Wisconsin as evidence that making declarations is more likely to lead to long-term success.[7]

3. *Failing to create a vision for a better future.* While several institutional consolidation efforts have been attempted to reduce costs, saving money is not always inspiring. Increasing student access, sup-

porting students to complete their degrees, and improving regional prosperity are more engaging goals. The University System of Georgia's success in completing nine institutional consolidations in the past decade is largely viewed as a function of helping stakeholders imagine a better Georgia.[8]

4. *Creating too much uncertainty*. Change often requires moving from what is known to the uncomfortable and often anxiety-producing state of uncertainty. As Harvard professor Rosabeth Moss Kanter aptly noted, "People will often prefer to remain mired in misery than to head toward an unknown."[9] Failing to provide road maps and time lines can prompt stakeholders to imagine the worst and actively engage in shutting down change efforts.

5. *Demanding too much change at once*. During the initial stages of the Iraq War, the US military employed "Operation Shock and Awe," a strategy to paralyze the Iraqi's perception of their battlefield and crush their will to fight. The shock and awe strategy was intended to be sudden, unexpected, and so overwhelming that opponents felt unequipped to mount a viable opposition.[10] The approach was not new, of course, and had been applied in past military incursions, such as dropping nuclear weapons on Hiroshima and Nagasaki.[11]

In an organizational setting, a shock and awe strategy may include terminating several people at once, reorganizing structures suddenly, and introducing one change after another to make it difficult for organizational members to mount opposition. While a shock and awe approach can accomplish change quickly, its results may not be enduring, and the destruction of morale it causes may weaken the organization in the long term.

6. *Leaning on data to make a case for change*. Members of the higher education community like data and evidence, so making the case for change based on logic and statistics seems to make sense. While this approach will work for some people, it will not work for everyone. Savvy change agents turn to Aristotle's advice on persuasion, often called the "rhetorical triangle" when crafting a comprehensive strat-

egy for change. This model asserts that when it comes to creating buy-in for a new idea, we should consider logic, ethos, and pathos.[12]

Logos involves appealing to logic and reason, for example, facts, statistics, and research. Ethos involves appealing to personal credibility, ethics, and character. Pathos involves appealing to emotions.

A reliance on logos—for example, "Here is our financial situation; the need to cut staff is obvious"—is typically insufficient to win both the hearts and minds of those likely to be affected by change. Likewise, appealing only to emotion—for example, "Merging with another institution will destroy the deep sense of connection our alumni have enjoyed for more than 100 years"—is unlikely to reverse a data-oriented board's decision to pursue a more financially sustainable merger.

7. *Not honoring the past*. When charting the path to merge Augusta State and Georgia Health Sciences Universities, the Georgia Board of Regents originally decided to call the new entity "Georgia Regents University." The name faced derision from multiple stakeholders and prompted Chris Gay, a sportswriter at the *Augusta Chronicle*, to write: "I guess we should congratulate the Board of Regents on the birth of their son today because many of us will now call this new university 'Georgia Board of Regents University.' How narcissistic can you get?"[13] Recognizing the sense of alienation it has created, the Georgia Board of Regents changed course and in 2015 voted to rename the new entity Augusta University, a nod to the community in which had long supported both institutions.[14]

8. *Moving too fast*. While there are some who believe that moving quickly is important to maintain momentum, there are others who advocate for a more deliberate approach that provides time to work through unintended consequences. In opposing the New Hampshire higher education consolidation, former trustees from the University System of New Hampshire and the Community College System of New Hampshire called the merge a "hasty proposal" in an open letter to state senators and representatives. The former trustees called for the governor to remove the merger proposal from his bud-

get and to establish a commission composed of legislative, executive, and public members to study the benefits of a future merger.[15]

Advocating caution and urging change leaders to avoid haste to reduce the likelihood of embarrassment later is a common strategy to block change.[16] Being viewed as rash can reduce the credibility and likely success of a change initiative, however.

9. *Ignoring skeptics*. When we believe we have a good idea, it can be annoying to be questioned by skeptics. That is why many change advocates believe it is best to simply ignore the skeptics and focus on building strong alliances with supporters instead. This is faulty thinking. In his book *Making Sustainability Stick: The Blueprint for Successful Implementation*, Kevin Wilhelm writes, "Skeptics can be one of the greatest resources you can have with any implementation project or change initiative because they are the ones who have concerns, see potential hiccups, notice blind spots, and think they know what's wrong with your idea. They might know the answers to the unspoken questions."[17]

10. *Failing to consider that change often means loss*. In their book *The Practice of Adaptive Leadership*, Ronald Heifetz, Alexander Grashow, and Martin Linsky assert, "People do not resist change, per se, but loss."[18] When planning for change or attempting to analyze why change efforts tend to fail, it is essential to acknowledge that there is nothing appealing about losing autonomy, status, identity, comfort, resources, control, feelings of competence, or relationships. We are sometimes open to loss or sacrifice if we can see the possibility of a better future, but if we are not personally advantaged by a change, it can be hard to garner enthusiasm.

When asked to explain why the Marlboro College and Bridgeport University merger talks broke down, Marlboro president Kevin Quigley explained, "We were really attracted by the compelling vision that Bridgeport had for us, but despite our repeated efforts to understand how that vision would be implemented programmatically and financially, we really never got any details over three months of negotiations. We wanted to understand how Marlboro endures."[19] Note the phrase "how Marlboro endures." Clearly, the potential loss of identity and cherished autonomy were considered insurmountable obstacles.

Fear of loss was another factor that doomed the University of Michigan's initial attempt at creating a shared services center. The 842 faculty who signed a petition opposing the Administrative Service Transformation Project feared losing control of valued administrative resources and resisted having to make their own copies, schedule their own meetings, and engage with administrative staff via email rather than in person.[20] The petition also expressed concern that faculty were not appropriately consulted during the planning process. Administrative staff resisted the change as well because it would mean losing the sense of community they enjoyed as members of an academic department.

A fear of loss also surfaced during conversations related to merging New Hampshire's two- and four-year institutions. In addition to citing research that demonstrated that community colleges are not affected by the same enrollment challenges as those challenging four-year institutions,[21] the interim chancellor of the New Hampshire Community College System expressed concerns about community colleges losing their ability to meet the needs of their communities. "When we look at other mergers that have happened, the first voice that goes away is the voice of the community colleges," she explained.[22]

What Does Change Management Research Tell Us?

Having reviewed common change management gaffes, let's turn now to what research on change management theorists advise change agents to do to be more successful. Here we summarize models advanced by five well-known change management theorists and consider how their recommendations might be applied in higher education systems. It is worth noting that much of the available change management research has been designed for corporate settings that are far more hierarchical than colleges and universities. Even so, there are kernels of advice from popular models that can prove useful in higher education settings. Let's review them.

John Kotter's Eight-Step Change Model

According to John Kotter, change agents should follow eight steps:

1. *Create a sense of urgency*. Help others see the need for change and the importance of taking swift action.
2. *Build a guiding coalition*. Build a broadly representative team to guide, coordinate, and communicate the change effort.
3. *Form a strategic vision and initiatives*. Describe how the future will be different and better than the present.
4. *Enlist a volunteer army*. Encourage mass support for the opportunity by building a movement rather than a change project.
5. *Enable action by removing barriers*. Focus on eliminating silos and inefficient processes to make change possible.
6. *Generate short-term wins*. Celebrate success at each project milestone.
7. *Sustain acceleration*. Build on past success by pushing harder for more change.
8. *Institute change*. Ensure that organizational members see the link between new behaviors and organizational success, and work to see that new habits replace old habits.[23]

Implications for Higher Education Systems

Three of Kotter's steps hold promise for change initiatives in higher education. Creating a sense of urgency is critical to encourage attention and engagement. Building a broadly representative guiding coalition is essential to establish a sense of legitimacy. And creating small, achievable milestones for change initiatives and recognizing success along the way is a practical strategy for sustaining energy and enthusiasm.

Prosci's ADKAR Model

The change management consulting firm Prosci developed the ADKAR Model to explain factors critical for transformational change. The firm asserts five key elements are critical for change.

- Awareness of the factors driving the need for change
- Desire to participate in and support the change effort
- Knowledge regarding how to change
- Ability to demonstrate the skills and behaviors required given the change
- Reinforcement to sustain the change[24]

Implications for Higher Education Systems

Awareness of the factors driving the need for change is essential and is a fundamental foundation for generating support for doing things in new way. Providing individuals with the skills they need to be successful when navigating change is also essential. When we consider efforts to install enterprise resource planning systems such as financial, human resources, student information systems, institutions that invest in preparing users to master the new platforms are far more successful than those that provide little or no support. As we observed in 2020 during the COVID-19 pandemic, assuring faculty that they would be given the tools to transition to online teaching and learning was instrumental in the successful and relatively quick transition from in-person to digital instruction.

Nudge Theory

Popularized in their 2008 book *Nudge: Improving Decisions about Health, Wealth, and Happiness*, University of Chicago scholars Richard Thaler and Cass Sunstein created broader interest in using nudge theory as a positive and ethical method for influencing behavior.[25] Nudges can include putting water in vending machines to offer a healthy alternative to soft drinks, encouraging donors to use monthly credit card deductions to encourage continuous giving, and giving customers a small discount for bringing in their own grocery bags to reduce plastic bag use. A frequently cited nudge was attempted at Schiphol Airport in Amsterdam. There, a black housefly was etched into urinals as a strategy for improving aim. Did it work? It did. In fact, studies indicated an 80 percent reduction in spillage.[26]

Thaler and Sunstein offer several ideas for influencing behavior, key among them:

1. Make change easy.
2. Make change fun.
3. Make change popular and socially desirable.[27]

Implications for Higher Education Systems

When attempting to encourage change in higher education, make doing things differently as simple as possible. Also, look for opportunities to make adopting a change a popular and high-status behavior.

Elisabeth Kübler-Ross's Five Stages Model

Those familiar with Elisabeth Kübler-Ross may be surprised to see her work included among change management theories. That is because she is best known for her work in explaining the dynamics of grief, specifically the stages that terminal patients and their loved ones may go through when learning that death is inevitable. But given that change can be associated with loss, her work is useful in understanding the emotional cycles that individuals experience when anticipating or facing profound change. Kübler-Ross noted that individuals experiencing grief often go through five stages: denial, anger, bargaining, depression, and acceptance.[28]

Using the Kübler-Ross model, consider how members of a financially struggling small college might react to news that their system board has voted to merge with a larger and better resourced university in the system. In such a case we might expect faculty, staff, students, alumni, and donors to work through the stages of grief in the following way:

1. Denial ("This can't happen.")
2. Anger ("How dare they swallow us up.")
3. Bargaining ("Give us a year to launch a fundraising campaign to turn our situation around.")
4. Depression ("Things aren't like they used to be; I am miserable.)
5. Acceptance ("There are definitely some benefits to being part of a

better resourced institution; I can see why our board supports the merger.")

The Kübler-Ross model is useful for understanding how people affected by change might behave. Feelings of denial and anger are common, and savvy change leaders recognize that organizational members often need time to process the pending change before they can fully embrace it. Being attuned to potential bargaining is also important because a flurry of activity to block proposed change is common.

Kübler-Ross noted that not all people experience the five stages of grief, the stages of grief are not necessarily sequential, and that it is possible to get stuck in one of the stages. Eventual acceptance is not guaranteed.

Implications for Higher Education Systems

Understand that change often feels like (and may even be) loss, so anticipate and attend to common stages of grief. For example, expect denial by giving those to be affected by change advance notice, allowing them time to reflect on and process what is coming. Be prepared for anger and depression, which may be manifested in low morale and declines in performance and engagement. Importantly, respect feelings of grief by honoring what has been lost and expressing gratitude for what served the institution in the past.

William Bridges's Transition Model

In his book *Managing Transitions: Making the Most of Change*, William Bridges advanced the concept that we should think about transitions rather than change. According to Bridges, change is something that happens to people, while transitions are what happen to people as they experience change. According to Bridges, when going through change, people move through three stages:

1. Ending, Losing, and Letting Go
2. The Neutral Zone
3. The New Beginning[29]

During the Ending, Losing, and Letting Go stage, people may experience emotions that include fear, denial, anger, disorientation, and grief. While in the Neutral Zone, they may ponder what the change means for them and consider how it affects their personal and professional identity. In the New Beginning stage, the change is accepted and sometimes embraced.

Implications for Higher Education Systems

Actively honor the past while looking to the future, and respond to feelings of disorientation by providing as much information as possible to reduce uncertainty and feelings of disorientation.

A Higher Education System Change Checklist

Having considered various change theories and some of the lessons they offer, let's consider a 10-step process that higher education system leaders and policymakers can use to make their change efforts more successful.

Step One: Expose the Higher Education Community to the Outside World

Without exposure to emerging trends, external threats, and evolving expectations, it is hard for stakeholders to see the need for change. When everything seems to be working, potential change seems disruptive and unnecessary. This is especially true in academia, which can be highly insular. While people who work outside of higher education often engage with individuals in multiple industries, academics are more likely to talk among themselves. Exposing higher education members to emerging trends and ideas is critical.

Strategies to Consider

- *External advisory boards.* Form external advisory boards for each discipline, and invite faculty and staff to meet with their members to learn from outsiders about emerging trends and challenges.

- *Build financial and organizational acumen*. Regularly report on institutional data, and make it bite-sized and digestible. For example, report on net tuition revenue during one month, auxiliary revenue in the next, and health insurance costs after that. Share information on enrollment trends. Where are your applications coming from? Why are students choosing you? Report on which campuses and courses have the highest withdrawal and fail rates. When students drop out, what makes them leave? And what barriers are in the way of students transferring within the system or taking courses from more than one university? When possible, report on how information has changed over time to give faculty and staff a sense of context. For example, failing a class during their first semester could have been the top factor leading students to drop out three years ago, while lack of financial resources could be the primary factor revealed when students were queried most recently.

Step Two: Surface Dissatisfaction to Create Demand for Change

Consider lessons learned from social and political movements when crafting change strategies, especially those used most recently by the #MeToo and Back Lives Matter movements, which used outrage as a fulcrum for change. History reveals that outrage and a willingness to challenge the status quo have been essential foundations for transformational change.[30] Look for opportunities to put a face on the need for change and the need to fight for something better.

Step Three: Build a Team of Credible Advisors to Guide the Change Strategy

Bring together a broadly representative group of well-respected advisors to serve as strategy advisors.

Strategies to Consider

- Ask your strategy advisors to discuss the factors prompting the need for change within their networks and to bring back intelligence that might inform the change approach.

- Use your strategy advisors to explore the potential impacts of the change by asking: Who will be affected by the change? How many people will be affected by this change? Who stands to benefit from the change? How might they benefit? Who might be disadvantaged by the change? How soon does this change need to occur? Could the change be delayed? What happens if it is? What additional information do we need to consider our options? What are the pros and cons of the options we have surfaced so far? What opposition might we expect? What do those who might oppose this change know that we don't know?

Step Four: Provide Time for Reflection about Coming Change

Before launching the change effort, provide stakeholders with time to consider the need for change before expecting them to let go of their current reality. While too much reflection time can lead to uncertainty-related anxiety, it can be useful to give those likely to be affected by change some time to consider what it might mean to them, and to work through feelings of denial and anger before the real work begins.

Step Five: Engage Your Stakeholders

Change is more likely to be accepted when it is co-created rather than announced. To the degree possible, involve your stakeholders in the change planning process. Describe the challenge and ask for options. Importantly, report back what was learned during the information-gathering process to demonstrate that diverse voices have been heard and considered.

Strategies to Consider

- Form internal teams or engage ext.ernal consultants to conduct interviews and focus groups to gather broad input.

- Establish small project teams to work on various aspects of the change effort.
- Involve those most likely to be affected by the change to help design it.

Step Six: Embrace Your Skeptics

In partnership with your strategy team, identify likely skeptics and speak with them about the challenge you are trying to address.

Strategies to Consider

- Consider adding a known skeptic to your strategy team.
- Ask the skeptics for advice about how to think about the challenge and to share lessons learned from past change efforts. Invite them to answer following questions:
    - What might make this plan fail?
    - What have we failed to consider?
    - What would make this plan more viable?
    - Is there a better approach that we have not considered?
    - Who else feels the way you do? Do they have the same concerns?
    - What advice do you have?

Step Seven: Use Strategic Communication

Because uncertainty can be demotivating and even paralyzing, share as much information as possible. Share time lines, potential options, likely projections, and possible barriers. Let your stakeholders know what to expect, and commit to keeping them informed. Customize communication approaches to connect with stakeholders' varied interests and motivations.

Strategies to Consider

- Create a strategic communication plan that includes audiences, key messages, communication channels, time lines, and responsible parties.

- Customize messages to be responsive to different audience needs. Use logos, ethos, and pathos (i.e., logic, ethics, and emotion) to craft varied messages.
  - For those motivated by logic, cite examples, statistics, expert reports, and reliable studies.
  - To reach stakeholders' concerns about ethics, consider social norming strategies, testimonials from credible community members, and expressions of support from recognized experts.
  - To inspire those who are more likely to be moved by emotional appeals, use photos, personal stories, and inspirational language. Highlight common feelings of outrage or outline the path to a greater sense of belonging to build support.
- Use multiple communication channels, including presidential addresses, town halls, editorial board meetings with the local press, social media, and institution-wide messages. When seeking support for a change effort that involves community leaders and government officials, request one-on-one meetings to increase the likelihood of hearing genuine concern or support.
- Make it easy and safe to share ideas and concerns through online reporting mechanisms that allow comments to be made anonymously.
- Communicate what you know and what you don't know.
- Share how your thinking has evolved based on feedback.
- Give credit to individuals and groups who propose useful ideas.
- Report on the number of people who have provided input.
- Acknowledge the foundations that have made the new change possible, and recognize those who contributed to past success.

Step Eight: Make Change Possible

In some cases, change will require organizational members to learn new skills. When that is the case, be strategic about offering training and support to facilitate new learning.

Step Nine: Allow for Small Wins and Celebrate Success

Treat the change like a large, multifaceted project and establish multiple performance milestones. This approach keeps the project moving, but also allows for regular opportunities to recognize accomplishments and celebrate success. Publicizing success is important because it increases stakeholder confidence in the change initiative by demonstrating that change is truly possible.

Strategies to Consider

- Recognize individuals and groups who have been instrumental in moving the change initiative forward.
- Provide regular project updates and announce small wins through multiple communication channels.
- Hold celebration lunches or distribute modest "thank-you" gifts to change team members as project milestones are reached.

Step Ten: Allow for Rest

Finally, be intentional about allowing for rest between change initiatives to allow stakeholders to recharge and refresh.

What If There Is No Time to Work through the Higher Education System Checklist?

There will be times when change is urgently required, but there is no time to be methodical. A governor may make a huge cut to a university system budget without notice. A state legislature may unexpectedly schedule a vote to limit curriculum autonomy or demand a campus closure. A group of key donors may threaten to renege on their philanthropic pledges if system campuses execute plans to rename buildings named after confederate generals. In fast-moving and unexpected situations like these, how can sound change management change principles be applied?

This is a time when it makes sense to consider John Kotter's advice to create a sense of urgency. This may be accomplished by mobilizing supporters and key stakeholders and asking them to voice their concerns. It might involve a social media or traditional media campaign that creates a sense of outrage that makes others want to take action. It could also involve getting key influencers to engage in behind-the-scenes conversations with decision-makers to change hearts and minds.

When it comes to managing change, trust and information are generally our greatest tools. Savvy leaders understand the importance of building deep and diverse relationships, even with those who have different opinions and objectives. Because they stay in touch, listen, and offer support when possible, they establish a reputation for being reasonable and create a reservoir of goodwill that can be tapped when times are tough. They are less likely to be surprised, and they have a coalition of support that they can mobilize quickly when changing minds is critical. Friends are always important, but in times of crisis, they are essential.

Conclusion

Higher education's long-term survival requires openness to new approaches and high levels of adaptability, but higher education is known for being resistant to change. Further, the complexities of large university systems can make building support for change and then navigating it especially difficult. Given these truths, is change in university systems truly possible?

Absolutely.

Strategic change leaders know how to navigate organizational dynamics and build support for new approaches by using inclusive approaches and attending to the perceptions of loss that so often accompany change initiatives. They are respectful to those who may be affected by change and are careful to honor the past while looking to the future. Importantly, they recognize that achieving results is more important than getting credit. Change management is an essential competency for higher education leaders; the concepts in this chapter offer a reliable road map for initiating and executing both transformational and incremental change.

Notes

1. Dave Soloman, "How the Big USNH and Community College Merger Fizzled." *Business New Hampshire Magazine*, October 18, 2021, https://www.sentinelsource.com/news/economy/how-the-big-usnh-and-community-college-merger-fizzled/article_ae797374-6d90-53c0-9bff-f65e8a2fb4f0.html.

2. Colleen Flaherty, "No Deal," *Inside Higher Ed*, September 16, 2019, https://www.insidehighered.com/news/2019/09/16/marlboro-college-and-u-bridgeport-drop-plans-merge.

3. Ry Rivard, "U. of Michigan Delays Controversial 'Shared Services' Plan." *Inside Higher Ed*, December 3, 2013, https://www.insidehighered.com/quicktakes/2013/12/03/u-michigan-delays-controversial-shared-services-plan.

4. Martin Kurzweil, Melody Andrews, Catharine B. Hill, Sosanya Jones, Jane Radecki, and Roger C. Schonfel, "Public College and University Consolidations and the Implications for Equity," *Ithaka S+R*, August 30, 2021, https://doi.org/10.18665/sr.315846.

5. Arthur Levine and Scott Van Pelt, "The Future of Higher Ed Is Occurring at the Margins," *Inside Higher Ed*, October 4, 2021, https://www.insidehighered.com/views/2021/10/04/higher-education-should-prepare-five-new-realities-opinion#at_pco=cfd-1.0.

6. Kathy Johnson Bowles, "Why Can't Higher Education Change?," *Inside Higher Ed*, January 11, 2022, https://www.insidehighered.com/blogs/just-explain-it-me/why-can%E2%80%99t-higher-education-change.

7. Kurzweil et al., "Public College and University Consolidations."

8. Kurzweil et al., "Public College and University Consolidations."

9. Rosabeth Moss Kanter, "Ten Reasons People Resist Change," *Harvard Business Review*, September 25, 2012, https://hbr.org/2012/09/ten-reasons-people-resist-chang.

10. Melvin L. M. Mboa, "Operation Shock and Awe: Its Implications for the Future of Multilateralism and International Law," *Comparative and International Law Journal of Southern Africa* 37, no. 2 (2004): 253–66. http://www.jstor.org/stable/23252187.

11. Harlan K. Ullman, James P. Wade, L. A. Edney, Fred M. Franks, Charles A. Horner, Jonathan T. Howe, and Keith Brendley, *Shock and Awe: Achieving Rapid Dominance* (Washington, DC: National Defense University, 1996).

12. A. D. Brown, Susan Ainsworth, and David Grant, "The Rhetoric of Institutional Change," *Organization Studies* 33, no. 3 (2012): 297–321. https://doi.org/10.1177/0170840611435598.

13. Katherine Mangan, "What's in a Name? Merger of 2 Universities in Georgia Smells Anything but Sweet," *Chronicle of Higher Education*, August 10, 2012, https://www.chronicle.com/article/whats-in-a-name-merger-of-2-universities-in-georgia-smells-anything-but-sweet/.

14. Walter C. Jones, "Georgia Regents University Gets New Name with Augusta in It," *Florida Times-Union*, October 15, 2015, https://www.jacksonville.com/story/news/2015/09/16/georgia-regents-university-gets-new-name-augusta-it/15679828007.

15. "Our Turn: Hasty Higher Education Merger Is Dangerous," *Concord Monitor*, March 20, 2021, https://www.concordmonitor.com/OurTurn-39468523.

16. US Office of Strategic Services, *Simple Sabotage Field Manual* (Washington, DC: US Office of Strategic Services, 1944), https://www.hsdl.org/?view&did=750070.

17. Kevin Wilhelm, *Making Sustainability Stick: The Blueprint for Successful Implementation* (Upper Saddle River, NJ: Pearson Education, 2013).

18. Ronald Heifetz Alexander Grashow, and Martin Linsky, *The Practice of Adaptive Leadership* (Boston, MA: Harvard Business Press, 2009).

19. Colleen Flaherty, "No Deal," *Inside Higher Ed*, September 16, 2019, https://www.insidehighered.com/news/2019/09/16/marlboro-college-and-u-bridgeport-drop-plans-merge.

20. Jennifer Calfas, "Initiative Challenged by Faculty Petition," *Michigan Daily*, November 24, 2013.

21. Dave Soloman, "How the Big USNH and Community College Merger Fizzled," *Business New Hampshire Magazine*, October 18, 2021, https://www.sentinelsource.com/news/economy/how-the-big-usnh-and-community-college-merger-fizzled/article_ae797374-6d90-53c0-9bff-f65e8a2fb4f0.htm.

22. Emma Whitford, "New Hampshire Merger Proposal Takes Shape," *Inside Higher Ed*, March 3, 2021.

23. John P. Kotter, *Leading Change* (Boston, MA: Harvard Business Press, 1996, 2012).

24. Jeff Hiatt, *ADKAR: A Model for Change in Business, Government, and Our Community* (Loveland, CO: Prosci Learning Center Publications, 2006).

25. Richard Thaler and Cass Sunstein, *Nudge: Improving Decisions about Health, Wealth, and Happiness* (New Haven, CT: Yale University Press, 2008).

26. Christopher Ingraham, "What's a Urinal Fly and What Does It Have to Do with Winning a Nobel Prize?," *Washington Post*, October 9, 2017.

27. Ingraham, "What's a Urinal Fly?"

28. Elisabeth Kubler-Ross, *On Death and Dying* (New York: Macmillan, 1969).

29. William Bridges, *Managing Transitions: Making the Most of Change*, 4th ed. (London: Nicholas Brealey, 2017).

30. Ken Perlman, "Moving from Outrage to Real Change," Culture Sync, June 19, 2020, https://culturesync.net/moving-from-outrage-to-real-change/.

17 |

Systems Heads

NANCY ZIMPHER AND REBECCA MARTIN

SYSTEMS OF HIGHER EDUCATION face numerous internal and external challenges that are accelerating at a brisk pace. At the same time, systems possess unique capabilities to unleash innovation, advance social and economic mobility, and improve our quality of life. To realize their full potential, we need to reshape the future roles and functions of higher education systems, and to do that, we need the requisite leadership from system leaders. This dynamic situation, the evolution of systems, our vision for systems of the future, and the call for leadership are the focus for this final chapter of *Public University Systems: Leveraging Scale in Higher Education*.

The Rise of Public College and University Systems

Higher education systems are barely a century old. They were founded to oversee, regulate, and coordinate postsecondary education. Decades later, they were tasked with ensuring effective use of state resources and weeding out duplicative courses and programs within states. Aims McGuinness provides a recent documentation of this evolution, which can be broken down into six fairly distinguishable periods that "coincide with significant economic transitions in the United States" (McGuinness 2013, 48), as follows:

Period 1: Progressive Era (late 1880s to World War I). Consolidation of higher education began as states enacted laws that sought to eliminate corruption and modernize—and often centralize—state government, underscoring the notion that institutions were state agencies with no independent legal standing. Efforts to counter that assumption continue to advocate for increased institutional autonomy from state forces that might overregulate public systems of higher education.

Period 2: Consolidation Era (World War I through World War II). The severe economic conditions of the Great Depression coupled with rising concerns about political intrusion into higher education motivated states to take bold action to consolidate governance of their public colleges and universities, to insulate higher education from direct control of the governor, and to curb political intrusion, the dominant themes of this period.

Period 3: Capacity Building, Expansion, and Standardization (World War II to the 1970s). Herein states sought to accommodate demand for higher education by driving two trends: a significant increase in individuals pursuing higher education and calls for consolidation across all forms of state government, creating an architecture of state higher education coordinating and governing structures that remain essentially in place today.

Period 4: The Rise of Decentralization (1980s). This period witnessed the beginning of a fundamental shift away from the almost century-long trend toward centralization, resulting in considerable legislation enacted to increase the institutions' operational flexibility in establishing tuition levels, contracting, and human resources.

Period 5: Restructuring amid a Changing State Role (1990–2003). Specifically, states would establish a more aggressive position in promoting reforms designed to link higher education to the state priorities of holding colleges and universities accountable for student learning, developing research capacity, linking institutional capacity to explicit state goals, and sharing best practices about "what works" in system organization and leadership in bringing about major system changes and their effectiveness.

Period 6: Responses to Recession and Slow Economic Recovery (2003 *through the present*). States continue to press for improvements in productivity, cost containment, and innovation designed to improve student success and degree completion at lower cost to the state and to students.

In summary, McGuinness observes: "Overall, systems remain among the more stable elements of the nation's public higher education system. In this respect, systems can serve as a 'platform' for leading change and linking the component institutions to public priorities. At the same time, the 'closed' bureaucratic structure of systems and their dominant internal governing responsibilities can be significant barriers to the capacity of systems to respond to the demands of the 21st century" (48–64).

At the time systems were founded, there were no road maps, resources, or sources of support to chart the way. Even so, systems began to emerge and evolve organically as the idea of collective impact began to catch on. Today, systems of public higher education serve the largest proportion of students attending college in this country and within the states that fund these systems. They also serve an increasingly diverse population of students from both urban and rural settings, largely underrepresented in the general student population, providing systems of public higher education the great opportunity to help a generation of students of low economic status and racial and ethnic diversity to pursue increased economic and social mobility.

These systems are local assets and national treasures. They are powerful instruments for change to meet this country's promise and its commitments to low economic and highly diverse communities as well as to the youth and adults who seek a better education, gainful careers, and improved quality of life.

Even in this relatively young New World construct of organizational development, a century isn't very long compared to the amount of time and money invested over the years in the growth of individual hospitals, churches, primary schools, and college campuses, for example. We might consider postsecondary systems to be currently entrenched in their teenage years—experiencing awkward growth spurts, seeking clarity on identity and purpose, and eyeing pathways to future opportunities for meaningful roles in society.

As they advance toward the next phase of maturity, public university systems are distinctly poised to address some of the most significant challenges facing humankind, to leverage their unique ability to create value for society greater than the sum of their institutional parts. This is a historic moment for achieving equity, access, and success for all students across higher education in the United States. The closest parallel was undertaken 50 years ago by the Carnegie Foundation through its early studies of multicampus systems and its highly influential institutional classification system.

Our Vision for University Systems in 2030

Systems of higher education are important instruments of the state, no matter the varied efforts to improve or reform them. Looking forward, they will continue to be valued, repeatedly called upon to exhibit a sense of timeliness and leadership that puts the interests of their states, and the nation, on a trajectory of educating more people in service to economic and social mobility and national improvements in universal quality of life. In every dimension imaginable, they will advance the promise that a better educated population enhances the human condition: improved personal and public health, enhanced education for generations of children and grandchildren, strengthened civic infrastructure, higher levels of civic engagement, less dependence on social services, and enhanced individual mental wellness. This vision is a compelling call to action to systems of public higher education, which envisions more equitable access to higher education in one of two ways: (1) through the traditional pattern from early childhood, to elementary and secondary education, and through credential or degree completion into the workforce or (2) on a pathway that returns undereducated adults to the classroom and the prospect of better jobs. Both of these routes result in increased social and economic mobility. According to Lane and Johnstone (2013):

> to be successful in the future, higher education systems will move beyond their roles as allocators, coordinators and regulators. They will exert leadership in moving higher education institutions toward greater impact in society. They will identify and pursue ways that add value to the states they serve and the campuses of which they are comprised. . . . [H]igher education systems need to find ways to (1) promote the vibrancy of individual institutions by supporting their unique missions; (2) focus on smart growth by coordinating the work of campuses to improve access, control costs, and enhance productivity across the system; and (3) leverage the collective strengths of the institutions to benefit the states and community served by the system. (5)

We might ask at this stage of our chapter several probing questions regarding our vision that are addressed in the following sections: (1) How might systems of higher education prioritize the current issues concerning all of postsecondary education, with a clear view of which of these issues are most effectively addressed by systems as opposed to individual college campuses? (2) What are the necessary steps that only systems can take to address those issues? (3) What are the existing formative or futuristic strategies that systems must take to address calls for systems transformation in meeting the demands placed on them, within the current financial and political constraints that compromise or completely undermine change efforts? A quick look at the prevailing concerns about the capacity of higher education systems to meet contemporary demands sets the table for transformative proposals for change.

Dynamic Headwinds: The Accelerating Pace of Internal and External Challenges

Like all public institutions, during the past 100 years, higher education systems have endured waves of state, national, and global social, economic, and political ups and downs. Within that broader context, however, the public postsecondary education sector faces unique business and structural challenges in the twenty-first century. They may borrow strategy and solutions from other sectors and to some extent, and often do. Examples include strategic planning, outsourcing, public-private partnerships, shared services, globalization, and lean process improvement. But to a significant degree, postsecondary systems must rely on their own innovation, strategies for collective impact, and improvement science to adapt to, and get in front of, the headwinds of change. In other words, to lead.

These systems operate in an increasingly complex and diverse environment where they are expected to harness the collective contributions of their various campuses to benefit the students, communities, and other stakeholders that they serve. In 2013, Jason Lane and D. Bruce Johnstone captured the nature of these headwinds this way:

> Public higher education is confronting unprecedented challenges and demands. There is an ongoing and significant change in the demographics of the students being served. How education is being delivered to students is transforming in the wake of massive technological advancements. Employers are looking for graduates with better critical thinking skills and more specialized knowledge. Governments are increasingly recognizing the criticality of educating students and producing cutting-edge research for enhancing a state's or nation's economic competitiveness. In the midst of all of this, there has been a significant change in the higher education sector's revenue models and regulatory environment, creating new opportunities and constraints. (ix)

While this state of affairs summarizes primarily the impact state economies and expectations can level on systems of higher education, there is a prevailing national context that impacts systems as well. Despite their major roles that affect conditions ranging from the local to the global, systems are not recognized in the federal law governing American higher education, they receive virtually no direct federal financial support, they are largely left out of the accreditation process, and with a few notable exceptions, they receive little scholarly attention.

In less than a decade, a new wave of pressing and complex problems has begun to squeeze most institutions' notions of a reasonable time horizon within which to respond to strategic challenges. The issues facing our nation's higher education systems have grown even larger to include declining enrollments, state funding cuts, equity gaps in college attendance and completion, student debt, extended time to degree completion, perceptions of inefficiency and political partisanship, growth in competition from online and the for-profit sectors, lack of coordination with state and federal policymakers, gaps in meeting workforce demand for skilled talent, and more. At the same time, great expectations were put on the nation's systems. Examples include taking a leading role in the shift to a knowledge economy, educating students for the workforce and for citizen engagement, steering research into areas that produce financially valuable intellectual property, providing public services such as health care, expanding social mobility and economic opportunity, and advancing our knowledge of the causes of environmental change and methods of adaptation, all at a lower cost to students and funders.

During this most recent troubled time in which the COVID-19 pandemic magnified the forces described above, many systems have leveraged their abilities to scale innovation by setting collective visions and sharing resources across campuses. The results of these efforts include greater student access and mobility, sharing of student data to improve learning outcomes, combining research capacity, expanding health care, and adding impactful student support activities. While many systems have demonstrated their effectiveness in these areas, many other systems have been constrained by outmoded policies and practices, with the result that state attainment, completion, equity, and workforce goals are not being met.

The Promise of Systemness

University systems—and the institutions that comprise them—are more important than ever at this turbulent time. Their contributions of research and development, innovation, and application of new ideas are key to unlocking new futures. These systems provide workforce certifications through the most advanced professional and academic degrees. They serve their states and the nation through community outreach and public service. They contribute to economic development, social mobility, public and environmental health, civic engagement, and national defense. And they bring added value that only they can deliver.

Changing demographics, uncertain funding patterns, technological developments, and many other demands on the nation's higher education sector will require actions that systems are best positioned to lead. Systems will need to bring all the assets within their reach to tackle urgent statewide challenges. Among many strategic opportunities that can fuel equitable student success are:

- making the programs at all campuses in a system accessible to students wherever they live;
- eliminating barriers to transfer between and among campuses;
- using technology to streamline and consolidate administrative functions;
- designing new academic programs to prepare the workforce of the future;
- selecting and developing skilled campus leaders who collaborate rather than compete; and
- shifting and sharing resources to increase student-centered support services.

The dynamic flywheel of change inherently spins faster and faster. Lane and Johnstone (2013) cite pressing and complex issues in an era of increased accountability, greater calls for productivity, and intensifying fiscal austerity. A new term—"systemness"—was introduced in *Higher Education 3.0* to define the unique ability of higher education systems to better serve students and society by leveraging diverse campus assets within and across systems to create impact greater than the sum of the systems' institutional parts. As Nancy Zimpher notes in Lane and Johnstone (2013, 27), "Systemness is the ability of a system to coordinate the activities of its constituent campuses so that, on the whole, the system behaves in a way that is more powerful and impactful than what can be achieved by individual campuses acting alone.

Ideally, systemness permits systems to channel institutional activity and resources in order to improve the economic status of the state in which it operates and enhance the quality of life its citizens possess."

This notion of systemness sets the table for the kind of collaboration and collective action that will be required in the next decades of the twenty-first century. Since introducing the notion of systemness, its true meaning is beginning to come into focus. One could say that the greatest lessons learned from the COVID experiences of 2020 and the years following would be the instrumentality of systemness in the midst of a crisis. Systems had to oversee the intersection of state and federal policy around issues of testing, administering vaccines, mask-wearing, and other protections; crowd control; openings and closings; and, of course, transitioning to remote instruction. Because of the systemic response to COVID and campus safety issues, campuses made a major strategic shift in instructional delivery systems and everything that followed "on a dime." Since the orchestration of that shift was essentially made through the coordination of state policy at the system level, campuses and communities saw firsthand how much more effective they could be when campuses benefitted from more centralized crisis coordination. Systems also were able to address technological support in online delivery of instructions, lead decision-making relative to academic grading policies during massive remote instruction, enact changes in course additions and withdrawal processes, and much, much more. All of this produced numerous examples of the benefits of more centralized decision-making processes. From that experience, and over months of digesting what really happened amid such a confounding crisis, it was clear from the general commentary that these necessary crisis response steps simply could not have happened without the more coordinated, and in many cases "centralized," direction emanating from the system central office.

From these crisis lessons, we know several things about the conditions that foster systemness. We know this: systemness and collective action are inspired by vision, a "true north" that compels constituent groups to seek solutions that will positively affect the execution of shared goals, often derived at the hands of many. That said, systemness requires a form of discipline not necessarily the hallmark of higher education in the past. We can take a lesson in "greatness" from Jim Collins (2005), who notes: "We must reject the idea—well-intentioned, but dead wrong—that the primary path to greatness in the social sector is to be 'more like a business.' Most businesses—like most of anything else in life—. . . have a desperate need for discipline . . ., disciplined people who engage in disciplined thought and who take disciplined actions. . . . A culture of discipline is not a principle of business; it is a principle of greatness" (1–2).

We also know that systemness requires actions that are carefully constructed to meet the needs and desires of constituent groups and to reflect a well-articulated plan for execution and assessment, public accountability for the work at hand, and, where appropriate, the disaggregation of data to reflect the equity agenda within the larger goal. And finally, systemness requires a deep respect for "collective action," a concept coined by Kania and Kramer in 2011, derived from multiple examples of local community work wherein "the idea of genuine change, real improvement on any social issue, requires a cross-sector commitment from a group of passionate and dedicated leaders who are willing to set aside their individual agendas and work together to solve a specific social problem in which they all share an interest." As we turn to prospects for the future advancement of a transformational agenda for state systems of higher education, these conditions will be set forth as a "theory of action" for deep institutional adjustment to the societal challenges we are expecting systems to address.

The Power of Systems: Advancing Prosperity for the Nation

Addressing the challenges of these early decades of the twenty-first century requires an abundance of coordinated leadership across many sectors, and certainly within the postsecondary sector. It bears saying, leadership is often in scarce supply, especially leadership dedicated to coordinated action. Herein we make the case that the current organization of systems provided an opportunity to take a collective pause to assess our response to the COVID crisis, with the concomitant opportunity to identify the transformative changes necessary to respond and lead. When the pandemic forced immediate transition to 100 percent remote learning, system leaders were forced to reflect on the long-term big picture. The pandemic exposed barriers to health care for vulnerable populations, huge disparities in technology access, a dearth of expertise in pandemic crisis response, deep and systemic racial injustice, and extreme gaps in economic opportunity. These health- and social-justice-related issues immediately became the new drivers of higher education reform. Undaunted by the COVID crisis, system leaders seized the opportunity to "get on the balcony" to look at problems through a different lens, and to rethink and reimagine the roles American public higher education systems could and should play in strengthening our country going forward.

With a decade of experience under its belt utilizing a collective impact approach to address systems' top priorities, the membership of the National Association of System Heads (NASH) saw that its existing network of higher education systems could build on a tradition of collaboration in several areas to increase equitable student success. A network of systems could not only improve education outcomes, but also expand health care, address systemic racism, and strengthen the nation's economy and communities. In fact, increased educational opportunity is exactly the pathway to address other systemic challenges that often limit access to social services because of locale, economic loss, lack of education, and long histories of health care neglect. Campuses were responsive to these aspects of the crisis, given the role universities play in administering health care through their hospitals; meeting the demands of just-in-time upskilling and reskilling of health care workers; and, for many of our systems, increasing reliance on the pipeline of criminal justice officers, social workers, and educators. NASH saw its most immediate response to this crisis as one of student access to higher education that provided social and economic stability and success that only could be realized through advanced education.

NASH is uniquely positioned to scale existing evidence-based practices as well as innovations within and across systems, all in service to ensuring equitable student success. The diffusion of systemness across higher education systems has largely occurred via the leadership networks developed by NASH. It is a convener and a network of networks with a strong record of success in spreading and implementing the benefits of systemness at scale. Noteworthy examples include deep implementation of high-impact practices in Georgia, Montana, Tennessee, and Wisconsin, and extensive faculty development in evidence-based teaching practices in California, Missouri, New York, and Texas.

Applying this principle of networks and systemness to the future of higher education, a "Group of 100" leaders and design teams from systems developed the Big ReThink (BRT) Transformation Agenda over an 18-month period during 2020–21. System leaders endorsed the agenda in December 2021, and the NASH Board unanimously adopted it in January 2022.

The BRT Transformation Agenda centers on the power of systemness to close equity gaps in student access and college completion, both of which are necessary preparation for successfully entering the workforce. The agenda is built on a set of five imperatives to deliver equitable student success at scale, with particular emphasis on the redress of inequities and the promotion of cost-effectiveness and economic and social mobility.

Learning. System-wide support for flexible and responsive programs to meet the unique needs of each student.

Talent. A civically engaged and globally competitive workforce that contributes to community vitality and economic development.

Equity. Just and accessible opportunities that empower all students by removing structural and systemic barriers.

Investment. Collective resource-sharing and efficiencies to reinvest in student success.

Systemness. Leveraging the power of public higher education systems to better serve students and society.

With these imperatives at the center, the BRT Transformation Agenda set forth a vision for the next decade. It would move beyond competition toward integrated services, shared academic programming, and predictive data analytics to close equity gaps and deliver access, completion, and success for all students at scale, state by state, by 2030.

What if racial gaps in completion were closed? What if students could transfer within systems seamlessly? What if administrative costs were shared and reduced, slowing ever rising costs and reducing students' debt burden? What if learning management systems, email platforms, academic calendars, registration processes, and financial aid policies were consistent from campus to campus? What if faculty taught students across a system in addition to those on their own home campus? What if people with some college and no degree came back in large numbers and finished their degrees? Why not?

Realizing this ambitious vision by 2030 will require deliberate and determined focus—by leaders across university systems beginning now—on redefining student success, fundamentally reducing the cost base of higher education, and restructuring the education model for quality and equity.

What will it take to accelerate equitable student success? Collective impact (working with coalitions of the willing). Networks of systems using continuous quality-improvement cycles to solve problems of practice and identifying policy barriers. Scaling and sustaining of evidence-based practices is a must.

The commitment of NASH member systems to making the necessary changes has been demonstrated by their signing on to the Power of Systems: Advancing Prosperity for the Nation. This statement translates the BRT Transformation Agenda imperatives and vision into bold goals, corresponding system-level metrics, and a set of initiatives designed to create value for the nation that is greater than the sum of its individual parts. Member systems have agreed to the following commitments by 2030.

- Collectively increase degree and credential completion by 35 percent and reduce equity gaps by 50 percent from 2019–20 baseline levels, yielding an additional 60,000 credentials for minoritized students.

- Support upward social mobility such that the median income of students in the bottom percentile eight years after enrollment exceeds the national median. In addition, by 2040, advance 85 percent of students from families in the bottom 40 percent of the income distribution to the top 60 percent of the income distribution, and 65 percent of students in the bottom 40 percent to the top 40 percent.
- Collectively decrease the median debt borrowed by Pell students (completers and non-completers), by 25 percent from 2020–21 baseline levels. In addition, we propose that the equity gap in three-year repayment rates between Pell recipients and non-Pell recipients should be reduced by 50 percent from 2019–20 baseline levels (19 points). Achieving this goal in conjunction with the other NASH targets would result in an estimated $7 billion reduction in borrowing by low-income students by 2030.

Strategies to Achieve More Equitable Student Success

The Power of Systems strategy to achieve more equitable student success centers on three complementary components: (1) the Institute for Systems Innovation and Improvement, which applies the science of continuous improvement to student-facing processes in networks of systems; (2) the Systems Center for State Policy, which develops a diagnostic "tool kit" and annual report of system and state policies that support improvement in higher education outcomes; and (3) the Partnership to Increase Federal Support for Systems, a state-federal partnership to strengthen system contributions to national educational goals, including a timely initiative to leverage the unique capacities of public university systems to aid in refugee resettlement.

Institute for Systems Innovation and Improvement

The institute builds on NASH'S strong record of leading innovation at scale through multisystem initiatives that advance equitable student access, completion, and success. A partnership with the Carnegie Foundation for the Advancement of Teaching, a leader in improvement science (IS), will support the application of the process of IS to higher education. The institute has five components: (1) NASH Improvement Communities (NICs), (2) innovation initiatives, (3) leadership development, (4) system grants, and (5) credentialing.

While improvement science has proven successful in elementary and secondary education, as partners, the Institute and the Carnegie Foundation will test what works in postsecondary education, spread and scale improvements, and accelerate learning within systems and across networks of systems. An adapted version of the Carnegie Networked Improvement Communities model will align with NASH member systems' organizational structures, culture, and needs.

The first of these networks, called NASH Improvement Communities, were formed in 2022. Each NIC includes five systems teams and applies improvement science methodology to a specific problem of practice. The institute provides ongoing support to the NICs in the form of coaching, analytics, technical support, knowledge sharing, and onboarding new members.

NASH will continue to support existing and new innovation initiatives to solve problems that emerge between strategy formulation and strategy execution. The institute plans to maintain a strong focus on the management and progress of these large cross-system and cross-institutional initiatives, which must be successfully completed to achieve system goals. Grants to systems will provide resources and incentives to use improvement science methodology to solve problems of practice. System grants will also support competitive innovation initiatives.

Increase the Number of Transfer Students Who Complete Degrees

Research suggests that articulation agreements and bilateral relationships between institutions have not been effective in improving success for transfer students. Designing transfer opportunities to mirror the reality of how students actually move among institutions is more effective than focusing on the problem from an institutional perspective. The following are proven policy improvements adopted by higher education systems, in order of prevalence.

- *Transfer credit and/or course guarantees*. Reduce time to credential or degree by accepting general education or major completion requirements.
- *Aligning curriculum*. Institute system-wide general education frameworks and comparable introductory courses.
- *Transfer credit appeals*. Relatively new, the focus is on achieving parity in how institutions evaluate and award transfer credit.
- *Reverse transfer*. Post-transfer credits to community colleges so that students can complete an associate's degree.
- *Grading policies for transfer*. Standardize minimum grading standards to ensure credit transfer.

Another major solution to transfer issues lies in the technology arena, including standardizing data collection and sharing; accepting credits earned through prior learning assessment; using a common learning management system; standardizing student information tracked in data systems; and disaggregating student data by race, ethnicity, socioeconomic status, and gender. Highly recommended student-facing services include dedicated advisors to assist historically underrepresented students and orientation sessions that explain how transfer works. Owing to the significant number of students who attend NASH-member institutions, improving transfer rates by just 5 percent across NASH systems would yield more than 50,000 more graduates per year.

Use Proven High-Impact Practices for Student Success

High-impact practices, or HIPs, are experiential education offerings that help students acquire transferable skills. Employers consistently report that skills such as critical thinking and problem-solving, teamwork, and oral and written communication are less well developed and matter more than specific knowledge in a particular discipline. These skills are best built when students practice complex, problem-centered, applied learning through research, seminars, community-based learning, and internships.

The effects of HIPs on persistence and completion are especially important for transfer students (Zilvinskis and Dumford, 2018), first-generation students, and students of color (Finley and McNair, 2013).

By putting student-focused, problem-centered learning at the center of system-wide student success efforts, and lifting up the importance of and support for faculty development, systems can more tangibly connect state- and system-level goals, policies, and plans to the campus classroom. Good teaching and high-quality learning should be the core of "student success" initiatives.

Using Data to Help Close Equity Gaps

State systems of higher education have a particular responsibility to confront long-standing systemic inequity and institutionalized racism. NASH's Equity Action Framework expands an equity lens to encompass anti-racism. This framework is a tool that systems can use within colleges and universities to assess progress toward introducing equity practices and eliminating racist policies and practices.

Disaggregating data is a critical first step toward more equitable policies and practices. Although its importance should not be underestimated, disaggregating data is not how a system addresses equity, but rather a key tool to developing an equity strategy. When done well, disaggregating data makes it possible to see where gaps exist so that the reasons for those gaps—be they structural, institutional, pedagogical—can be explored.

Equity is not only about access. Access is important, but without nuanced shifts in policies, procedures, and culture, problems may persist, including the equity issues targeted by Power of Systems: gaps in completion, lack of social mobility, and student loan debt. Ultimately, understanding students' most pressing concerns requires information about student perceptions beyond quantitative data and participation counts. In Wisconsin, for example, the system is adopting a National Survey of Student Engagement module as one means to better understand the quality and impact of student experiences and to help guide improvement efforts.

The Systems Center for State Policy supports building better state policies based on proven practices to maximize the Power of Systems in service to students, institutions, and states. In partnership with the National Center for Higher Education Management Systems (NCHEMS), the center plans to develop a tool kit and to publish an annual progress report using evidence-based research on effective state and system policies, structures, roles, functions, and practices. An example of an effective practice would be that the system has goals and strategies at both institutional and system levels that align with and support state goals for degree completion, for example. The center also will assess the impact of federal policy on state policy and consult with states on policy matters.

The Partnership for Federal Support of Systems focuses on two priority initiatives. The first initiative is working with allies to advocate for sustained federal-level recognition and financial support for systems by the US Department of Education. A stronger partnership among the federal government, states, and public systems can advance the purposes of the Higher Education Act by supporting innovation and creating economies of scale that only systems can provide. Examples include expanding system and state access to federal "college completion" funds, strengthening and diversifying workforce development pipelines (especially for educators), channeling resources to student-facing quality credentials, and providing more cost-effective delivery of federal educational support.

A specific federal priority is the Refugee Resettlement Initiative, designed to leverage the unique social, learning, and workplace environments of system campuses to support refugee resettlement in the United States (initially from Afghanistan and Ukraine). In partnership with the federal government and Welcome US (https://welcome.us/), system leaders can contribute substantially toward building a more inclusive and tolerant world by expanding access and opportunity for diverse populations, including immigrants and refugees. A coalition of systems has formed a Welcome Campus Network. By March 2022, more than 30 states were working with their respective higher education systems and individual public/private colleges to house and educate refugees, building on lessons learned from working with underrepresented populations. The three components of the refugee resettlement strategy are: (1) offering a whole-campus approach such as Every Campus a Refuge (ECAR), (2) leveraging on-campus physical and academic resources, and (3) mobilizing campuses to create a welcoming environment.

NASH's Power of Systems story is about leadership—collective leadership. Never before has an entity of the size and scale of the 65 systems represented by NASH undertaken such an ambitious and collective venture. The verdict on impact is still out and will be until at least the end of the decade. But part of the leadership strategy here is to define our network of systems as the vehicle for transformation, spread, and scale, and to declare our intentions publicly. Our vision is in our tagline: Advancing Prosperity for the Nation. Our goals are threefold: increased credentials and degree completion, enhanced social and economic mobility, and reductions in student debt. Our shared metrics track our progress and our impact. This is a case of transformation, leadership, collective impact, and strategic interventions to achieve equitable student success outcomes, once and for all. The task is to develop and recognize the leadership required to move this dial going forward.

Where Systems and Campuses Lead, Together

Systems are beginning to reimagine their roles, shifting from hierarchical relationships with their component institutions to a collaborative one based on centralized resources and shared problem-solving connected to the social and economic needs of the states they serve.

Systems commonly share core business functions to achieve efficiencies by coordinating resources across multiple campuses (table 17.1). While these functions are also discussed in chapter 1 in this volume, a summary of business functions sets the stage for differentiating value-added roles and the future potential to expand these roles even further in service of excellence for students, states, and the nation. Beyond

Table 17.1 Shared functions of systems to coordinate resources across multiple campuses

Core Business Functions	Value-Added Functions
Governance, regulation, and oversight of constituent institutions	A vision for the system that goes beyond its constituent parts, differentiating campuses to better meet diverse student needs
Financial policy and administration	Common goals across campuses within systems, linking system/campus goals to state priorities
Private fundraising	Public policy and resources: shaping a public higher education agenda for the state, advocating for resources and support for higher education within systems' respective states
Capital and operating resource allocation	Developing partnerships and collaborative relationships with other public and private institutions, allocating funds to promote goal achievement, and investing in system-wide assets such as common learning management system
Academic policy and administration	Maximizing access for aspiring students with choices of opportunities, institutions, and programs
Program assessment, addition, and recission (including content delivery alternatives)	Easing student pathways through institutions within the system, faculty development
Marketing/branding and public relations	Emphasizing partnerships and coordination, rather than competition across the education pipeline
Institutional leadership selection	Developing institutional leaders, selecting leaders with demonstrated orientation toward collaboration

business basics, the competitive advantage of having a state system can be realized by stepping outside of operating policy and administration roles and stepping into cross-campus collective impact in academics and student support services.

To be successful in the future, however, higher education systems will need to pivot quickly in order to move beyond their traditional roles as allocators, regulators, and coordinators, and even further than the current state to the next tranche of value-added roles and functions.

What do systems need to not only sustain excellence in the business functions, but also to aspire to greater excellence in delivery of equitable student success? What needs to change? What will system leadership look like a decade from now?

Through the Power of Systems, NASH aspires to partner with system and campus leaders to add even greater value to students, states, and the nation by achieving a transformational increase in equitable student outcomes in the next decade. Realizing such an ambitious goal will require greater adaptive leadership skills, upskilling for system heads using a renewed and refined focus on professional development, working in networks and improvement cycles to solve persistent problems of practice, building better state policies based on proven high-impact practices, and finding cost savings that can be reinvested in core teaching and learning activities.

Specific opportunities for working in networks, using collective impact and improvement science methodologies, include the following strategies. At the macro (multisystem and multistate) level, networks will need to develop specific strategies to:

- intentionally develop a culture of collaboration
- develop and implement a shared public agenda for federal resources and support for higher education systems
- set common goals across systems and states to make contributions to the nation and globally
- streamline transfers across systems
- ease student pathways to and through institutions in other systems
- develop partnerships and collaborative relationships across systems and states, and with political, civic, and business leaders, to link higher education to the future of the nation
- engage in multisystem, multistate, regional, national, and global partnerships to contribute to quality of life and economic vitality
- serve as permanent partners to address big national issues like workforce preparation, economic competitiveness, and racial equity

At the system and campus level, they will need to:

- reduce costs and reallocate funding to student-facing services
- redesign programs and courses so all students have clear pathways to completion
- close gaps in access, opportunity, and equity
- harness economic development activity
- focus on meeting states' needs for an educated population
- close skill gaps to meet states' needs for a prepared workforce
- support public engagement in civic life

The ultimate value of systems will be determined by their ability to steer campuses to meet the needs of their states. Leadership from system heads and boards is central to success in making this conversion. By working together, public university systems can reenvision and innovate to achieve their full potential.

If systems do all of this by acting together, as a nation we can reasonably expect our students to complete quality certifications and degree credentials at a higher rate, increase graduates' social and economic mobility, and reduce student loan debt.

This is, by definition, equitable student success.

Conclusion

The work of adaptive leadership involves deciding what is core to an organization's mission and purpose, discarding what is no longer core, and investing freed-up resources into the capacity to innovate and thrive in a rapidly changing environment. NASH's Power of Systems is providing the leadership and support to systems across the nation to support their ability to adapt, to renew collectively their sense of mission and purpose, and to determine what practices and policies they can shed or simplify in service to our vision of equitable student success.

References

Collins, Jim. (2005). *Good to Great and the Social Sectors*. New York: Harper.
Finley, A., and T. McNair. (2013). *Assessing Underserved Students' Engagement in*

High Impact Practices. Washington, DC: AC&U Publications. http://www.aacu.org/assessinghips.
Kania, John, and Mark Kramer. "Collective Impact." *Stanford Social Innovation Review* 9, no. 1 (Winter 2011): 36–41.
Lane, Jason E., and D. Bruce Johnstone (2013). *Higher Education* 3.0. Albany: State University of New York Press.
McGuinness, Aims. (2013). "The History and Evolution of Higher Education Systems in the United States." In *Higher Education* 3.0, edited by Jason E. Lane and D. Bruce Johnstone. Albany: State University of New York Press.
Zilvinskis, John, and Amber D. Dumford. (2018). "The Relationship between Transfer Student Status, Student Engagement, and High-Impact Practice Participation." *Leadership, Counseling, Adult, Career and Higher Education Faculty Publications* 304.https://digitalcommons.usf.edu/ehe_facpub/304.

Conclusion

JAMES R. JOHNSEN

AS THE PREVAILING FORM of organization and governance for public universities in the United States, university systems play a critical role in advancing a wide variety of societal interests that all rely on an educated population. From preparing a skilled workforce to developing and implementing new technologies in fields as diverse as health care and national security, university systems have a broad set of responsibilities they must carry out in a highly dynamic environment, pushed and pulled by powerful forces within and without, political and economic, social and demographic, constantly facing the challenge of how to adapt and change if they are to realize their promise to the students and states they serve.

Realizing the promise of university systems is a complex set of adaptive challenges, only partly achievable through technical, authoritative expertise. Rather, realizing that the promise of these systems requires the kind of adaptive practices that Ronald Heifetz has taught and that the authors in this volume have articulated in the context of their specific fields of expertise. Framing all these adaptive practices into a single "tool kit" or integrated model for policymakers, board members, and university leaders is beyond the scope of this book, although we take a strong first step here by asking two provocative questions: What if? Why not?

What if system leaders seeking the benefits of "systemness" did not get bogged down with restructuring and its predictable pushback by forces with interests in protecting their roles in current structures, but rather understood clearly the dual role of the university system in relation to the political, economic, and cultural environment outside the system and to the institutions in the system, with a focus on rationalizing and streamlining internal functional effectiveness, reducing barriers to student access and success, and demonstrating accountability to the states they serve? An example would be the option being considered in several systems to repurpose campuses in locations experiencing population and enrollment decline from degree-granting institutions with their own faculty and curriculum to learning centers with coaches and mentors who support students as they complete courses developed by other larger campuses in the system. So, while the structure does not change—there is still a campus providing both economic and educational value to the community—the function of that campus changes as it adapts to external conditions by serving local students with resources from elsewhere in the system.

What if systems contributed their expertise and resources to the quality and accountability functions advanced by institutional accreditation and were recognized by regional accreditors as possessing unique expertise, perspective, and authority in relation to governance of institutions in their systems? At least one system (Florida) has challenged the power of the regional accreditors by requiring its campuses to periodically change accreditors and by suing the federal government over its accreditation policies. Another, perhaps less controversial step would be to add system representatives to the boards of the accrediting agencies, for as of 2023 just one out of 204 accrediting agency board members across the nation is employed by a system.

What if the collective bargaining process were based on shared rather than particular interests, where adaptability to market conditions, freedom of expression, and productivity were advanced, and where there are clear distinctions between collective bargaining over terms and conditions of employment and shared governance of academic issues? While it is reasonable to expect unions to assert the interests of their members in relation to the employer, many unions have become influential players in state capitols, providing an additional valuable voice of support for state funding for higher education, as well as a barrier to state, system, and institutional efforts to implement policies they see as detrimental to their members, even as some of those policies may have been advanced by policymakers and university leaders in order to benefit students.

What if the complex models for how states finance public higher education were aligned with state attainment goals and federal financial support, all the while encouraging cost effectiveness, innovation, performance, accountability, and return on investment? If they were, more students and their families would understand the costs of benefits of higher education and be able to manage the cost of higher education without the risk of burdensome debt. An interesting example of alignment in student finance are mandates by numerous states and cities across the country for completion of the Free Application for Federal Student Aid as a condition for high school graduation. This requirement has resulted in a dramatic increase in federal support to students in those states. Another interesting possibility for diversifying financial support is if state income tax credits (in conjunction with extant federal deductions) were provided to private donors who contribute to higher education institutions in their states, as is the case presently in Alaska.

What if administrative services and academic programs were regularly and systematically reviewed in order to reallocate scare resources from lower to higher priorities not only within an institution but also across a system as a whole? Such reallocation decisions, if boards exercised the will to implement them, would not only focus scarce resources on high-value programs and services, but also those decisions would communicate to policymakers, employers, and students that the system and its campuses are responsible stewards of resources, relevant in the eyes of the state's population, innovative leaders of beneficial change, and effective agents of social and economic mobility.

What if systems were truly student centric rather than just collections of more or less independent institutions, where credits transferred seamlessly and grading policies, calendars, learning management systems, and student financial aid and registration processes were aligned? If such innovations as the Momentum Year, Nexus Degree, course redesign, curricular pathways, and the use of predictive analytics and intrusive advising were extended across more systems at scale, it is likely we would see increases in college completion rates and decreases in racial completion gaps. Imagine the improvement in student interest, employee morale, and public support for those campuses with completion rates under 50 percent, if they improved to the point of producing more graduates than dropouts?

What if systems adopted lean process improvement practices, placing primacy for determining value in the hands of students and consumers of university research and outreach, primacy for determining how best to maximize that value to the faculty and staff on the front line of delivering it, and primacy for allocating resources and support for value creation with those in governing roles? While there are examples of institutions and systems that have pursued lean initiatives, they generally are confined to administrative processes. What if they were more widely applied, including to the process of academic curriculum design?

What if institutional barriers to system-wide collaboration in development and delivery of online courses and programs were reduced, if not eliminated altogether, thus enabling greater adaptability to changing market demand, production of the highest-quality course content, increased coordination and standardization of course offerings, and reduced administrative cost? Large market segments of students not well served by traditional institutions include people living in rural locations far from campus and working adults who cannot take the time to attend class on campus. These potential students can be better served if they were provided convenient access to programs that are online, affordable, and relevant—access that is enhanced at the system level by shared faculty, standardized general education requirements, and common learning management systems, academic calendars, grading policies, financial aid processes, and student services.

What if students were able seamlessly to access courses and programs across systems in their own states as well as also across systems in other states through a regional compact or other "system of systems" model, enabling students to gain access to programs not delivered in their own state and providing states the ability to offer student access to specialized and costly programs without the need to build those programs themselves? Multistate consortia have proven effective at expanding cost-effective access to specialized academic programs. On this foundation of system-level collaboration, much more is possible, particularly with regard to the important role of higher education systems in addressing through research, teaching, and service that growing list of issues that transcend state boundaries, such as economic development, environmental protection, food security, energy, health care, immigration, pandemic response, and transportation.

What if systems encouraged intra- and intersystem collaboration on smaller, voluntary, and time-bound projects that better meet the interests of specific stakeholders, where, for example, a group of Hispanic-serving institutions might work together within and across systems on a project, thus bringing the benefits of scale and network to the effort? The lessons from the experience and study of consortia—forging and sustaining a shared vision, fostering internal alignment for lateral alignment, staying agile with minimum viable structures, and establishing rules to change the rules—are most applicable to attempts to capture the benefits of systemness without some of the bureaucratic constraints of the system.

What if systems fostered relations with systems in other countries in ways complementary to work at the institutional level, in order to reduce the cost and broaden access to the many well-documented benefits of international programs for both American and international faculty, students, and employers? What if instead of contracting such international initiatives in the face of rising tensions, those initiatives were expanded? Might they create the kinds of relationships that could enhance mutual understanding and international cooperation, especially on problems that transcend national boundaries such as climate change, immigration, and pandemics?

What if systems brought their expertise and resources to strengthen institutional efforts to increase diversity, equity, and inclusion (DEI) through common data sets, evidence-based research into practices that work, innovative outreach efforts that are inclusive and accessible, and faculty and staff training programs that are consonant with institutional culture? In the ongoing debate over DEI, what if these efforts provided an empirical basis for the effectiveness of certain DEI initiatives in improving student outcomes and meeting state educational attainment goals?

What if systems brought together the needed resources to ensure security of critical computing networks and the ethical use of artificial intelligence, taking advantage of system scale and expertise not available at the institutional level, and perhaps even creating a system of systems for this purpose? What if the historical pattern of society responding to technological innovation rather than laying the ground for the new technology, often with highly disruptive results, were reversed, and we put ethical and social interests ahead of the introduction of new technologies?

What if faculty governance were organized at the system level—which in many systems is where the governing board operates, setting policies and priorities, approving new programs, closing programs, setting tuition, and distributing resources? Could increasing faculty awareness of and opportunity to contribute to decisions at the system level build intercampus relationships, break down barriers to institutional collaboration, expand opportunities for faculty to conduct research and teach students across the system, and improve access to the benefits of systemness not available solely at the institutional level?

What if governing boards were more adept at playing that difficult dual role of insulating the system and its campuses from partisan political pressures while also ensuring system and institutional accountability and responsiveness to elected officials and the public? What might be possible if boards insisted upon clear system- and institution-level goals and strategic plans aligned with and in support of state-level goals for an educated populace?

What if processes for leading change were managed intentionally using research-based best practices rather than two prevailing approaches, neither of which are effective? The first is to avoid change and to pursue stability at the expense of improvement. The second is to make ad hoc decisions based on raw political power, short-term interests, political expediency, or in reaction to the fears of a particular constituency. The tools and methods for managing change are well known and have been applied with success in a variety of organizational contexts. We would be wise, though, to recall the observation that people do not fear change; they fear loss. Managing the change process so that people understand any potential losses in the context of what might be gained, though often uncertain, is critical.

What if system leaders effectively leveraged their systemness, devoting the myriad human, intellectual, technological, financial, leadership, and cultural assets of their campuses to achieve state and national educational goals, providing value to society greater than the sum of their institutional parts? The same logic and potential for systemness at the state level applies at the national level, where systems could work together on such national educational imperatives as increasing postsecondary completion rates, improving social and economic mobility, and reducing the burden of student debt.

Finally, what if higher education system leaders adopted an innovative process not normally associated with higher education, leadership, strategic planning, and change management. That process—worldbuilding—is commonly used in futuristic film and game design to imagine a desired future state, a world with all its social, economic, environmental, governance, and many other aspects fleshed out, visualized in digital media and realized through narrative. Alex McDowell, well-known film designer (*Minority Report*, among others) and director of the Worldbuilding Institute at the University of Southern California, has applied the deeply interdisciplinary worldbuilding process to explore what is possible in the future for cities, research and innovation centers, refugee camps, tribal wellness centers, and yes, even a university system of the future.

Contrasted with standard strategic planning processes, worldbuilding looks out into the future, not so close to the present that one is inclined to merely extrapolate trends, yet not so far out that it's fantasy. The University of Alaska System—serving a state with a huge geography, a small and declining population, a high-income/low-education economy, and among the lowest college-going and completion rates in the nation—worked with McDowell and his team to create a deeply researched interdisciplinary and hopeful vision for higher education in the state in the year 2040. A vision that would create "pull" of the state's students through postsecondary education into a future for the state marked by their agency rather than continued debilitating dependence on the major political and economic decisions made outside the state. The process involved hundreds of faculty, staff, students, and community leaders exploring the many positive aspects of the university system—its strong research on a variety of topics related to the Arctic, campuses in rural and urban locations, faculty dedicated to student success, and generous funding from the state—through workshops, surveys, and research driven by two simple yet profoundly provocative questions: What if? Why not?

The result is a website (https://alaska.edu/ua2040) with a powerful student-centric theme, UA, Your Way. A video describes the process and result (https://youtu.be/MIN5vrGF8mc). At the center of the site are students, faculty, and alumni along with dozens of new academic programs, research institutes, and outreach centers that would be available to people across Alaska by 2040. And with those positive possibilities that aim local interests toward a compelling state-level vision, the system and its campuses would inspire broad public support and student interest in pursuing higher education, set ambitious yet practical mid- and long-term goals, and take the necessary steps realize those possibilities.

What if other university systems used a worldbuilding process to create a compelling visual and narrative vision for what they could be, rooted in the unique culture and history of their state, including the myriad elements that comprise a university system, reaching for what is possible? And once they were able to envision an aspirational future that integrated all parts of the system into a synergistic whole—a system that seamlessly meets the needs of students wherever they are geographically and educationally, one that pulls the university system out of its inward focus to be of even greater service to its stakeholders—then the task is to identify the practical steps needed to realize that vision through the provocations and adaptive processes suggested by the expert contributors to this volume.

The chapters in this book have explored these questions in a wide variety of structural and functional contexts. The diversity of topics and how they are treated reflects the diversity of systems, how they are organized and governed, what they do, how they do it, as well as their relationships internally with the institutions that comprise them and externally with the stakeholders they serve. Despite the wide variance across the nation's university systems, they all share the need to adapt to changing conditions, and to do so, they must answer the question that Ronald Heifetz posed in his foreword—in the face of a rapidly changing world with competing and contradicting demands, a world of adaptive challenges that require adaptive responses, what must university systems shed in order to create the capacity to adapt while continuing to serve their core purpose of delivering on the promise of our higher education systems? While there necessarily will be different responses to this question across the nation's many systems—their number and variety are themselves beneficial attributes of our nation's higher education systems—by pursuing the adaptive strategies offered in this book, we can advance the enormous potential of America's public university systems to fully realize their promise to the people they serve.

CONTRIBUTORS

George Blumenthal is a faculty affiliate and former director of the Center for Higher Education Studies at the University of California, Berkeley. As the tenth chancellor of the University of California, Santa Cruz, a role he served in for 13 years, he oversaw rapid growth and successfully positioned the campus to be selected to join the American Association of Universities. Prior roles include chair of the UC System Faculty Senate, faculty representative to the UC Board of Regents, and professor of astronomy. He is also author of two astronomy textbooks.

Wallace E. Boston served as president and CEO of American Public University System from 2004 through 2020, when he retired. He was an executive in multiple publicly held health care companies from 1985 to 2002. He earned an AB in history from Duke University, an MBA from Tulane University, and a doctorate in higher education management from the University of Pennsylvania. He lives in Austin, Texas, and blogs about higher education at www.wallyboston.com.

Joel Cutcher-Gershenfeld is professor and associate dean at Brandies University and a member of the Stakeholder Alignment Collaborative, which has as its other members Karen Baker, University of Illinois, Urbana Champaign; Nicholas Berente, University of Notre Dame; Helen M. Berman, University of Southern California and University of California, San Francisco; Alan Blatecky, RTI International; Anita Say Chan, University of Illinois, Urbana Champaign; Alysia Garmulewicz, University of Santiago, Chile; Ron Hutchins, University of Virginia; Alyssa Mikytuck, Randolph-Macon College; Barbara B. Mittleman, WayMark Analytics; Alyson Gounden Rock, McGill University; Rajesh Sampath, Brandeis University; Namchul Shin, Pace University; Pips Veazey, University of Maine; Susan Winter, University of Maryland; and Kimberly E. Zarecor, Iowa State University.

Tristan Denley is deputy commissioner for academic affairs and innovation at the Louisiana Board of Regents. His widely recognized work that combines education redesign, predictive analytics, cognitive psychology, and behavioral economics with college completion initiatives at statewide scale has significantly improved student success in several states and serves as a national model. He also developed and launched the Nexus Degree, the first new degree structure in the United States in more than 100 years.

Robert C. Dickeson is president emeritus of the University of Northern Colorado. He has served as chair of governors' cabinets in two states, as president and CEO of Noel-Levitz Centers, and as visiting scholar at the University of Michigan. He has authored more than 200 publications in higher education policy, including widely recognized work on academic program prioritization, and served as the senior policy adviser to the Spellings Commission on the Future of Higher Education.

Peter T. Ewell is president emeritus of the National Center for Higher Education Management Systems. Ewell's work focuses on assessing institutional and system effectiveness and involves both research and consulting with institutions and state systems on planning, evaluation, and budgeting. He has consulted with more than 425 colleges and universities and 24 higher education systems and authored or coauthored eight books and numerous articles on improving undergraduate instruction through the assessment of student outcomes.

Mark Hagerott is chancellor of the North Dakota University System. He is a certified naval nuclear engineer and previously served in campus administration and in the faculty as an historian of technology and professor of cybersecurity. His proposals for national education reform in response to digitization and artificial intelligence have been published in multiple publications, including the *Chronicle of Higher Education*, and have been presented on Capitol Hill and in the White House.

Dr. Ronald Heifetz is among the world's foremost authorities on the practice and teaching of leadership. He founded the Center for Public Leadership at Harvard Kennedy School, where he is the King Hussein Tala Senior Lecturer in Public Leadership. Ron played a major role in establishing leadership as an area of study and education and published numerous highly acclaimed books on adaptive leadership. A graduate of Columbia University and Harvard Medical School in psychiatry, Ron is also an accomplished cellist.

James R. Johnsen is vice president of executive search at Greenwood Asher and affiliate faculty in the Center for Studies in Higher Education at the

University of California, Berkeley. He also serves on advisory boards at the University of Pennsylvania and the University of Wisconsin-Madison. Previous roles include president of the University of Alaska System, senior fellow at the National Association of System Heads, and commissioner of the Western Interstate Commission on Higher Education.

Dennis P. Jones is president emeritus of the National Center for Higher Education Management Systems. He has more than 50 years of experience in research, development, technical assistance, and administration in higher education management and policy. Mr. Jones is widely recognized for his work in strategic planning, financing and budgeting, and how systems can meet the higher education needs of states and their citizens. He received undergraduate and graduate degrees from Rensselaer Polytechnic Institute.

Daniel J. Julius is a senior fellow at the Center for Global Work and Employment, School of Management and Labor Relations at Rutgers University, a visiting fellow at the School of Management at Yale University, and an adjunct professor at the Weatherhead School of Management, Case Western Reserve University. For more information, visit his webpage at DanielJJulius.com.

Jason E. Lane is special advisor to the president of the University of Illinois system and president of the National Association of System Heads. Previously, Lane served as the dean at Miami University in Ohio and at the State University of New York and in leadership roles in the SUNY system. Jason has published extensively on the changing role of colleges and universities and the power of systems.

Paul E. Lingenfelter is president emeritus of the State Higher Education Executive Officers (SHEEO). He advanced educational policies and practices to increase opportunity and attainment for over 40 years as deputy director for finance at the Illinois Board of Higher Education, vice president of the MacArthur Foundation, and president of SHEEO; and as author of more than 40 articles, chapters, and the book *Proof, Policy, and Practice—Understanding the Role of Evidence in Improving Education.*

Rebecca Martin was the executive director of the National Association of System Heads—which includes system heads in 40 states, more than 5.6 million students, and 75 percent of all students in public four-year colleges and universities—and its transformative Power of Systems project.

Previous roles include director of higher education and senior fellow at the Education Delivery Institute and senior vice president for academic affairs for the University of Wisconsin System.

Aims C. McGuinness Jr. is a senior fellow with the National Center for Higher Education Management Systems. He is the author of several influential publications on the history, functions, and issues facing public university systems. He has consulted in all 50 states and internationally on projects related to strategic planning, governance reform, and other issues. Prior roles include director of higher education policy at the Education Commission of the States and chief of staff to the chancellor of the University of Maine System.

Demarée K. Michelau is president of the Western Interstate Commission for Higher Education, which shares knowledge, creates resources, and develops innovative solutions for society's most pressing needs through high-quality, affordable postsecondary education, strategic technology investments, and impactful behavioral health research and training programs. Demi is the author of numerous reports and policy briefs on higher education policy issues, including those related to equity and attainment, governance, strategic planning, adult learners, transfer, accelerated learning options, affordability, and workforce.

Steven J. Patin is a senior executive with diverse leadership experience in banking and financial services, higher education, publicly traded corporations and 22 years of service as a US Army officer with multiple worldwide deployments. He has also served as a university department head, course director, and faculty member. His research interests include process transformation, program and project management, ethical business practices, and equal employment opportunity. He serves on the board of several academic, health care, and nonprofit institutions.

Kevin P. Reilly is president emeritus and regent professor with the 26-campus University of Wisconsin System. He came to Wisconsin from the State University of New York System, where he was associate provost for academic programs and then secretary of the university. As secretary, he was the chief staff officer for the SUNY Board of Trustees. Currently he has an appointment as senior fellow with the Association of Governing Boards of Universities and Colleges.

Jessica Schueller is a PhD student in educational leadership and applied statistics at Miami University of Ohio. She holds an Erasmus Mundus joint master's degree in research and innovation in higher education from Tampere University (Finland) and Danube University Krems (Austria). Previously, she held roles in international education, career services, and higher education research in the United States and Europe. Her current research interests include the internationalization of career services, transnational education, and ethical advising practices.

Khaleel Seecharan and Darren Greeno are cofounders of DEI Ready, a coaching firm committed to diversity, equity, and inclusion. Seecharan's research and practice explore how organizations improve. He was educated at Harvard and the University of Pennsylvania. Greeno's research explores the relationship between institutional performance and organizational culture. He was educated at the University of Pennsylvania. They were assisted by Jasmine Kaduthodil, University of California, San Diego, and Pamela Felder-Small, DEI consultant.

Allison M. Vaillancourt is a vice president and senior consultant at Segal, a leading human resources and organizational strategy consulting firm. She brings more than 30 years of faculty and leadership experience in research universities across the United States. Prior to joining Segal, Allison was at the University of Arizona, where she served as vice president for business affairs and human resources and was an award-winning faculty member in the School of Government and Public Policy.

Nancy Zimpher is chancellor emeritus of the State University of New York and senior fellow at the National Association of System Heads. Previous roles include president of the University of Cincinnati and chancellor of the University of Wisconsin-Milwaukee. Throughout her career, Nancy has embraced the expansive responsibilities of public higher education in the twenty-first century. More recently, she has championed the unique power of public university systems to reach state and national goals.

INDEX

academic courses and programs, 51, 55, 58, 102, 116–18, 119, 134, 155, 162, 178, 192, 304, 328, 386; consortia-based access, 10, 192–93, 208–9, 387; core courses, 130–31, 134, 136, 138, 273; cost and funding, 18, 83, 107, 119, 185–86; duplication/redundancy, 18, 58, 116, 122, 192, 308; enrollment relationship, 173–74, 323–24; new, 36–37, 38, 113, 187, 229, 235, 308, 312, 367; prioritization, 107, 108, 109–10; scheduling, 133, 158–59, 174–75, 181, 183, 187, 190, 191, 204, 330
academic degrees, 112, 157–58, 234–35, 267, 304, 375
academic departments, 119, 121, 176, 190, 304, 317n3
academic focus areas, 129, 130, 134, 138
academic freedom, 64–65, 118, 163, 305–6, 310, 313, 315
academic majors, 29, 120, 128–29
academic senate, system-wide, 301–18
Acadeum course-sharing platform, 192–93
accreditation, 26, 50–58, 52–53, 55, 58, 90, 99–100, 113, 154–55, 175, 187, 191–92, 208–9, 242, 337n9, 365, 384; regional commissions, 57, 113
Adams, John, 96
administration, 3, 21, 22; interaction with governing boards and academic senates, 301, 303, 304, 309–10, 313, 315, 327; in lean systems, 146, 158, 160–61, 162, 163. *See also* leadership, academic; presidents of colleges and universities; system offices
administrative functions and processes, 4, 6, 18–19, 102, 107, 155, 176, 226, 367, 372, 386; academic senate's authority in, 304, 313–16; assessment scheme, 116–18; centralization, 51, 53–54, 57–58; consolidation/collaboration approach, 339–40, 345–46, 367, 386–87; in lean systems, 9, 146, 150, 154, 386; new, 20–21; in online systems, 176, 180; resource sharing in, 42, 379, 385; traditional, 18–19
admissions, 181, 185, 186, 201, 235, 236–37, 289, 304, 309, 311–12, 328
adult students, 34, 101, 174, 178, 181, 186, 192, 203, 204, 321, 322, 331–32, 363–64, 372, 386–87
advising: as academic senate's function, 304; for change initiatives, 351, 352–53; of students, 121, 133, 136, 157, 176, 181, 190, 193, 330, 375, 386
advocacy, 34, 37, 51, 159, 233, 248, 277, 278, 326, 332–35
aging population, 85, 97, 98, 198–99
Alaska, 385; university system of, 3, 43, 54, 154–55, 228, 385, 390
Alfred P. Sloan Foundation's Anytime, Anyplace Learning Program, 171
Algonquin College, 153–54
American Association of Colleges and Universities (AAC&U), 96, 103, 332; Inclusive Equity and Excellence Frameworks, 269–70, 275
American Association of University Professors (AAUP), 63–64, 65, 305, 306
American Council on Education, 271, 331
American Federation of Teachers (AFT), 63, 65
American Indian / Alaskan Native students, 132, 227, 231–32, 266, 267, 271

American Institutes of Research (AIR), 56
American Military University, 174, 190
American Psychological Association, 265
American Public University, 174
American Public University System (APUS), 174–75, 190
American Rescue Plan, 200
Americans with Disabilities Act (ADA), 187
Antioch University, 42
Arizona, University of (UofA), 172; Global Campus, 172, 174, 175, 185
Arizona State University, 157, 235
Arkansas State University System, 246
artificial intelligence (AI), 78, 189, 224, 281, 283, 284–85, 286, 288–89, 292–93, 388
Ashford University, 172, 174
Asian / Pacific Islander students, 267, 271
Associated Colleges of the Midwest, 42
associate's degree, 140, 267
Association of American Universities (AAU), 62–63
Association of Governing Boards of Universities and Colleges, Task Force on System Board Governance, 326
Association of Public and Land-Grant Universities (APLU), 206
athletes and intercollegiate athletics, 83, 88, 102, 157, 174–75, 191
Augusta State University, 344
Austin Peay State University, 127
autonomy, 62, 63, 64, 70, 154, 155, 159, 207, 228, 345–46, 356, 361

bachelor's degree, 120, 137, 140, 266, 304, 321–22, 332, 339; applied, 331–32
back-office operations, 18, 38–40, 176, 207–8
Biden, Joseph, 285, 292, 296
Big 10 Academic Alliance, 42
BioMarkers Consortium, 225–26, 232–33
Black Lives Matter movement, 352
Black students, 132, 136, 137, 191, 220, 266–67, 330
board of trustees or regents, 42, 54, 67–68, 107, 111, 155, 207, 317, 325; in lean systems, 155–56; relationship with academic senate, 301, 303, 304, 310, 311, 314; resource allocation role, 108, 109, 110–12, 118
Bowen, Howard, 82
Bowling Green State University, 153
Boyer, Earnest, 99
Brandman University, 172, 179
brands and branding, 159, 172, 175, 179, 185, 326, 379
Brewer, Catherine, 266
Bridgeport (CT), University of, 339, 345–46
Brown, Michael, 269
Brown University, 61–62, 265
budgets and budgeting, 26, 32, 76–77, 87, 190, 207; academic senate's role, 304, 305, 306, 309, 313; cuts, 107, 112, 356; governing board's role, 324, 327; resource allocation and, 107, 112, 113, 114; state government's role, 19, 356; strategic, 21
buy-ins, 31, 213, 305, 310, 344

Calbright College, 179
calendar, academic, 158–59, 330, 386–87
California, university system of (UC system), 43, 53, 177, 219, 271–72, 302; academic senate, 12, 307–11, 312, 314, 315; international education activities, 246, 252; Master Plan for California Higher Education, 222; mission, 60–61, 62, 154; Santa Cruz campus, 62
California Board of Governors, 302
California Community Colleges (CCC) system, 53, 271–73, 302, 310–11
California State University System, 43, 53, 61, 246, 247, 271–72, 302, 310–11
Campus Research Computing Consortium (CaRCC), 225–26
Canada, 95, 96
Cardiff University, 153
career planning and placement, 134, 136, 138, 140, 157, 231, 251, 328
Carlos Albizu University, 42

Carnegie Commission on Higher Education, 85–86
Carnegie Foundation for the Advancement of Teaching, 2, 101, 153, 222, 363, 373–74
Carnegie Networked Improvement Communities, 374
centralization, 234, 361, 378; of administration, 51, 53–54, 57–58; of crisis coordination, 368; of data collection and analysis, 50–51; of functions, 326; of governance, 211; of institutional quality review, 50–51, 53–54, 57–58; in international activities, 243, 247; of online systems, 171–73, 176; regional, 207; of services, 25, 39, 190, 192
Central Oklahoma, University of, 153
certification/certificate programs, 1, 175, 204, 208, 211, 321, 322–23, 331, 366–67
chancellors, resource allocation role, 109, 110, 111, 114
change initiatives, 13, 27–28, 31, 233–34, 339–59, 362, 364–66, 369, 389; barriers, 13, 341–46, 350, 362; emotional responses to, 345–46, 349–50, 351, 357, 389; errors in, 341–46; models, 346–51; sense of urgency, 347, 356–57; 10-step process checklist, 351–56. *See also* consortia, multi-stakeholder; Power of Systems initiative
Chapman University, 172, 179
ChatGPT, 285
Cheyney University, 266
Chicago, University of, 348
chief executive officers, 18–19, 111, 115, 154–55, 335
China, 252–53
CHIPS and Science Act, 293
Choi, Mun Y., 270
citizenship/civic education, 93–94, 96–97, 211, 363, 366, 367
City University of New York (CUNY), 60–61, 250, 251
Claremont Colleges, 42
codes of conduct, 310, 313, 316
collaboration in higher education, 27–29, 197–98, 211–14, 217–18, 368, 370, 378, 380; among constituent campuses and institutions, 18, 23; cross-disciplinary, 235; examples, 202–9; among faculty, 102, 235, 312; in international education, 243–44, 245, 247, 253–60; pressures for and against, 196–209, 214; in research, 258, 312; stakeholder-focused, 387; strategic approach, 197, 200, 202, 205, 212, 214. *See also* consolidations and mergers; consortia, multi-stakeholder; consortia for course-sharing; partnerships in higher education
collective bargaining / labor negotiations, 7, 21, 59–80, 229, 313, 384–85; academic administrators/leaders in, 69–70, 71, 72–73, 74, 78, 79; academic senate in, 306, 315, 317n4; in lean systems, 159, 161; legal issues, 66, 67–68, 71, 73, 74, 75, 78, 79; obstacles, 60, 68–70, 74; political factors, 67–68, 69, 71–72, 74, 75, 76–77, 78–79, 230. *See also* labor unions in higher education
"Collective Impact" (Kania and Kramer), 369
College and University Personnel and Human Resources Association (CUPA-HR), 59
college education / educational attainment, 92–93, 95–96, 100–102, 388; economic and social benefits, 82, 92, 97–98, 100, 201, 202, 363; gender and racial/ethnic differences, 236, 267, 386; public attitudes toward, 321, 324–25, 386; public funding–based, 92–93, 98, 103, 104; state goals for, 366, 385, 388; of workforce, 92, 95, 100
College of William and Mary, 265
Collegiate Learning Assessment (CLA), 51, 52
Collins, Jim, 369
Colorado State University System, 249, 250, 307, 326–27
community colleges, 84, 97, 130, 131, 134, 136–37, 228, 287, 331; applied baccalaureate degrees, 331–32; California System, 53, 271–73, 302, 310–11; consolidations, 344–45, 346;

community colleges (*cont.*)
DEI initiatives, 271–73; enrollment, 17, 196, 252–53; governance and academic senates, 302, 307, 310–11, 319–20; New Hampshire System, 344–45, 346; system organization, 42, 43–49, 222, 302, 307, 328; transfer policies, 29, 307, 308, 309, 310–11, 375; workforce development funding, 184
community engagement/partnerships, 34–35, 157–58, 337n9, 364, 367, 369; cyberinfrastructure initiatives, 232; DEI initiatives, 269–70, 276–77; lean process benefits for, 9, 157–58, 162, 163; systems' services to, 32, 34–35, 332
commuting students, 176, 183
competency-based education, 56, 204, 321, 329–30
competition: with for-profit sector, 366; global, 1, 106, 365; industrial, 222; inter-institutional, 102, 157, 176, 197, 203, 210, 340; as obstacle to collaboration, 203; regional, 18
Complete Georgia, 136
Connecticut: State Colleges and Universities System, 331; University of, 52–53, 63, 206
consolidations and mergers, 22, 111–12, 207, 323, 332, 337n9, 342–43, 361; of back-office operations, 38–40; barriers and opposition, 339–40, 344–46; Consolidation Era, 221–23, 361; for cost savings, 323, 342–43; in lean systems, 149; of online universities, 172, 174, 179, 185; of processes, 27; support for, 342, 349–50; system office's role in, 27–28
consortia, multi-stakeholder, 217–41; internal and lateral alignment, 218, 229–32, 238, 387; minimum viable approach, 218, 232–34, 238, 387; minority-serving institutions and, 227, 231–33; rules to change rules, 218, 234–36, 387
consortia for course-sharing, 10, 192–93, 208–9, 387
constituent campuses and institutions of systems: branch campuses, 18, 43–49, 254–55, 258–59, 337n9, 379n1; centralized crisis response, 368; collaborative relationships, 378–79; flagship campuses, 228, 270, 319, 324, 337n9; in homogeneous systems, 302; institutional priorities, 228; in lean systems, 155–56, 158–59, 163; linked to main campus, 42–49; online operations, 178–79; resource allocation, 108, 111, 114; shared functions, 378–79; students' educational options within, 328–32; students' sequential attendance, 51, 321–22
continuous improvement, 99–100, 101, 103, 148, 211, 372, 373; in lean systems, 9, 148, 150–51, 152, 153–54, 156, 161, 162, 163
Coronavirus Aid, Relief, and Economic Security (CARES) Act, 199–200
Coronavirus Response and Relief Supplemental Appropriations Act (CRRSA), 200
corporation-higher education partnerships, 222–23, 294, 331
corporatization, 64, 221–23
cost of public higher education, 1, 81, 82–84, 86, 89; access and quality relationship, 103; cost-benefit analysis, 85–86, 107; cost-effectiveness, 4, 56–57, 101–3, 147, 175, 385, 387; costs and revenues per student, 84; cost-savings and cost containment strategies, 321, 323, 362, 366, 372; enrollment and, 173–74; of online programs, 173–77, 185–86; operating costs, 148, 173–74, 175, 182; public attitudes toward, 325; resource allocation and, 106–8, 118. *See also* public funding of higher education; tuition
COVID-19 pandemic, 1, 36, 56, 67–68, 75, 76–77, 195–96, 199–200, 202, 203, 228, 267–68, 289, 296n3, 321, 323, 335, 366, 368, 369–70; international education and, 242–43, 252, 258–59; online instruction and, 173, 175–76, 179, 183, 188, 191, 195, 208, 287, 348, 368
credentialing/credentials, 34, 36, 140, 184, 204, 205, 211, 224, 235, 322, 374

credit hours, 31, 120–21, 134, 138, 204, 256; prior learning–based, 30, 321, 329–30; student success relationship, 130, 131, 133, 134; of transfer students, 29, 31, 177–78, 329
critical thinking skills, 96, 97, 365, 375–76
Cross-National Regional Universities, 244
culture wars, 68, 325
curriculum: academic senate's jurisdiction over, 304, 316; Common Core, 29, 101, 158, 177–78; core, 130, 134, 187; curricular analysis, 135; curricular pathways, 130, 133, 139, 141, 386; curriculum creep, 107–8, 112; in cyber/digitization education, 294; for educational attainment, 100; faculty jurisdiction over, 63, 304; foundational material, 130–32; internationalization, 247–48; in lean systems, 160; Momentum Year framework–based innovation, 9, 133–42; online, 182, 187, 192; in proprietary institutions, 89; shared governance over, 304
cyberinfrastructure (CI), consortial approach to, 225–27, 231–32
cyber-resilient systems, 11–12, 281–98, 296n3; adaptability, 282, 285, 286, 287, 288, 289, 291; advanced robotics and, 283, 284–85, 286, 289, 292–93; human-centric, robotic, and cyber framework, 284, 288–89, 290–93, 295; reliability, 282, 285, 286–87, 288, 289, 291; resilience theory of, 286–89, 297n8; transformability, 282, 285, 286, 287, 288, 289, 291
cybersecurity, 12, 184, 187–88, 227, 289, 290–93, 388; workforce development in, 184, 292

D2L, 189
data collection and analytics, 1; certificate programs, 331; for change initiatives, 343–44, 352; cloud data storage, 159, 187–88, 224, 226, 227, 283, 284, 288, 291; data disaggregation, 369, 375, 376–78; in educational attainment monitoring, 101; in employer-system partnerships, 205; in equity gap closure, 376–78; in institutional quality review, 50–52, 57; in resource allocation, 109–10, 113, 114, 115; in transfer processes, 375. *See also* cyber-resilient systems
deans, 71, 114, 175, 230
decentralization, 234, 361
Degree Qualifications Profile, 103
Delta Cost Project, 84
demographic factors/changes, 1–2, 41, 62–63, 198–99, 203, 205, 206, 207, 210, 214, 316, 320–21, 340, 365, 367, 390
Digital Bill of Rights, 285
Digital-Cyber Land-Grant program, 293–96
digital technology / digitization, 1, 176–77, 282–83, 340; adverse and disruptive effects, 281–83, 284–85; cloud data storage, 159, 187–88, 224, 226, 227, 283, 284, 288, 291; multistakeholder consortia model, 217–38; as postindustrial digital era, 223–38. *See also* cyber-resilient systems; online higher education
distance learning, 171, 288
District of Columbia, University of, 266
diversity: college students, 1–2, 204–5, 274, 320–21, 362; as educational value, 97; faculty, 236, 274
diversity, equity, and inclusion (DEI) initiatives, 36, 236–37, 264–80, 329, 369, 371–73, 388; communication and transparency, 270, 271, 273, 275, 276–77; community engagement, 269–70, 276–77; data disaggregation, 369, 375, 376–78; frameworks, 268–69, 270–71, 272–73, 275; leadership, 269–70, 272, 276; mandates and incentives, 275–76, 277. *See also* Power of Systems initiative
doctoral degree/programs, 267, 333–34

economic development, 3, 4, 20, 35, 157–58, 259, 367, 371, 381, 387
economies of scale, 21, 159, 163, 207, 244, 312, 377

Education Commission of the States (ECS), 184
Educause, 176–77
Elementary and Secondary Education Act (ESEA), 200
elite institutions, 61–62, 66–67, 77, 82, 83, 87–88, 222, 264
employees: DEI performance criteria, 271–72; governmental, 204; growth-of-duties factor, 122–23; health insurance coverage, 76, 309–10; in lean systems, 148–49, 151, 152–53, 159, 160–61, 162, 163; unionization and collective bargaining, 61–63, 65–66, 67, 71–72, 74, 79–80. *See also* staff; workforce capability development
employers/businesses, systems services for, 6, 17, 32, 34, 41, 51. *See also* workforce capability development
endowments, 87–88, 199
English as a Second Language (ESL) courses, 248, 250, 253
enrollment, 17–18, 87, 264, 268; adult students, 192; declines, 1–2, 28, 66, 199, 201, 207, 323, 366; dual, 329; impact of COVID-19 pandemic on, 196, 323; increases, 86, 361; international students, 252–53, 258–59; management, 83; as online process, 172; in online programs, 56, 174–75, 180–83, 185, 190, 191, 193–94; open, 134; program demand relationship, 158; relation to cost of higher education, 173–74
environmental issues, 150, 336, 366, 367, 387, 389
equity in higher education, 265, 270, 363–64, 367, 369, 370, 377–78; gaps, 127, 135, 329, 366, 371–72, 376–78. *See also* diversity, equity, and inclusion (DEI) initiatives; Power of Systems initiative
Erasmus Program, 256
European Union (EU), 256
European Universities Initiative (EUI), 244, 256
evidence-based practices/research, 7, 79, 115, 116, 132, 135, 138, 370–71, 372, 377, 388
faculty: adjunct, 62; administrative duties, 121; autonomy, 62, 63, 64; in change initiatives, 351; clinical, 315, 318n8; collaboration among, 102, 235, 312; of color, 236, 274; contingent, 315, 318n8; in DEI initiatives, 272–73, 274, 275; discipline and termination, 305, 317n4; in electronic online instruction, 171; female, 236; full-time, 122, 174; full-time-equivalent (FTE), 120–21; in industry-university partnerships, 333, 334; innovative groupings, 235; interaction with governing boards, 331, 388; international education activities, 247–48, 249, 251, 254, 256; in lean systems, 158, 159, 160, 162; number per academic department, 119; in online education, 174, 181–82, 183, 188, 348, 386–87; part-time, 62, 89, 122, 174, 181, 182, 314; political/ideological orientations, 69, 201–2; research capability, 98–99, 388; in resource allocation, 110, 111, 114, 119, 120–21; reward system, 123–24; salaries and benefits, 64, 89, 122, 309–10, 313; of small or redundant programs, 55; state and regional problem-solving role, 35–36; temporary, 315, 318n8; of virtual campuses, 316; workload and working conditions, 21, 62, 64–65, 67, 102–3, 120–21, 236. *See also* academic senate, system-wide; promotion of faculty; tenure
faculty-to-student ratio, 83
faculty unionization. *See* labor unions in higher education
federal funding of higher education, 51, 92, 93, 94–95, 99–100, 196, 199–200, 265–66, 365, 377, 380. *See also* financial aid
federal government: cybersecurity-based collaborations, 292–93; intersection with state policies, 368, 377; oversight of institutions' international activities, 252–53; recognition of public university systems, 4, 365, 377; student debt issue, 56–57
financial aid, 81, 83–84, 86–87, 90, 92,

98, 328; application for, 181, 330, 385, 386; barriers to, 101; consortial agreements and, 193; during COVID-19 pandemic, 199; in lean systems, 158–59; merit- or need-based, 85, 87, 330; state policies, 85–86; student decision-making about, 139–40; system-wide policy, 329
financing of higher education, 2, 66, 81–105, 379; governing bodies' and, 319; of public service, 81; of research, 81; revenue-raising activities, 82; role of tuition in, 86–87; state and national policies for, 85–86, 92–93. *See also* philanthropic funding of higher education; private investment in public higher education; public funding of higher eduction
first-generation college students, 1–2, 128–29, 132, 136, 137, 235, 273
first-year college students, 128–31, 133, 178; Momentum Year framework, 133–42
"Five Ways Consortia Can Catalyze Open Science" (Stakeholder Alignment Collaborative), 226–27
Florida: State University System of, 62, 302; University of, 62
Floyd, George, 321
Food and Drug Administration (FDA), 232–33
Ford Motor Company, 147
for-profit institutions, 82, 84, 88–90, 92, 98, 101, 366; online programs, 9–10, 172, 174–75, 192; state financial support, 85–86; student failure/attrition rates, 89–90, 91
functions and processes of systems, 6, 17–49, 268; approval processes, 149–50; of early systems, 17–20; efficiency, 25–27, 33–34, 41; evolution, 20–21; internal vs. external, 19–20; inward facing, 21–23; in lean systems, 149; monitoring of results, 31; outward facing, 21, 23–24, 33–37, 40; shared, 27–28, 378–79; structural changes and, 37–41, 384; system role changes and, 6, 21–37; variability by state, 18
function-structure relationship of systems, 37–41
fundraising, 26–27, 379

Gallagher, Sean, 322
Gay, Chris, 344
gender issues, 220, 236, 237, 266–67, 320, 375
general education courses and programs, 120, 177–78, 187, 309, 329, 375, 386–87
Georgetown University, 61–62
Georgia, University System of (USG), 53–54, 127–28, 129, 134, 154–55, 265, 337n9; CASSIE initiative, 249; Chancellor's Learning Scholars Program, 132; consolidations, 342, 343, 344; ESL program, 250; international education activities, 246, 247, 248, 249, 250; Know More Borrow Less initiative, 139; Momentum Year framework, 133–37, 139; Nexus Degree program, 140; student success rates, 9, 128, 130, 131, 137; System Council on International Education, 248
Georgia Board of Regents, 344
Georgia Health Sciences University, 344
Georgia Institute of Technology (Georgia Tech), 137
"Get with the Program . . ." (Jenkins and Cho), 130
GI Bill, 92, 97, 221
Gonzalez, Daisy, 273
governance, 42, 67, 154–55, 337n9, 361, 379; accreditors' standards, 54; adaptable approach, 234–35; centralization, 211; in early systems, 18; of independent voluntary systems, 42; of lean systems, 157, 160, 161; as non-value-creating activity, 159; of online programs, 175, 178–79; overhead, 157; systemic goal-oriented mode, 256
governing boards, 154–55, 242, 302, 319–38; advocacy role, 332–35; in collective bargaining, 69–70; of cross-national regional universities, 257; of early systems, 18–19, 20; enterprise management tools, 326–28, 336;

governing boards (*cont.*)
higher education trends affecting, 12–13, 320–36; of lean systems, 160; single-institution, 319, 320; strategic planning role, 326, 327, 388–89
Governor's Emergency Education Relief (GEER) Fund, 199–200
grading policies, 158–59, 188, 304, 308–9, 311, 330, 368, 375, 386–87
graduate courses, degrees, and programs, 82, 85, 100, 116, 120, 304, 308, 312, 333–34
graduate students, unionization of, 61–62, 65, 73–74, 77, 78
grants, 26, 83–84, 86, 89, 90, 106, 171, 199–200, 232, 374
Great Upheaval, The (Levine and Van Pelt), 340
Greenstein, Daniel, 323–24
growth-of-duties factor, 122–23
guild model of higher education, 218, 219–21

Hampton Institute, 60
Harvard College, 265
Harvard University, 61–62, 343
Hawaii: Fifteen-to-Finish initiative, 133; university system of, 154–55, 246, 247
health care system, 86, 94–95, 103, 195, 203, 370; insurance, 309–10; lean systems, 9, 145–46, 149, 153; for students, 366; systems' services to, 3, 4, 24, 34–35, 36, 38, 366, 367, 370, 383, 387; university partnerships with, 35, 332–33
Heifetz, Ronald, 2, 383
higher education: historical development, 10, 85, 92–93, 97, 217–24, 265–67, 360–63; perceived value, 201–2, 211, 214
Higher Education Act, 93, 377
Higher Education Emergency Relief Fund (HEERF), 199, 200
Higher Education Research Institute, 202
higher education systems, definition and types of, 42–49
Higher Education Systems 3.0 (Lane and Johnstone), 11, 244, 245, 337n1, 364, 365, 367–68
high-impact practices, 101, 138, 141, 238, 371, 375–76, 380
high school graduates, 1–2, 34, 36, 97, 198, 201, 203, 205, 321, 323, 325
high school students, 97, 100, 309, 323, 329, 330, 331, 385
hiring practices: for academic leaders, 2, 32–33, 330–31; DEI-based, 272, 275; for faculty and staff, 139, 275, 304–5, 313–14; in lean systems, 149–50; skills-based, 322; system-wide policies, 313–14
Hispanic/Latino/Latina students, 132, 136, 191, 267, 271, 273, 330
Hispanic-serving institutions (HSIs), 134, 227, 231–32, 387
historically Black colleges and universities (HBCUs), 134, 137, 210, 220, 227, 231–32, 266
Howard University, 60
human resources departments/systems, 21, 26, 35–36, 59, 73, 122, 149, 159, 348, 361

Idaho, University of, 172, 180; Online Idaho, 179–80, 208
identity: institutional, 212, 345–46; intersectional, 237
Illinois, university system of, 60, 154–55, 171, 228, 252; Urbana-Champaign campus, 234–35
Illinois Board of Higher Education, Proprietary Advisory Committee, 81
improvement science model, 5, 153, 365, 373–74, 380
independent institutions, 42, 97, 386
industrialization eras, 219–23; post-industrial digital, 223–38
industry–higher education partnerships, 140, 203, 205–6, 222–23, 231–33, 294, 332–34
inequities. *See* racial and social inequities
information technology (IT), 21, 35–36, 159, 176–77, 185, 331; certificate pro-

grams, 331; collaboration in, 207–8; costs, 83; digital transformation, 176; as shared service/consolidation, 26, 159. *See also* digital technology / digitization
Institute for Systems Innovation and Improvement, 373–74
institutional priorities, 121, 228, 362, 370, 385
instruction. *See* teaching
intellectual property, 253, 290–91, 366
interdisciplinary courses/collaboration, 123–24, 235
Interdisciplinary Earth Data Alliance (IEDA), 225–26
interdisciplinary worldbuilding process, 389–91
internationalization of higher education systems, 42, 242–63, 365, 387–88; collaboration and partnerships, 243, 244, 245, 246, 247, 248–49, 253–60; planning, steering, and coordination functions, 245, 247, 248–49; policies and policing functions, 245, 247, 248, 252–53; promotion, research, and recruitment functions, 245, 247, 248, 259; student exchanges and study abroad initiatives, 242, 243, 245, 247, 248, 249–50, 251, 254, 328; supranational systems, 255–58; system offices' functions in, 244, 245–53
Internet, 171, 173, 188, 295
Internet2, 225, 232
internships, 140, 158, 251, 328, 333, 375–76
Iowa, University of, 153
Ivy League institutions, 60, 90, 287

Jefferson, Thomas, 96
Johnson Controls, 333–34
Johnstone, D. Bruce, 11, 244, 245, 337n1, 364, 365, 367–68
Jones, Dennis, 197
just-in-time education, 340, 370

K–12 education, 63, 90, 92, 98, 101, 153, 173, 200, 363–64
Kanter, Rosabeth Moss, 343
Kaplan University, 172
Kerr, Clark, 2, 222
Kotter, John, 347, 356–57
Kübler-Ross model applied to change, 348

labor unions in higher education, 21, 60–61, 63–65, 66, 68, 69, 121, 221, 331; academic senate's relationship with, 306, 315; leadership, 64, 67, 69–70, 78, 79; in private sector, 61–62, 66; in public sector, 60–61, 62–63, 64, 66, 67–68, 384–85. *See also* collective bargaining / labor negotiations
land-grant universities, 4, 16, 18, 34–35, 206, 220–21, 228, 265–66, 287, 337n9
Lane, Jason E., 245, 246, 252–53, 255, 364, 365, 367–68
Latino/Latina/Hispanic students, 132, 136, 191, 267, 273, 330
law schools, 88, 302
leadership, academic, 36, 317, 360–82; of academic office, 38, 58; adaptive, 360–82; change management role, 13, 342, 369–70; of collaborations/ partnerships, 203–4, 212, 213; of early systems, 18–19; faculty development in, 314; hiring and evaluation process for, 330–31; of lean systems, 152–53; of multi-stakeholder consortia, 230, 231; NASH strategy for, 370–72, 374, 378, 380; partisan politics and, 2; proactive, 36–37; in quality review and accreditation, 54, 58; in resource allocation, 109, 110–11; as shared service, 26, 379; of system office, 30–31. *See also* presidents of colleges and universities
lean systems and value creation, 9, 145–70, 365, 386; benefits to students, 9, 146, 150, 157–59, 160, 161, 162, 163; conditions for, 152–53, 155–59, 161–62, 365; definition and concepts, 9, 148–51; evolution and history, 9, 145, 146–48; future developments, 161–64; leadership, 152–53, 157, 160, 161, 162; non-value-creating activities, 154, 158, 159, 161, 163; in public university systems,

lean systems and value creation (*cont.*) 145, 153–64; standard work processes and procedures, 150–51, 152, 160–61, 162; value stream, 152, 153–54, 162–63; waste reduction in, 9, 149–50, 154, 162, 163
learning: adaptive, 178, 189; applied, 375–76; blended, 321; centers, 384; collaborative, 321; community-based, 375–76; competency-based, 321; cooperative, 328; hybrid, 191–94; lifetime, 140; management systems (LMSs), 173, 177, 187, 188–89, 330, 372, 386–87; mindsets, 131–32, 134; outcomes-based, 340; service, 328; work-based, 205, 211
liberal arts education, 4, 119, 140, 219, 222, 323
Liberty University, 186
Lincoln, Abraham, 293
Lincoln University, 266
Long-Term Ecological Research Network, 225
Louisiana State University System, 250
low-income students, 1–2, 97–98, 136, 273, 329, 362, 373, 390
Lumina Foundation, 191

Machine That Changed the World, The (Womack, Jones, and Roos), 147–48
Maine, university system of, 52–53, 206, 247, 250, 337n9
Making Sustainability Stick (Wilhelm), 345
Managing Transitions (Bridges), 350–51
market: demand, 22, 82, 182–83, 386; growth, 108; share, 84, 102, 108
marketing, 159, 181, 182–83, 185, 186, 250–51, 258–59, 379
Marlboro College, 339, 345–46
Maryland, University System of, 157, 177, 184, 246; Global Campus (UMGC), 182; University College, 171
Massachusetts, university system of, 63, 171–72, 179; international education activities, 246, 251, 252, 254; Medical School, 171–72, 179; Umass Global, 172, 175, 185; Umass Online, 171–72, 179
Massachusetts Institute of Technology, 61–62; International Motor Vehicle Program, 147–48
Massachusetts State College, 60–61
master's degree, 267
McDonald, Kevin G., 269–70
McDowell, Alex, 389–90
McGuinness, Aims, 360–62
medical schools, 88, 228, 265
mentoring, 236, 272–73, 384
mergers. *See* consolidations and mergers
#MeToo movement, 352
Michels, Robert, "iron law of oligarchy," 230, 234
Michigan, University of, 60, 339, 346
Middle States Commission on Higher Education (MSCHE), 52–53
Midwestern Higher Education Compact (MHEC), 209
mindsets: academic, 138; lean, 148; learning, 131–32, 134
Minnesota State University system, 248, 251
minoritized/underserved/marginalized students, 191, 235, 237, 264, 274; racism and discrimination toward, 220, 266–67; student success rates, 135, 136–37, 267–68, 375. *See also* Black students; diversity, equity, and inclusion (DEI) initiatives; Hispanic/Latino/Latina students; low-income students; Native American / Alaska Native / Indigenous students
Minority Serving Cyberinfrastructure Consortium (MS-CC), 225–26, 227, 231–33
minority-serving institutions (MSIs), 210, 227, 231–32
Mintzberg, Henry, 244
mission creep, 107
Missouri, University of (UM), 269–71
Momentum Year framework, 133–38, 142, 386; Momentum Approach expansion, 137–42
Montana University System, Montana Virtual Campus, 208
More Student Success (SHEEO), 100–101
Morrill Land-Grant Acts, 34, 88–89, 92, 220–21, 265–66, 294–95

National Association of Community College Trustees, Equity Award, 271
National Association of System Heads (NASH), 3, 13, 211, 338n19, 370–71, 373–74, 375; Big ReThink (BRT) Transformation Agenda, 371–73; Equity Action Framework, 275, 376; Improvement Communities, 153; improvement science model, 5, 153. *See also* Power of Systems initiative
National Center for Higher Education Management Systems (NCHEMS), 2, 51n1, 197, 326–27, 336, 377
National Data Service, 233
national defense and security, 94, 367, 383
National Defense in Education Act, 92
National Education Association (NEA), 63–64, 65
National Institutes of Health (NIH), 232–33
National Labor Relations Board, 61–62
National Science Foundation (NSF), 232
National Student Clearinghouse Research Center, 196, 321–22
Native American / Alaska Native / Indigenous students, 132, 227, 266, 267, 271
Nebraska: State College System, 250; university system of, 246n1, 252
networks, 322, 328, 329, 332, 352–53, 371, 372, 373, 374, 380–81
Nevada System of Higher Education (NSHE), 246, 252, 254, 337n9
New England Association of Schools and Colleges (NEASC), 52–53
New England Board of Higher Education (NEBHE), 209, 210
New Hampshire, State University System of, 339, 344–45; Community and Technical College System, 344–45, 346
New Hampshire, University of, 63
New Orleans, University of, 153
New School for Social Research, 60
New York University, 61–62
Nexus Degree program, 140, 386
noncredit courses, 131, 329
"normal" (teacher training) schools, 90, 92, 219, 220, 222
North American Agricultural Advisory Network, 249
North Carolina: Community College System (NCCCS), 51, 52, 54; University of (UNC), 51; university system of, 180–81, 185–86, 246, 265
North Dakota University System, 251
Northeastern University, Center for the Future of Higher Education and Talent Strategy, 322
Northwest Commission on Colleges and Universities, 54
Nudge (Thaler and Sunstein), 348–49
nursing education, 36, 208, 333

Oberlin College, 220
Ohno, Taiichi, 147
Oklahoma State System of Higher Education, 53
O'Neill, Tip, 320
online higher education, 1, 171–94, 287, 321, 329, 366; applied baccalaureate degrees, 331–32; campus-based enrollment and, 175–77, 180, 181, 191; constraints, 178–79; content development and sharing, 188–89; course-sharing agreements, 193–94, 208–9; COVID-19 pandemic and, 173, 175–76, 179, 183, 185, 224; in cyber/digitization education, 294; development costs, 185–86; enrollment, 56, 180; fixed vs. variable-cost models, 173–77; hybrid models, 191–94; learning assessment and, 56, 58; learning management systems, 173, 177, 187, 188–89; for nondegree credentials, 322; online program management, 172, 185–86; operation at scale, 180–83; partnerships in, 184–86, 194; standardization, 177–78, 187–89; student support infrastructure, 189–90, 192; white labeling or licensing of, 187
Online Idaho, 179–80, 208
OpenAI consortium, 285
opportunity gaps, 273
Oregon: University of, 62; University System, 62, 246, 246n1

Organisation for Economic Co-operation and Development (OECD), 95–96
organizational structure, 10; back-office operations, 38–40; bureaucratic, 19–20, 160–61, 238, 242, 362, 387; change initiatives and, 233–34; corporate logic–based, 221–23; effectiveness-based changes, 40–41; environmental instability and, 244; heterogeneous systems, 302, 307, 311, 313–14, 315–16; historical development, 219–20; homogeneous systems, 302, 307, 313–14; hybrid, 302; learning centers, 384; of NASH member systems, 374; as obstacle to collective bargaining, 72; outward facing functions, 40; system effectiveness and, 40–41; three-tier, 222; transformability, 287; variations among systems, 155. *See also* centralization; collaboration in higher education; consortia, multi-stakeholder; consortia for course-sharing; governance
outsourcing, 123, 159, 365

Pan African University (PAU), 257–58
partnerships in higher education, 211–14, 322, 365, 380–81; with corporations, 222–23, 294, 331; with industry, 140, 203, 205–6, 222–23, 231–32, 294, 332–34; in international education, 244, 248–49, 253–55, 258–59; for redesigning system resources, 206–8; scaling, 203–6; for state and regional problem solving, 23–24, 35, 40, 332–35; university system–employer, 184–85, 192, 194, 203–6
Patterson, Mary Jane, 266
peer review, 74, 100
Pell Grants, 373
Pennsylvania: State College, 60–61; State System of Higher Education (PASSHE), 52–53, 206, 246, 250, 323–24; State University, 171, 324; University of, 265
Pew Research Center, 201, 325
philanthropic funding of higher education, 81, 82, 87–88, 93, 94, 99, 106, 199, 232, 294, 319, 379
Phoenix, University of, 172, 180
political factors/issues in higher education, 66, 366, 383, 384; academic freedom, 118; affecting system leadership, 36; attitudes toward higher education, 201–2, 325; citizenship education, 93–94, 96–97; consolidation, 361; culture wars, 68; DEI initiatives, 273–74, 278; digital technology, 286; faculty's political orientation, 69, 201–2; governing boards' responses to, 334–35, 388–89; labor-management relations, 66, 68; resource allocation, 107, 110, 118
Politics, Economics, and Welfare (Dahl and Lindblom), 95
Power of Systems initiative, 2, 5, 13, 196–97, 214, 268–69, 372–73, 378, 380; Institute for Systems Innovation and Improvement, 373–74; Partnership to Increase Federal Support for Systems, 373, 377–78; Systems Center for State Policy, 373, 377
practical education programs, 88–89, 340
Practices of Adaptive Leadership, The (Grashow and Linsky), 345
predictive analytics, 136, 371–72, 386
presidents of colleges and universities, 69–70, 79, 175, 109, 110, 111, 114, 327, 331, 336
prior learning, college credits for, 30, 321, 329–30, 375
private investment in public higher education, 81, 82, 88–90, 93, 94, 99; income tax credits for, 385
private nonprofit institutions, 61–62, 82, 84, 85–86, 87, 90, 93; online, 172, 174, 192
procurement functions, 19, 21, 149, 153–54, 159, 207–8
productivity, 56, 102, 116, 117, 151–52, 362, 364, 367, 384–85
professional development, 132, 314, 371
professional education, 88–89, 120, 221–22, 228, 312, 323–24, 366–67
promotion of faculty, 63, 64–65, 124, 204, 294, 313–14
Protein Data Bank (PDB), 225

provosts, 79, 114, 127, 180, 314
Public Agenda, 201
public funding of higher education, 34, 81, 82, 85–86, 90–93, 94–95, 98, 100, 103–4, 199; alignment in, 385; decreases, 319, 323, 340, 366; influence of online programs on, 173–74, 180; public objectives, 93–94, 95–99; for research, 93, 94, 98–99, 199
public good, systems' contributions to, 8, 33–36, 41, 55, 85, 100, 102–3, 104, 316, 363, 366, 367–68, 383, 387; governing board's role, 332–35; public funding and, 93–94, 99–104; worldbuilding, 389–91. *See also* cybersecurity; economic development; environmental issues; health care system; research / research and development; workforce capability development
public university systems: definition and purpose, 154, 306–7; with multiple colleges and universities, 42–49; number of, 171; post-WWII expansion, 92–93, 97, 221, 361; rationale for, 17–18, 22; roles and responsibilities, 99–104; state-by-state listing, 42–49. *See also* land-grant universities; *names of systems under individual states*
Purdue University, 157, 172; Purdue Global, 172, 175, 185

quality of higher education, 50–58, 88, 90, 100, 103, 155, 157; academic senate's role, 303, 306, 311–12; assessment, 51–53, 54, 57–58; federal regulation and, 99–100; institutional competition and, 86, 106; resource allocation and, 117, 157; technology-based, 102; unit of analysis problem, 52–53, 55, 58
quality of life, 360, 363, 367–68, 380–81
Queensland (Australia), University of, 254
Quigley, Kevin, 345–46
Quilt consortium, 225–26

Race against the Machine, The (McAfee), 284
racial and social inequities, 2, 196, 220, 235, 236–37, 266–68, 267, 271, 321, 371, 376, 381
racial/ethnic factors in student population composition, 198, 199
recruitment of students, 83, 89–90, 98, 102, 181, 244, 245, 247, 250–51, 252–53, 258–59
refugee resettlement, 5, 373, 377–78, 389–90
regional compacts and partnerships, 209–11, 380–81, 387
regional institutions: cross-national, 257–58; governing boards, 319–20
regionalism in higher education, 219
religious institutions, 218, 219–20, 265
remedial (developmental) education, 178, 273, 329; corequisite model, 131–32, 135–36
Rensselaer Polytechnic Institute, 153
reputation/prestige, institutional, 62, 102, 106, 111, 112, 119, 176
research / research and development (R&D), 26, 40, 83, 98–99, 100, 103, 157, 188, 206, 224, 226, 231, 285, 290–91, 365, 366; of cross-national regional universities, 257; faculty time allocated to, 102–3, 121; federal oversight, 252, 253, 255; funding and grants, 9, 92, 93, 94, 98–99, 103, 255, 312; international initiatives, 242–43, 244, 247–48, 250, 251, 252, 255, 256, 258; in lean systems, 9, 157, 163; multicampus centers, 312; student, 375–76; university-industry partnerships, 222–23, 231–32, 333–34
research universities, 53, 84, 99, 100, 134, 154, 219, 220–21, 222, 258, 302, 307, 324
resource allocation/reallocation, 95, 103, 106–24, 379; for DEI initiatives, 273, 275; for international activities, 244; in lean systems, 149–50, 152, 153–54, 162; prioritization and decision-making for, 8–9, 107, 108, 109–15, 385
Rio Salado College, 174
robotics, 283, 284–85, 286, 289, 292–93, 295

Russel, Stuart, 285
Rutgers University, 62–63

Scranton (PA), University of, 153
secondary education, 90, 92, 98, 100, 374. *See also* high school graduates; high school students
Second Industrial Divide, The (Piore and Sabel), 219, 221, 223
Sederburg, William, 328
services corporations, 39–40
shared governance, 63, 64, 68, 301–18, 327, 331, 384–85, 388
shared services and resources, 25–29, 35–36, 268, 289, 346, 365, 366, 367, 371, 378–79
Sloan Consortium of Colleges and Universities, 171
social and economic mobility, 3, 13, 40, 97–98, 100, 360, 362, 363–64, 366, 367, 371–73, 376, 385, 389
social media, 78–79, 284–85, 288, 295, 321
societal institutions, higher education's coevolution with, 10, 217–24
South Dakota Board of Regents, 207
Southern California, University of, Worldbuilding Institute, 389–90
Southern Illinois University System, 252
Southern New Hampshire University (SNHU), 179, 182
Southern Regional Education Board (SREB), 209, 210
Spellings, Margaret, 88
staff, 60–61, 65, 122–23, 158, 160–61, 274
Stakeholder Alignment Collaborative, 218, 229
stakeholders: broad range, 32, 33, 34, 37, 38, 41, 50, 387; in change initiatives, 341, 342, 343, 344, 351, 353–54, 355, 356, 357; in lean systems, 9, 146, 150–51, 152, 155–56, 160, 161, 162; in resource allocation, 108, 109; systems' services for, 32, 33, 34, 37, 38, 41
St. Andrews (Scotland), University of, 153, 162
state and regional problems, systems' responses to. *See* public good, systems' contributions to
state governments, 18, 20, 21–22, 67, 204, 291, 292, 296, 361–62
state legislatures, 18, 19, 63, 110, 207, 303, 310, 314, 356, 379
State University of New York (SUNY), 53–54, 171, 197–98, 221–22, 228, 229, 230, 302, 307; Agricultural and Technical Colleges, 55; Association of Council Members and College Trustees, 236; Buffalo campus, 62; Center for Leadership and Sustainable Development, 254; Collaborative Online International Learning (COIL) Center, 250; faculty and staff unionization, 60–61, 62; Faculty Council of Community Colleges, 236; international education initiatives, 243–44, 246, 247, 248–50, 251, 252–53, 254; Korean campus, 254, 259; Office of Global Affairs, 247, 251, 252–53; role-alike groups, 230, 236; Stony Brook campus, 62; Student Assembly, 236
statewide coordinating/regulatory entities, 42, 43–49
STEM education, 92
strategic planning, 20, 107, 113, 151, 155, 229, 248–49, 365, 388–89
Strayer University, 186
structural barriers to student success, 128–42; evidence of, 128–33; Momentum Year/Approach strategies for, 133–42
student-centric systems, 127–44, 386; Momentum Year framework, 133–42, 386; University of Alaska, 390
student debt, 56–57, 98, 330, 340, 366, 372, 373, 376, 381, 385, 389
student exchanges, international, 245, 247, 248, 249–50, 251
student experience, 30–31, 83, 157, 376–77; systemic barriers in, 138–42
student information systems (SISs), 177
student loans, 83–84, 85, 89, 90, 330
student retention and graduation. *See* student success
students: as DEI focus, 277; full-time-equivalent (FTE), 120–21, 182, 190; as higher education customers,

156–57, 340; involvement in state and regional problem-solving, 35–36; multiple educational options, 320–21, 328–32; nontraditional, 181, 191, 204–5; out-of-state, 157; part-time, 190; shared governance participation, 331; transitions of, 86, 136, 138–39
student success, 2, 21, 31–32, 56–57, 123, 130, 176, 340, 362, 389, 390; adult students, 178; assessment, 51–52, 53, 56, 57; BRT Transformation Agenda, 371–73; core courses and, 130–31, 134, 136, 138; DEI initiatives, 273, 371–72; at for-profit institutions, 89–90, 91; institutional and structural barriers, 128–42; Momentum Year strategies for, 133–42
study abroad programs, 242, 243, 245, 247, 248, 249–50, 251, 254, 328
support services, 26, 28, 34, 83, 90, 157, 176, 189–90, 192, 366, 379, 386–87
systemness, 31–32, 268, 367–68, 371, 384, 389
system offices, 8, 19, 26, 39–40, 155, 230, 252; centralization, 25, 26, 159; cybersecurity and, 292; international functions, 244, 245–53; inward and outward facing relationships, 23–25, 33–36, 40; in lean systems, 155–56, 159, 163; roles and responsibilities, 8, 27–37, 155; roles and responsibilities (traditional), 18–20

taxation policies, 85, 294, 295, 385
teaching, 101, 98–99, 102–3, 121, 123–24, 132, 371, 376
technical/vocational schools, 88–89, 184, 221–22, 228, 319–20, 328, 331
technological change, 66, 82–83, 108, 217, 220–38, 281–82, 292–93, 316, 365, 388
Tennessee, university system of, 52, 54, 337n9; community colleges, 131, 134, 136–37; student success, 9, 128, 130, 131, 136–37
Tennessee Board of Regents, 52, 127–28, 134
tenure, 19, 21, 63, 121–22, 124, 159, 204, 272, 293–94, 340
Texas: A&M University System (TAMUS), 193, 255; Higher Education Coordinating Board, Texas General Education Core Curriculum, 177–78; multiple higher education systems, 219; Tech University, 255; university system of, 51, 246, 252, 253
Toyota Production System (TPS), 147
transfer process/policies/students, 29, 31, 38, 177–78, 193, 307, 308, 309, 310–11, 316, 329, 367, 374–75, 376, 380, 386
tribal colleges and universities (TCUs), 227, 231–32
tuition, 10, 28, 81, 84, 85–86, 87, 98, 99, 157, 180, 181, 183, 192, 204, 209–10, 323, 340
tutoring, 131, 176, 190, 328
2U, 186
two-year institutions, 62, 91, 177, 179, 201, 330, 331–32

University of California Press, 309
US Department of Education, 88, 90, 199, 200, 249, 377
US Supreme Court, 51, 52, 143, 167

value-added functions, 1, 150, 251, 367, 378
Vermont, University of, 206
viable approach, 218, 232–34, 238
Virginia Community College System, 52
virtual campuses, programs, technology, 57, 208, 249, 312, 316
vision/visioning process, 108, 212, 218, 226–29, 337n9, 342–43, 363–64, 387, 390
voluntary systems/associations (colleges and universities), 42, 43–49

Washington State University, 246, 247, 250–51, 337n9
Wayne State University, 63
Webster University, 42
Welcome World Campus, 377–78
Wesleyan College, 266
Western Governors University, 56, 182

Western Interstate Commission for Higher Education (WICHE), 205, 209, 210, 211; Knocking at the College Door, 198; Western Regional Program, 209; Western Undergraduate Exchange (WUE), 209
West Indies, University of the (UWI), 254
"Why Can't Higher Education Change?" (Bowles), 341
Wilberforce University, 266
Wisconsin, university system of, 154–55, 246, 247, 254, 302, 332–34, 342; National Survey of Student Engagement, 376–77
workforce capability development, 3, 4, 10, 20, 24, 35, 45, 92, 97, 100, 211, 271, 292, 295, 323, 324–26, 363–64, 366–67, 371, 377, 381, 383; employers' needs in, 41, 96, 184–85, 203, 205, 331–32, 340, 365, 366, 375–76; employer-university partnerships for, 51, 184–85, 192, 194, 202, 203–6; funding, 92, 93–94, 95–96, 97, 98, 100, 103, 184; for low-income/marginalized groups, 5, 36, 98, 231, 268, 271; online/digital technology–based initiatives, 184–85, 192, 293–94, 295; remote work, 283
Workforce Innovation and Opportunity Act, 184
worldbuilding, 389–91

Yale University, 61–62, 265
Yeshiva University, 61–62

Zimpher, Nancy, 197–98, 211, 212, 367–68